C000088175

HERE IS
THE NEWS

THE BBC AND THE
SECOND WORLD WAR

RICHARD HAVERS

SUTTON PUBLISHING

First published in the United Kingdom in 2007 by
Sutton Publishing, an imprint of NPI Media Group Limited
Cirencester Road · Chalford · Stroud · Gloucestershire · GL6 8PE

British Library Cataloguing in Publication Data
A catalogue for this book is available from the British Library.

Hardback ISBN: 978-0-7509-4121-1
Paperback ISBN: 978-0-7509-4122-8

*For Bettina, John and Douglas,
who were there*

Typeset in Photina.
Typesetting and origination by
NPI Media Group Limited.
Printed and bound in England.

CONTENTS

INTRODUCTION

In 1915 David Sarnoff, the man who would become President of the Radio Corporation of America (RCA), said, 'I have in mind a plan of development which would make a radio a "household utility" in the same sense as the piano or phonograph. The idea is to bring music into the house by wireless. While this has been tried in the past by wires, it has been a failure because wires do not lend themselves to this scheme. With radio, however, it would seem to be entirely feasible.' Almost 90 years later Patricia Hodgson, the Chief Executive of the Independent Television Commission, said, 'Nearly 80 per cent of the British public say, television is their main source of world news. Most of us do read newspapers, but fewer than one in ten regard them as our main source of international information.'

There was a period between these two statements when the first of them came true in a way that no one would have predicted. But it was also a time when the technology that has allowed television to become the news vendor to the world was unavailable, a period when such a concept would have been looked upon as fanciful, the very stuff of science fiction.

In 1939, and throughout the Second World War, the wireless was king, radio ruled supreme and a man with a cultured accent saying, 'and here is the news' meant only one thing: the British Broadcasting Corporation – the BBC – London – facts – information – and, most importantly for nearly everyone, it meant . . . THE TRUTH.

Towards the end of the war the BBC, in one of its publications, described its mission to inform by quoting from the preface to Dryden's poem 'Annus Mirabilis': 'To describe the motives, the beginning, the progresses, and successes of a most just and necessary war.' It summarises perfectly what the BBC's correspondents, editors, newsreaders, commentators, givers of talks and its thousands of other dedicated employees achieved.

When the war began the BBC had no more of a clue than anyone else about how the war would progress, how long it would last – other than that it would probably be long – nor its outcome. They had to adapt to changing circumstances against pressures that ranged from the cultural to the technical, both on a personal level and on a global scale. In particular, the expansion of the war into far-flung corners of the world placed enormous demands on the broadcaster, and in particular a growing exigency for correspondents, the longer the conflict went on. Throughout it all the BBC had to face criticism at home, attacks from the newspapers, carping from MPs and sometimes the wrath of its own listeners – but, broadly speaking, Britain and the world never lost faith in the Corporation.

Today the BBC has a reputation that has been built upon its achievements during the Second World War. There have been some who have tried to bring the harsh glare of a revisionist's spotlight on the work of the Corporation: theirs have been cheap shots and, as often as not, they have been misinformed. The BBC provided the soundtrack to six of the most turbulent years in Britain's history, and did so while showing great resilience during the early years of the war in what were very extreme circumstances. The BBC's employees did so with great skill, flair, imagination, dedication and tremendous tenacity, and they did it while never losing sight of their own imperative: 'To tell the truth – in war as in peace.'

Prologue

THE VOICE OF FREEDOM

Can you imagine living in a world where you are unable to hear, let alone watch, the news before six o'clock in the evening? A world in which before 6 p.m. your only information as to what was happening, at home or abroad, was from the pages of a newspaper? Well, this was the situation just before the outbreak of the Second World War, when 6 p.m. was the earliest time that the BBC was allowed to broadcast the news under an agreement with the newspaper owners. It was also an era during which BBC radio faced no competition from commercial radio, or its own fledgling television service. In any event, who on earth would want to watch news? When it was time for the radio to reveal all, a man would enunciate, in perfect, received English, that immortal phrase: 'Here is the news'. It was said in such a way as to verify that there really was nowhere else, other than on the BBC, where the news could be heard. The facts that followed, devoid of the type of comment that constitutes much of our news today, would be delivered in a style of language that has become known throughout the world as 'BBC pronunciation': a form of speech that would be recognised, with the advent of war and the growth in the BBC's global service, as 'the voice of freedom'.

For the first seventeen years of the BBC's existence the news had been something akin to a reserved preserve of the newspapers. This rather odd – to our modern-day minds – arrangement had been agreed between the Newspaper Proprietors' Association and the British Broadcasting Company, in the days before it was a 'Corporation'. Such was the BBC's desire to appease the newspaper owners that BBC Director Sir William Noble confirmed the Corporation's position as supplier of mostly second-hand news by saying, 'We want to act in such a way that broadcasting may be an incentive to the public to buy more newspapers.' This peculiar agreement between the purveyors of the written and the spoken word also barred news bulletins from being broadcast after 2 a.m. Such was the BBC's view of the news in the first decade or so of the company's existence that it felt comfortable in saying it would cancel bulletins if there was no news. This is precisely what happened on at least one occasion: 'Good evening, today is Good Friday. There is no news.' The deal with the newspaper owners did allow for extra bulletins to be broadcast 'in the case of urgent national emergency', which is what happened at the time of the Munich Crisis in September 1938; as well as during the 1926 General Strike. A year after 'Munich', on 25 August 1939, as the crisis in Europe came to a head, the situation warranted two additional bulletins: one at 10.30 a.m. and the other at 1 p.m. It was the start of a new news order.

The extra bulletins came just four days after BBC newsreader Stuart Hibberd told the country that Soviet Russia and Nazi Germany had agreed to 'a non-aggression pact'. This bolt from the ether was an early example of radio being first with the news; because the story had come in after the daily papers had gone to press. In the evening of the following day, 22 August, a special announcement broadcast by the BBC prompted the recall of Parliament. Britain and the rest of Europe were on course for war and the BBC was already playing a significant role by disseminating not just regular news items but also through special announcements. In pre-war Britain there were so few domestic tele-phones, or the other paraphernalia of our overcommunicating world, that the radio was the fastest and most effective way of reaching almost every part of the country.

Hibberd spoke of these momentous events in his diary: 'This may of course mean nothing – it may be "grandstand play" as the Americans say; on the other hand it may be of vital importance to every one of us.' The six o'clock bulletin on 23 August began with news of a rail strike that coming Saturday, 25 August. The later bulletins carried news of a Cabinet communiqué announcing that more men were to be called up into the armed forces. It was that peculiar mix of the ordinary and the extraordinary that seemed to characterise the run-up to war.

When war broke out there were over nine million radio licences issued to British households, meaning almost three-quarters of British homes legally had a wireless. In Scotland 63 per cent of homes had one, in Wales 64 per cent, and in Northern Ireland 43 per cent. The region of Britain in which wireless cover-age was densest was the west of England, with 83 per cent; in Dorset and Wiltshire it reached 90 per cent. At the other end of the country the north of Scotland (Caithness, Orkney, Ross and Cromarty, Shetland and Sutherland) could only muster 42 per cent – the lowest on the mainland. Fermanagh and Tyrone, in Northern Ireland, where just over a quarter of homes had a licence, had the lowest overall. Interestingly, there was about the same level of radio ownership in German homes at the outbreak of the war: 75 per cent of households had a wireless.

The remarkable historian of all things radio related, Asa Briggs, said, 'Words do not win wars' when writing about the role of the BBC during the Second

World War. Maybe not directly, and certainly not in isolation, but Britain and Germany, along with the rest of the world, were about to find out just how important 'wordy warfare', as someone else described the BBC's news bulletins and war reports, was to become. A German newspaper described the BBC's broadcasts as a 'spiritual danger, intellectual poison, and a weapon more paralysing and deadly than cannon and machine gun'. Numerous commentators have looked back to the years between 1939 and 1945 as a period in which the BBC came to represent truth, freedom and democracy for most of the free world. It's a premise that has underpinned much of what the Corporation has stood for ever since; it's a principle of which any broadcaster would be proud. These are fundamentals that need to be jealously guarded by today's reporters, journalists and news managers in a world where news has gone from being reportage to something more akin to a business. Unquestionably the Second World War was when radio came of age, setting in train practices and techniques that have been revolutionised through technology, as well as experience, but at the same time essential principles were established that are still practised by the BBC and countless other broadcasters around the world.

THE WIRELESS

A radio at the outbreak of war was most often referred to as a wireless – why? We tend to think of radios from that era being connected to the electricity supply, rather than the battery-powered transistor radios that became so popular in the 1960s. In fact, radios were often large, wooden affairs that were built in such a way as to accommodate accumulators – big, heavy batteries that needed recharging every two weeks or so, often by a local garage. Although the Central Electricity Grid, which supplied Britain's homes, had been set up in 1935, coverage was a long way short of complete. Even by the third year of the war as many as one-third of Britain's homes were not connected to the grid. This was also a time when a family did not immediately run out and buy the latest new piece of consumer electronics.

Chapter 1

LET US BEGIN

The years between the end of the First World War and the beginning of the Second went by in a flash in the timeline of history. And yet the First World War was like the media's Dark Ages when compared to the way that news was reported a little over two decades later. Between 1914 and 1918 people at home could only find out about the progress of the war through the pages of their newspaper; twenty years on and the power of broadcasting came into its own.

Between 1939 and 1945 radio reporters, through their capacity for observation, remarkable journalistic skills and their way with words, brought death, heroism, glory, sadness, the fantastic and the farcical into homes up and down the length of Britain, and across the world via the BBC's worldwide transmissions. Of course it hadn't happened in the First World War for one simple reason: the BBC, or any other radio station, did not exist. Between the wars technology moved at an incredible pace, changing almost everything much faster than anyone could have imagined. For politicians in Britain and in the rest of the world – many of whom, like Winston Churchill, had gone into battle on horseback – the advent of the wireless was a revelation, and not necessarily one that they were very comfortable with. Indeed, Churchill never did feel totally at ease with radio, and he certainly loathed appearing before a camera. It is therefore somewhat ironic that Churchill's broadcasts throughout the conflict performed myriad functions, and most importantly they helped win the war.

When the British Broadcasting Company began daily transmissions on 14 November 1922 there can have been few who imagined just how important a role radio was to play in the lives of the average person in Britain. It wasn't long before it became clear that people really enjoyed listening to the wireless, and within two years there were a million licence-holders, but more often than not they were being entertained rather than informed. A typical Saturday's broadcasting in late November 1924 featured musical programmes ranging from 'The Wireless Quartet' to the 'All Blacks' Concert Party', beamed live from Cardiff. There were occasional talks like the one on Saturday 22 November 1924 by a West End butler, who explained to what must have been a rapt audience, all glued to their wireless sets, the 'Domestic Service Problem'. On the same day there were just two news broadcasts, one at 7.30 p.m. and the other at 9 p.m. Such was the fascination around the world with broadcasting that the following week had been decreed 'International Radio Week'. The novel idea was for broadcasters to 'exchange' programmes in this publicity stunt, organised by the Wireless Retailers' Association to help increase the sales of wireless sets.

In May 1926 the BBC had its first real chance to demonstrate the effectiveness of radio as a medium for spreading the news. The General Strike began at midnight on 3 May and the print unions were among the many that stopped working, which meant that the newspapers were out of circulation for nine days; the radio had a virtual monopoly on reporting the dramatic events. BBC General Manager John Reith dominated the Corporation in 1926, and for many years after. His vision for the company was that it should be an independent broadcaster, free from political interference, where commercialism took something of a back seat. During the strike Reith was instrumental in broadcasting pro-government propaganda; he even went as far as to prevent the somewhat more 'worker-friendly' Archbishop of Canterbury, Randall Thomas Davidson, from speaking on the radio. When some of the newsreaders were accused of sounding 'panicky' during the strike Reith decided that the only solution was to read the bulletins himself.

It was during this period of domestic unrest that Winston Churchill had his first brush with the feisty Scot Reith. During the strike there were five daily news bulletins and Churchill, who was Chancellor of the Exchequer at the time, suggested to the Prime Minister, Stanley Baldwin, that the government should take the BBC into state control for the duration of the industrial action, the better to manage the flow of information. Reith saw this as a personal threat to his own position, and, having no affection for Churchill, railed against the suggestion, managing to convince Baldwin of the BBC's need to be 'seen to be independent'. This largely explains Reith's stance throughout the period of unrest.

One far-reaching outcome of the strike was that instead of relying on the news agencies for its information, the BBC set up its own fledgling news-gathering team, one that would eventually grow into the sophisticated machine – by the standards of the time – that was operating by the end of the Second World War. During the early stages of the war the Corporation proudly proclaimed that, 'the BBC does not only edit news, it goes out and gets it', which at that time was new and groundbreaking.

In his capacity as stand-in newsreader Reith had the distinction of being one of the first people to broadcast a momentous event live on air. On 12 May he announced the end of the General Strike:

> I had just begun to read the news when I was told I was wanted urgently on the phone from Downing Street. So I broke off and said I would stop for a moment, as it might be more important news was coming. Waterhouse gave me a message, which I went back to the microphone and read, to the effect that the TUC leaders had visited the PM and announced their intention of calling off the strike forthwith. It was rather wonderful to have been the first to give the news.
>
> *Lord Reith's diary entry, 12 May 1926*

On 1 January 1927 the BBC was awarded a Royal Charter; simultaneously the word 'company' was dropped and replaced by 'corporation'. In recognition of his work in creating the BBC, the 38-year-old John Reith was knighted and appointed its first Director General. It was not long afterwards that a number of significant events occurred that helped to change the face of radio. Perhaps most notably the ban that prevented the BBC from broadcasting 'controversy' was removed in 1928; what would the BBC be like now if that had been maintained? Four years later the short-wave transmitter at Daventry in the West Midlands became operational; this allowed the BBC to broadcast to the whole of the British Empire, a particularly important factor when war broke out. Seven months earlier, in May 1932, the Corporation's London head-quarters at Broadcasting House, in Portland Place, opened. Six years later the BBC's Arabic Service began; these were the Corporation's first broadcasts in a foreign language. Over the next twelve months regular transmissions in French, German, Portuguese, Italian and Spanish began.

During 1938 the crisis with Hitler's Nazi Germany steadily worsened, prompting the BBC to begin planning for the possibility of wartime broadcasting. Most of the detailed plans remained secret from all except those that needed to know or were directly involved. The government was also making secret plans to introduce a broadcasting service that could be 'trained on an enemy' in the event of war. Although broadcast propaganda was in its infancy no one at the Foreign Office wanted Britain to be left behind, especially given that the Germans seemed to be developing formidable skills in this area. Initially the plan to set up a propaganda unit came under the wing of the Foreign Office, but they most definitely wanted it to be sited well away from their offices, to avoid any stigma attaching itself to their artful form of politics.

Initially the propaganda section was set up in Electra House, the headquarters of Cable and Wireless, on the Victoria Embankment, which gave rise to the section most often being called 'EH'. This group of specialists would eventually form the nucleus of what became known as the Political Warfare Executive.

On 27 September 1938 Prime Minister Neville Chamberlain broadcast three days before he flew to Munich to meet German Chancellor Adolf Hitler. Chamberlain famously and ironically said: 'How horrible, fantastic, incredible it is that we should be digging trenches and trying on gas masks here because of a quarrel in a far away country between people of whom we know nothing.' Chamberlain's policy of appeasement has been the subject of almost ceaseless historical debate ever since. But at the heart of the issue lies the fact that he seems to have viewed much of what happened with detachment, demonstrating an attitude that was perhaps emblematic of the age. Then again, it could have been the cancer which was to be the cause of Chamberlain's death in late 1940 that may also have played a part.

Hitler himself was under no illusions and is reported to have told those close to him, 'If ever that silly old man comes interfering here again with his umbrella, I'll kick him downstairs and jump on his stomach in front of the photographers.' The Italian dictator, Benito Mussolini, shared his fellow tyrant's views: he called Chamberlain an 'old man' and a 'bourgeois pacifist'. With enemies like that Chamberlain didn't need fellow countrymen – or members of his own party – saying, 'The Prime Minister has believed in addressing Herr Hitler through the language of sweet reasonableness. I have believed that he was more open to the language of the mailed fist.' This is how the First Lord of the Admiralty, Duff Cooper, vented his anger during his resignation speech on 3 October 1938. All this left the field wide open for the arch-opponent of appeasement, Winston Spencer Churchill, to speak out in Parliament on 5 October, and eleven days later to broadcast to the United States from the BBC in London.

> We have passed an awful milestone in our history, when the whole equilibrium of Europe has been deranged, and that the terrible words have for the time being pronounced against the Western democracies: 'Thou art weighed in the balance and found wanting.' And do not suppose that this is the end. This is only the beginning of the reckoning.
>
> *Winston Churchill, House of Commons, 5 October 1938*

We must arm. Britain must arm. America must arm; we shall no doubt arm . . . But arms . . . are not sufficient by themselves. We must add to them the power of ideas. People say, many people, we ought not to allow ourselves to be drawn into a theoretical antagonism between Nazidom and democracy – but the antagonism is here, now. You see these dictators on their pedestals, surrounded by the bayonets of their soldiers and truncheons of their police. They are afraid of words and thoughts, words spoken abroad, thoughts stirring at home – all the more powerful because they are forbidden . . . It is the very conflict of spiritual and moral ideas which gives the free countries a great part of their strength . . .

Winston Churchill, US radio, 16 October 1938

Churchill was prophetic when he talked of 'words spoken abroad'. It was this powerful notion that focused the minds of those who were involved in pointing the pistol of propaganda at Britain's enemies. It may also have struck a chord with anyone at the BBC who heard the 63-year-old backbencher's forceful rhetoric. Not that everyone in Britain felt the same way. One newspaper report accused 'Mr Churchill, Mr Eden, Mr Duff Cooper, and the opposition leaders of delivering . . . somewhat truculent and bellicose speeches'. A German paper, rather bizarrely, called Churchill 'a political tyro'. If some at the BBC shared the view of Churchill and the others as troublemakers it did not prevent them from moving forward with their planning. Within three months the senior management of the BBC were hard at work deciding how best to cope with the task of broadcasting during a conflict; one that now seemed inevitable.

When the BBC committee charged with deciding how the Corporation would deal with wartime broadcasting first met in January 1939 it was not the first time that such internal conversations had taken place. Back in the spring of 1938, soon after Austria was annexed by Germany, a small group of BBC executives, including the Director of Planning, had decided that most listeners would be hungry for 'the reception of news, of official statements and instructions'. There was much discussion about the maximum length of programmes that would be listened to during a war; it was eventually settled at thirty minutes. They agreed that children's programmes, and the daily service, were to remain, but the quantity of entertainment programmes would be reduced. One of their other recommendations was that a supply of 1,000 gramophone records should be dispatched to each of the BBC's regional offices, marked to be 'kept for use in time of war'. However, by January 1939 views had changed somewhat, and among the new recommendations was that the BBC should be 'on air' for 22 hours a day, which was up from the 17 hours recommended during the earlier discussions. It was also felt that a gradual increase in entertainment programmes would be necessary after the initial phases of any conflict. For the BBC its overriding mission was clear: 'The maintenance of public morale should be the principal aim of war-time programmes.'

By April 1939 the Director of Programme Planning was actively devising a week's worth of suggested wartime programmes; a dawn-to-closedown run-through of what listeners would actually hear in a typical week. Scripts were prepared and the records to be played were chosen; all the minutiae of such plans became the subject of a flood of inter-office memoranda. In one exchange there was a debate as to whether it was really necessary for Admiralty announcements to be broadcast three times a day in both English and Gaelic. While these plans had obviously been meticulously discussed it was almost inevitable that come the day, and come the hour, things were not going to be quite as easy to organise in a real war scenario. There would often be disagreement about what was broadcast and what was not. Differences of opinion among the BBC's management would be echoed by those in the newspapers, as often as not for competitive reasons, as well as by politicians, and inevitably by letter-writers to *The Times* and other newspapers.

Not that the BBC was working in a vacuum. Sir Samuel Hoare, the Home Secretary, was working on a plan to establish a Ministry of Information. In July 1939 Hoare told the House of Commons:

A third organ of publicity is the wireless. The plan would not be that the Government would take over the BBC in wartime, but, on the whole, the wise course would be to treat broadcasting as we treat the other methods of publicity, the press and the films, and leave the BBC to carry on, but obviously in wartime, with a very close liaison between the Ministry of Information and the Broadcasting Corporation, with definite regulations as to how the work should be carried out.

Naturally this was not the last word on the subject. There were others, particularly those working in the upper echelons of the BBC, who saw things differently. From the very first days of the conflict there was disagreement between the BBC's Director General, Sir Frederick Ogilvie, who had been appointed to succeed Sir John Reith in the summer of 1938, and the Ministry of Information, other ministers and the Cabinet. While he was a fighter for BBC independence from government interference, Ogilvie, a former economics academic, was not really the best man for the job. He demonstrated a lack of leadership, and a penchant for the hallowed halls of university life, like Queen's University, Belfast, from where he came, and Jesus College, Oxford, where he went after leaving the BBC in 1942.

It was not just what the public heard broadcast that was of concern to the government. It was realised as early as 1936 that there was a need to find a way to prevent enemy aircraft from using the valuable direction-finding capabilities that radio waves offered – but at the same time there was a need to keep on broadcasting. The solution that was agreed upon, just as Ogilvie was appointed Director General, was comparatively simple. There were to be a northerly and a southerly group of transmitters, with each group using one of two wavelengths. In this way enemy aircraft could not use the transmitters as beacons to fix their positions. If an individual transmitter was shut down for any reason listeners were able to continue to get a signal, albeit a weaker one, from one of the other masts in their region. On top of everything else, and a situation that no one wanted to envisage, was in the event of an invasion or devastating bombing it was important, vital even, for the BBC to continue to broadcast. It was imperative, particularly if the south-east and London were overrun, that the government should continue to control the airwaves, and the rest of the country should be held together somehow.

During the build-up to the conflict it was difficult for everyone involved in planning for wartime broadcasting to maintain secrecy, while at the same time developing effective arrangements to allow for the continuous operation of all the BBC's departments. As one BBC staffer said, '[things] were getting more and more complicated'. Of course, some things were not secret. On 25 August 1939 gas-doors to protect Broadcasting House were put in place; ever since the First World War a gas attack was almost everyone's worst fear in the event of war. Later that evening the call went out from the news department that everyone should stand by, as 'the first warning had come in'.

While the consensus continued to be that news and information would dominate the airwaves, immediately following the outbreak of war plans were well advanced for other departments of the BBC to provide as seamless a service as humanly possible. On 29 August 1939 the first party of BBC staff moved to Wood Norton Hall, Evesham; set in over 100 acres of the Worcestershire countryside, it was the former home of the Duc d'Orléans. The BBC had bought the mansion house earlier in the year with the specific aim of moving staff out of London in the event of war. To maintain some secrecy the BBC encouraged the rumours that government had bought Wood Norton Hall to be a home for the Duke and Duchess of Windsor. Following the move to Evesham the Variety and Religious Departments, along with the BBC Orchestra and the Children's Hour team, all moved to Bristol. Given their duties there was to be no trip to the country for the news staff; they were to remain at Broadcasting House for the duration.

If the BBC planners had thought of everything in minute detail the DG had another last-minute brainwave, one that made minutiae seem like grand design. On the eve of war Ogilvie decreed that the BBC should broadcast the 'song of the nightingale', recorded in Oxfordshire's Bagley Woods, to Germany; he felt it would demonstrate Britain's peace-loving intentions. As we all know, it failed, and rather than signalling peaceful intent it acted as a call to arms for the BBC.

In the early evening of Friday 1 September someone at the Ministry of Information was instructed to telephone Welbeck 3368 to order the BBC to adopt 'war stations'. The same message was then relayed to every BBC office in Britain, where those in charge opened their sealed orders and set about following their specific instructions. Immediately announcements were played on all stations telling listeners to retune to one of two frequencies.

Within the next two hours you will be asked to adjust your sets to a wavelength of 391 metres or 449 metres – that is to say, to the wavelengths of Scottish Regional or North Regional. From that time on broadcasting throughout the United Kingdom will, until further notice, be confined to those two wavelengths. Meanwhile, all stations of the BBC are closing down except the three medium-wave national transmitters in the London, North, and Scottish regions on 261 metres, on which you will hear the Bow Bells interval signals. After that we shall give you news and announcements until the time comes for the further change of the wavelengths to Scottish Regional and North Regional on 391 or 449 metres. Until further notice a single programme without alternatives will be broadcast continuously on those two wavelengths only from 7 a.m. to 12.15 midnight.

There will be news bulletins at 7 a.m., 8 a.m., 9 a.m., 12 noon, 1 p.m., 2 p.m., 4.30 p.m., 6 p.m., 7.30 p.m., 9 p.m., 10.30 p.m., and 12 midnight. In addition, there may be news announcements at the following hours: 10 a.m., 11 a.m., 3 p.m., 4 p.m., 5 p.m., 7 p.m., 8 p.m., 10 p.m., 11 p.m., 1 a.m., 3 a.m., and 5 a.m. If announcements are going to be made at 1 a.m., 3 a.m., 5 a.m., they will be preceded by a five-minute interval signal – Bow Bells.

Details of programmes will be issued daily to the Press, and arrangements have been made for a special issue of the *Radio Times* to be published within the next few days, giving full details of programmes for at least a week from the day of issue.

BBC announcer, 1 September 1939

To ensure total coverage telegrams were sent to every post office in the country to be prominently displayed in their windows; the press were issued with the same information. At 8.15 p.m. on 1 September 1939 the new single-station wartime service was launched with words that were to become so familiar to every listener: 'This is the BBC Home Service.' And with this all 4,889 members of the BBC staff were officially at war, even if the rest of the country had to wait a couple of days.

The first casualty of war as far as the BBC was concerned was the fledgling television service. It had begun broadcasting in 1936 and was just beginning to find its feet, even if there were precious few people who could actually see what the BBC was televising as there were just 23,000 TV sets in Britain, and it was only in the south that the broadcasts could be watched. The viewing had been a mix of programmes, such as Peggy Ashcroft starring in *The Tempest*, coverage of the Derby, *Me and My Girl* broadcast from the Victoria Palace and coverage of the King and Queen on their return from a state visit to Canada. Around midday on 1 September an announcer had just told viewers what was in the schedule for the coming week. Ten minutes later, having received the order to cease broadcasting, the TV network closed down. The final programme was an eight-minute Mickey Mouse cartoon; there would be no TV for the duration of the war.

EVACUATION

On Friday 1 September the evacuation of children from London began. The previous day the BBC had warned that this was going to happen. In a typical piece of government-speak the BBC told listeners that 'no one should conclude that this decision means that war is now regarded as inevitable'. School-teachers, along with MPs, were recalled to their posts, the former to deal with the logistics of a huge evacuation.

The evacuation of British children is going on very smoothly and efficiently. The Ministry of Health says that great progress has been made with the first part of the government arrangements. Railways and road transport organisations, the local authorities and teachers, the voluntary workers and not least the householders in the reception areas are all playing their part splendidly.

Alvar Lidell, BBC, 1 September 1939

We're on number twelve platform at Waterloo Station, one of the ten big metropolitan stations that are engaged today on the evacuation of London's schoolchildren. We're on number twelve platform, the train's in, and the children are just arriving, coming along in their school groups with a banner in front saying what school they are. This lot, St John's School Walworth, which is south of the river. The tiny tots in front, leading up to the bigger ones, the 12- and 13-year-olds behind. Behind them a High School, 14-, 15-, 16-year-olds, they're being evacuated too.

S.J. de Lotbinière, BBC, 1 September 1939

Many now think that the evacuation purely involved Londoners, but it also included children – and sometimes their parents – from cities throughout Britain; they were all heading for the relative safety of the countryside. Almost 1.5 million left the urban areas in the first three days of September. This number was made up of 834,000 schoolchildren and 103,000 teachers, along with over 500,000 mothers and children under school age, along with 13,000 expectant mothers. It had been envisaged that the number was going to be closer to 3.5 million.

The people in the countryside who accommodated the children and the attendant adults were paid 10s 6d per week (the equivalent of around £73 today, based on average earnings) by the government for taking a child, and 8s 6d for each additional child. This was expected to cover living expenses. If, in addition to a child or children, a mother and an underage child were accommodated, then mothers paid 5s (£35 today) for themselves and 3s for each child, but this excluded the cost of meals. For many the evacuation turned into little more than a few months in the country, with over two-thirds who had left in the September exodus returning to their homes by January 1940. For most it was the lack of a German offensive that encouraged them to return home; others were simply homesick.

With the beginning of the German bombing raids in 1940 many children, and some of their parents, were once again evacuated. One who went in the second evacuation was a 4½-year-old Bill Perks, who 23 years later would become the bass player for the Rolling Stones and change his name to Bill Wyman. 'My family was evacuated to Pembrokeshire in Wales during 1940; we only stayed for two weeks, as we didn't like it. Back in London I started infants' school in September 1940, around the same time as the Battle of Britain began. I vividly remember standing in the street with lots of our neighbours; we were all looking up at the sky that seemed to be filled with German bombers. Everyone cheered as we watched the white trails of our fighter planes diving in and out of the German formations. We were eventually evacuated to Mansfield Woodhouse, Nottingham.'

At the other end of the social scale was the BBC reporter who was at Waterloo station covering the evacuation. He was old Etonian Seymour Joly de Lotbinière, known to his colleagues as Lobby. He was the BBC's Director of Outside Broadcasts, and later became Assistant Controller of Programmes. He had a reputation as one of the politest people working at the BBC in those pre-war years, an era when just about everyone at the Corporation was exceptionally polite. While in charge of Outside Broadcasts he took on John Snagge, Howard Marshall, Tommy Woodruffe and Wynford Vaughan-Thomas. Later, along with Cecil Madden, who was one of his producers, he helped the singer Petula Clark by providing a fund that paid for her singing and dancing lessons. Lotbinière also gave Peter West his start at the BBC, commentating on the cricket.

Alvar Lidell, who perhaps more than anyone came to epitomise the quint-essential 'BBC voice', was a master of pronunciation; as one observer said, 'The Queen's English was never more safe than in the hands of, and at the micro-phone of, Alvar Lidell.' He was 31 when war broke out, and given his perfect accent it's somewhat surprising to learn that his parents were Swedish and lived in Wimbledon. Lidell, who possessed a fine baritone voice, started his career as a singer, giving recitals as well as being a sought-after narrator for Walton's *Façade* and other classical pieces. Besides reading the news during the war he presented various programmes, including one about music called 'I Know What I Like'. Briefly, from early 1943, Lidell went missing from the airwaves because he joined the RAF, but it was not something that lasted awfully long as he was invalided out! He worked at the BBC for over thirty years, retiring in 1969.

THE COMING OF WAR

Just before 6 a.m. on 1 September 1939 the German army crossed the Polish border; their invasion followed an intense aerial bombardment. The leading German divisions were the spearhead of an attack by over one million men, including six armoured divisions.

> These are today's main events. Germany has invaded Poland and has bombed many towns. General mobilisation has been ordered in Britain and France. Parliament was summoned for six o'clock this evening. Orders completing the mobilisation of the navy, army and air force were signed by the King at a meeting this afternoon of the Privy Council. Details will be given later in this news. The British Cabinet met from half past eleven this morning until half past one. Both Houses of Parliament were summoned for six o'clock this evening. We hope to give the first part of Mr Chamberlain's statement later in this broadcast.
>
> *Alvar Lidell, BBC, 6 p.m. news, 1 September 1939*

Later that evening Neville Chamberlain told the House of Commons: 'I do not propose to say many words tonight. The time has come when action rather than speech is required. Eighteen months ago in this House I prayed that the responsibility might not fall upon me to ask this country to accept the awful arbitrament of war. I fear that I may not be able to avoid that responsibility.'

One of the enduring misconceptions about what happened in the first few days of the war concerns the Polish Air Force. One myth that has grown up over the years is that in the first few hours of the German Blitzkrieg ('lightning war') the Polish Air Force was largely destroyed on the ground. In reality many of its aircraft had been dispersed to secret locations to prevent just such a thing happening. The Luftwaffe bombed and shot up mostly empty airfields but was none the wiser because of the early morning mist that enveloped many of the aerodromes. The problem for the Polish Air Force was keeping one step ahead of the super-fast advance of the German army, with the Blitzkrieg in full swing; communications, detachment from spares, shortage of fuel and poor communications all took their toll. Following the defeat many Polish fighter pilots and other personnel escaped to England, where they were to make a significant impact during the Battle of Britain.

Midway through the 'Daily Service', which began at 10.15 a.m. on that fateful day from Studio 3E, James Welch, the BBC's Director of Religious Broadcasting, was handed a piece of paper. On it was written 'Germany invaded Poland early this morning'. It was the cue to change the broadcast and a prayer was offered for the people of Poland. By five o'clock that evening the whole of the Religious Affairs Department was on its way to Bristol.

The German radio, Reichs-Rundfunk-Gesellschaft, broadcast a wonderful piece of propaganda on the day after the German military's attack on Poland; it was their attempt to justify their invasion. The Propaganda Ministry (Reichministerium für Volksaufklärung und Propaganda) was established when the Nazis seized power in 1933. RRG was an integral part of the Ministry because, in the words of Dr Joseph Goebbels, 'Radio is the most modern, most powerful and most revolutionary weapon which we possess . . . in the struggle for the new Third Reich'.

> For the sake of history, however, the facts must be nailed down that the numerous border incidents in Silesia and East Prussia and especially the Polish bombardment of Boynton created a situation which made it incompatible for that series of military transgressions to go by unpunished. Germany's actions are an act of defence.
>
> *German radio, 2 September 1939*

Chapter 2

TODAY'S THE DAY

In the BBC's news department on Saturday 2 September 1939 things were almost unnaturally quiet; Britain 'became tensely calm', as one writer put it. The only news was that there was no news; Britain had not received a reply to its ultimatum to Germany. For the newsreaders it almost became a mantra as it was repeated over and over again; people were actually getting restless for something to happen. As day broke on 3 September it was a warm and sunny morning. It was much like any other late summer Sunday morning, except for the newspapers' headlines: 'Plans for a Long War' and 'War Cabinet Ready for Long War; Will Win at All Costs'. At around 8.30 a.m. Alvar Lidell was told to make the short trip from Broadcasting House to Downing Street, where he would be needed to make announcements as the morning's events unfolded. His first job, at 10 a.m., was to tell listeners of what had taken place in Berlin earlier that morning – or more precisely what hadn't taken place.

> Following the midnight meeting of the cabinet, the British Ambassador at 9 a.m. this morning gave the German Government two further hours in which to decide whether they would, at once, withdraw their troops from Poland. This ultimatum expires at 11 a.m. The Prime Minister will broadcast to the nation at 11.15 a.m.
>
> *Alvar Lidell, BBC, 10 a.m., 3 September 1939*

For the next seventy-five minutes the Home Programme played gramophone records, punctuated every fifteen minutes or so with the information that the Prime Minister would make an announcement at 11.15. There were also a number of recurring public service messages telling listeners, among other things, 'how to make the most of tinned foods'. Everyone knew what was coming, which only made the waiting harder.

> I am speaking to you from the Cabinet Room at 10, Downing Street. This morning the British Ambassador in Berlin handed the German Government

a final Note stating that unless we heard from them by eleven o'clock that they were prepared at once to withdraw their troops from Poland a state of war would exist between us. I have to tell you now that no such undertaking has been received, and that consequently this country is at war with Germany. You can imagine what a bitter blow it is to me that all my long struggle to win peace has failed. Yet I cannot believe that there is anything more or anything different that I could have done and that would have been more successful.

Up to the very last it would have been quite possible to have arranged a peaceful and honourable settlement between Germany and Poland. But Hitler would not have it. He had evidently made up his mind to attack Poland whatever happened, and although he now says he put forward reasonable proposals, which were rejected by the Poles, that is not a true statement. The proposals were never shown to the Poles, nor to us, and, though they were announced in a German broadcast on Thursday night, Hitler did not wait to hear comments on them, but ordered his troops to cross the Polish frontier. His action shows convincingly that there is no chance of expecting that this man will ever give up his practice of using force to gain his will. He can only be stopped by force.

We and France are today, in fulfilment of our obligations, going to the aid of Poland, who is so bravely resisting this wicked and unprovoked attack upon her people. We have a clear conscience. We have done all that any country could do to establish peace, but a situation in which no word given by Germany's ruler could be trusted and no people or country could feel themselves safe had become intolerable. And now that we have resolved to finish it, I know that you will all play your part with calmness and courage. As such a moment as this the assurances of support that we have received from the Empire are a source of profound encouragement to us.

When I have finished speaking certain detailed announcements will be made on behalf of the Government. Give these your closest attention. The Government have made plans under which it will be possible to carry on the work of the nation in the days of stress and strain that may be ahead. But these plans need your help.

You may be taking part in the fighting Services or as a volunteer in one of the branches of civil defence. If so you will report for duty in accordance with the instructions you have received. You may be engaged in work essential to the prosecution of war for the maintenance of the life of the people in hospitals, in factories, in transport, in public utility concerns or in the supply of other necessaries of life. If so, it is of vital importance that you should carry on with your jobs.

. . . Now may God bless you all and may he defend the right. For it is evil things that we shall be fighting against, brute force, bad faith, injustice, oppression and persecution. And against them I am certain that the right will prevail.

Neville Chamberlain, BBC, 11.15 a.m., 3 September 1939

At 11.27 a.m., just as Chamberlain's speech was ending, there was an air-raid warning and sirens sounded across London and the south in what would have been one of history's greatest moments of synchronicity – had it been a German attack. The warning had been triggered by an unidentified aircraft flying at about 5,000ft over an Observer Corps position at Maidstone in Kent; it was on course for London. Fighters were put on alert, but it was soon found to be a French aircraft that hadn't filed a flight plan. 'My wife commented favourably upon the German promptitude and precision and we went up onto the top of the house to see what was going on . . . [there] were already slowly rising thirty or forty cylindrical balloons. We gave the Government a good mark', wrote Winston Churchill. Twenty minutes later the all-clear sounded, but not before one Londoner is reported to have died of heart failure – the shock of hearing the siren sound had all been too much. Britain had suffered its first casualty of the war. Almost immediately the rumour mill went into overdrive; some people living in Chelsea told anyone who would listen that the East End had in fact been flattened. Nor was this the last false alarm of the day. The sirens went off again in the evening, and then again at 3 a.m.; half an hour earlier in some other parts of the country. Stuart Hibberd was reading a news bulletin when the air-raid warning sounded. He admitted later that 'It was difficult to concentrate: automatically my mind was trying to picture the scene outside.'

For years after the war, and even today, people who heard Chamberlain's speech could tell you exactly where there were, and how it made them feel. A man named Richard Brown kept a diary throughout the war in which he made a very perceptive contemporary comment: 'Chamberlain sounded quite annoyed and, at the same time, sorrowful and I noted that he referred to "Hitler" and not the usual diplomatic "Herr Hitler".' For Richard Brown, and many millions of Britons, as well as Germans, French, and other European nationalities, it was the second time in their lifetime that they found themselves at war. The horrors of the First World War were etched on their minds, horrors that modern technology would make even more horrific in this impending conflict. Wynford Vaughan-Thomas, who became a well-known war reporter for the BBC, was at the time of the Prime Minister's broadcast working as an Outside Broadcasts Assistant for BBC Wales. He was in

Llandudno and heard Chamberlain's speech on a wireless at the hotel in which he was staying. 'It was hardly a clarion call to action, "Commence hostilities" was not the message. Rather it was stop broadcasting for the BBC.'

Following the Prime Minister's speech the BBC's news department was just about the only section of the Corporation to have any real broadcasting to do. There were hourly news bulletins, but much like today with a rolling news format there was little new news, just a repetition of what had already been said. There was one significant idiosyncrasy of pre-war news bulletins that was about to change forever. In that pre-war age of elegance the announcer who read the news did so while wearing a dinner jacket. With the outbreak of hostilities he, for it was always a man, was allowed to wear 'normal' clothes – even a sports jacket. But in early 1941 there were still two dinner jackets hanging in a dressing room in the basement of Broadcasting House for some unknown emergency or another – in fact they may still be there. Neither Reith, nor his successors, saw reading the news as woman's work – people would never trust a female speaking of world events for goodness' sake. Not that the men solely read the news. They were also the continuity announcers who were required to 'fill in' the gaps between programmes and to play the gramophone records that were frequently needed to provide for a seamless broadcast. News-reading was not something the BBC identified as a dedicated profession.

The BBC's wartime newsroom and studios were situated three floors below ground to help protect them from the potential bomb damage. What it didn't do was to prevent the noise of the underground trains on the Bakerloo line to occasionally accompany the man reading the news. Besides the sounds of the underground there was competition from a noisy lavatory cistern that was next to a little studio, adjacent to the main news studio, from which news talks were frequently made. Although quite how much anyone heard of either the trains or the flushing toilet, given that the sound quality on the medium wave was nothing like as good as the VHF transmissions that we are more used to today, is not clear.

The hourly news bulletins, which became increasingly repetitious, were interspersed with special announcements from the government. These too tended to repeat themselves, but perhaps only one actually annoyed some people.

Closing of Places of Entertainment – All cinemas, theatres and other places of entertainment are to be closed immediately until further notice. In the light of experience it may be possible to allow the reopening of some places in some areas. They are being closed because if they were hit by a bomb large numbers would be killed or injured. Sports gatherings and all gatherings for purposes of entertainment and amusement, whether outdoor or indoor, which involve large numbers congregating together are prohibited until further notice. This refers especially to gatherings for purposes of entertainment, but people are earnestly requested not to crowd together unnecessarily in any circumstances. Churches and other places of public worship will not be closed.

BBC, 3 September 1939

In Australia Chamberlain's broadcast was heard on the short wave at 8 p.m. local time. It was followed, an hour and fifteen minutes later, by a broadcast from Mr R.G. Menzies, the Australian Prime Minister: 'It is my melancholy duty to inform you officially that, in consequence of a persistence by Germany in her invasion of Poland, Great Britain has declared war upon her and that, as a result, Australia is also at war.' New Zealand followed suit and later in the afternoon, the French ultimatum to Germany also expired; and so at 5 p.m. France too declared war on Germany. South Africa followed on 6 September, and Canada on the 10th. An hour after the French declaration, King George VI broadcast to Britain and the whole of the Empire from Buckingham Palace. The King's message of duty and fortitude contained the prophetic, and worrisome, words, 'and war can no longer be contained to the battlefield'. Both King George VI and his Queen would stand as shining examples of defiance throughout the war, and particularly during the Blitz on London.

In this grave hour, perhaps the most fateful in our history, I send to every household of my peoples, both at home and overseas, this message, spoken with the same depth of feeling for each one of you as if I were able to cross your threshold and speak to you myself.

For the second time in the lives of most of us we are at war. Over and over again we have tried to find a peaceful way out of the differences between ourselves and those who are now our enemies. But it has been in vain. We have been forced into a conflict. For we are called, with our allies, to meet the challenge of a principle, which, if it were to prevail, would be fatal to any civilised order in the world.

It is the principle which permits a state, in the selfish pursuit of power, to disregard its treaties and its solemn pledges; which sanctions the use of force, or threat of force, against the sovereignty and independence of other states. Such a principle, stripped of all disguise, is surely the mere primitive doctrine that might is right; and if this principle were established throughout the world, the freedom of our own country and of the whole

British Commonwealth of Nations would be in danger. But far more than this – the peoples of the world would be kept in the bondage of fear, and all hopes of settled peace and of the security of justice and liberty among nations would be ended.

This is the ultimate issue, which confronts us. For the sake of all that we ourselves hold dear, and of the world's order and peace, it is unthinkable that we should refuse to meet the challenge.

It is to this high purpose that I now call my people at home and my peoples across the seas, who will make our cause their own. I ask them to stand calm, firm, and united in this time of trial. The task will be hard. There may be dark days ahead, and war can no longer be confined to the battlefield. But we can only do the right as we see the right, and reverently commit our cause to God. If one and all we keep resolutely faithful to it, ready for whatever service or sacrifice it may demand, then, with God's help, we shall prevail.

King George VI, BBC, 6 p.m., 3 September 1939

The government planned to send a copy of the speech to every household, but such was the coverage of the radio that it was felt to be both an unnecessary strain on the Post Office and a waste of paper, which was in short supply. The radio had proved, for the first time, its power as a medium for instantaneous news dissemination that had every other method of communication beaten hands down. Within a matter of a week to ten days the Ministry of Information published a pamphlet that carried transcripts of all the important speeches by the King, the Prime Minister, and members of the Opposition, as well as a broadcast made to the French by their Prime Minister, Edouard Daladier. Was it information overload, or the Ministry taking the view that the radio didn't reach everywhere with such important messages?

Lionel Marson read the news bulletin that followed the King's broadcast and he told listeners that the War Cabinet of nine would include Winston Churchill as First Lord of the Admiralty. Moments after the bulletin a message was flashed to every Royal Navy ship at sea, and to every land base; it simply said: 'Winston is back'. Following the King's broadcast there were speeches by Arthur Greenwood, Deputy Leader of the Labour Party, whose theme was 'We Believe in Liberty', and by Sir Archibald Sinclair for the Liberals; his was called 'The Common Cause'. The Archbishop of Canterbury gave an address in the 'Evening Service'.

Mollie Panter-Downes, an American living in London who wrote about the day in the *New Yorker* magazine, seemed to see it all through thirties gaiety-tinted glasses:

Today was a day of unprecedented activity in the air. Squadrons of bombers bustled in all directions and at midday an enormous number of vast planes, to which the knowing pointed as troop carriers, droned overhead toward an unknown destination that was said by two sections of opinion to be (a) France and (b) Poland. On the ground, motor buses full of troops in bursting good humor tore through the villages, the men waving at the girls and howling 'Tipperary' and other ominously dated ditties that everybody has suddenly remembered and found to be as good for a war in 1939 as they were in 1914. London and the country are buzzing with rumors, a favorite one being that Hitler carries a gun in his pocket and means to shoot himself if things don't go too well; another school of thought favors the version that he is now insane and Goering has taken over. The English were a peace-loving nation up to two days ago, but now it is pretty widely felt that the sooner we really get down to the job, the better.

Chapter 3

WHAT WAR?

FOOD GLORIOUS FOOD

The months that followed the outbreak of war have perhaps most famously been called the Phoney War, and, most amusingly, the Bore War. And while it's true that there was not a great deal of actual fighting there was no shortage of activity in just about every office, section and department of the BBC. Within twenty-four hours of war being declared there was a feverish round of memoranda expounding all sorts of theories as to what constituted the best type of broadcasting for Britain and the world.

Possibly the most perceptive was John Green, who worked in the BBC's Talks Department. He was eager to have programmes about farming and gardening, designed to inspire listeners to cultivate. The need to supplement a family's food supply, which would be severely diminished by rationing, would be a key feature of the war on the Home Front. Green's boss, Sir Richard Maconachie, the Head of the Talks Department, felt the same but suggested the Cabinet via the Ministry of Information should take the lead. These first seedlings were to bear fruit within nine months when a series entitled 'The Kitchen Front' went on air in June 1940; by October it was attracting close to 5.5 million people in its regular 8.15 a.m. slot. Food rationing was introduced on 8 January 1940, largely as a result of the losses inflicted by German U-boats on British merchant shipping bringing food to the country from around the world. Such was the success of 'The Kitchen Front' that German radio regularly poked fun at it. But there's no doubting its importance as it gave all sorts of valuable advice to wives and mothers who were struggling with rationing. The first presenter was Marguerite Patten, one of the government's food advisers. Later, Elsie and Doris Waters – better known as Gert and Daisy – Freddie Grisewood, and Grandma Buggins – 'a difficult woman', who had first appeared on children's radio played by the actress Mabel Constanduros – would all be featured in the programme to keep up the interest level with the audience. George Orwell's wife, Eileen O'Shaughnessy, and the novelist Lettice Cooper, who both worked for the Ministry of Food, prepared scripts and recipes for the show.

By the time the war ended there had been close to 1,200 radio broadcasts on the subject of food. With the levels of rationing imposed on the British public it's fair to say that food had become something of a national obsession. Besides 'The Kitchen Front' there was also 'In Your Garden' (3 million listeners in October 1940), which had been on air since before the war, but now had an added reason to be there. Another programme, 'Back to the Land', was specifically aimed at smallholders, an increasingly important source of home-grown food. By 1942 there was also 'The Radio Allotment', which was an outside broadcast; it was rather like the radio equivalent of television's 'Gardener's World' without the flowers. In the strictest sense of the word these programmes were of course not news, but they provided very valuable information throughout the period of the war when for some the Home Front seemed like the front line.

Not that it was just in Britain that food rationing was an issue. On German radio in September they were offering menu suggestions for the first three days of the week. It was far from a balanced diet.

MONDAY

Breakfast: Malt coffee, wholemeal bread, apple tart prepared with windfalls.

Lunch: Elderberry soup, hotpots prepared with apple potatoes, and white cabbage.

Dinner: Potatoes, with horseradish salad, one slice of bread and sausage.

TUESDAY

Breakfast: Flour soup, bread and fat.

Lunch: Cucumbers filled with bread, potatoes with parsley, carrot salad.

Dinner: Pudding with stewed pears and bilberries.

WEDNESDAY

Breakfast: 'German' tea, wholemeal bread and jam.

Lunch: Hotpot, consisting of beans, carrots, potatoes and bacon.

Dinner: Stewed fruit, wholemeal bread and junket.

German radio, c. 25 September 1939

LIMITED NEWS

In the early hours of 4 September, less than twenty-four hours after war had been declared and even less time since President Roosevelt had declared US neutrality, two things happened that underlined sharply the dichotomy of war. The Cunard liner SS *Athenia* was torpedoed by a U-boat off the west coast of

Scotland; on board were many American passengers who were leaving the UK and Europe for the safety of their own homes. At Broadcasting House, when the news first came through, the duty editor and newsreader were standing alongside Ed Murrow, an American reporter for CBS based in London. Murrow, who would establish his reputation during the war for his broadcasts from Britain, then heard the Germans' claim that they had mistaken the liner for an armed merchantman. Within twenty-four hours many of the survivors from the *Athenia* landed at Greenock in Scotland and the BBC was there to record their accounts for broadcasting on the news; there had been 1,103 passengers on board, and mercifully only 118 lost their lives. The recording was made by one of the two BBC mobile recording units, carried in a Wolseley saloon car. The other Wolseley had secretly been driven to Paris a few days before war had been declared, where it had been hidden in an underground car park.

In stark contrast to the 'real news' of people who lost their lives on the *Athenia* was a letter in that morning's edition of *The Times* complaining about the closure of places of entertainment, news of which had been announced on the radio two days earlier.

> May I be allowed to protest vehemently against the order to close all theatres and picture houses during the war? It seems to me a masterstroke of unimaginative stupidity . . . What agent of Chancellor Hitler is it who suggested that we should all cower in darkness and terror 'for the duration'?
>
> > Why brother soldiers, why
> > Should we be melancholy boys?
> > *George Bernard Shaw*, The Times, 5 September 1939

Another early victim of war was the BBC Board of Governors, whose numbers were immediately reduced from seven to two, a move that was hoped would allow for speedier decision making. Simultaneously control reverted, for some aspects of broadcasting, to the Ministry of Information; most notably it allowed for 'the possible control of the service in emergency'. The issue of censorship was a vital one and it was made clear that the BBC, like the newspapers, was subject to rigorous controls. Put simply, the BBC 'must not broadcast information likely to be of military value to the enemy'. In the Corporation's *Handbook* of 1940 it was pointed out that this was only 'a small diminution of its peacetime liberties that the BBC has suffered'. On 7 September there was the first meeting of the Advisory Council of the Ministry of Information. While it was reiterated that censorship was a key issue it was also made clear that the news on the BBC should be 'truthful and objective'. After the war there were those, including Duff Cooper, who would argue that the Ministry's only real function was as a censor. Its abilities to inform were woefully inadequate, in his view. Labour MP Aneurin Bevan put it another way: 'If the Germans did not manage to bomb us to death the Ministry of Information will bore us to death.'

During the first week of war, and for a number of weeks more, there were ten news bulletins each day; the only problem was that they were a bit short of content. The enduring memory for those who sat glued to the radio during the opening weeks of the war was the tidal wave of announcements, regulations, and instructions. There were even counter-instructions when it was realised that the first one wouldn't necessarily work. There were broadcasts by ministers, public information bulletins, and talks about the strictures that war would place on the country. However, not all the talks could be said to be inspirational: 'The Louse' by Professor Buxton of Cambridge University would probably fall into that category. As one commentator put it, 'your wireless seemed to have changed from an agreeable companion to an official bully'. Added to which the stockpiles of records that had been earmarked for use during this period were already becoming repetitive; even good old Sandy Macpherson at the theatre organ, giving up to three performances each day, was struggling to liven up the proceedings. It was a question of who would succumb soonest – the audience from over-exposure or Macpherson from exhaustion.

To lighten the proceedings, in a way that children often seem unconsciously to manage, there were reports from those who had been evacuated ten days earlier.

Hello mum and dad don't get worried about us we're very happy here. I don't think anybody wants to go home – yet. We go on the moors nearly every night and watch all the cows and the sheep grazing and the river flowing – we're quite near it now. We go playing football on the football pitch and watch the colliery. Last week the girls and boys had a match of netball, there were 14 girls and three boys, the girls won us.

Boy evacuee, BBC, 10 September 1939

Almost inevitably the BBC came under attack from the press, but in fairness they really were only reflecting public opinion. As the novelist Naomi Mitchison noted in her diary, 'After supper and the 9 o'clock news – and we've made up our minds not to listen too much, as this constant dripping of the wireless gets on our nerves badly'. Not everybody took such a firm stance; at the time it was estimated that 50 per cent of the population listened each night to the 9 p.m. BBC news. At the same time the newspapers got up a head of steam, accusing radio entertainment of being 'puerile'. Other complainants said it was a 'scandal', 'a travesty', and that the BBC broadcast 'second-rate programmes'. One listener in Scotland grumbled about the lack of programmes specifically about his own country and then summed up what most people felt about the general level of the Corporation's output: 'We could do with a little less organ music and fewer records.'

Even so, the fact was that the BBC was in a no-win situation. To begin with, the logistics of moving all but essential BBC staff out of London would have been a mammoth undertaking in peacetime, without the added complications brought on by war. With almost all the 'entertainment' departments having been relocated it was something of a minor miracle that any programmes other than news and talks were heard at all. Against the odds on Wednesday 6 September the first variety programme went on air from the Bristol studios. Pretty soon the Drama, Schools, Religious and Variety Departments were all managing to generate something akin to their peacetime output. While some, including the newspapers, continued to complain there were others who were impressed with what the Corporation had succeeded in doing. The 68-year-old Sir Seymour Hicks, the great actor–manager, wrote from the Garrick Club to one of the BBC's announcers to say, 'I should only like you to know that an ordinary member of the public – who earns his living by serving his country – appreciates to the full that you are doing.' One change that was noticed, and applauded, by everyone was the fact that the Variety Department could at last lampoon Hitler, and the rest of his 'gang of Nazis'. All pretence at the diplomatic niceties was dropped, and comedies like 'Adolf in Blunderland' parodied Hitler with songs like 'The Voice of the Führer'.

Come the end of September, when around eighteen hours of records were being played each week, Clement Attlee told Parliament, 'There is very wide criticism of broadcasting'. To be fair the objections had been as much about the lack of decent entertainment programmes as they were about the quality of the news. One significant problem for the BBC, and the newspapers too, was that when real news did come along it was more often than not bad news. There had been the sinking of an aircraft carrier, HMS *Courageous*, with the loss of 500 men, while on the Home Front income tax was raised to 7s 6d in the pound (37.5 per cent) to help meet the cost of the war. To cap it all 250,000 conscripts were called up on 1 October; while people anticipated such things, they still found it very disheartening. With the absence of hard news bulletins were soon reduced to seven each day, much to the delight of the newspapers, for they had never enjoyed the competition from the BBC, especially for their evening editions. There had been no choice but to put the BBC into war mode, but it was a move which anticipated that things would happen, and while there were some things happening there were not enough of them to make for interesting bulletins. In the post-declaration lull there was no invasion, no bombing; there was nothing that seemed like a real war.

Five days before Attlee spoke in Parliament about broadcasting the BBC carried an important relay of a speech by the US president. Roosevelt, speaking to Congress about American neutrality, finished with these words:

. . . I should like to be able to offer the hope that the shadow over the world might swiftly pass. I cannot. The facts compel my stating, with candor, that darker periods may lie ahead. The disaster is not of our making; no act of ours engendered the forces which assault the foundations of civilisation. Yet we find ourselves affected to the core; our currents of commerce are changing, our minds are filled with new problems, our position in world affairs has already been altered.

In such circumstances our policy must be to appreciate in the deepest sense the true American interest. Rightly considered, this interest is not selfish. Destiny first made us, with our sister nations on this hemisphere, joint heirs of European culture. Fate seems now to compel us to assume the task of helping to maintain in the western world a citadel wherein that civilisation may be kept alive. The peace, the integrity, and the safety of the Americas – these must be kept firm and serene. In a period when it is sometimes said that free discussion is no longer compatible with national safety, may you by your deeds show the world that we of the United States are one people, of one mind, one spirit, one clear resolution, walking before God in the light of the living.

Franklin D. Roosevelt, BBC, 21 September 1939

Few who heard Roosevelt's words would have realised the significance of what he had said, nor the level of behind-the-scenes support for Britain from the US president.

PROBLEMS AT HOME

Life on the Home Front in the first month of the war brought problems that have often been overlooked by historians. The switch from a peacetime, albeit one that had been gearing up to war, to a wartime economy brought significant issues; although some were far from unique, having also occurred during the First World War. It was hoped that the experiences of the earlier conflict, when there was widespread unemployment during the first weeks of hostilities, would not be repeated. Sir Samuel Hoare, the Lord Privy Seal, spoke on the BBC in the third week of war on the issue of the Home Front:

. . . Too many workers had been dismissed, and I appeal to employers to refrain from dismissing employees whose services may be needed later. It is natural that those employers who find the market for their products restricted by war-time conditions should seek to economise by reducing their staffs, since they cannot be expected to conduct business on a philanthropic basis. But they might be well advised to wait until the nation has settled down to the changed situation before they dispense with the services of employees. Industries which are severely hit during the period of transition may recover to an unexpected degree when people become accustomed to conditions of war. Employers who hasten to dismiss may find that they have effected an unnecessary and ill advised economy, besides increasing the hardships which can scarce be avoided in the first stage of a war.

Sir Samuel Hoare, BBC, 22 September 1939

While unemployment among men had dropped by some 75,000, there were 175,000 more women who were out of work in September, some of which could be attributed to the closure of places of entertainment.

. . . When more men are called to the colours there is likely to be a marked shortage of labour, and the country will need at no very distant date the services of every able-bodied man and woman. Apart from the fighting services, the defence industries, and the trades and professions which are essential for the conduct of the everyday life of the nation, the export industries must be maintained, and with all those calls on labour there should be little unemployment, except in the case of the unemployable . . . I urge people to refrain from excessive economy. With the additional taxation the Chancellor of the Exchequer imposed in his War Budget most people will perforce have to exercise a certain amount of economy, and the drastic action against profiteering which the Government intends to take will not prevent increases in prices necessitated by the additional costs of war risks insurance and other factors. But economy does not mean refusing to buy anything beyond the bare necessities of life. Such a misguided zeal for saving would paralyze the economic activity of the nation. 'No misers, no hoarders, and no profiteers', should be our slogan whether we are producers or consumers.

Sir Samuel Hoare, BBC, 22 September 1939

Just over a week later the BBC began a new series called 'Home Front', in which aspects of life in the changing scenario brought about by war were featured. Other shows like 'In Britain Now' (first broadcast on 17 November 1939) and 'Go to It' were soon added to let people hear how others all around Britain were coping with war at home.

From very early in the war it was recognised that 'farming was as important as arming' if Britain was to stand any chance of winning. The toll taken by U-boats on merchant shipping soon began to mount, which is partly what inspired the bright idea of the 'Dig for Victory' campaign. It was a simple notion that encouraged everyone to use any spare piece of land, and especially allotments, to cultivate vegetables. It was the perfect way to supplement what would become an increasingly worrisome diet that shortages would impose on Britain. As early as October 1939 the slogan began to be touted, and the philosophy was seen as a huge opportunity. Naturally the BBC was central to the strategy in being the most effective way not just to communicate ideas but also to inspire people in all sorts of creative ways; by the spring of 1940 'Digging for Victory' was everywhere. Activities were launched right across the country and at local events speakers urged people to give over 'a few square yards of garden to the cultivation of potatoes which would produce 45 times as much human food as the same square yards of pasture'. This was one of the great triumphs of the war on the Home Front, and by 1943 it was estimated that over a million tons of vegetables were being grown in Britain's gardens and allotments. As a BBC announcer said in the spring of 1940, 'Today we begin a new Dig for Victory campaign. The successful Dig For Victory campaign this autumn was one of the best answers to Hitler's attempts to damage our overseas food supplies and interrupt our communications. We must try to rope in every single person.'

THE STORY SO FAR

With the war just a month old it fell to Winston Churchill to talk to the nation on the BBC; his theme was the progress of the war so far. In fact what Churchill did was not, as his biographer Roy Jenkins has noted, to talk to the nation at all. What he gave were 'broadcast declarations'. This declaration was almost a year to the day after Churchill's speech in which he had urged, 'We must arm . . .':

The British Empire and the French Republic have been at war with Nazi Germany for a month tonight. We have not yet come at all to the severity of fighting which is to be expected. But three important things have happened.

Poland has again been again overrun by two of the great powers that held her in bondage for 150 years, but were unable to quench the spirit of the Polish nation. The heroic defence of Warsaw shows that the soul of Poland is indestructible . . . The second event is of course the assertion of power of Russia. Russia has pursued a cold policy of self-interest. We could have wished that the Russian armies could be standing on their present line as the friends and allies of Poland instead of as invaders. But that the Russian armies should stand on this line was clearly necessary for the safety of Russia against the Nazi menace. At any rate the line is there, and an Eastern Front has been created that Nazi Germany dare not assail . . . I cannot forecast to you the action of Russia. It is a riddle wrapped in a mystery inside an enigma: but perhaps there is a key. That key is Russian national interest.

What is the third event; here I speak as First Lord of the Admiralty, with especial caution. It would seem that the U-boat attack upon the life of the British Isles has not so far proved successful. It is true that when they sprang out upon us as we were going about our ordinary business with 2,000 ships in constant movement every day upon the seas they managed to do some serious damage. But the Royal Navy has immediately attacked the U-boat and is hunting them night and day . . . And it looks tonight that it is the U-boat that is feeling the weather and not the Royal Navy.

. . . Directions have been given by the Government to prepare for a war of at least three years. That does not mean that victory may not be gained in a shorter time. How soon it will be gained depends on how long Herr Hitler and his group of wicked men, whose hands are stained with blood and soiled with corruption, can keep their grip on the docile, unhappy German people. It was for Hitler to say when the war would begin, but it is not for him, or for his successor, to say when it will end. It began when he wanted it and it will end only when we are convinced that he has had enough . . .

Winston Churchill, BBC, 9.15 p.m., 1 October 1939

Among the many millions who listened to Churchill was Neville Chamberlain, who wrote about it to his sister in glowing terms: 'I take the same view as Winston, to whose excellent broadcast we have just been listening.' Five days later Hitler took a somewhat different view of the First Lord of the Admiralty's radio declaration when he spoke in the German Parliament. The German Chancellor singled out Churchill as the main protagonist, which was extremely perceptive of him given the fact that Chamberlain was still Prime Minister, and would remain so for over seven months. But then again, Hitler's views on Chamberlain had already been made clear.

Mr Churchill and his companions may interpret these opinions of mine as weakness or cowardice if they like. I need not occupy myself with what they think; I make these statements simply because it goes without saying that I wish to spare my own people this suffering. If, however, the opinions of Messrs Churchill and followers should prevail, this statement will have been my last. Then we shall fight. Neither force of arms nor lapse of time will conquer Germany. There never will be another November 1918 in German history. It is infantile to hope for the disintegration of our people.

Mr Churchill may be convinced that Great Britain will win. I do not doubt for a single moment that Germany will be victorious. Destiny will decide who is right.

Adolf Hitler, broadcast on German radio from the Reichstag,
6 October 1939

Not everyone was so concerned with such serious matters. H. Wilson Harris, the editor of the *Spectator*, writing as Janus in the 6 October 1939 edition, was taking a more obtuse view of the war:

What, by the way, is the BBC coming to? Twice on Wednesday (very likely there were other opportunities of which I failed to take advantage) news about Moscow, Berlin, Rome, the Western Front, sinkings of neutral ships, was followed by the singular observation that 'A walk in the country is urged by the Ramblers' Association as . . .', if I remember, specially beneficial for nerves, limbs and other organs or fibres; farmers, therefore, ought not to be allowed to plough up footpaths. The Ramblers' Association is no doubt an admirable body. So, to take a random example, is the Governesses' Benevolent Institution – and ex-governesses are likely to have a particularly bad time during war. Will the BBC give them a show? If not, why not? If so, what other estimable organisations may apply?

Janus, Spectator, *6 October 1939*

It was all rather redolent of the times; it was almost as though, for many British people, the war was something that barely concerned them. There were many life-changing aspects of war, not least the blackout, which affected everyone, but it was one thing that actually had a positive benefit. Coincident with the blackout being fully enforced was the fact that crime in Britain was at an all-time low. The police instead turned their attention to rounding up suspected aliens; by the end of September they had interned 6,000.

THE SOUNDS OF WAR

Beginning in early October the war started to seem more real to those listening to the radio. In part this was because the BBC began airing reports from the mobile recording unit that had been hidden in the underground car park in Paris. The men who reclaimed it were 26-year-old Richard Dimbleby, along with an engineer and another BBC employee. Dimbleby knew exactly where to find the car as he had driven it to France the week before the war broke out. He had been with the BBC for three years, having joined in 1936 as the first of their Topical Talks Assistants, which was something akin to a roving reporter. Dimbleby's vision for his job was a combination of what many years later Alan Whicker, John Simpson and Rageh Omaar became; unfortunately, it was a vision not always shared by his superiors. Colleagues talked of his 'remarkable energy' and said he was a 'pioneer', but to those he worked for he was something of a maverick. Nicknamed 'Bumble' by his colleagues, most of whom were at least five years older than Dimbleby, and were graduates, Richard Dimbleby had not been to university; he was merely a former newspaper reporter for the *Richmond and Twickenham Times* – a paper edited by his father – and a former employee of the *Advertisers' Weekly*, among other not very prestigious papers. In fact, Dimbleby was lucky even to be in France, as his first broadcast for the BBC was almost his last. Sir Cecil Graves, the Deputy Director General, heard it and contacted R.T. Clark, the Senior News Editor, to report that the BBC's newest recruit 'started his piece with an inverted sentence . . . Dimbleby is not to broadcast again'.

Accompanying Richard Dimbleby on his French adventure was David Howarth, who had the somewhat unusual title of a 'Programme Official'; Howarth would later join the Royal Navy, and later still the Special Operations Executive. There was also the all-important engineer, the wonderfully named Harvey Sarney. All three men had been kitted out in military-style uniforms, at the insistence of the War Office; Dimbleby had bought his from Austin Reed, ensuring he was the very model of a modern army officer. From Paris the BBC men drove to Arras, the headquarters of the British Expeditionary Force (BEF), and introduced themselves to both officers and men. Once ensconced in an attic at General Headquarters Dimbleby set about trying to root out suitable stories; it proved to be hard work, despite the fact that there were already over 158,000 British troops in France.

We are standing in the pouring rain at the side of a French road, a road squelching with mud and lined right away over the plain to the far skyline with the inevitable double row of poplars. It's a grey, cold, dismal day. A few lorries only are splashing by to and from the forward areas. But coming down the road towards us is a battalion that I know to be of a famous Irish regiment. They are marching in threes, and in their full battledress and kit they blend with the dripping green grass of the roadside and the brown of the haystacks . . . As they passed us on that road, with their brown capes glistening and their tin hats perched on their heads, I thought how similar this must be to pictures of the last war: the road, the trees, the rain and the everlasting beat of feet.

Richard Dimbleby, BBC, 13 October 1939

Sarney had caught the skirl of the bagpipes as an atmospheric background to the commentary. It was all designed to make it sound as if something was happening. Given the lack of action the three men managed to inveigle their way into an attachment to the French Army and drove to Saar on the frontier with Germany; from there they could at least see the enemy.

I could hear the birds singing in the wood, the rustle of a hare that leapt away from us . . . this wood had been shelled. Nearly every night it was visited by German patrols . . . We found a machine gun mounted in a small trench, manned by three men. Fifty yards along the edge of the wood was the second gun. We were only three hundred yards from the German position . . . I suppose we were in full view of the Germans . . .

Richard Dimbleby, BBC, autumn 1939

Soon afterwards the BBC's trio managed to record the sounds of the French guns firing from the Maginot Line. Sarney had set up his recording equipment on a truck on the miniature railway that ran through the underground fort. The recording of the guns was treated by the BBC, and the *Radio Times* in particular, as something approaching a world scoop, which in its own small way it was. But rather than stirring a passionate response from the public all it seemed to do was to incite the press yet again to complain about the BBC. The Newspaper and Periodicals Emergency Council insisted that these reports 'should not be transmitted until after newspaper reports of the same event had already been published'. It was not the first time that the BBC had broadcast gunfire, nor the sounds of bombs exploding. Dimbleby had covered the hostilities in Spain at the tail end of the Civil War. He recorded a piece that was broadcast in the 10 p.m. news about Republican soldiers fleeing across the border with France to escape Franco's troops. It was arguably the BBC's first piece of war reporting, and it had helped Dimbleby's career no end.

Other reports from France remained optimistic, with lines like 'these people don't think they will win – they KNOW it'. But keeping the listeners' spirits raised at home was a tricky task when Dimbleby's spirits were at a low ebb. He just wanted something to happen so that he could stop having to make silk news out of sows' ears. With Christmas approaching one correspondent was led to claim that 'boredom is their worst enemy' when talking about the Allied troops, but it was a sentiment that could equally be applied to war reporters.

On 16 October, three days after Dimbleby's report 'from beside a French road', the war arrived in Britain by way of Scotland, and more precisely Edinburgh, when nine Junkers Ju88 attacked the Rosyth Naval Dockyard, on the north shore of the Firth of Forth; it was the Luftwaffe's first attack on Britain.

To-day, October 16, between 9 a.m. and 1.30 p.m., several German aircraft reconnoitred Rosyth. This afternoon, about half-past two, a series of bombing raids began. These were directed at the ships lying in the Forth, and were conducted by about a dozen machines. All the batteries opened fire upon the raiders, and the Royal Air Force fighter squadron ascended to engage them. No serious damage was done to any of His Majesty's ships. One bomb glanced off the cruiser *Southampton* causing slight damage near her bow, and sank the Admiral's barge and pinnate, which were moored empty alongside. This was the first hit which German aircraft have made during the war upon a British ship. There were three casualties on board the *Southampton* and seven on board the cruiser *Edinburgh* from splinters. Another bomb fell near the destroyer *Mohawk*, which was returning to harbour from convoy escort. This bomb burst on the water, and its splinters caused 25 casualties . . . On the other hand, four bombers, at least, out at the twelve or fourteen were brought down, three of them by fighters of the RAF.

BBC News, 9 p.m., 16 October 1939

Around 2.30 p.m. the German aircraft were sighted, and Spitfires of No. 603 (City of Edinburgh) Squadron, Auxiliary Air Force, were scrambled from RAF Turnhouse (the site of modern-day Edinburgh airport) to intercept the raiders. Additionally, Spitfires from No. 602 (City of Glasgow) Squadron, based at RAF Drem, located to the east of Edinburgh, in East Lothian, were on patrol at 20,000 feet.

At around 2.35 p.m., the Luftwaffe bombers began their attack and were met with anti-aircraft fire. The Spitfires of 603 Squadron that had taken off from Turnhouse were the first to engage the Junkers and soon shot down one of the bombers. The Spitfires from 602 Squadron were then ordered into the attack and they shot down another. During the action the Royal Navy suffered three officers and thirteen ratings killed and a further forty-four wounded on board the light cruisers HMS *Southampton* and *Edinburgh* and the destroyer HMS *Mohawk*. There were also two people injured on the ground in Edinburgh by falling shell cases.

Probably on the following day the BBC broadcast an interview recorded by the mobile unit of several eyewitnesses to the raid. One of the men, a bricklayer working to the west of the city, was very pleased to see the RAF do so well.

. . . one of the bonniest siehts I ever saw . . . I got no farther than one brick when over they came and, my word, the fighters were fairly pepperin' the Nazi.

Did you take shelter? [asked the reporter]

Nae fear. Yon was the sieht o' a lifetime and I wouldn'te missed it for all the Nazis in the world.

BBC News, 17 October 1939

There is an amusing postscript to the story involving a Luftwaffe pilot who was taken prisoner after his aircraft was shot down. He was taken to Bletchley Park to be interrogated by British Intelligence. By all accounts he was the archetypal Nazi, smartly dressed and capable of the full gambit of actions considered *de rigueur* for German officers. A party of four was assembled for the interrogation, including one of the cryptographers, who were more at home in the halls of academia than questioning a prisoner. The interrogators felt it was vital to adopt an air of superiority and so they sat behind a long table as the prisoner was marched in. He came to a halt, stood to attention, snapped his heels, gave the Nazi salute and said 'Heil Hitler'. At this the cryptographer jumped to his feet, saluted and repeated the 'Heil Hitler'. Realising his mistake, he sat down, or tried to, missed the chair and ended up on the floor. Needless to say, the interrogation team learned nothing.

MORE VARIETY

Besides having some real war to report on, and much to listeners' relief, the BBC managed by the middle of October to reduce from eighteen to just six hours per week the playing of gramophone records. This reduction had been achieved by an increase in the number of documentary-type programmes, as well as an upsurge in variety and entertainment programmes as the various BBC departments settled more fully into their new out-of-London homes. All in all it meant that the Home Programme was broadcasting for seventeen hours each day, whereas before the war a 'BBC day' lasted for just fourteen. On 1 November the first public appearance of the BBC Symphony Orchestra at Bristol's Colston Hall was broadcast. Four days later there was the first broadcast of a complete Gilbert and Sullivan opera, *Trial by Jury*. Equally as important as the reduction in records was the fact that there was less Sandy Macpherson at the theatre organ, and definitely more 'Variety'.

On Thursday 2 November, by no means an atypical evening, listening to the wireless would have provided a pretty mixed bag. Following the six o'clock news was a talk for the amateur handyman and then the first broadcast of an ENSA concert at an army camp 'somewhere in England', featuring Jack Buchanan, Elsie Randolph, Fred Emney and Sid Millward and his Orchestra. ENSA – the Entertainment National Services Association – had been formed specifically to entertain the troops, and many similar thirty-minute programmes were featured on the radio throughout the war. Following ENSA there was an orchestral concert, one of several during the evening, and then an adaptation of A.E.W. Mason's *The Four Feathers* – not inappropriate for wartime – several talks and thirty minutes of Government announcements, as well as the regular news bulletins, at 9 p.m. and midnight. Somewhat amusingly on this particular evening the talk scheduled to be given by the amateur handyman W.R. Mathews was given by Stuart Hibberd, as Mr Mathews was held up on the tube. It was no mean achievement having to sightread complicated instructions about maintaining lavatory cisterns! Ten days after the first ENSA concert there was the inaugural ENSA broadcast from France at which Sir Seymour Hicks was the master of ceremonies.

Just over a week later the ambition of the BBC was ably demonstrated when a short series called 'The Shadow of the Swastika' was inaugurated, in which a dramatic reconstruction of the rise of the Nazi party was attempted. One letter-writer to the newspapers congratulated the BBC on their use of incidental music, saying it 'suggested the cacophonies of what one of our poets has called "the cohorts of the damned"'. A thirty-year-old actor named Marius Goring, who would later regularly broadcast on the BBC's German Service, played the part of Hitler. In 1939 he had played the part of a U-boat captain in *The Spy in Black*; after the war he played a Nazi in *Ill-Met by Moonlight*, as well as having a successful career in TV and films.

From mid-November, with little or no real war to talk about, it really did become 'jaw war', with government ministers as well as their political opponents lining up to broadcast to the nation. Inevitably among the ministers was the First Lord of the Admiralty, who talked about the early stages of the war. His upbeat speech highlighted 'how well the war has turned for the Allies during the first ten weeks'. Prophetically, Churchill spoke of the superior quality of the RAF against the Luftwaffe, and commented that the 'mists and storms of winter' would act in Britain's favour. In a veiled comment he spoke of 'a marked advantage in the higher range of science applied to war'. Then on 26 November the Prime Minister spoke on 'The War and Ourselves'; it was his first broadcast since the day war broke out. On the following day Herbert Morrison, Labour MP for Hackney, added his contribution in a speech entitled, 'What are we fighting for?':

In my own mind I make a distinction between war aims and peace aims. Our war aim can be stated very shortly. It is to defeat our enemy, and by that I do not merely mean the defeat of the enemy's military forces. I mean the defeat of that aggressive, bullying mentality, which seeks continually to dominate other people by force, which finds a brutal satisfaction in the persecution and torture of inoffensive citizens, and, in the name of the interest of the State, justifies the repudiation of its own pledged word whenever it finds it convenient. If the German people can be convinced that that spirit is as bad for themselves as for the rest of the world, they will abandon it.

If we can secure that they do abandon it without bloodshed so much the better, but abandoned it must be. That is our war aim, and we shall persevere in this struggle until we have attained it.

Neville Chamberlain, BBC broadcast, 26 November 1939

Morrison summed up the mood of the time with his opening remarks of a BBC broadcast on 27 November 1939: 'This is a queer war. First we had had four years of a peace that was anything but peaceful, now we had a war that, so far, was not nearly so – warlike as we expected.'

As 1939 drew to a close the pattern of wartime broadcasting became ever more stable; it was against this background that the BBC took a decision that would have long-lasting ramifications. It was decided that separate programmes should be broadcast, one for those at home and the other specifically for the Forces. The BBC had naturally covered the visit of the King to the BEF in France in early December, which was of interest to everyone, but a more tailor-made service for the Services was deemed more appropriate in wartime.

A week after the King's visit the BBC began a series of eight broadcasts entitled 'The Voice of the Nazi', in which Scot W.A. Sinclair discussed Nazi propaganda.

In the second of these programmes, on Boxing Day 1939, Sinclair talked about German radio's problems when discussing the sinking of the *Graf Spee*. On 15 December Germany had announced that their 'pocket battleship' had won a famous victory, but from there it all went downhill.

> Then, on the following days the Nazi announcements became hopelessly contradictory. First of all the German wireless said that the *Graf Spee* had soundly beaten three British cruisers, that she was undamaged, and had gone into Montevideo only because her food supply had been tainted by our alleged mustard-gas shells. Not long after, as you know, they had to admit that the ship was unseaworthy, and they then protested that she could not be repaired in the time allowed her by the Uruguayan Government.
>
> But the facts are common knowledge now, and the Nazis have had to admit that the *Graf Spee* has been scuttled and that her commander has committed suicide. This must have done more than any other single incident since the war began to arouse mistrust of the Nazi news in the ordinary German's mind.
>
> *W.A. Sinclair, BBC, 26 December 1939*

JARMANY CALLING

For almost everyone who lived through the Second World War the only person who truly qualified for the epithet 'Voice of the Nazi' was William Joyce, or 'Lord Haw-Haw', as he became known to everyone.

The enduring image of William Joyce is one bound up in ridicule. However, for a short while the man who made the phrase 'Jarmany Calling' his trademark had an extremely negative effect on some of those who listened to his broadcasts in Britain. His biographer Mary Kenny has described him, quite correctly, as 'one of the twentieth century's most notorious voices'. Many also found the Irishman one of the most irritating. Even sixty years later his clipped tones sound authoritarian, smug, and hectoring – all within the same sentence.

Born in New York in April 1906 to an English mother and an Irish father, Joyce moved with his family to Ireland three years later, where he grew up in County Mayo. The family moved to England when Joyce was fifteen, and two years later he was demonstrating strongly anti-Semitic views, although he was far from alone in Britain. Having joined the Conservative Party, Joyce by 1932 was almost inevitably drawn to Sir Oswald Mosley's British Union of Fascists. In contrast to Mosley, who had a relaxed, some said an almost charming manner, Joyce was by all accounts a nasty, angry man, and by 1937 the latter had split from the BUF and formed his own party, the British National Socialist League. A week before war broke out Joyce, together with his family, fled to Berlin after a tip-off that his arrest was imminent.

In Berlin he quickly ingratiated himself with the German Foreign Ministry, which is how he came to have a job on German radio, broadcasting in English. Lord Haw-Haw, as the *Daily Express* dubbed him, was a name that stuck and as he had not revealed his true identity it was the perfect cover-up.

With his broadcasts seeming to reveal details that only a man with a network of spies and informers could possibly know, the attraction to listeners starved of what they saw as real information by the BBC who were merely doing as much as they were allowed by the Ministry of Information, it was easy to see why millions tuned in to Radio Bremen during the early months of the war. Such was the Haw-Haw effect that in May 1940 the Ministry finally snapped and issued a statement that was broadcast on the BBC.

> Rumours attributing to the German wireless an intimate knowledge of British local events through secret channels are without foundation, states the Ministry of Information. It is clearly important that no individual should help to undermine confidence by repeating these rumours at all events unless he has personally tuned in to Germany and heard the statement for himself. If Germans possessed secret channels in British towns for obtaining such information they would scarcely be likely to advertise the fact. On some occasions there may be a perfectly simple explanation of German broadcast descriptions of local events in Britain.
>
> *BBC News, 29 May 1940*

Quite apart from the slightly odd notion that it was only men who tuned into German radio, there is an inference that things were only untrue if they were repeated!

> Win, the fat-head, is in a stew because she listened to Lord Haw-Haw who said Ipswich was being made a garrison town therefore it would be bombed and specially mentioned the Mansion. I mention it to show how they try to put the wind up us and succeed with some people.
>
> *Richard Brown's diary, 15 September 1940*

After the Battle of Britain and the start of the war on the Eastern Front Haw-Haw's collateral went steadily downhill, although on occasions he continued to hit the mark. Joyce took German citizenship, which failed to stop him from being tried in Britain for treason – the fact that he was born in

America and was more Irish than English did nothing to help him either. Joyce was executed in January 1946.

CENSORSHIP?

Winston Churchill had been bullish in his speech of 12 November 1939, speaking optimistically and forecasting that Britain would 'gain the first campaign of the war'. But behind the scenes he was unhappy with one aspect of the BBC's coverage of the war so far. At a cabinet meeting on 16 December Churchill, who had turned sixty-five two weeks earlier, agreed with Lord Halifax, who spoke of 'the depressing losses . . . which had been unduly advertised in neutral countries'. Churchill 'deplored the unrelieved pessimism of the BBC broadcasts which unfailingly opened with a long account of ships sunk'. He went on to say that they were having 'a demoralising effect on the fleet itself, and it would be sufficient to broadcast shipping losses once a week'.

The difficulties for the BBC in maintaining something that resembled a balanced radio service were illustrated on Christmas Eve. Just before 'Pictures in the Fire', which featured a military band, it was necessary to broadcast a special announcement from the Admiralty about a new minefield. While there was no getting around the fact that the bulletin was necessary, it lasted for seventeen minutes and played havoc with the continuity – not an uncommon occurrence, particularly during this phase of the war. What was published in the *Radio Times* and the newspapers was incorrect, as the programme schedule would frequently get changed at the last minute; timings were, as often as not, approximate.

> 'Ere's to a happy Christmas to you lads and let's hope all this nonsense will be over next Christmas.
>
> *Gracie Fields in concert, BBC, 9.15 p.m., 25 December 1939*

At the end of the first four months of the war the King broadcast a Christmas Day message on all the BBC networks at home and overseas. There was also a concert given by Gracie Fields, 'the queen of Lancashire', from an RAF base 'somewhere in France', using the same mobile unit that Richard Dimbleby had taken to Paris; it was the only BBC recording equipment in the whole of the country. Britain had suffered relatively few casualties at this stage and so the mood of the nation was less pessimistic than many had anticipated. Not that it was all light-hearted banter on the radio, because just three days after Christmas there was news of yet more rationing; this time it was sugar and meat. The King's broadcast managed to ensure a sense of reality into Christmas; there was even a hint of optimism.

A new year is at hand. We cannot tell what it will bring. If it brings peace, how thankful we shall be. If it brings us continued struggle, we shall remain undaunted. In the meantime I feel that we may all find a message of encouragement in the lines, which, in my closing words, I should like to say to you:

'I said to the man who stood at the Gate of the Year, "Give me a light that I may tread safely into the unknown." And he replied, "Go out into the darkness, and put your hand into the Hand of God. That shall be to you better than light, and safer than a known way."'

May that Almighty Hand guide and uphold us all.

King George VI, BBC, 3 p.m., 25 December 1939

Chapter 4

MISINFORMATION

O n New Year's Day 1940 nearly two million men aged between 19 and 27 years old were called up, which certainly brought home the reality of war to millions more of their family members. The need for such action was underlined ten days later, when a German Messerschmitt Me108, having got lost in fog, crashed in Belgium, near Mechelen-sur-Meuse. On board were two officers who were carrying plans for the German offensive against Belgium and Holland, which showed it was to begin on 17 January. The capture of the two men, and those papers they did not manage to burn, led to Hitler postponing the offensive. In any event General Gamelin, the Commander-in-Chief of the French Army and the Allied Commander-in-Chief, thought the whole thing was a trick.

In the early months of 1940 it seemed for some that the only war was the one between the BBC on one hand and the Ministry of Information and other government departments on the other. An army officer had been appointed to oversee the flow of information from the military to the Corporation in an effort to curb what they believed would be mistakes made by the BBC. While much of this went on behind the scenes in Whitehall and Broadcasting House the absurdity of the situation facing the BBC was clear for all to hear on 5 January. The Secretary of State for War, Leslie Hore-Belisha, resigned; this news was broadcast by German radio before the BBC got the story. It was episodes like this that added to the 'Haw-Haw effect' and convinced many that Germany was winning the propaganda war. While 16 million people in Britain usually listened to the 9 p.m. BBC news, around 6 million switched over to Hamburg to catch Haw-Haw at 9.15 p.m.

On the same day as Hore-Belisha resigned Sir John Reith, the BBC's former Director General, was appointed Minister of Information, much to his annoyance as he was hoping for greater things. Within ten days Reith clashed with Churchill over his 'ridiculous idea', according to Reith, of broadcasting shipping losses weekly. Not that there was any love lost on Churchill's part either. He accused Reith – whom he called 'old Wuthering Heights' on account of the fact that he was 6ft 4in tall – of 'keeping him off the wireless for eight years'. A few days later and Churchill was very definitely on the wireless, when he spoke for fifteen minutes on the state of the war.

Everyone wonders what is happening about the war. For several months past the Nazis have been uttering ferocious threats of what they are going to do to the Western Democracies – to the British and French Empires – when once they set about them. But so far it is the small neutral states that are bearing the brunt of German malice and cruelty. Neutral ships are sunk without law or mercy – not only by the blind and wanton mine, but by the coldly considered, deliberately aimed, torpedo. The Dutch, the Belgians, the Danes, the Swedes, and, above all, the Norwegians, have their ships destroyed whenever they can be caught upon the high seas. It is only in the British and French convoys that safety is to be found. There, in those convoys, it is five-hundred-to-one against being sunk. There, controlling forces are at work, which are steadily keeping the seas open, steadily keeping the traffic going, and establishing order and freedom of movement amid the waves of anarchy and sea-murder.

We, the aggrieved and belligerent Powers who are waging war against Germany, have no need to ask for respite. Every week our commerce grows; every month our organisation is improved and reinforced. We feel ourselves more confident day by day of our ability to police the seas and oceans and to keep open and active the salt-water highways by which we have, and along which we shall, draw the means of victory. It seems pretty certain that half the U-boats with which Germany began the war have been sunk, and that their new building has fallen far behind what we expected. Our faithful Asdic detector smells them out in the depths of the sea and, with the potent aid of the Royal Air Force, I do not doubt that we shall break their strength and break their purpose . . .

. . . In the bitter and increasingly exacting conflict which lies before us we are resolved to keep nothing back, and not to be outstripped by any in service to the common cause. Let the great cities of Warsaw, of Prague, of Vienna banish despair even in the midst of their agony. Their liberation is sure. The day will come when the joy bells will ring again throughout Europe, and when victorious nations, masters not only of their foes but of themselves, will plan and build in justice, in tradition, and in freedom a house of many mansions where there will be room for all.

Winston Churchill, BBC, 20 January 1940

Lord Halifax at the Foreign Office was furious with Churchill, accusing him of taking a different line from the government's. He wrote to the First Lord of the Admiralty and appended some unfavourable press from Norway, Denmark and Belgium, among other neutral countries. Although Churchill replied in somewhat conciliatory terms, it affected his inner resolve not one jot.

A week after his broadcast Churchill spoke to a crowd of 2,500 at a meeting in Manchester's Free Trade Hall. Just before he spoke a heckler was heard shouting 'We want Mosley', referring to the man who had been a Conservative MP at 21 and later founded the British Union of Fascists Party in 1932. Churchill, on being asked if he wanted the man thrown out, said, 'No, let me deal with him, I've had forty years' experience of this kind of thing'. There were, in fact, no more interruptions. In his speech he urged people not to become downhearted at the shipping losses, 'as reiterated by the BBC'.

In late February, to help counteract the negative effects of Germany's ability seemingly to broadcast 'better news', the new Minister of Information met with the BBC's Director General to discuss a daily series of talks of 'the heartening kind', as some kind of antidote to information emanating from German radio. Soon after, the BBC changed from airing talks such as 'Trade unions in wartime' and 'India and the war' by the Marquis of Zetland, and moved to a series of Sunday evening talks dealing with other, more appropriate and stimulating subjects. There was also a greater variety among weekday talks, but it was those broadcast at the end of the week – the 'Sunday Postscripts' – that were to become one of the most widely listened-to programmes on the BBC. While these were not news as such they were an integral part of the information flow broadcast to the majority of British homes. Barrister Maurice Healy gave the first of twelve in March 1940, succeeded by J.B. Priestley until October 1940. Priestley was replaced by a number of speakers, including playwright Emlyn Williams and actor Leslie Howard, before he returned in January 1941. In fact there was a whole string of eminent speakers, including an American, Raymond Gram Swing, and George Hicks MP, who spoke in this fifteen-minute slot. Raymond Gram Swing was regularly listened to by HM the King, Churchill and Roosevelt, and like Ed Murrow became extremely important to the British cause, as his talks were repeated on the BBC's North American Service. These talks were deliberately broadcast at 9.15 p.m. to harness as much verbal firepower as the BBC (and the Ministry of Information) could muster to go head to head with Haw-Haw.

A bonus of this comparative lull in the 'real war' was that the BBC was given the opportunity to introduce programming designed specifically for the Forces. In the late autumn of 1939 the Director General, Sir Frederick Ogilvie, who had been an army captain in the First World War, went to France to find out what the soldiers of the BEF wanted to hear. The overriding demand from the men in France, and probably at home too, was that they wanted programmes that cheered them up, and so on 11 January at 11.30 a.m. an announcer began the new service with the words 'This is the BBC calling on 342 metres'. A little over a month later, on Sunday 18 February, there was a switch to 373.1 metres on the medium wave. This coincided with an increase in the limited hours that the service had initially provided and from then on the Forces Programme was given over mostly to music and variety shows – although there were appropriate talks. The first day of the expanded service featured Jay Wilbur and his Band, a variety concert and a commentary on the second half of a French versus British Army football match at Lille. Over the next couple of days there were performances by Harry Leader and his Band, Billy Merrin and his Commanders, the Clydebank Burgh Band, Reginald Dixon at the Organ, Eddie Carroll and his Band, Dave Frost and his Band, and Harry Roy and his Band.

SOMEONE ELSE'S WAR

Given the lack of war on the Western Front, mostly as the result of the weather, it was ironic that the only serious fighting in Europe was in Finland, between the Russian invaders and the Finnish defenders. In temperatures of 57 degrees below zero the far smaller Finnish army constantly frustrated the numerically superior Russians. The BBC's Edward Ward, son of Viscount Bangor, was present to send back reports of the fighting. Ward, a man with a penchant for drawing exotic Chinese characters, was one of the first reporters to capture for radio some of the horror of war.

Never, I should think, has there been such a scene of frozen horror since the retreat of Napoleon's Grand Army from Moscow, and even that cannot anywhere have been so concentrated. Some of the best war material had been taken away, but the bodies were there – the ground was far too hard for them to be buried – they were there in their thousands, frozen as hard as stone in the ghastly attitudes in which they had fallen. There was a terrifying unreality about these bodies. Somehow they didn't look human. The terrific cold had made them look like rather badly executed waxworks, they were a curious brown colour and when, once, I stumbled and hit a dead man's hand, his finger snapped off as if it had been plaster. The bodies were everywhere: on the sides of the road, in the makeshift shelters and dug-outs where they had tried to escape the relentless fury of the Finnish ski patrols.

Edward Ward, BBC, mid-February 1940

The might of the Russian forces eventually achieved a breakthrough, but on

12 March they were forced to abandon plans to occupy the whole of Finland. The peace agreement saw Finland cede 10 per cent of its territory to the aggressors, but Finland itself remained free of occupation and a separate country. The 450,000 Finns who lived in the 16,000 square miles that were lost to Russia were resettled in the rest of Finland.

> Yesterday afternoon was one of the most depressing I have ever spent. For a couple of hours or so I walked around the streets of Helsinki; the flags were at half-mast, the streets were everywhere more crowded than I had ever seen them. I suppose the people, while the war was on, spent most of their time at home for fear of air raid have come out into the town. The stoicism of the crowd was extraordinary. To look at their faces you'd never guess their real feelings: the consternation and humiliation this peace has brought them.
>
> *Edward Ward, BBC, 13 March 1940*

No matter how upbeat Winston Churchill was in his broadcasts, and whatever the British government said about the vulnerability of Germany, there were people all over Britain hearing Ward's broadcast who were thinking 'what if?' Back home in London at the end of March, Ward made a radio appeal on behalf of the Finland Fund, one in the regular series of weekly appeals by the BBC. In 1941 Finland allied itself to Germany to battle against Russia and the Finns temporarily regained control of the lands they had lost. Another of the hundred or so press correspondents who covered the war in Finland was Donald Day of the *Chicago Tribune*. He joined the Finnish Army in 1942 and a year later became a broadcaster for the German Ministry of Propaganda; at the end of the war, Day was one of eight Americans accused of treason.

NAVAL SENSITIVITIES

Just before 4 a.m. on 18 February the destroyer HMS *Daring* was torpedoed and sunk off the Pentland Firth by a German U-boat; just five of the crew of 162 survived. The Ministry of Information was keen to suppress news of the disaster, especially given that it was the sixth destroyer to have been lost since the war began; consequently, the Admiralty delayed announcing the news until the following morning.

> HMS *Daring*, a destroyer, has been torpedoed and sunk with the feared loss of 157 lives, nine officers and 148 ratings. Among the missing is the commander, Commander S.A. Cooper. An official Admiralty communiqué issued yesterday morning stated: 'The Secretary of the Admiralty regrets to

announce that the destroyer *Daring* has been torpedoed and sunk. One officer and four ratings have been picked up. Nine officers and 143 ratings are missing and it is feared have been lost. The next of kin have been informed.'

BBC News, 19 February 1940

The incident brought to something of a head relations between the BBC and the Ministry. While the BBC agreed that distressing details such as 'sunk in one minute' were best left out of news reports the Corporation felt strongly that it had a duty to be more than just a mouthpiece for the Ministry of Information.

The tension was relieved between the parties when Reith and Ogilvie agreed that Lindsay Wellington would be transferred from the BBC to the Ministry to act as Director of Broadcasting Relations. A month later the fiasco surrounding British reporting of the German raid on Scapa Flow galvanised thinking at the highest levels of government over how the BBC should be handling news.

During the evening of 16 March German aircraft attacked Scapa Flow and inflicted some minor damage on the base. The attack also resulted in the first British civilian killed as the result of direct military action. Shortly after 7 a.m. the next day, in what was in danger of becoming an all-too-familiar scenario, the Admiralty asked the BBC not to broadcast news of the raid, despite the fact that BBC monitors had heard a German broadcast during the night provide details of the attack. By mid-morning French radio had broadcast a statement issued by the German High Command and it was only on the 1 p.m. news that the BBC was finally allowed to broadcast the Admiralty's statement.

At 7.50 p.m. on Saturday German aircraft made a raid on the fleet anchorage at Scapa Flow. About fourteen enemy aircraft reached the objective. A considerable number of bombs were dropped, one hitting a warship, which sustained minor damage. Bombs were also dropped on land, no military objectives being hit; but one civilian was killed and seven wounded, including two women in the village of Bridge of Waith; five cottages were damaged. There were seven casualties to naval personnel; the next of kin have been informed. Ships' batteries, shore defences and fighter aircraft combined to drive off the enemy. One aircraft was shot down and others were believed damaged.

BBC, 1 p.m. news, 17 March 1940

The Germans had been doubly quick off the mark in getting their story on air. Not only had they told of it in their news bulletin but they also had pilots who took part in the raid regale listeners two days after the raid:

We were forced to turn back very soon, because we found two British fighters behind us before our attack started. The cry 'Fighters' was given in our plane, and consequently we dropped all our bombs at once on a landing ground; we then flew back. I can assure you that one is highly pleased to get back to Germany after such a trip.

Observer, German radio, 18 March 1940

Among the British ships which were attacked were the *Hood, Renown*, and *Repulse*. The bombs scored either direct hits or dropped into the water near the capital ships, which were lifted by the explosion.

Leader of the German raid, German radio, 18 March 1940

I was surprised at the number of ships anchored there. None of us had ever seen so many. There were good pickings. I dropped a bomb over one and thought I had missed, when I suddenly saw her stern lift out of the water.

German pilot, German radio, 18 March 1940

It's not difficult to understand the sensitivity of the Royal Navy. In October 1939 they had lost the HMS *Royal Oak*, which had served during the First World War, at Scapa Flow; it went down with the loss of 833 lives. However, for the BBC and the British government to have any credibility at all it was vital to be 'truthful and objective'. According to Reith's diary entry of 27 March the Prime Minister told him that 'we weren't taking Propaganda seriously enough in this country'. Chamberlain also told his Minister of Information that he thought the war was going to go on 'more or less indefinitely as it is now'. This was typical of how Reith was hearing such things, at one-on-one meetings with the PM, because for some reason or another he was not in the War Cabinet. Given the importance of the Ministry's role it seems somewhat absurd, especially from the perspective of sixty years on. Ironically, it was one of the few things that Reith and Churchill agreed upon.

Shortly after the Scapa Flow fiasco, in order to try to get a better control of the whole business of news, Ogilvie requested that A.P. Ryan, who was on loan from the BBC to the Political Warfare Executive, be allowed to return to the Corporation to assume the position of Controller (Home). It was agreed to and so, by dint of their own skills, some good fortune and not much help from the Ministry of Information, the BBC was in improving shape. Good news indeed, as the war was about to enter a new phase. Despite Chamberlain's thoughts on how little was to change, the end of the 'Bore War' was just around the corner.

When Churchill spoke on the radio on 30 March he talked about 'a sterner war'. He also spoke of how valuable it had been to have had six months in which everything had been focused upon improving the British military position. He could have made the same remarks about the BBC – they were now far more ready for war than before.

Almost from the start of hostilities the BBC's monitoring service was recognised as a vital part of the propaganda war, essential in the process of gathering news. To begin with, the department had numbered fewer than a hundred people, but soon grew to have a staff in excess of 500 men and women. Many of the monitors were foreign nationals, and some, like those who broadcast on the various BBC Overseas Programmes, were refugees from occupied countries; there were also refugees from those countries doing the occupying. By 1941 monitors were listening to broadcasts in over thirty different languages.

In 1939 there were no tape machines or dictaphones to record the broadcasts, so the monitors had to be very good listeners, and also very quick to document what they heard. One of the BBC's monitors was blind and took down his notes on a Braille typewriter. Given that these monitors were taking down a million words a day it was a prodigious feat, and one that has failed to be recognised by many looking back at the war – a period when people-power in broadcasting was pivotal.

Early in the war a monitoring team listened to Hitler's broadcast speech at Danzig. The Foreign Office's own translation of this speech that had been passed to the Prime Minister had caused Chamberlain great alarm, as it spoke of a 'secret weapon'. The scientist R.V. Jones, who worked for MI6, was asked to hypothesise about what kind of secret weapon it could be. There was even a rumour that the Germans might possess a death ray! After much frustrating research Jones contacted the BBC to ask if the Corporation's monitors had a translation of the speech. He thought there might be some additional clue as to what the 'secret weapon' might be. According to the BBC's translation, what Hitler said was '. . . the moment could arrive very quickly, when we would employ a weapon with which we cannot be attacked'. The Foreign Office translators had translated what Hitler had said as 'to which no defence would avail'. Hitler's reference, far from being to a secret weapon, was actually to the vast superiority in numbers of the Luftwaffe, coupled with his myopic view that the RAF were no conceivable match for the German Air Force.

NORTH TO NORWAY

In his speech at the end of March Churchill spoke of it being 'all quiet on the Western Front', but there were over a million men of the German Army ranged along the frontier with France and the neutral countries and it was just a matter of time before there was an attack. Ten days after his speech Germany acted, but not where expected.

It was about dawn this morning that the first reports came in saying that German troops are crossing the frontier with Denmark. At the same time attacks were being delivered from the sea on a number of Norway's biggest ports. The Oslo Radio is still working and it's announced that German troops have disembarked at Egersund on the south coast of Norway and that Kristiansand has been attacked.

Alvar Lidell, BBC News, 9 April 1940

The supreme command of the German defence forces announces the operation to occupy Denmark and the Norwegian coast have proceeded according to plan today. On marching into and landing on Danish territory no incidents have occurred anywhere. No significant resistance was offered along the coast of Norway except near Oslo. Resistance there was broken during the afternoon and Oslo itself was occupied . . .

Lord Haw-Haw, German radio, 9 April 1940

The following day the BBC's news bulletins carried an important announcement to the ships of both Denmark and Norway that were at sea. 'Do not be deceived by the message broadcast telling you to proceed to Spanish and Italian ports; it was put out by Germany. Come to Allied ports, where you will be treated as friends.' Two days before the invasion of Norway a British naval task force had sailed from Scapa Flow; its mission was to mine the waters off the coast of Norway. One of the ships, the destroyer HMS *Glowworm*, had become detached from the main fleet during a violent storm and was spotted by a German destroyer and a cruiser, the *Admiral Hipper*. With his vessel badly damaged by the cruiser's guns and unable to outrun it, the skipper of the *Glowworm*, Lieutenant-Commander Roope, took the decision to ram the *Admiral Hipper*. The action badly damaged the cruiser and the *Glowworm* blew up, killing all but thirty-seven of the crew, including Roope, who was awarded a Victoria Cross – the Navy's first of the Second World War.

One day later a Polish submarine sank a German ship laden with troops, some of whom were rescued, which confirmed the belief in London that

Norway was about to be attacked. This notion was reinforced by a Short Sunderland's sighting of the *Admiral Hipper* and its destroyer escort heading towards Trondheim. The warships were carrying part of a German force assembled for the invasion of Norway. The conditions, the advanced state of the German invasion and the length of coastline that they were to attack all made it impossible for the Royal Navy to have any significant impact on their strategy. Despite some stout Norwegian defence in some areas, particularly around Oslo, the result was a forgone conclusion. South Norway eventually fell around the beginning of May, and on 7 June 1940, King Haakon and his government left Norway on board HMS *Devonshire*. In Denmark the King ordered his troops not to resist, against overwhelming German odds, and the country capitulated immediately – the war on the Western Front had begun.

German radio's boast of 'no significant resistance' in Norway was not entirely true. Germany's newest cruiser, the *Blücher*, was sunk by the 55-year-old guns of Oslo's coastal fort; around 1,000 men, mostly soldiers, lost their lives. The pocket battleship *Lützow* was also damaged.

Two days after the German invasion of Norway three Wellington bombers from 115 Squadron, along with two Bristol Blenheims of 254 Squadron, attacked the airfield at Stavanger. On the following day six Hampdens and three Wellingtons were lost during an attack on Stavanger. In all there were fifteen more RAF raids on the airfield over the coming days as the RAF tried to prevent the Luftwaffe using Stavanger and other Norwegian airfields. At the end of April aerial reconnaissance photos showed the whole thing to have been something of a failure, as there were well over one hundred German aircraft at Stavanger.

None of this dissuaded the RAF and the BBC from demonstrating something of a 'gung-ho' spirit during two broadcasts in April. Three Bomber Command pilots talked about their exploits on missions over Norway on 'Air Log', which was broadcast on the Forces Programme.

We ourselves made four raids in six days. The first was a raid over Bergen. We had had a report that there were two German cruisers in the fjord. We found one cruiser alongside the shore, but didn't attack her for fear of injuring Norwegians.

The other ship seemed to be making towards the shore about as quickly as it could, probably guessing that we would not attack it there but it did not get there in time. The aircraft, flying low for greater precision in bombing, got a very hot reception from anti-aircraft guns of the ship and on the shore, but they pressed home the attack. It was the leader of the formation who got in a direct hit on the stern of the cruiser. Other bombs fell very close. Another bomber squadron, we believe, scored a hit on the same ship that evening, and, as announced by Mr Churchill, the cruiser has not been heard of since.

We didn't get away unscathed. One aircraft was hit by pom-poms and a shell took a nasty chunk out of its starboard wing. The pilot was afraid that one of the tyres had been punctured as well and was trying to hurry home so as to make a landing before dark, while all the time the section leader – seeing this big hole in the wing – was aiming at preventing him going too fast because he was afraid that flying at any sort of high speed would increase the damage. Still, he got down without mishap in the end.

Back at the base we had been making all sorts of emergency arrangements in case there were any casualties, but, fortunately, they proved unnecessary. Naturally we were eager to know all about what had happened, but most of the fellows seemed to have been so impressed by the beauty of the Norwegian scenery that at first it was difficult to get them to talk about anything else.

The following evening we called in on Stavanger aerodrome. As we knew there were fighters there, we planned to arrive in the failing light to make it more difficult for them to intercept us. We were also relying on the cloud to cover our approach, but it rather let us down, so we descended to water level. We thought that there we should be less likely to be seen. That attack really was a magnificent sight: the sort of thing that will always remain in one's memory. We had split up into sections of three. Each section seemed to be trying to race the other to the target. We were simply streaking across the water. The other section – not the one I was in – got there first.

The Germans put up a terrific barrage over the target before we got there, but our chaps simply went straight in. We flew across that aerodrome just below 1,000 feet and at about 200 miles an hour with our front and rear gunners letting loose their full fire and the bombs exploding in our wake. With different coloured tracer bullets coming up and our own tracer bullets going down, it was like a gigantic firework display.

Unfortunately we lost one aircraft. Two others were badly damaged but got home. The pilot of one of these aircraft was wounded in the left side and the left shoulder and his second pilot got a splinter wound in the head. The tail gunner was hit, too. The second pilot wanted to relieve the more seriously injured captain of the aircraft but they dared not risk changing places because the control trimming gear, which enables you to trim the aircraft to fly itself for a short period, had been damaged. To make matters even worse, the hydraulic system had been put out of action, so that they were faced with the prospect of having to land, not being able to let the undercarriage down. They made the three-hour flight in the dark through very bad weather with heavy rainstorm and unusually bumpy conditions to reach their base.

Reaching home, the pilot circled the aerodrome three times, waited until everything was ready down below. Then he put the machine down on its belly. They deserved to get away with it – and I am very glad to say they did. In the other machine the navigator was shot in the chest. The second pilot attended him and gave him morphia. Having done that, he took over the injured man's chart and maps and navigated the aircraft home.

The next day we were standing by for another attack on Stavanger, but it was eventually decided to postpone the raid until dawn the following morning. We had to wake the pilots and crews in the middle of the night and they took off in the small hours of the morning, while it was still dark.

In the weather conditions we were expecting I had been doubtful whether it would be possible for the machines we were sending to keep formation in the dark. I did not want them to go in separately and stir up trouble for one another. But the captains of the aircraft were dead keen to go. They said they could do it; in fact, they almost tried to bully me into sending them. At first they were able to fly with their navigation lights on. That's all right, but as they got nearer Norway their lights had to be put out.

After that, flying over the North Sea in darkness, the pilots of the two following aircraft managed to keep formation by watching the exhaust flames from the leading machine. When they arrived off the Norwegian coast it was too dark for them to find their target with any degree of accuracy, so they hung about for half an hour – keeping well away and out to sea – until the light improved.

The Germans opened fire as soon as the aircraft came in to attack. The machines dived to about four to five hundred feet. Their front gun raked the enemy aircraft on the ground and the bombs, aimed at the runway, the aircraft and the hangar, began to fall. In addition to attacking the aerodrome we shot up their seaplane base there on both these Stavanger raids . . .

RAF wing commander and squadron leader,
BBC, probably Tuesday 23 April 1940

The second broadcast, possibly on the same date, was entitled an 'Attack on German Cruisers in Norway'. The raid probably took place on 17 April and the aircraft may well have been a Blackburn Skua of the Fleet Air Arm. On that day there was a combined operation with RAF bombers, three of which were shot down.

It was in the late afternoon that we set off across the North Sea to carry out our attack. The weather going over was good, but when we got there the sky was absolutely cloudless.

We approached the Norwegian coast at a height of 7,000 feet, flying in two sections of three machines each. Then when we were about ten miles from the harbour where the cruisers lay I gave the prearranged signal for the second section to detach itself from mine and to take its position astern and to our right.

By this time we could see the two cruisers. I told the leader of my other section to attack the one which was lying at anchor near the shore while, for our formation, I chose the one in the middle of the harbour. The ships and the shore batteries had opened fire during our approach, but none of our aircraft was hit. We went in to attack in line astern, making a steep dive from 7,000 to 1,000 feet. The aircraft followed one another quite closely.

At about 1,000 feet I gave the order to my bomb-aimer to release his bombs. Owing to a misunderstanding, however, we flew right over the ship without letting them go.

It happened like this. I was anxious that my bomb-aimer should not drop his bombs too close together so I said to him before we started: 'Don't pull your lever over too quickly, but take your time from me. As I say "bomb . . . bomb . . . bomb", let them go.' Well, he must have got a bit excited. We were all excited of course at the idea of getting in our crack at the cruiser. Anyway, he mistook my 'bomb . . . bomb . . . bomb' for 'Oh . . . Oh . . . Oh', thinking I had been wounded, and didn't release his bombs.

The only thing to do was to have another shot at it. For about ten minutes we cruised up and down one of the fjords, hoping that the enemy would think we'd gone home. But, unfortunately, this little ruse failed because there were some guns on top of the cliff. They spotted us and apparently decided to have a little practice at our expense.

We were flying then at about 100 feet above the water and they were shooting down on us. They came pretty close but didn't hit us. By now the other chaps had carried out their attacks and had left, so we decided after a few minutes that it was about time to make our second attempt. We climbed up over the mountains to about 5,000 feet, and approached from the land side instead of from the sea as we had done before.

This time, of course, being alone, we were the gunners' only target and they gave us a really hot reception. By now, the cruiser was under way and making for the open sea. Again we went down in a steep dive at over 300mph. Accurate bombing with the aircraft being shaken by shell bursts is very difficult. I'm afraid we didn't get a direct bit, but we came within twenty feet of her.

It was now dusk, and having dropped all our bombs, we decided to follow the others and make for home. One might have thought that the day's adventures were over then, but there was still another to come. For, shortly afterwards, we ran into an enemy flying boat, a Dornier. We were going west and he was flying east, so we turned and gave chase. The minute he saw us, he dived towards the sea. We dived after him. As we came into range we opened fire with our front guns and he replied with his rear guns. Eventually, we drew alongside where we could bring our other guns to bear.

We must have been flying side by side for about a minute, exchanging shots from about sixty yards' range. First his rear guns stopped firing and then one engine was put out of action. Clouds of smoke were coming from it and we could see that the propeller had stopped. He continued for a bit on one engine. Then that stopped too and he went down into the sea. Again we set course for home.

When we landed and inspected the aircraft, we found that we had been hit a good many times. There were bullet holes in the wings, fuselage, and the tailplane and a bullet had even gone through one of the propeller blades, but whether this damage was done by the Dornier or by the AA fire over Bergen we could not say. The main thing was that no member of the crew had been hit and that we had got home.

An RAF squadron leader, BBC, probably Tuesday 23 April 1940

On 26 April the decision was taken to withdraw British troops from Norway. Two or three days later newspaper editors were informed of the decision, but for some inexplicable reason the BBC was not told. This led to criticisms of the Corporation when the news was finally announced, as the BBC seemed unprepared and ill-informed. Robert Boothby MP had already complained in Parliament about the BBC, saying it should not have reported an Admiralty communiqué about the destroyers being lost at Narvik on the grounds that it 'would spread alarm and despondency'. With hindsight this seems daft, but the BBC, having prepared itself to report on a war with the nation's enemies, was fighting one of its own on the Home Front. It was not just disagreements with the Ministry of Information but also at the most senior levels of government; there was a whispering campaign against the BBC in which some people referred to the Corporation as 'an enemy within the gates'. The level of absurdity is no better illustrated than when the Secretary of State for Air, Sir Samuel Hoare, gave a broadcast following the 9 p.m. BBC news on Saturday 27 April. He delivered a speech in which he spoke of the government's determination to 'prosecute the war in Norway with the utmost energy and resolution'. This was in full knowledge of the decision to pull out.

It led to many in Britain believing that the BBC was out of touch with what was happening. Sir Howard Kingsley Wood even accused the BBC of allowing 'pacifist sermons' to be broadcast and questioned whether everyone working for the Corporation was sufficiently patriotic. In an ever-changing world it seems as though some things never change.

With the end of the Phoney War there were better things for politicians and the BBC to be doing than arguing among themselves. Less than two weeks later Germany invaded Holland and Belgium – things were getting much closer to home. And with the war about to engulf France Richard Dimbleby, much to his frustration, was not there to witness it. He had been recalled to London and told to get some warm weather clothing together as he was being dispatched to Egypt. Dimbleby's place with the BEF had been given over to Bernhard Stubbs.

THE BIRTH OF THE BBC WORLD SERVICE

Ironically on the very morning of the German invasion of Norway Leif Konow had been asked to visit Broadcasting House in order to start a Norwegian language programme. It was all part of the BBC's expansive plans to provide European language broadcasts for as many countries as possible. The first had begun on 27 September 1938, when Neville Chamberlain's eve of Munich speech was transmitted in French, German and Italian. Daily news bulletins quickly followed in these languages, as well as Spanish and Portuguese. During September 1939 Czech, Greek, Polish, Rumanian and Serbo-Croat were added. During 1940, besides the Norwegian service, Albanian, Bulgarian, Danish, Dutch, Finnish, Swedish and Turkish were added. Not all language broadcasts were as ambitious as the German service, where there were eight news bulletins each day – interestingly, during 1940 the BBC's Home Service reduced news bulletins from seven to six. All of these foreign language broadcasts were on the short wave.

The European service was built around the framework provided by the pre-war Empire Service. Besides the English-language short-wave broadcasting there were also daily broadcasts in Afrikaans, Hindustani and French. Weekly, and slightly more frequent, bulletins were also given in Burmese, Cypriot and Maltese. These were all added to the Arabic service, the first of the BBC's foreign language services, which had started in January 1938.

In July 1940 the North American service of the BBC went into operation, building upon a successful relationship with the Canadian Broadcasting Corporation (CBC). The BBC received the approval of the New York Times: 'A review of the first new set of programmes showed that England isn't wasting time on fairy tales.' A couple of weeks later Time magazine said: '"Britain

Speaks" is at its best when novelist–playwright John Boynton Priestley holds forth'. During the whole of the war, and over the coming months in particular, the BBC's broadcasts to the USA proved vital in winning the hearts and minds of many Americans.

When America was attacked at Pearl Harbor there were broadcasts in twenty-one different languages from the USA. They were beaten by Russia, which managed twenty-two, and the Germans' thirty-six. The BBC beat everyone with thirty-nine.

Chapter 5

REAL WAR

A BEGINNING AND AN END

In the period leading up to the violation of Dutch and Belgian neutrality there was feverish activity on the political front in Britain – and none of it was aimed at the BBC. The Prime Minister was feeling the heat from several different directions. Members of his own party, as well as the opposition, were getting restless. But it was not something that seemed to bother the PM unduly when he met Sir John Reith on 3 May. He told him that he was confident regarding his own situation, although he admitted that Churchill's reputation was 'inflated' and was based on the reaction from throughout the country to his frequent radio broadcasts – Chamberlain had obviously changed his mind since writing to his sister a few months earlier.

Within days the situation for Chamberlain proved to be far from comfortable when a debate was called for by the Labour opposition to discuss the Norwegian debacle – it was in effect a debate on the Prime Minister's conduct of the war. In the House of Commons on 7 May Chamberlain spoke first, but only really succeeded in rambling for almost an hour in which the best he could do was to praise the courage of the soldiers; according to John Reith's diary he was 'dispassionate'. Given the air of defeat that hung around the whole Norwegian campaign it was difficult for Chamberlain to find anything positive to say, but his performance was so uninspiring that at least one Ambassador in the Strangers' Gallery fell asleep. Among the Tory members who spoke out against Chamberlain was Leo Amery, a man not noted for his oratory but who on this occasion surpassed himself: 'You have sat too long for any good you have been doing. Depart, I say, let us have done with you. In the name of God go!' The following day both Socialist and Liberal MPs were ranged against Chamberlain and two of his closest advisers – Sir Samuel Hoare and Sir John Simon, the Chancellor of the Exchequer. Labour MP Herbert Morrison called for all three to resign.

This is London – I spent today in the House of Commons, the debate was opened by Herbert Morrison – one of the ablest members of the Labour

Party. He doubted that the Government was taking the war seriously. He said the Labour Party had decided to divide the house – in other words called for a vote. Mr Chamberlain, white with anger, intervened in the debate and accepted the challenge, in fact he welcomed it. He fairly spat the words. He said he had friends in the house and he appealed to them to support him. When he'd finished Mr David Lloyd George rose and placed his notes upon the dispatch box and members surged into the room from both doors as though the little square grey-shouldered white-haired Welshman were a magnet to draw them back to the seats. He swept the house with his arm and said, 'If there is a man here who is happy with our production of planes or guns or tanks or the training of troops let him stand on his feet.' No one stood.

Ed Murrow, US radio, 8 May 1940

Chamberlain's confidence was unfounded, or perhaps events moved too quickly behind the scenes for the man, who had long seemed detached, to be able to keep up. Chamberlain's 'friends in the lobby tonight' failed to support him in sufficient numbers and while he won by 281 votes to 200 his majority should have been around 213 votes. Too many Conservatives had voted against their leader, or abstained, for him to survive. It was an awful night, with friends from within the Conservatives often voting on different sides – Churchill voted in support of Chamberlain. At just after 1 p.m. on 8 May Neville Chamberlain left the House against shouts of 'resign' – but he had other ideas.

For the next thirty-six hours Chamberlain seemed to show no signs of relinquishing his hold on power. His only hope of survival was to form a coalition, something he had steadfastly rejected to this point. Negotiations with the Labour Party, from Chamberlain's point of view, didn't go too well, but the alternative of Winston Churchill was not popular with the Socialist leadership or rank and file; Lord Halifax, a possibility, had ruled himself out because he felt he couldn't sit in the Lords and be prime minister. Halifax said he thought Churchill should be prime minister. Ultimately Clement Attlee told Chamberlain that there was no hope for him to continue – neither the Opposition, nor the country as a whole, would support him. Late in the evening of 9 May Churchill's son Randolph telephoned his father from his army base in Northamptonshire and was told, 'I think I shall be Prime Minister tomorrow'.

The Germans had not been shown a copy of the script; with impeccable timing, before anything could happen in London, they invaded Belgium and Holland. Churchill was woken with the news, along with telegrams from everywhere, and everybody, or so it seemed. The rest of the country heard the news from Alvar Lidell a few hours later.

This is the BBC Home Service – here is a short news bulletin. The German army invaded Holland and Belgium early this morning by land and by landings from parachutes. The armies of the Low Countries are resisting. An appeal for help has been made to the Allied governments and Brussels says that Allied troops are moving to their support.

Alvar Lidell, BBC News, 7 a.m., 10 May 1940

Events moved fast during the morning following a meeting of the War Cabinet at 8 a.m. Ministers reviewed the plans that had been so long in the formulation and were now being set in train. Chamberlain's position was very much a secondary consideration for everyone, especially Churchill, who told his son when he called him that morning, 'Nothing matters now except beating the Germans'. Two more War Cabinet meetings took place, vainly trying to keep pace with events that were unfolding under the German Blitzkrieg. At the third, after taking more decisions and reviewing the day's events, the question of Chamberlain's position was the only thing left on the agenda. A short discussion ended with Chamberlain telling his colleagues that he intended to seek an audience with the King that evening. Later George VI and his Prime Minister discussed who should take over the running of the country. His Majesty favoured Halifax, but Chamberlain told him that Churchill was the only choice. At 8.15 p.m. the decision was announced, and less than an hour later the man who had been Prime Minister for three years broadcast to the nation from 10 Downing Street.

Early this morning, without warning or excuse, Hitler added another to the horrible crimes which have already disgraced his name, by his sudden attack on Holland, Belgium, and Luxembourg. In all history no other man has been responsible for such a hideous total of human suffering and misery as he. He has chosen a moment when, perhaps, it seemed to him that this country was entangled in the throes of a political crisis, and when he might find it divided against itself. If he has counted on our internal differences to help him, he has miscalculated the mind of this people.

I am not now going to make any comment on the debate in the House of Commons which took place on Tuesday and Wednesday last, but when it was over I had no doubt in my mind that some new and drastic action must be taken, if confidence was to be restored to the House of Commons, and the war carried on with vigour and energy, which are essential to victory. What was that action to be? It was clear that at this critical moment in the war, what was needed was the formation of a Government which would include members of the Labour and Liberal Oppositions, and thus present a united front to the enemy. What had to be ascertained was the conditions which would be necessary to enable such a united Government to be formed, and to this question I devoted myself, with the assistance of some of my colleagues, yesterday afternoon.

By the afternoon of to-day it was apparent that the essential unity could be secured under another Prime Minister, though not under myself. In those circumstances my duty was plain. I sought an audience of the King this evening, and tendered to him my resignation, which His Majesty has been pleased to accept. His Majesty has now entrusted to my friend and colleague Mr Winston Churchill the task of forming a new Administration on a national basis, and in this task I have no doubt that he will be successful.

Neville Chamberlain, BBC, 9 p.m., 10 May 1940

Neville Chamberlain, despite his offer to help Churchill in whatever capacity, was in poor health. He was to broadcast only once more on the BBC on 11 October, when he recorded a farewell from his home, too ill to go to the studio; he died less than a month later, on 9 November 1940.

John Reith was scathing in his diary about Churchill's appointment: '. . . being Defence Minister as well as PM – Heaven help us. The three service departments are Sinclair, Eden, and Alexander. This is obviously so that Churchill can ignore them more or less and deal direct with the chiefs of staff. Awful.' Next day Reith lost his job as Minister of Information to Duff Cooper. More importantly, the Labour Party issued a statement saying that their Executive had 'unanimously decided to take their share of responsibility . . . under a new Prime Minister who could command the confidence of the nation'. Sir Archibald Sinclair, the Liberal leader, offered a similar message of support.

In the days following Churchill's appointment attention was focused on the situation across the Channel. French generals scornfully dismissed reports that the Germans were massing in the Ardennes sector – only to feel the full might of the German armoured forces 24 hours later. They soon crossed the Meuse as well as continuing their advance into Belgium – the Allied forces could find no way of countering the speed and power of the German advance. Bernhard Stubbs, the BBC correspondent who had been sent to France to replace Richard Dimbleby, gave one of the first reports from the Franco-Belgian border; by this time the BBC had managed to get two mobile recording units to the Continent. Broadcast on 13 May the recording was probably made on 11 May, as the BEF were moving into Belgium. His report was set against a background of cheering people applauding the Allied forces – an upbeat and positive message. But the second part of his report offers an alternative, and soon to become all too common, view of what war meant to ordinary Europeans.

. . . But the enthusiasm of the people from this part of Belgium makes a sharp contrast with the sufferings of the refugees from such places as Liege. We saw several lorry loads of these unhappy people and at one point on another road we met a straggling little party of Belgians, old men, and women, and children, some of them with rolled blankets tied over their shoulders, their few pathetic belongings strapped on their backs or carried in cheap suitcases in their hands.

Bernhard Stubbs, BBC News, 13 May 1940

On the same day as Stubbs was broadcasting from close to the front line, the war on the Home Front took a somewhat unusual turn when two bogus messages were broadcast by the BBC. One called for all men of the RAF Volunteer Reserve to report to their bases, while the other warned children to keep away from RAF facilities. Both messages had been received at the BBC by telephone from the Air Ministry, or so it was thought. Three hours later the instructions were countermanded, and it has never been properly established who made the calls. It certainly forced everyone involved to look carefully at the system by which such potentially vital announcements were communicated. It highlighted the need for everything to be channelled through the Ministry of Information.

THE HOME GUARD

The day after Stubbs's broadcast from Belgium the Secretary of State for War, Anthony Eden, was tackled in the House of Commons about plans for the defence of Britain if the Germans were to mount a similar campaign to the one they had waged against Holland and Belgium. The fear of an attack by parachutists was uppermost in many people's minds, especially given all the talk of Germans disguised as civilians, or Dutch or Belgian soldiers, being dropped behind their lines. On 14 May Eden made an appeal following the 9 p.m. news for 'local defence volunteers' – the Home Guard or Dad's Army as we have come to know them.

I want to speak to you to-night about the form of warfare which the Germans have been employing so extensively against Holland and Belgium, namely, the dropping of troops by parachute behind the main defensive lines.

The success of such an attack depends on speed. Consequently, the measures to defeat such an attack must be prompt and rapid. It is upon this basis that our plans have been laid. You will not expect me to tell you, or the enemy, what our plans are, but we are confident that they will be effective. However, in order to leave nothing to chance, and to supplement, from sources as yet untapped, the means of defence already arranged, we are going to ask you to help us in a manner which I know will be welcome to thousands of you. Since the war began the Government have received countless inquiries from all over the Kingdom from men of all ages who are for one reason or another not at present engaged in military service and who wish to do something for the defence of the country.

Now is your opportunity. We want large numbers of such men in Great Britain who are British subjects between the ages of 17 and 65 to come forward now and offer their service in order to make assurance doubly sure. When on duty you will form part of the armed forces and your period of service will be for the duration of the war. You will not be paid but you will receive uniform and will be armed . . . Your loyal help, added to the arrangements which already exist, will make and keep our country safe.

Anthony Eden, BBC, 14 May 1940

In the days following Eden's broadcast newspaper reports spoke of a 'spare time corps' and told of how hundreds of men rushed to their local police station to volunteer within minutes of hearing the broadcast. The first actual recruit seems to have been in Newcastle, where a man arrived within four minutes of the broadcast ending; in Edinburgh there had been seventy volunteers by midnight.

The BBC TV series *Dad's Army*, based on a mythical Home Guard unit somewhere on Britain's coast, has helped to create an 'Ealing comedy' image for the men, but at the same time it has turned them into folk heroes. Given that they were never really called upon to perform the tasks that Eden said they might be expected to carry out this perhaps is hardly surprising. There was another factor in mythologising the Home Guard, and it stems from a wartime need to try to put a positive spin on just about everything during the period of the BEF's retreat and its aftermath.

It now transpires that during the air raids on Sunday a few Home Guards in the South London area were attacked by machine-gun fire from an enemy dive bomber. The Home Guards retaliated with rifle fire, and, after firing 180 rounds, caused the enemy aircraft to crash. This is the first occasion on which the Home Guard have succeeded in bringing down a German bomber.

BBC News, 19 August 1940

According to newspaper reports describing the events in more detail it was perhaps not quite as it seemed. There was an eyewitness account from the officer in charge of the Home Guard unit:

> I was in charge of the post at the time. All the men had been issued with their rifles and ammunition. My observer noticed the plane coming in our direction. He recognised it at once as a German machine, which had evidently been hit. It was flying at a height of about 400 feet. As soon as we had satisfied ourselves that it was an enemy plane some of the men with rifles took up position and we 'plugged off' about 180 rounds into the machine. I gave the order for rapid fire, and my second in command directed the distance and the height of the firing. We saw the machine stagger and lose height, and then smoke began to issue from it. We saw the German plane crash between the road on which our posts were situated and the next village.
>
> *Home Guard officer*

There seems little doubt that this aircraft was already in serious trouble and it is very doubtful that the Home Guard did anything but boost their ego by shooting at it. That day, 18 August, was a bad one for the RAF, the first day of serious British losses in the Battle of Britain; 35 aircraft were lost.

During the war 1,206 men of the Home Guard were killed and 557 were seriously injured. Two George Crosses and thirteen George Medals were awarded for the bravery of the men of the Home Guard before they were disbanded in November 1944.

BLOOD, TOIL, TEARS AND SWEAT

Just before Anthony Eden broadcast his plans for the Home Guard there was an Admiralty announcement on the BBC asking all owners of self-propelled boats between 30 and 100 feet in length to notify the government within the next fourteen days. It was the first sign of the build-up to the Dunkirk evacuation, and it was clear that things were inexorably going downhill across the Channel.

With the changes in ministerial positions it brought about a flurry of government broadcasts from most of the new appointees – all with a clear message of the need for resolute defence. There was also a subtle change in the role of the Ministry of Information, now under the 50-year-old Etonian ex-Guards officer, Duff Cooper. Churchill had decided that Cooper, from this point on, would attend all Cabinet meetings. Cooper also told Reith that he would 'control the BBC'. Another changing sign of the times was the much more audible presence of the new Prime Minister, compared to Neville Chamberlain.

On 19 May Winston Churchill made his first prime ministerial broadcast, the first of nine during the remainder of such a crucial year for Britain:

I speak to you for the first time as Prime Minister in a solemn hour for the life of our country, of our empire, of our allies, and, above all, of the cause of Freedom. A tremendous battle is raging in France and Flanders. The Germans, by a remarkable combination of air bombing and heavily armoured tanks, have broken through the French defences north of the Maginot Line, and strong columns of their armoured vehicles are ravaging the open country, which for the first day or two was without defenders. They have penetrated deeply and spread alarm and confusion in their track. Behind them there are now appearing infantry in lorries, and behind them, again, the large masses are moving forward. The re-groupment of the French armies to make headway against, and also to strike at, this intruding wedge has been proceeding for several days, largely assisted by the magnificent efforts of the Royal Air Force . . .

. . . It would be foolish, however, to disguise the gravity of the hour. It would be still more foolish to lose heart and courage or to suppose that well-trained, well-equipped armies numbering three or four millions of men can be overcome in the space of a few weeks, or even months, by a scoop, or raid of mechanised vehicles, however formidable. We may look with confidence to the stabilisation of the Front in France, and to the general engagement of the masses, which will enable the qualities of the French and British soldiers to be matched squarely against those of their adversaries. For myself, I have invincible confidence in the French Army and its leaders. Only a very small part of that splendid army has yet been heavily engaged; and only a very small part of France has yet been invaded. There is a good evidence to show that practically the whole of the specialised and mechanised forces of the enemy have been already thrown into the battle; and we know that very heavy losses have been inflicted upon them. No officer or man, no brigade or division, which grapples at close quarters with the enemy, wherever encountered, can fail to make a worthy contribution to the general result. The Armies must cast away the idea of resisting behind concrete lines or natural obstacles, and must realise that mastery can only be regained by furious and unrelenting assault. And this spirit must not only animate the High Command, but must inspire every fighting man.

In the air – often at serious odds hitherto thought overwhelming – we have been clawing down three or four to one of our enemies; and the relative balance of the British and German Air Forces is now considerably more favourable to us than at the beginning of the battle. In cutting down the German bombers, we are fighting our own battle as well as that of France. My confidence in our ability to fight it out to the finish with the German Air Force has been strengthened by the fierce encounters which have taken place and are taking place. At the same time, our heavy bombers are striking nightly at the tap-root of German mechanised power, and have already inflicted serious damage upon the oil refineries on which the Nazi effort to dominate the world directly depends.

We must expect that as soon as stability is reached on the Western Front, the bulk of that hideous apparatus of aggression which gashed Holland into ruin and slavery in a few days will be turned upon us. I am sure I speak for all when I say we are ready to face it; to endure it; and to retaliate against it – to any extent that the unwritten laws of war permit. There will be many men and many women in the Island who when the ordeal comes upon them, as come it will, will feel comfort, and even a pride, that they are sharing the perils of our lads at the Front – soldiers, sailors and airmen, God bless them – and are drawing away from them a part at least of the onslaught they have to bear. Is not this the appointed time for all to make the utmost exertions in their power? If the battle is to be won, we must provide our men with ever-increasing quantities of the weapons and ammunition they need. We must have, and have quickly, more aeroplanes, more tanks, more shells, more guns. There is imperious need for these vital munitions. They increase our strength against the powerfully armed enemy. They replace the wastage of the obstinate struggle; and the knowledge that wastage will speedily be replaced enables us to draw more readily upon our reserves and throw them in now that everything counts so much.

Our task is not only to win the battle – but to win the war. After this battle in France abates its force, there will come the battle for our Island – for all that Britain is, and all that Britain means. That will be the struggle. In that supreme emergency we shall not hesitate to take every step, even the most drastic, to call forth from our people the last ounce and the last inch of effort of which they are capable. The interests of property, the hours of labour, are nothing compared with the struggle for life and honour, for right and freedom, to which we have vowed ourselves.

I have received from the Chiefs of the French Republic, and in particular from its indomitable Prime Minister, M. Reynaud, the most sacred pledges that whatever happens they will fight to the end, be it bitter or be it glorious. Nay, if we fight to the end, it can only be glorious.

Having received His Majesty's commission, I have formed an Administration of men and women of every Party and of almost every point of view. We have differed and quarrelled in the past; but now one bond unites us all – to wage war until victory is won, and never to surrender ourselves to servitude and shame, whatever the cost and the agony may be. This is one of the most awe-striking periods in the long history of France and Britain. It is also beyond doubt the most sublime. Side by side, unaided except by their kith and kin in the great Dominions and by the wide empires which rest beneath their shield – side by side, the British and French peoples have advanced to rescue not only Europe but mankind from the foulest and most soul-destroying tyranny which has ever darkened and stained the pages of history. Behind them – behind us – behind the Armies and Fleets of Britain and France – gather a group of shattered States and bludgeoned races: the Czechs, the Poles, the Norwegians, the Danes, the Dutch, the Belgians – upon all of whom the long night of barbarism will descend, unbroken even by a star of hope, unless we conquer, as conquer we must; as conquer we shall.

Today is Trinity Sunday. Centuries ago words were written to be a call and a spur to the faithful servants of Truth and Justice: 'Arm yourselves, and be ye men of valour, and be in readiness for the conflict; for it is better for us to perish in battle than to look upon the outrage of our nation and our altar. As the Will of God is in Heaven, even so let it be.'

Winston Churchill, BBC, 19 May 1940

Churchill finished his brilliant oratory with a quote from the Old Testament's First Book of Maccabees. Churchill slightly misquoted, 'And Judas said, arm yourselves, and be valiant men . . .', but in so doing made the phrase his own, for this speech has ever since been referred to as 'Be Ye Men of Valour'.

Six days before this maiden broadcast as Prime Minister, Churchill had given a speech in the House of Commons that showed what he was made of, and that he expected the rest of the country to be cast in the same mould.

I say to the House as I said to ministers who have joined this government, I have nothing to offer but blood, toil, tears, and sweat. We have before us an ordeal of the most grievous kind. We have before us many, many months of struggle and suffering. You ask, what is our policy? I say it is to wage war by land, sea, and air. War with all our might and with all the strength God has given us, and to wage war against a monstrous tyranny never surpassed in the dark and lamentable catalogue of human crime. That is our policy. You ask, what is our aim? I can answer in one word. It is victory. Victory at all costs – Victory in spite of all terrors – Victory, however long and hard the road may be, for without victory there is no survival.

It's ironic that one of Churchill's best-known speeches should be one that was not broadcast.

Before May was out other ministers spoke on the radio, mostly in terms that echoed Churchill's defiant message, even if they lacked the power of his oratory. On 22 May Clement Attlee, the Deputy Prime Minister, spoke about the Emergency Powers Bill. He said: 'Our men at sea, on land and in the air, have shown the bravery, devotion and skill which we expected of them. We must be worthy of them.' Ernest Bevin, the Minister of Labour and National Service, spoke eloquently and was true to his socialist roots when he said, 'When these boys do come back . . . [we want] to reabsorb them into normal civil life and to secure the ushering in of a better age, based upon social justice and peace.' Herbert Morrison, who had been given the job of Minister of Supply, spoke after the 9 p.m. news in the third week of May; his theme was 'a call for arms'.

> Today we are at grips with a more deadly menace than has threatened the people of these islands since Philip's great Armada set out to storm our coasts and bring us under his yoke. Indeed the present threat looms nearer. Today there is not 'time enough to finish the game and beat the enemy too'. There is time for nothing but an intense concentrated effort of muscle and mind and will. It must begin now.
>
> *Herbert Morrison, BBC, 22 May 1940*

Morrison finished his speech by saying, 'Work is the call; work at war speed. Goodnight – and go to it.' These last three words began appearing on posters to encourage a greater sense of urgency in the production of arms, and especially Spitfire and Hurricane fighters that were to become pivotal in the defence of Britain.

Despite any, or all of, the urging from government ministers, the mood of the country in the second half of May was intensely gloomy. Children were being evacuated from along the coastline facing the Continent; almost everyone, almost everywhere, was preparing for invasion. Talk was rife that Hitler had a firm date in mind as to when he would invade; some even said they knew for certain that he would drop parachutists inland to disrupt Britain's defences. Others talked of how the Luftwaffe would overrun Britain's pitifully small number of modern fighter aircraft. Even with Duff Cooper's appointment at the Ministry of Information there was still unrest in some circles, particularly among Conservative MPs, that the BBC had done a poor job in prosecuting the war. One MP spoke about the radio building up 'personalities that should never have been built up in the national interest'. He went on to blame the BBC for broadcasting talks by Middleton Murry, 'a communist, a pacifist, and a principal member of the Peace Pledge Union'. Given the gravity of the situation facing Britain it seemed a little off the point.

On the same day the Belgian Army surrendered on the orders of their King. Leopold had in fact acted against the orders of his government, but it really was a no-win situation. The power of the German Army and Air Force was awesome; but in fact many officers and men of the Belgian Army continued to fight alongside the British and French soldiers. Churchill again spoke to the House of Commons saying that the British and French forces would fight on. Two days earlier German radio had announced that British troops were 'laying down their arms and fleeing towards the coast'. Shortly after the Prime Minister spoke to the House, Lord Haw-Haw's broadcast from Hamburg poured scorn on the Allies. Much of his speech attempted to be divisive, in that he criticised 'those that conducted war from luxury hotels' while contrasting them to those that actually did the fighting.

> The last week has been supremely eventful in the history of the world – it has witnessed the climax of the first great German campaign against the forces of the Allies. And as for the result there is now no doubt whatsoever. We were confident of victory from when it was announced that our forces had entered Holland and Belgium for the purpose of frustrating the Allied attack that had been planned against the Ruhr. On the other hand the capitulation of Holland within five days was something that we shouldn't have ventured to predict . . . The Allied forces have been routed so thoroughly that it must be wondered if there is any parallel for such a defeat in military history . . . The number of British and French prisoners that have been taken is beyond computation.
>
> Lord Haw-Haw, German radio, 28 May 1940

Haw-Haw went on to lambaste Duff Cooper and the Ministry of Information for deceiving the British people. Although not directly responding to specific German propaganda the Ministry were forced to issue a statement on 29 May to try to quell the rising tide of rumour-mongering and disquiet that Haw-Haw's broadcast seemed to engender in some quarters.

Such was the speed of the news and unfolding events in this period, with the German Blitzkrieg in full cry, that newsreaders were on a rota that kept them sleeping at Broadcasting House every night. It was a situation that would became standardised to a working pattern of three days on, two days off, with the news staff sleeping at the BBC during their nights on. In fact the whole news operation was working in shifts with the increasing volume of news flooding into Broadcasting House. Each shift had an editor in charge, with half a dozen sub-editors, along with typists to pull things together. There were also specialists in various subjects, who along with everyone else, reported to R.T. Clark, the Senior News Editor. The logistics were complex, and given that they didn't have computers, e-mail, the web and every other piece of time-saving technology at their disposal, it was a triumph for all concerned in getting the news on air. R.T. Clark was one of the most important men in the BBC's news team, and it's been said that he seldom left Broadcasting House during the war. While this may be artistic licence it gives an indication of his significance to the operation. He was also a brilliant writer who had the ability to produce scripts 'to length', that is to say, if it needed to run for 48 seconds, that's how many words he wrote – apparently he rarely got it wrong.

The sense of paranoia over what the Germans knew, and whether their news was better than the BBC's, led to a great deal of time being spent at Broadcasting House simply trying to keep up with events. Noel Newsome, the BBC's Director of European Broadcasts, keenly felt the frustration of the times when he wrote to the Director General: 'If our propaganda remains superficial, unprincipled and opportunist it cannot, however clever or cunning, contribute . . . towards shortening the war, still less towards laying the foundations of a postwar world fit for anyone to live in.' The task for the BBC, in European broadcasts as well as at home, was to raise the level of confidence in the listener, and at the same time keep morale as buoyant as possible. Newsome's comments were not well received and he found himself marginalised for speaking out.

Such was the hunger for news that many jumped on any morsel of information and often in the re-telling it became more outrageous. The situation in France, and especially in the area around Dunkirk, needed no exaggeration or manipulation. It was desperate. A German army that numbered around 750,000 men encircled what remained of the BEF in France. At this time Stuart Hibberd, one of the BBC's best-known announcers, had been back working in Broadcasting House for a few days, having been transferred to Bristol a few weeks earlier, and was returning on the train from London. He noted in his diary: 'In my carriage when travelling to Bristol were a number of race-goers, who got out at Bath; they were returning to London again by the 5.40. Nobody seemed in the least perturbed about the serious plight of our army before Dunkirk.' It seems surreal, but then again how often when one is not directly involved in something it is easier to blank it out, to park it in a part of the brain that allows what counts for normal life to carry on.

On the last day of May Bernhard Stubbs, who had been retreating with the BEF, managed to make his way back to Britain and broadcast of the plight of the men who had also made it home.

For days and nights ships of all kinds have plied to and fro across the Channel under the fierce onslaught of the enemy's bombers, utterly regardless of the perils, to bring out as many as possible of the trapped BEF. There was every kind of ship that I saw coming in this morning and every one of them was crammed full of tired, battle-stained and blood-stained British soldiers. Soon after dawn this morning I saw two warships steaming in, one listing heavily to port under the huge load of men she carried on her decks. In a few minutes her tired commander had her alongside and a gangway was thrown from her decks to the quay. Transport Officers counted the men as they came ashore, no question of units, no question of regiments, no question even of nationality, for there were French and Belgian soldiers who had fought side by side with the British in the battle of Flanders. All of them were tired, some were completely exhausted, but the most amazing thing was that practically every man was reasonably cheerful and most of them managed a smile. Even when a man was obviously on the verge of collapse from sheer fatigue you could still tell by his eyes that his spirit was irrepressible. That is a thing that all the bombs in Germany will never crush.

Bernhard Stubbs, BBC, 31 May 1940

Stubbs joined the Navy shortly after this broadcast, and lost his life a year later when the *Bismarck* sank the battleship HMS *Hood*. The day after Stubbs's report on the defeated BEF Lewis Ricci, a retired Royal Navy captain, broadcast another eyewitness account of the evacuation. Ricci worked for the Ministry of Information as a naval eyewitness and broadcast under the name Bartimeus.

All day Thursday I spent at the South Coast base where the ships that brought off the British Expeditionary Force came and went. For days and nights there had been a continuous stream to and fro of transports and destroyers, sloops and trawlers, coming back crammed to their utmost capacity with men. They had been shelled by coastal batteries and bombed almost ceaselessly from the air. They embarked thousands from beaches, men wading out to their armpits to reach the boats. They embarked tens of thousands from piers and jetties, beating off the German bombers with their guns while the troops climbed on board. They told me of men of a Scottish Regiment who scrambled on to a destroyer's fo'c'sle in the last stages of exhaustion and joined in the fusillade with their rifles, trying to shoot down the low-diving bombers.

I was on board a destroyer in the afternoon that had just come back from the beaches. She had had fifty-two bombs dropped over her, and she had lost her captain, but she came back crammed to capacity. They had only one boat, a whaler; to bring them off – the other boats were splintered and out of action. What seemed to worry them most was the behaviour of a German bomb that burst in shallow water on the bottom of the sea and deluged the whole ship and everybody on board with grey mud . . .

. . . I sailed in another destroyer about midnight. We riddled our way through the minefields till we were nearing Dunkirk. The oil tanks were still blazing furiously, and there was an occasional sound of distant gunfire. Once a shell landed in one of those blazing tanks and a huge red glare blazed up almost to the zenith. It died down again and the moon came out from behind a cloud, giving the sea and the sky a queer semblance of peace, in contrast to the blazing inferno ashore. It was light enough to see the outlines of the town buildings still standing, black against the glare of the fire, and the vast clouds of smoke billowing away eastward. And it was light enough to see, assembled on the whole length of the Mole, thousands of men of the British Expeditionary Force waiting patiently for embarkation. There was a French destroyer already alongside filled up with men. There was a trawler alongside also; but she had been sunk by bombs, and only her masts and funnels were above water. The White Ensign was still flying bravely at her mast-head. We went alongside between them, watched by those thousands of patient eyes under the shrapnel helmets. It was nearly low water, and the top of the Mole was level with our bridge. Scaling ladders were lowered, and down they came as fast as fully equipped, fully armed men could climb. This was no army in defeat: they looked in magnificent fettle, ruddy and burly, and wearing full equipment; dog-tired after fighting rearguard action day and night for a week, as well they might be; but for the matter of that, the Navy that was bringing them off could have done with a bit of sleep themselves. Every man as he got on board grinned and said 'Thank God', and settled down quietly on a bit of deck space, like a well-behaved school-treat packing into a motor-coach for an outing.

Then a bomber appeared overhead and we opened fire. A French destroyer came in through the entrance, firing as she came, followed by a British destroyer. The embarkation continued as calmly as if nothing out of the ordinary was happening. German shells began bursting at the end of the Mole with methodical regularity, hitting nobody, about one a minute. The English Channel was an extraordinary sight as the sun rose. It looked something like Henley Regatta, as if every craft on the south coast that could float was heading for Dunkirk and the beaches to finish off the job. There were barges and wherries, yachts and launches. Little boats in tow of bigger boats, and presently up through the middle of them came an overseas convoy from the other side of the world. There was something about them – their bright Red Ensigns, and their guns cocked up on the stem, that suggested an indescribable jauntiness. On board our ship, every inch of space on deck and below was crammed with men. Already many of them were asleep where they lay, and many of those who slept had smiles on their faces as if they were congratulating themselves, even in sleep, on a good job well done. They were just a haphazard collection of men from any number of regiments, but in physique and bearing they might have been the pick of the crack regiment of an army. We all felt happier that morning than we had felt since the war started. 'Give us a chance for a wash and brush-up and a bit of sleep, and let's get back: we've got Jerry beat.' That is, in effect, what they all said.

                                            Bartimeus, BBC, 1 June 1940

Broadcasts like this were the closest people could get to have any inkling of what it was like to be in such a desperate situation. Without television or any kind of on-the-spot reporting like that to which we are accustomed to today, this was as good as it was going to get. The newsreels failed to provide anything but a delayed reaction, and they were often even more sanitised than the reports carried by the radio. There was another factor at work here. Listening to the thoughts of the broadcasters on the resilience of the British 'Tommy' was a vital weapon in the armoury for the defence of Britain. The fear of invasion was enormous, especially after hearing what had happened in Holland and Belgium. What shone through so much of the reporting at this time was a sense of hope. At the time some would have said it was a triumph of optimism over reality, but hindsight has proven the optimists right. Who can precisely say how much of a part the positive and hopeful BBC broadcasts – whether news, talks, or even comedians just poking fun at the Nazi leaders – played in getting the mind set of Britain right for the fight? Like almost everything else during this period, for every vote in favour of a particular course of action, or point of view, there was someone else against it.

In particular, for the BBC that someone was the Ministry of Information. They constantly urged the BBC to spare listeners 'unnecessary frightening details'. To be fair, some of what the Ministry and MPs were getting exercised over was the dramatisation of events in radio programmes. A forty-minute reconstruction of Narvik – 'a great Naval feat of arms' – was broadcast on

13 May and came in for particular condemnation: 'vulgarly sensational' was how one MP put it. On the positive side, and in a piece of programming good fortune, the BBC Symphony Orchestra under Sir Adrian Boult broadcast a concert at 7.30 p.m. on 1 June. The concert's running order had been planned weeks before and began with Tchaikovsky's 1812 Overture – music that had been completed in 1882 to celebrate the seventieth anniversary of Russia's victory over Napoleon. If you allowed for some changes in allegiances, the sentiment and feelings stirred by this heroic music perfectly suited the times.

ACTS OF DEFIANCE

Before the start of the plan to bring the beleaguered troops of the BEF back to Britain on 26 May, codenamed Operation Dynamo, it was hoped that the audacious strategy might allow for a few tens of thousands to be saved, maybe 50,000 at most. When it ended on 4 June over 300,000 men, two-thirds of them British, were saved. There were around 34,000 Allied soldiers and airmen taken prisoner and a similar number killed, along with nine destroyers sunk and over two hundred smaller ships lost. The confusion that reigned supreme during the evacuation was keenly felt by the BBC, which tried as best it could to provide news bulletins based around the facts supplied by the Ministry of Information.

A superb example of how easily things can get out of control during such an intense period of fighting occurred on 30 May. The BBC announced that a squadron of twelve Defiant fighters had shot down thirty-seven enemy aircraft; this was a gross distortion. There has been much criticism of the BBC, both then and with hindsight, but they were victims of the system, the whole information flow, as they were unable to 'gather news' in the sense of how we see the process today. It is easy to be critical, but at the same time news of a 'success' like this helped to balance an equation heavily stacked in favour of the reality of bad news. It was bad news that the BBC could not, and did not want to, hide and bad news that the German radio exploited to the fullest extent.

Although the Germans stated three days ago that the British Army in Flanders was surrounded and annihilated, four-fifths of it, and tens of thousands of French troops, have already been brought over, and the evacuation goes on.

Anthony Eden, 9 p.m., BBC, 2 June 1940

The Prime Minister said what had happened at Dunkirk was 'a miracle of deliverance'. Perhaps it was the first of several 'miracles' that saved Britain.

We shall not flag nor fail. We shall go on to the end. We shall fight in France and on the seas and oceans; we shall fight with growing confidence and growing strength in the air. We shall defend our island whatever the cost may be; we shall fight on beaches, landing grounds, in fields, in streets and on the hills. We shall never surrender and even if, which I do not for the moment believe, this island or a large part of it were subjugated and starving, then our empire beyond the seas, armed and guarded by the British Fleet, will carry on the struggle until in God's good time the New World, with all its power and might, sets forth to the liberation and rescue of the Old.

Winston Churchill, BBC, 4 June 1940

It was a pity that what the country heard of Churchill's speech to Parliament on 4 June was an edited portion of his thirty minutes of sustained oration repeated by a BBC announcer. Although it resonated with enough power for poet and novelist Vita Sackville-West to write to her husband Harold Nicolson MP, to say: 'It sent shivers (not of fear) down my spine'. Following the reading of Churchill's speech there was another broadcast concert from Bristol's Colston Hall.

We have heard from the Prime Minister, and from the French military communiqués, that the withdrawal of the Allied Armies in Flanders is complete. To mark the occasion of this great deliverance, and by way of tribute to the heroism of those who have fallen, and those who are saved, we perform the Eroica Symphony by Beethoven.

BBC, 4 June 1940

There was no hint of irony in the announcement.

Chapter 6

IN THE END ALL WILL COME RIGHT

ORATORY AND ALCHEMY

On the day following Churchill's fighting speech the first in the series of J.B. Priestley's talks was broadcast on the BBC. While this one was on a Wednesday evening most of those that followed were on a Sunday immediately following the 9 p.m. news. They were to prove incredibly popular over the next four, crucial, months – so much so that almost a third of the adult population of Britain would tune in to hear his 'Yorkshire stoicism', as the *Daily Mail* reported on 2 July.

I wonder how many of you feel as I do about this great battle and evacuation of Dunkirk. The news of it came as a series of surprises and shocks, followed by equally astonishing new waves of hope. It was all, from beginning to end, unexpected. And yet now that it's over, and we can look back on it, doesn't it seem to you to have an inevitable air about it – as if we had turned a page in the history of Britain and seen a chapter headed 'Dunkirk' and perhaps seen, too, a picture of the troops on the beach, waiting to embark?

And now that this whole action is completed, we notice that it has a definite shape, and a certain definite character. What strikes me about it is how typically English it is. Nothing, I feel, could be more English than this Battle of Dunkirk, both in its beginning and its end, its folly and its grandeur. It was very English in what was sadly wrong with it; this much has been freely admitted, and we are assured will be freely discussed when the proper moment arrives. We have gone sadly wrong like this before; and here and now we must resolve never, never to do it again. Another such blunder may not be forgiven us.

But having admitted this much, let's do ourselves the justice of admitting, too, that this Dunkirk affair was also very English (and when I say English I really mean British) in the way in which, when apparently all was lost, so much was gloriously retrieved. Bright honour was almost 'plucked from the moon'. What began as a miserable blunder, a catalogue of misfortunes and miscalculations, ended as an epic of gallantry. We have a queer habit – and you can see it running through our history – of conjuring up such transformations. Out of a black gulf of humiliation and despair rises a sun of blazing glory . . .

J.B. Priestley, BBC, 5 June 1940

In Priestley's talk there is a subtle mix of the everyman and the intellectual that at all times makes the listener feel comfortable. It was not just in Britain that his talks were well received; by September it was estimated that 18 million Americans were also hearing his broadcasts on the BBC's North American Service. Not every giver of talks met with similar acclaim, and Priestley to some was much too far to the left in his political leanings. A letter to the *Scotsman* on 5 August from someone in Edinburgh – they failed to give their name – thought that there was no place for such discourse: 'Surely 9 o'clock in the evening is a bad time for talks full of hatred and anger with Hitler and a repetition of his crimes'. The letter-writer went on to say that good music and more interesting subjects would be better to ensure that listeners had an undisturbed night's sleep. Perhaps, therefore, it really was a case of timing, rather than the talks themselves. Priestley's broadcasts played a significant role in keeping British wirelesses tuned to the BBC, and not to Haw-Haw, during a crucial period. However, he eventually fell foul of those in high places; Churchill was not a supporter, and the Ministry of Information wrote to the BBC in the spring of 1941 saying his series was to cease on the 'instruction of the Minister'.

Five days after Priestley's talk the need to conjure up transformations in the news content was to be stretched to the limit.

The hour marked with the seal of destiny has struck, the hour of irrevocable decisions! Our declaration of war has been handed to the Ambassadors of Britain and France! . . . This gigantic struggle is the struggle of peoples poor but rich in workers against exploiters. It is a struggle of the fruitful and young peoples against the sterile on the threshold of their decline.

Mussolini at the Palazzo Venezia, Radio Rome, 6 p.m., 10 June 1940

Four days later the Germans entered Paris, and within forty-eight hours the new French Premier, Marshal Pétain, sued for peace. The bleakness of the outlook for Britain cannot be overstated. If France could fall, what other than the Channel was stopping the Germans from invading immediately? Those who had been saying that Hitler had the date of the invasion already planned may just have known what they were talking about. On 17 June Churchill broadcast a short statement on the Home, Forces and Overseas Services of the BBC saying that Britain expected that France would rise again. He finished his statement with words of hope, words that are the very essence of Churchillian greatness – simple, effective and totally understandable by everyone: 'We are sure that in the end all will come right.' Politicians today try to emulate his delivery, to copy his style, but he had the power of alchemy – they do not.

The following afternoon the Prime Minister was once again in the House, cajoling, demanding, and seeming once again to conjure up mystical powers to ensure that no one failed to comprehend what was at stake. At the close of the speech he said:

> What General Weygand called the Battle of France is over. I expect that the Battle of Britain is about to begin. Upon this battle depends the survival of Christian civilisation. Upon it depends our own British life, and the long continuity of our institutions and our Empire. The whole fury and might of the enemy must very soon be turned on us. Hitler knows that he will have to break us in this Island or lose the war. If we can stand up to him, all Europe may be free and the life of the world may move forward into broad, sunlit uplands. But if we fail, then the whole world, including the United States, including all that we have known and cared for, will sink into the abyss of a new Dark Age made more sinister, and perhaps more protracted, by the lights of perverted science. Let us therefore brace ourselves to our duties, and so bear ourselves that, if the British Empire and its Commonwealth last for a thousand years, men will still say, 'This was their finest hour.'
>
> *Winston Churchill, BBC, 18 June 1940*

Reading them now still sends a bolt of pride through the body; hearing them in the Commons would have been electrifying. In fact Churchill was so tired from his efforts to keep the French fighting, as well as marshalling greater endeavour at home, that the first part of this long speech was not delivered as well as many of his earlier efforts. However, according to everyone who heard it, the end of the speech was 'magnificent' – all came right. When he broadcast the same speech on the radio that evening he sounded even less inspiring. According to Harold Nicolson, in a letter to his wife the following day, '. . . it sounded ghastly on the wireless. All the great vigour he put into it seemed to evaporate.' By way of contrast, the self-appointed leader of the Free French in London, General Charles de Gaulle, broadcast an emotional appeal for resistance against the Germans to all Frenchmen and -women who had managed to flee France: 'Whatever happens the flame of French resistance must not and shall not die.' Churchill personally authorised his broadcast on the European Service of the BBC, much against the wishes of some of his cabinet.

At this point in the war few French people were listening to the BBC and so it's doubtful whether very many people actually heard de Gaulle's first broadcast. However, the BBC repeated it several times over the coming days and newspapers based in the south of France carried extracts from it. Gradually word spread that there was a French resistance movement, but for now it was to be found only in London.

With the acute sense of timing that was even then expected of Germans, the Luftwaffe launched some exploratory raids on the east coast of England and the Thames Estuary during the night of 18 June. Reports the following day spoke of many raids and how people travelling on a late train saw one take place over the Thames Estuary. Across the whole east of the country there was little damage on the ground and only one German raider was shot down. Hitler and the Luftwaffe had laid down a marker, although the Battle of Britain proper was not to begin for another three weeks.

. . . IT'S ALL IN THE EYE TIE OF THE BEHOLDER

One aspect of Italy's involvement in the war that caused senior BBC managers considerable consternation was the propensity for comedians to make the Italians the butt of their jokes. Not that the Germans got away scot-free; jokes at the expense of Goering's girth were legion. On 17 June 1940 a ban on jokes about Italians was made by the BBC, not because anyone was particularly concerned about them getting upset, but because it was feared that they might not be quite as soft a touch as they were in the First World War. Not that jokes about Italian soldiers were a twentieth-century phenomenon; as far back as the 1500s the Italians were getting some stick. Normal service was resumed within a year, when jokes about Italian tanks and their reverse gears were once again deemed acceptable. As this exchange proves, normal service was resumed in January 1941 on the Forces Programme, when the comedians Bennet and Moroney were back picking on the Italians.

Bennet: Here's a new riddle, very funny, highly topical. What is it that has feathers on the head but isn't a bird – has two legs but runs faster than a hare?

Moroney: I don't know, what is it?

Bennet: An Italian soldier . . . We'll sing the Italian generals' theme song.

Moroney: What's that?

Bennet: 'If I only had wings'.

TIMING IS EVERYTHING

With the fall of France came something of a pause in proceedings; everyone needed to draw breath. The speed of the German advance had been breathtaking and they needed to regroup. Despite this brief respite a message from the Prime Minister was read out on the news on 27 July; it finished with the words: 'Do not relax because the enemy has not yet attempted invasion.' In other words, it was only a matter of time.

With the seriousness of the situation it's interesting that this was the time that the BBC decided to introduce a new variety show. It was to become synonymous with the radio both during the war and for the two decades after it was over. The philosophy behind 'Music While You Work' was simple. There was a need to raise morale on the production lines, for it was work done in factories that was vital in building up Britain's stocks of aircraft and guns, as well as other, less obvious, war materials. It had been shown that workers' attention spans showed signs of wandering at 10.30 a.m. and 3 p.m. – so that was when the show was aired. 'Music While You Work' was first broadcast on 23 June and over the course of the war it was transmitted live from thousands of factories all around the country, soon attracting audiences of 3.5 million. In one factory not far from Croydon in Surrey it proved not totally to the liking of Elsie Whiteman. She and a friend, Kathleen Church-Bliss, kept a diary while they worked at Morrisons, an aircraft parts manufacturer: 'The new loud-speakers have been tried and "Music While You Work" blared out for half an hour this morning. It may be all right for those who are not near a loud-speaker, but Els is not one of those, so to her it is bedlam. She thinks she may have to ask for her release on account of a £600 wireless.'

A year later 'Workers' Playtime' went on the air with the aim of cheering up the men and woman on the production line by way of a steady diet of comedians. It was broadcast at lunchtimes and was originally intended to run for just six weeks; in the end it lasted for well over twenty years. In speaking on the radio about both programmes Ernest Bevin, the Minister of Labour and National Service, said: 'The BBC is a factory for entertainment and education, and must be regarded as one of the vital services.'

The attention paid to improving the standard of the variety and non-news-related programming by the BBC was essential in helping maintain a sense of proportion. Those in charge at the BBC took the view that broadcasting is like a good meal, in that it requires a balance of flavours, textures and a blend of the sweet and the savoury to satisfy the palate. It was not a view entirely shared by one letter-writer to the *Scotsman* in early August 1940:

Since the war started, hundreds of thousands of listeners must have wasted in the aggregate astronomical amounts of time, listening to radio news bulletins, the greater part of which they had already heard earlier in each day. Surely it would have occurred to anyone to announce – say, after the one o'clock bulletin, 'The following are new items since our previous bulletins to-day'. When the fresh items had been read, the old news could be repeated for the benefit of those who had not heard it before. Similarly, any items which had to be amplified could be put near the beginning, with an appropriate intimation. Surely it is at least as important to save time as anything else, but the present method of the BBC puts a premium upon waste, besides being a weariness to the flesh.

Factual talks, many by serving military personnel, continued to be broadcast. They provided some 'colour' compared to the more sterile feel of the news bulletins; giving people at home a taste of what it was like to be in the forces. Talks by RAF personnel were particularly popular; theirs were stories of 'derring do' in what was still the most glamorous arm of the Forces. A broadcast in June by a Hurricane pilot gave a graphic account of the excitement of war in the air. Of course, he was a survivor; there was no one telling the tales of the many that lost their lives. Called 'The Story of an American Fighter Pilot with the RAF', it was obviously useful in generating interest in the war in the USA and was probably also broadcast on the North American Service of the BBC.

I was born of Welsh parents in Bernardsville, near Morristown, New Jersey, in 1913. My father ran a big farm there. I went to school first at the Morristown High School, and when we left there for Connecticut, I went to the Gilbert School in Winstead, Connecticut. We lived for a long time in New Hertford, Connecticut, and I have many friends over there. I left the United States when I was about eighteen or nineteen years old. My parents, who had gone out to America two years before I was born, came back and settled down in Bridgend, South Wales. I went to Cardiff College to study wireless for a while, and after doing this and that for a year or two, I took a short service commission in the RAF. That was in 1936. I was posted to a squadron immediately I had finished my training, and here I am still a fighter pilot, and liking it more and more each day.

I got my first German in November 1939. It was the first enemy aircraft to be shot down in the Straits of Dover in this war. I was on patrol between Deal and Calais, leading a section of Hurricanes from my squadron when we spotted, at 12,000 feet, a Dornier 17 'Flying Pencil'. He was about 2,000 feet below us, and as we hadn't seen a German machine up to then, we went down carefully to make sure. We soon recognised him as an enemy, and as I turned to attack he tried to attack me. My Hurricane quickly out-manoeuvred him; I got on his tail, and gave him three sharp bursts of fire. Another member of the section got in three bursts too, as he dived towards the clouds. The last I saw of him was just above sea level. He had turned on his back, and a moment later crashed into the sea. When we got back to the mess we were handed a parcel. It contained a bottle of champagne – with the compliments of the Station Commander. You see it was our first fight – and we'd won. In those days, one German aircraft was something to celebrate.

We went over to France on May 10th, when Hitler invaded the Low Countries. We went up that same afternoon. That time we didn't see anything, but the next day we really started. We carried out three patrols east of Brussels, and on the third patrol we saw three Heinkel 111s. We shot down one, and badly damaged the other two. The day after that, we got two Heinkel 111s, one of which was credited to me. I shot mine down from 12,000 feet.

All the same, those skirmishes were child's play to what was to come later. On May 14th, after we had escorted a number of Blenheim bombers into enemy territory, we were on our way back when we saw three Dornier 17 'Flying Pencils'. It was a trap, for when we gave chase to the Dorniers, we suddenly found ourselves in the middle of between fifty and sixty Messerschmitt 109s and 110s. I was leading the flight that day and when I realised how hopelessly outnumbered we were, I gave orders to the boys to sort out their own targets and not to keep formation.

We broke up and began to set about the Messerschmitts. I got four Me110s, and other members of the flight got four more. On the way back to our base, I saw two Heinkel 126s, one of which I shot down, and damaged the other with the rest of my ammunition. It was a good day. We routed an overwhelming number of enemy fighters, beat up two of their Army reconnaissance planes, and we all got home safely. Our bag on that day was six. There were six of us, so we averaged one each.

There were several other days when we ran into heavy odds of enemy fighters. It is really amazing, looking back, that we should have had the success we had. But it certainly was a success each day. We never ran into the Germans without shooting some down. When we were patrolling

Dunkirk, for instance, giving protection day after day to the BEF, we always got a few. I remember once, when we found ourselves in the thick of six squadrons of Me109s and 110s, we saw an unusual type of new fighter. They were the new Heinkel 113s. Naturally we couldn't resist the appointment. We got one of each type, and three or four of what we call 'probables'. I was attacking an Me110 when I suddenly realised that there were six Heinkel 113s on my tail. I made a very quick turn to get away from them, and then shot down the Heinkel 113 on the extreme left of that particular formation.

That was in the afternoon. We had an 'appetiser' before lunch, when we met twenty Heinkel 111 bombers. I got one. He went down in flames. And others of the squadron got their share.

The smoke from innumerable fires in Dunkirk and other French coast towns was terrific about that time. A fellow pilot described it as being like a gigantic piece of cotton-wool lying right across the seashore, following the coast down the Channel as far as he could see, even from two or three miles up . . . We were stationed in France for eleven days. I remember that, when we went away, the roses were in bud; and when we came back they were in full bloom. In between we'd had eleven glorious days of action, but it was very hard work.

RAF flight lieutenant, 'Air Log', BBC, June 1940

In all the talks by serving military personal the speaker went unnamed. In this case it was Flight Lieutenant J.W.E. 'Jimmy' Davies, who was dark, slim and apparently something of a loner compared to most of the pilots who had come from overseas to fight with the RAF. The incident he talked about back in November 1939 had been reported on the radio that evening.

An enemy aircraft approached the east coast this morning. It was engaged and shot down by RAF fighter aircraft. There was no anti-aircraft fire, and no air-raid warning was sounded in Deal. The destruction of this bomber means that at least 20 enemy planes have been destroyed either over, or near Britain, since the raid on the Firth of Forth on October 16.

BBC News, 21 November 1939

The action involved two Hurricanes from 79 Squadron, and the Dornier Do17P they shot down belonged to 3(F)/122, a Luftwaffe long-range recon-naissance unit. At the time Davies was a flying officer based at Biggin Hill in Kent, although he and the three aircraft of Yellow Section of 79 Squadron had been ordered to operate from Hawkinge, which was on the cliffs above

Folkestone. Having been scrambled, one of the Hurricanes had engine problems, which meant that only two got airborne, the second being flown by Flight Sergeant Brown. Having made contact with the Dornier they opened fire from 60 yards and set one engine alight. The Dornier crashed and the destroyer HMS *Boreas* found pieces of wreckage floating on the sea some hours later. During their ten-day stay in France in support of the BEF 79 Squadron was based at Merville, 15 miles west of Lille, in the north of the country.

On the afternoon of 27 June, maybe a week or ten days after Davies made his broadcast, he was due to be given a medal, along with other pilots from Biggin Hill, by the King. Davies and others from his squadron had a protracted dogfight with German fighters during the morning and instead of making it back to their base in time for the ceremony, those that survived were diverted to Hawkinge; Flight Lieutenant Davies was not among those that got back. He was shot down and his Hurricane was spotted diving straight into the sea in a cloud of white spray. The 26-year-old James William Elias Davies's Distinguished Flying Cross remained on the ceremonial presentation cushion and was taken to the Adjutant's office; possibly they were unaware at this point that he was dead. His career as a fighter pilot effectively lasted nine months, which was longer than many of his contemporaries and a lot longer than those who would take the places of pilots who were killed in the coming Battle of Britain.

Chapter 7

THE BATTLE OF BRITAIN

The Battle of Britain began on 10 July 1940; on that everyone agrees. However, there has been debate ever since among historians as to how long it lasted and how many phases of the battle there were. Most agree that the first stage of the campaign was very much a 'testing the enemy' phase for the Luftwaffe. By attacking ships in the Channel, mounting small raids on the north of England and sending over reconnaissance aircraft the Germans were able to probe and test the preparedness of the RAF fighters. It also allowed them partially to test the RAF's tactics, as well as its strength in numbers. For the Germans there was the bonus that every RAF fighter lost was one less with which Britain could defend herself come the main attacks. As well as revealing aspects of Britain's defensive capabilities the attacks on Merchant Navy convoys in the Channel were helping to rob Britain of valuable food and materials.

In another 'Air Log' broadcast a pilot officer gave his version of events in a dogfight over the English Channel, probably on the opening day of the Battle of Britain:

. . . Our squadron was ordered to fly to the spot where ships were being attacked. In a few minutes we had reached the scene. We were at 8,000 feet, the clouds were about 2,000 to 3,000 feet above us, and below we saw very clearly a line of ships and a formation of bombers about to attack.

The bombers were between 100 to 200 feet below us. There were twenty-four Dorniers altogether and they apparently intended to attack in three waves. The first bunch of bombers had already dropped their bombs when we got there and the second formation was about to go in. The third wave never delivered an attack at all. It was a thrilling sight I must confess, as I looked down on the tiny ships below and saw two long lines of broken water where the first lot of bombs had fallen. There were two distinct lines of disturbed water near the ships and just ahead were fountains of water leaping skywards from bombs newly dropped. In a second or two the sea down below spouted up to the height of about 300 feet or more in two lines alongside the convoy.

Our squadron leader gave the order to attack. Down we went. He led one flight against a formation of bombers and I led my flight over the starboard side. It was a simultaneous attack. We went screaming down and pumped lead into our targets. We shook them up quite a bit. Then I broke away and looked round for a prospective victim, and saw, some distance away, a Dornier lagging behind the first formation. I flew after it, accompanied by two other members of my flight, and the enemy went into a gentle dive turning towards the French coast. He was doing a steady 300 miles an hour in that gentle dive, but we overtook him and started firing at him. He was in obvious distress. When fifteen miles out from the English coast we turned back to rejoin the main battle.

I was just turning round when I saw an Me109 come hurtling at me. He came from above and in front of me, so I made a quick turn and dived after him. I was then at about 5,000 feet and when I began to chase him down to the sea he was a good 800 yards in front. He was going very fast, and I had to do 400 miles an hour to catch him up, or rather to get him nicely within range. Then, before I could fire, he flattened out no more than 50 feet above the sea level, and went streaking for home. I followed him, and we still were doing a good 400 miles an hour when I pressed the gun button. First one short burst of less than one second's duration, then another, and then another, and finally a fifth short burst, all aimed very deliberately. Suddenly the Messerschmitt port wing dropped down. The starboard wing went up, and then in a flash his nose went down and he was gone. He simply vanished into the sea.

I hadn't time to look round for him, because almost at the precise moment he disappeared from my gun sights I felt a sting in my leg. It was a sting from a splinter of my aircraft, which had been hit by enemy bullets. There were some Messerschmitts right on my tail. Just as I had been firing at the enemy fighter, which had now gone, three of his mates had been firing at me. I did a quick turn and made for home, but it wasn't quite so easy as all that. My attacker had put my port aileron out of action, so that I could hardly turn on the left side. The control column went rough on that side too, and then I realised that my engine was beginning to run not quite so smoothly. There were no clouds to hide in except those up at 20,000 feet and they seemed miles away. Practically all my ammunition had gone, so it would have been suicide for me to try and make a fight of it. All I could hope for was to get back home. I watched my pursuers carefully. When they got near me I made a quick turn to the right and saw their tracer bullets go past my tail. I gained a bit on them and then they overtook me again, and once more I turned when I thought they had me within range. I did that at least twelve times. All the time I was climbing slightly and when I reached the coast I was at 2,000 feet. My course had been rather like a staircase. They had not hit my aircraft after that first surprise attack and finally, on the coast, they turned back.

I went on and landed at my home aerodrome, got a fresh Hurricane, and rejoined my squadron before going on another patrol.

RAF flying officer, 'Air Log', BBC, July 1940

It seems very likely, given the circumstances described by the flying officer, that this took place in the afternoon of the first day of the battle. The day was very cloudy, with intermittent showers, and shortly before 2 p.m. a large German formation showed up on the radar; it was just west of Calais and heading towards the Kent coast. There were close to eighty aircraft in all, including twenty-four Dornier Do17s and the rest being a fighter escort of around thirty Messerschmitt Me110s and a similar number of Me109s. Initially it was mostly Hurricanes that were scrambled from Manston, Biggin Hill and Croydon, along with Spitfires of No. 74 Squadron from Hornchurch; later on around half a dozen Spitfires were also sent up from Kenley.

While the Hurricanes of No. 111 Squadron from Croydon attacked the Dorniers, who themselves were busy attacking the convey, the remaining fighters engaged the escorting fighters. With so many aircraft the sky quickly became a mass of vapour trails and soon aircraft were going down. Later that day a force of around seventy bombers attacked both Swansea and Falmouth. During the night bombs were dropped in a number of locations in the south, and on the Isle of Mull in Scotland. RAF losses for the day amounted to eight aircraft, with two pilots killed. The Luftwaffe lost twenty, including badly damaged, aircraft, and twenty-three aircrew either killed or missing as well as ten more wounded; one of the ships in the convey was sunk. That was not how German radio reported the day's events.

Our bombers yesterday achieved effective successes on an airfield in south-eastern England, and on harbour installations on the south and south-west coast, and upon armament works. Especially at the munitions depot near Pembroke, and in the harbours of Plymouth and Swansea, heavy explosions and large fires were observed. The oil storage tanks at Pembroke and Portland were also set ablaze. Further, in the course of an attack on a convoy in the Channel, ten enemy fighter planes were shot down in air battle. During the air battle yesterday 35 enemy planes and one barrage balloon were shot down. Seven of our own planes are missing.

German radio, 11 July 1940

Not so much a case of 'this is my truth; tell me yours', as 'our propaganda's better than your propaganda'.

IT'S JUST NOT CRICKET . . .

Four days later there was the opportunity for something of a rematch when Stuka dive-bombers attacked the same convoy that was slightly further south in the Channel:

For now the Germans are dive-bombing a convoy out at sea; there are one, two, three, four, five, six, seven German dive-bombers, Junkers 87s. There's one going down on its target now. Bomb! No! Missed the ships, it hasn't hit a single ship; there are about ten ships in the convoy, but he hasn't hit a single one and there, you can hear our anti-aircraft going at them now. There are one, two, three, four, five, six – there are about ten German machines dive-bombing the British convoy, which is just out to sea in the Channel.

I can't see anything. No! We thought he had got a German one at the top then, but now the British fighters are coming up. Here they come. They come in an absolute steep dive, and you can see their bombs actually leave the machines and come into the water. You can hear our guns going like anything now. I am looking round now. I can hear machine-gun fire, but I can't see our Spitfires. They must be somewhere there. Oh! Here's one coming down.

There's one going down in flames. Somebody's hit a German and he's coming down with a long streak, coming down completely out of control, a long streak of smoke, and the man's baled out by parachute. The pilot's baled out by parachute. He's a Junkers 87, and he's going slap into the sea, and there he goes. [SMASH!] A terrific column of water and there was a Junkers 87. Only one man got out by parachute, so presumably there was only a crew of one in it.

Here comes one Spitfire. There's a little burst. There's another bomb dropping. Yes. It has dropped. It has missed the convoy. You know, they haven't hit the convoy in all this. The sky is absolutely patterned with bursts of anti-aircraft fire, and the sea is covered with smoke where the bombs have burst, but as far as I can see there is not one single ship hit, and there is definitely one German machine down. And I am looking across the sea now. I can see the little white dot of parachute as the German pilot is floating down towards the spot where his machine crashed with such a big fountain of water about two minutes ago. Now, then, oh, there's a terrific mix-up over the Channel! It's impossible to tell which are our machines and which are Germans. There was one definitely down in this battle and there's a fight going on. There's a fight going on, and you can hear the little rattles of machine gun bullets. [Crump] That was a bomb, as you may imagine.

Well, now, everything is peaceful again for the moment. The Germans, who came over in about twenty or twenty-five dive-bombers, delivered their attack on the convoy, and I think they made off as quickly as they came. Oh yes, I can see one, two, three, four, five, six, seven, eight, nine, ten Germans haring back towards France now for all they can go – and here are our Spitfires coming after them. There's going to be a big fight, I think, out there, but it will be too far away for us to see. Of course, there are a lot more German machines up there. [Can you see, Phil?] Yes, there are one, two, three, four, five, six, seven on the top layer, one, two, three – there's two layers of German machines. They are all, I think, I could not swear to it, but they were all I think Junkers 87s.

[There are two more parachutists? No, I think they are seagulls.] You can hear the anti-aircraft bursts still going. Well, that was a really hot little engagement while it lasted. No damage done, except to the Germans, who lost one machine and the German pilot, who is still on the end of his parachute, though appreciably nearer the sea than he was. I can see no boat going out to pick him up, so he'll probably have a long swim ashore.

Well, that was a very unsuccessful attack on the convoy, I must say.

Oh, there's another fight going on, away up, now – I think about 20, 25, or even 30,000 feet above our heads, and I can't see a thing of it. The anti-aircraft guns have put up one, two, three, four, five, six bursts, but I can't see the aeroplanes. There we go again. [What?] Oh, we've just hit a Messerschmitt. Oh, that was beautiful! He's coming right down. I think it was definitely that burst got him. Yes, he's come down. You hear those crowds? He's finished! Oh, he's coming down like a rocket now. An absolutely steep dive. Let us move round so we can watch him a bit more. Here he comes, down in a steep dive, the Messerschmitt. [Looking for a parachute?] No, no, the pilot's not getting out of that one. He's being followed down. What, there are two more Messerschmitts up there? I think they are all right. No, that man's finished. He's going down from about 10,000, oh, 20,000 to about 2,000 feet, and he's going straight down, he's not stopping. I think that's another German machine that's definitely put paid to. I don't think we shall actually see him crash, because he's going into a bank of cloud. He's smoking now. I can see smoke, although we cannot count that a definite victory because I did not see him crash. He's gone behind a hill. He looked certainly out of control.

Now we are looking up to the anti-aircraft guns. There's another! There's another Messerschmitt. I don't know whether he's down or whether he's trying to get out of the anti-aircraft fire, which is giving him a very hot time. There's a Spitfire! Oh, there's about four fighters up there, and I don't know what they are doing. One, two, three, four, five fighters fighting right over our heads. Now there's one coming right down on the tail of what I think is a Messerschmitt and I think it's a Spitfire behind him. Oh, darn! They've turned away and I can't see. I can't see. Where's one crashing? No, I think he's pulled out. You can't watch these fights very coherently for long. You just see about four twirling machines, you just hear little bursts of machine-gunning, and by the time you've picked up the machines they've gone. Hullo, there are one, two, three; and look, there's a dogfight going on up there, there are four, five, six machines wheeling and turning around. Now, hark at the machine guns going! Hark! One, two, three, four, five, six; now there's something coming right down on the tail of another. Here they come; yes, they are being chased home, and how they are being chased home! There are three Spitfires chasing three Messerschmitts now. Oh, boy! Look at them going! Oh, look how the Messerschmitts! Oh boy! That was really grand! There's a Spitfire behind the first two. He will get them. Oh, yes. Oh, boy! I've never seen anything so good as this. The RAF fighters have really got these boys taped. Our machine is catching up the Messerschmitt now. He's catching it up! He's got the legs of it, you know. Now right in the sights. Go on, George! You've got him! Bomb, bomb. No, no, the distance is a bit deceptive from here. You can't tell, but I think something definitely is going to happen to that first Messerschmitt. Oh yes, just a moment, I think I wouldn't like to be in that first Messerschmitt. I think he's got him. Yes? Machine guns are going like anything. No, there's another fight going on. No, they've chased him right out to sea. I can't see, but I think the odds would be certainly on that first Messerschmitt catching it. [Oh, look!] Where? Where? I can't see them at all. Just on the left of those black shots. See it? Oh, yes, oh yes, I see it. Yes, they've got him down, too. I can't see. Yes, he's pulled away from him. Yes, I think that first Messerschmitt has been crashed on the coast of France all right.

Charles Gardner, BBC News, 9 p.m., 14 July 1940

As the first 'ringside' commentary at a dogfight it's perhaps not too surprising that Charles Gardner's excitable commentary met with mixed reactions. Several letters to *The Times* were less than complimentary. 'As a pilot in the last War, will you allow me to record my protest against the eye-witness account of the air fight over the Straits of Dover given by the BBC . . . Some of the details were bad enough; but far more revolting was the spirit in which these details were given to the public. Where men's lives are concerned, must we be treated to a running commentary on a level with an account of the Grand National or a cup-tie final?' wrote R.H. Hawkins from Dalston Vicarage, Carlisle. Another writer from London agreed with Mr Hawkins, going on to say, 'The BBC standard of taste, feeling, understanding, and imagination is surely revolting to all decent citizens.'

Other sections of the press thought differently. The *Manchester Guardian* called it 'brilliantly exciting', while one of the Press Association reporters said 'the attack resembled a circus'. The BBC resolutely defended Gardner's commentary and decided to keep on with this kind of reporting. The Director General also wrote to *The Times* to explain the BBC's views on the matter.

> This broadcast gave an eye-witness account of an air action, successful without loss of British aircraft, against enemy attack on a convoy. The business of news broadcasting is to bring home to the whole public what is happening in the world and, at a grim time like this, to play some part in maintaining civilian morale. British fighting men do not wage war with long faces. The high gravity of German troops is alien to them. Theirs is a spirit of cheerful realism, and, in a total war, is it not also the spirit of the British people as a whole? That young men, on a fine July Sunday afternoon, fight to the death over the Channel instead of bathing in it is horrible. But it is, alas, through no fault of our country, a fact. The young men face this fact without loss of their native high spirits. Do civilians want it presented to them in any other way? . . . One group of 15 listeners voted it 'the finest thing the BBC has ever done'. Many have suggested that the record should be sold for the Red Cross. Others hoped that it would be relayed to America [as in fact it was], to show the British spirit at this moment.
>
> The Times

Interestingly, within a month the sporting theme was taken up by the newspaper sellers in the south when they began quoting the previous days' tally of losses as though it were a cricket score. Gardner's excitement is totally understandable given the scenes that he was witnessing and the circumstances that Britain was facing. Many of those that listened to the commentary failed to accept that they were occupying the same moral high ground as the letter-writers to *The Times*, a fact borne out by the BBC's own listener research. Listeners were more than happy to hear what sounded, to all intents and purposes, like the Germans being sent packing with a flea in their ear. Who could fail to be caught up in the excitement of it? Britain was under attack – the enemy was at the gates. Germany had overrun almost all of Western Europe and all that stood between Britain and a Nazi invasion, defeat, and occupation were a few fighter pilots and their machines. Of course men were being killed, but it was the men who were trying to kill people on the ground – those same people who sat around their wireless sets listening to what sounded like a win for the home team.

As with just about every piece of news, commentary or talk on the radio about events during the war there were subtle, and not so subtle, differences between what was reported and what actually happened. In Gardner's piece the Junkers 87, or Stuka as it was more commonly called, that he describes in its death throes was in fact an RAF Hurricane of 615 Squadron, Kenley, that had been shot down by an Me109. Pilot Officer M.R. Mudie, the Hurricane pilot, baled out and was later picked up by the Navy; he died of his injuries the following day. Of course events had moved on; it was an incident that left many listeners with a sense of both pride and relief that their side was winning. There was no retraction of the reporting to say, 'Sorry, Charles Gardner got it wrong – it was a young Englishman that was shot down and killed in a hail of bullets'. And would it have done any good if the BBC had issued such a retraction?

Gardner may well have stayed, or at least stopped in for a drink, at the Grand Hotel in Dover, which had become the unofficial headquarters of reporters from all around the world. Two months after the events of 14 July the hotel was bombed and Guy Murchie of the *Chicago Tribune* fell four floors and lived to tell the tale. The reporters staying at the Grand frequently took up vantage points on the cliffs or along the coastal wall to watch convoys being attacked or aircraft streaming across the Channel to attack somewhere in England, or fleeing to the safety of their temporary home in France. And while it was safer than being in a dogfight there were reporters who were lucky to escape serious injury. One reporter was very fortunate not to be badly hurt after being hit by a machine-gun cartridge that fell from the sky. James Gemmell of Paramount News was probably the luckiest when a bomb fell three feet away from him but failed to explode. As a footnote to the controversy generated by Charles Gardner he actually went on to join the RAF as a pilot, although he did occasionally broadcast anonymously. Gardner was another who was lucky and almost didn't get the chance to take up a career as a pilot because on one occasion a Heinkel He111 dropped a bomb so close to him that the recording equipment that he was using was blown into the air.

PERHAPS, PERHAPS, PERHAPS

In the evening of the Gardner's transmission Winston Churchill once again broadcast to the nation, as well as on the Overseas and North American Services of the BBC; it was estimated that 64 per cent of Britain's adult population heard him. Churchill's listening figures were helped by the fact that 9,132,000 wireless licences had been issued by this time.

This has been a great week for the Royal Air Force, and for the Fighter Command. They have shot down more than five to one of the German aircraft which have tried to molest our convoys in the Channel, or have ventured to cross the British coastline. These are, of course, only the preliminary encounters to the great air battles which lie ahead. But I know of no reason why we should be discontented with the results so far achieved; although, of course, we hope to improve upon them as the fighting becomes more widespread and comes more inland. Around all lies the power of the Royal Navy. With over a thousand armed ships under the White Ensign, patrolling the seas, the Navy, which is capable of transferring its force very readily to the protection of any part of the British Empire which may be threatened, is capable also of keeping open communication with the New World, from whom, as the struggle deepens, increasing aid will come. Is it not remarkable that after ten months of unlimited U-boat and air attack upon our commerce, our food reserves are higher than they have ever been, and we have a substantially larger tonnage under our own flag, apart from great numbers of foreign ships in our control, than we had at the beginning of the war? Why do I dwell on all this? Not, surely, to induce any slackening of effort or vigilance. On the contrary. These must be redoubled, and we must prepare not only for the summer, but for the winter; not only for 1941, but for 1942; when the war will, I trust, take a different form from the defensive, in which it has hitherto been bound . . . But all depends now upon the whole life-strength of the British race in every part of the world and of all our associated peoples and of all our well-wishers in every land, doing their utmost night and day, giving all, daring all, enduring all – to the utmost – to the end. This is no war of chieftains or of princes, of dynasties or national ambition; it is a war of peoples and of causes. There are vast numbers, not only in this Island but in every land, who will render faithful service in this war, but whose names will never be known, whose deeds will never be recorded. This is a War of the Unknown Warriors; but let all strive without failing in faith or in duty, and the dark curse of Hitler will be lifted from our age.

Winston Churchill, BBC, 14 July 1940

Elsewhere in his 18-minute broadcast the Prime Minister spoke warmly about France, and those that were continuing the fight. He also talked of the threat of invasion.

Perhaps it will come tonight, perhaps it will come next week, perhaps it will never come . . . we shall seek no terms, we shall tolerate no parley – we may show mercy – we shall ask for none.

Is it any wonder that people listened? Is it any wonder they felt comforted?

. . . AND THIS IS FRANK PHILLIPS READING IT

With the threat of invasion an ever-present danger, there was an increased level of concern over whether or not news bulletins were genuine. Some felt there was a serious danger of fifth columnists infiltrating the BBC in some way – an obsession for many after the fall of Norway – and so it was decided that newsreaders should announce themselves by name rather than continuing to say simply, 'This is the Home Service, here is the news'. On 13 July 1940 Frank Phillips became the first reader to identify himself on air. But concern persisted that all newsreaders sounded the same. Regardless of whether or not they announced their name it was felt that it would not be too hard for the Germans to imitate them.

Frank Phillips's other claim to fame is that he might well be the only announcer to read the news in just his pyjama top! One morning after sleeping in late at the makeshift facilities in Broadcasting House Frank went in to read the news having been sleeping pyjama-bottomless – he thought it a trifle too warm to wear them. He only noticed his mistake when he sat down on the rather cold chair. Apparently the Production people kept sending in the youngest girl on the news team with additional pieces of news for Frank to read out. Who needs a picture? I'm sure your imagination is presenting a perfect image!

A SHIFT IN TACTICS

While raids on convoys, as well as towns and cities, continued through the end of July and into the first week of August there was a shift in tactics soon afterwards. Hitler had issued his Directive No. 17 concerning the invasion:

The Luftwaffe will use all the forces at its disposal to destroy the British air force as quickly as possible. August 5th is the first day on which this intensified air war may begin, but the exact date is to be left to the Luftwaffe and will depend on how soon its preparations are complete, and on the weather situation.

Adolf Hitler, 1 August 1940

It was on 8 August that the shift in emphasis took place and fighter bases in the south of England came under attack, along with the radar stations that were a vital cog in directing the Spitfires and Hurricanes to be in the right place, somewhere close to the right time. It was imperative if the Germans' Operation Sealion, the invasion of Britain, was to become reality that RAF Fighter Command had effectively to cease to exist. German intelligence reports that filtered back to Berlin stated that the Luftwaffe had drastically reduced the RAF's strength and so the date for Sealion was set as 15 August. But it came and went, as was reported in a broadcast following the BBC's 9 p.m. Thursday night news by a regular giver of such talks – American Raymond Gram Swing.

Yesterday was a 'day of destiny' awaited by Britons and Germans alike, but Britain wasn't razed and wasn't in ruins. The day of destiny came, but it will take more days – many more days – before Britain is laid waste or brought to the point of surrender . . . I received a cable from an American journalist describing an interview with a Dover newspaper editor who told the correspondent how the Press advertising of summer sales, dances, and movies was still continuing. Department store sales in Dover were advertised on August 15 – that's a revealing commentary on the state of Dover, and it may well be the state of Britain after many similar days. The war that went into full dimension yesterday was primarily a war to establish air supremacy. Not till Germany has established that will it be even halfway safe to invade. The war cannot be won in the air, but it can be decided there. At least it can be decided if Germany can establish air supremacy, and so be able to knock out Britain.

Raymond Gram Swing, BBC, 16 August 1940

Throughout this period RAF losses were heavy. There were an increasing number of situations where new pilots would join a squadron and be thrust straight into battle. Given that sometimes they had as little as 20 minutes' training in dogfights the RAF pilots were more than holding their own. In the middle of the second phase of the Battle, when the full might of the German offensive was concentrated on the airfields of southern England, there was what has become known among historians as 'The Hardest Day' – 18 August 1940.

A communiqué issued just before 9.15 stated – In the raids upon this country at midday to-day bombs were dropped in the outer fringes of the South London area, in Kent, in other parts of the south-east and in southern England. Information so far available shows that some civilian casualties were caused in the neighbourhood of Croydon. Elsewhere the number of casualties was small, and damage to property was slight. This evening large formations of enemy aircraft again crossed the south-east coast near Dover and the North Foreland. These formations attempted to penetrate the London defences along both sides of the Thames Estuary but were broken up by our attacking fighters and driven back over Kent and Essex. The available information is incomplete but it appears that very little damage was done and few casualties were caused in this evening's raids. Reports received up to 8 p.m. show that at least 86 enemy aircraft have been destroyed in today's battles. Seventy-three of these were shot down by our fighters, twelve by anti-aircraft fire, and one by a searchlight crew. Sixteen of our fighters have been lost in combat, but the pilots of eight of these are safe.

BBC News, midnight, 18 August 1940

The German plan was simple, audacious and potentially catastrophic for the RAF as the Luftwaffe set out to destroy the fighter bases at Kenley and Biggin Hill. From all available research it would seem that the Luftwaffe, by the end of the day, had lost ninety-six aircraft damaged or destroyed, but the RAF losses were around fifty aircraft damaged or destroyed. There were also ten pilots killed and sixteen wounded. By this point in the conflict the RAF was destroying two German aircraft at the cost of one of their own fighters. Given that British aircraft were being produced more quickly than German it was, on the face of it, good news. The only potential problem was the fact that the Luftwaffe started the battle with more than twice the number of aircraft than those at the disposal of Fighter Command. All of these are the statistics of war, and given the severity of the situation it is also amazing to marvel at the formality of the language of official communiqués issued by the Ministry and broadcast by the BBC. It's little wonder that Gardner's broadcast was much loved by most people.

Two days after 'The Hardest Day' Winston Churchill rose from his seat in the Commons to talk to the House on the progress of the war. He spoke first about the Navy, before turning his attention to the war in the air. He spoke of how everyone should be grateful to the airmen who were facing such overwhelming odds yet were 'turning the tide of war'. The Prime Minister concluded with words that have become synonymous with the battle: 'Never in the field of human conflict was so much owed by so many to so few.'

THE BOMBERS ARE COMING

On 7 September the battle entered its third phase. The Luftwaffe began its intensive bombing campaign against London and other major cities; not that they hadn't already hit central London. Their first attack on the City was on

24 August when St Giles's Church, Cripplegate, was damaged. The view of the German High Command was that it would break the resolve of the British people if large numbers of civilians were killed. Goering took personal charge of the bombing campaign, justifying it by saying it was in retaliation for the attacks on Berlin. In Britain, German secret military communiqués, decrypted by the Enigma machine at Bletchley Park, had given the British government cause for great alarm. Messages indicated that the possibility of an invasion was highly likely – indeed 'imminent'.

The day started quietly, with no German raiders on the radar; by shortly after 3 p.m., however, the radar screens lit up. When the Observer Corps made their first sighting of the enemy they quickly realised it was a massive raid; initial reports stated '100 raiders at 20,000ft'; they quickly doubled then trebled the number. In fact these estimates kept on growing and ultimately the raid amounted to around 1,100 aircraft, of which 300 were bombers – the rest made up of their fighter escorts. The damage to the capital was enormous, the East End was ablaze and the Woolwich Arsenal was just one important factory that was destroyed. Later that night a similar number of Heinkel He111 bombers attacked the still burning city. Almost 500 people were killed and over 1,300 were seriously injured; the Luftwaffe had dropped over 300 tonnes of bombs to devastating effect. In all the RAF scrambled twenty-three squadrons. Losses on both sides were also very large, with the final tally being over forty RAF aircraft destroyed or damaged with the loss of eighteen pilots. The German losses were sixty-two aircraft, with sixty-eight aircrew killed.

One effect of the night-time raids was that they made the 9 p.m. news bulletins difficult for listeners to hear in some parts of Britain. The BBC announced that it was because 'a broadcasting station is a very good navigational help to anybody flying towards it. To avoid giving this help to the Germans we established a system of shutting down transmitters during air raids.' During the latter part of the year two new transmitters were introduced, which meant that even if one was shut down then it was still possible to hear a signal, albeit a weaker one, from a neighbouring transmitter. In any event, during a raid people who were down in the shelters couldn't hear anything – other than the exploding bombs.

Three days later Churchill was back on the wireless speaking of the Battle of Britain. Given the severity of the recent raids the need to reinforce the will of the people was paramount; everyone needed to keep fighting, whatever the cost. No one had ever witnessed this type of warfare and there were real doubts as to whether or not Londoners would hold firm – Goering could still be proved right. Churchill went to inspect the damage in the East End on the morning after the raid. Visiting the scene of a direct hit on an air-raid shelter Churchill broke down and cried. Scenes like that were the realities of the bombing campaign and his main concern was one of how people's resolve would stand up if the invasion, which was still very much on the cards, were quickly to follow such an aerial bombardment. Churchill again turned to the theme of the Armada, and how it had been repulsed, to demonstrate that when things were at their darkest, victory could spring from the jaws of defeat. These conflicting issues, along with the success of the RAF, were the interlocking themes of the Prime Minister's broadcast.

A great air battle is being fought out between our fighters and the German Air Force. Whenever the weather is favourable, waves of German bombers, protected by fighters, often three or four hundred at a time, surge over this island, especially the promontory of Kent, in the hope of attacking military and other objectives by daylight. However, they are met by our fighter squadrons and nearly always broken up; and their losses average three to one in machines and six to one in pilots. This effort of the Germans to secure daylight mastery of the air over England is, of course, the crux of the whole war. So far it has failed conspicuously. It has cost them very dear.

On the other hand, for him to try to invade this country without having secured mastery in the air would be a very hazardous undertaking. Nevertheless, all his preparations for invasion on a great scale are steadily going forward. Several hundreds of self-propelled barges are moving down the coasts of Europe, from the German and Dutch harbours to the ports of Northern France; from Dunkirk to Brest; and beyond Brest to the French harbours in the Bay of Biscay.

Besides this, convoys of merchant ships in tens of dozens are being moved through the Straits of Dover into the Channel, dodging along from port to port under the protection of the new batteries which the Germans have built on the French shore. There are now considerable gatherings of shipping in the German, Dutch, Belgian and French harbours – all the way from Hamburg to Brest. Finally, there are some preparations made of ships to carry an invading force from the Norwegian harbours.

Behind these clusters of ships or barges, there stand very large numbers of German troops, awaiting the order to go on board and set out on their very dangerous and uncertain voyage across the seas. We cannot tell when they will try to come; we cannot be sure that in fact they will try at all; but no one should blind himself to the fact that a heavy, full-scale invasion of this island is being prepared with all the usual German thoroughness and method, and that it may be launched now – upon England, upon Scotland, or upon Ireland, or upon all three.

If this invasion is going to be tried at all, it does not seem that it can be long delayed. The weather may break at any time. Besides this, it is difficult for the enemy to keep these gatherings of ships waiting about indefinitely, while they are bombed every night by our bombers, and very often shelled by our warships which are waiting for them outside.

Therefore, we must regard the next week or so as a very important period in our history. It ranks with the days when the Spanish Armada was approaching the Channel, and Drake was finishing his game of bowls; or when Nelson stood between us and Napoleon's Grand Army at Boulogne. We have all read about this in the history books; but what is happening now is on a far greater scale and of far more consequence to the life and future of the world and its civilisation than these brave old days of the past.

Every man and woman will therefore prepare himself to do his duty, whatever it may be, with special pride and care. Our fleets and flotillas are very powerful and numerous; our Air Force is at the highest strength it has ever reached; and it is conscious of its proved superiority, not indeed in numbers, but in men and machines. Our shores are well fortified and strongly manned, and behind them, ready to attack the invaders, we have a far larger and better-equipped mobile army than we have ever had before.

Besides this, we have more than a million and a half men of the Home Guard, who are just as much soldiers of the Regular Army as the Grenadier Guards, and who are determined to fight for every inch of ground in every village and in every street.

It is with devout but sure confidence that I say: Let God defend the Right.

These cruel, wanton, indiscriminate bombings of London are, of course, a part of Hitler's invasion plans. He hopes, by killing large numbers of civilians, and women and children, that he will terrorise and cow the people of this mighty imperial city, and make them a burden and an anxiety to the Government and thus distract our attention unduly from the ferocious onslaught he is preparing. Little does he know the spirit of the British nation, or the tough fibre of the Londoners, whose forebears played a leading part in the establishment of Parliamentary institutions and who have been bred to value freedom far above their lives. This wicked man, the repository and embodiment of many forms of soul-destroying hatred, this monstrous product of former wrongs and shame, has now resolved to try to break our famous island race by a process of indiscriminate slaughter and destruction. What he has done is to kindle a fire in British hearts, here and all over the world, which will glow long after all traces of the conflagration he has caused in London have been removed. He has lighted a fire which will burn with a steady and consuming flame until the last vestiges of Nazi tyranny have been burnt out of Europe, and until the Old World – and the New – can join hands to rebuild the temples of man's freedom and man's honour upon foundations which will not soon or easily be overthrown.

Our fighting forces know that they have behind them a people who will not flinch or weary of the struggle – hard and protracted though it will be; but that we shall rather draw from the heart of suffering itself the means of inspiration and survival, and of a victory won not only for ourselves but for all; a victory won not only for our own time but for the long and better days that are to come.

Winston Churchill, BBC, 11 September 1940

Almost as soon as Churchill finished his speech air raids on London and elsewhere began; the following day's newspapers called it 'a Super-Blitz'. It brought to an end a devastating week for British civilians. It was reported that 1,200 had been killed, with almost 1,000 of those in London alone. In fact the early indications of casualties were way under, and in a speech to parliament on 8 October the Prime Minister spoke of 6,000 casualties, that is people killed and seriously wounded, in this week alone.

The Luftwaffe's attempt to secure mastery of the air brought about a change in their tactics four days after Churchill's broadcast. On 10 September German radio had broadcast that 'the fact that the raids are now under the personal command of Field Marshal Goering can only be interpreted as the definite beginning of the invasion'.

This morning a large number of enemy aircraft crossed the coast near Dover in two waves. They were promptly met by strong formations of our fighters and an air battle ensued. In the course of this two small enemy formations succeeded in penetrating to the London area. Bombs were dropped and amongst the enemy objectives, Buckingham Palace was again hit. The Queen's private apartments were damaged by a bomb, which did not explode. Elsewhere in London area houses were hit, some fires broke out and damage was done to gas and water mains. From preliminary reports it is clear that the number of casualties was small. At least fifty enemy aircraft were shot down in this raid.

BBC News, 6 p.m., 15 September 1940

Here is the Midnight News and this is Alvar Lidell reading it. Up to ten o'clock one hundred and seventy-five aircraft have been destroyed in today's raids over this country. Today was the most costly for the German Air Force for nearly a month. In daylight raids between three hundred and fifty and four hundred enemy aircraft were launched in two attacks against London and south-east England; about half of them were shot down.

Alvar Lidell, BBC News, midnight, 15 September 1940

Almost every radio in Britain was tuned to the BBC that night, as well as on the following day, and the listeners would have been delighted by the news. Walter Musso noted in his diary:

That Germany is making a terrific bid for the mastery of London is certain; that we are more than holding our own in the air is equally certain. True, Buckingham Palace was again bombed, wrecking the Queen's private apartments, as well as many other buildings, but the announcement of the destruction by our grand RAF boys yesterday of no less than 185 planes out of some 400 launched against us, with a loss of no more than twenty-five, is the best evidence of the price Hitler is paying for his reckless disregard of our decencies.

What really happened on Sunday 15 September is very different from the events reported on the BBC. The day had dawned fair, with some patchy cloud; all in all, perfect weather for an attack. Intelligence officers had told the German crews that RAF Fighter Command was by this time an ineffectual force. The battle plan called for two major raids on London, with later smaller raids on the Southampton and Portland areas.

According to the RAF Campaign Diary the first attack on London was launched at about 1100 hours as enemy aircraft began to mass in the area between Calais and Boulogne. At 1130 hours the leading wave of 100 aircraft crossed the English coast between Dover and Dungeness; a second wave of 150 aircraft followed. The RAF's No. 11 Group sent up sixteen squadrons to meet the attack and approximately 100 enemy aircraft succeeded in reaching Central London. The second major attack began at 1400 hours, when approximately 150 enemy aircraft crossed the coast near Dover, followed by another wave of 100 aircraft. These formations spread over south-east and south-west Kent and the Maidstone area; about seventy penetrated Central London. Again, No. 11 Group sent up sixteen squadrons and No. 12 Group four squadrons.

According to the RAF they destroyed around 176 enemy aircraft (there are conflicting reports saying 179, while the BBC News on 16 September stated 185 aircraft) plus forty-one probable and seventy-two damaged. The RAF losses were put at twenty-five aircraft, with thirteen pilots killed or missing.

Such was the ferocity of the RAF attacks upon the bomber groups that they succeeded in breaking up the formations; this meant the German aeroplanes' bomb loads were spread far and wide across London and the suburbs, causing far less damage than if they had been concentrated. This raid turned out to be a lot less damaging than some of the raids earlier in September. Almost as important as defending the capital was the fact that the Spitfire and Hurricane pilots successfully defended Southampton and the Luftwaffe failed to damage the vitally important Woolston factory, where Spitfires were made.

A few days after the battle, Squadron Leader John Sample recounted his experiences on the BBC's 'Air Log'. Based at RAF Hendon, he commanded 504 Squadron, which flew Hurricanes.

At lunchtime on Sunday, my squadron was somewhere south of the Thames estuary behind several other squadrons of Hurricanes and Spitfires. The German bombers were three or four miles away when we first spotted them. We were at 17,000 feet and they were at about 19,000 feet. Their fighter escort was scattered around. The bombers were coming in towards London from the south-east, and at first we could not tell how many there were. We opened our throttles and started to climb up towards them, aiming for a point well ahead, where we expected to contact them at their own height.

As we converged on them I saw there were about twenty of them, and it looked as though it were going to be a nice party, for the other squadrons of Hurricanes and Spitfires also turned to join in. By the time we reached a position near the bombers we were over London – central London, I should say. We had gained a little height on them, too, so when I gave the order to attack we were able to dive on them from their right.

Each of us selected his own target. Our first attack broke them up pretty nicely. The Dornier I attacked with a burst lasting several seconds began to turn to the left away from his friends. I gave him five seconds and he went away with white smoke streaming behind him.

As I broke away and started to make a steep climbing turn I looked over the side. I recognised the river immediately below me through a hole in the clouds. I saw the bends in the river and the bridges, and idly wondered where I was. I didn't recognise it immediately, and then I saw Kennington Oval. I saw the covered stands round the Oval, and I thought to myself: 'That is where they play cricket.' It's queer how, in the middle of a battle, one can see something on the ground and think of something entirely different from the immediate job in hand. I remember I had a flashing thought – a sort of mental picture – of a big man with a beard, but at that moment I did not think of the name of W.G. Grace. It was just a swift, passing thought as I climbed back to the fight.

I found myself very soon below another Dornier, which had white smoke coming from it. It was being attacked by two Hurricanes and a Spitfire, and it was still travelling north and turning slightly to the right. As I could not see anything else to attack at that moment, I went to join in. I climbed up above him and did a diving attack on him. Coming in to attack I noticed what appeared to be a red light shining in the rear gunner's cockpit, but when I got closer I realised I was looking right through the gunner's cockpit into the pilot and observer's cockpit beyond. The red light was fire.

I gave it a quick burst and as I passed him on the right I looked in through the big glass nose of the Dornier. It was like a furnace inside. He began to go down, and we watched. In a few seconds the tail came off, and the bomber did a forward somersault and then went into a spin. After he had done two turns in his spin his wings broke off outboard of the engines, so that all that was left as the blazing aircraft fell was half a fuselage and the wing roots with the engines on the end of them. This dived straight down, just past the edge of a cloud, and then the cloud got in the way and I could see no more of him.

The battle was over by then. I couldn't see anything else to shoot at, so I flew home. Our squadron's score was five certainties – including one by a sergeant pilot, who landed by parachute in a Chelsea garden.

An hour later we were in the air again, meeting more bombers and fighters coming in. We got three more – our squadron, I mean. I started to chase one Dornier, which was flying through the tops of the clouds. Did you ever see that film *Hell's Angels*? You remember how the Zeppelin came so slowly out of the cloud. Well, this Dornier reminded me of that.

I attacked him four times altogether. When he first appeared through the cloud – you know how clouds go up and down like foam on water – I fired at him from the left, swung over to the right, turned in towards another hollow in the cloud, where I expected him to reappear, and fired at him again. After my fourth attack he dived down headlong into a clump of trees in front of a house, and I saw one or two cars parked in the gravel drive in front. I wondered whether there was anyone in the doorway watching the bomber crash.

Then I climbed up again to look for some more trouble and found it in the shape of a Heinkel 111 which was being attacked by three Hurricanes and a couple of Spitfires. I had a few cracks at the thing before it made a perfect landing on an RAF aerodrome. The Heinkel's undercarriage collapsed and the pilot pulled up, after skidding fifty yards in a cloud of dust. I saw a tall

man get out of the right-hand side of the aircraft, and when I turned back
he was helping a small man across the aerodrome towards a hangar.

RAF squadron leader, 'Air Log', BBC, September 1940

Squadron Leader Sample, who was 27 years old at the time of the broadcast,
had joined the Auxiliary Air Force in 1934 and had shot down a Dornier Do18
flying boat when flying a Gladiator biplane in 1939. After service in France
flying Hurricanes, for which he was awarded the DFC, he was given command
of 504 Squadron, having been promoted squadron leader on 1 September; four
days later he and his squadron had been transferred to Hendon on the western
fringes of London. Sample survived the Battle of Britain and then had a spell as
an operational controller before going back to flying. He was tragically killed,
not by enemy fire, but on a training flight, on 28 October 1941. His Westland
Whirlwind collided with another from his squadron. Sample's aircraft lost its
tailplane and went into an uncontrollable spin, crashing just south of Bath in
Somerset.

The sergeant pilot he refers to was R.T. Holmes, who baled out after his
Hurricane had been damaged by a Messerschmitt Me109, but not before he
shot down a Dornier Do17 that crashed on top of Victoria station where it
adjoins Buckingham Palace Road. The Heinkel He111 described in the
broadcast landed at RAF West Malling in Kent.

In reality the German losses were somewhere between sixty and eighty
aircraft, and probably closer to the lower number, but it was still the Luftwaffe's
worst day since 18 August; generally the confusion of battle accounted for the
exaggerated figures. Different pilots often claimed the same kills and ground
gunners were also mistaken in their claims, sometimes thinking they had shot
down an aircraft that was already crashing. RAF losses were around thirty
aircraft, with thirteen pilots killed. What makes the RAF pilots' achievement all
the greater is that by this time the average level of combat experience was
woefully inadequate. Many of the experienced pilots had been killed, or were
recovering from injuries, and while pilots were receiving better training it was
no substitute for the real thing. The German pilots, having been told that the
RAF was a spent force, found out to the contrary in the hardest way
imaginable. Such was the success of the RAF that it has been commemorated
ever since as 'Battle of Britain Day'.

While this day marked the end of any realistic hopes that Hitler may still have
had of invading Britain it did not bring to an end the daylight raids on London,
or the attacks on the fighter bases around London and throughout the south-
east. This phase of the battle lasted until the end of September, at which time
there was a switch to night-time bombing raids that achieved little in military

value for the Germans. All it did do was to see more and more Luftwaffe aircrew lose their lives. By the end of October the Battle of Britain would be over.

Two years later the writer George Orwell gave a talk on the BBC's Indian Service in which he spoke of the importance of 15 September 1940:

> Four days ago, September 15th, was celebrated throughout this country and the world as the second anniversary of the Battle of Britain . . . The whole manoeuvre, however, was a failure and in about two months of air warfare the Germans lost between two and three thousand planes, with some thousands of irreplaceable airmen.
>
> September 15th is celebrated as the anniversary because on that day the Royal Air Force shot down no less than 185 German planes, and it was about that date that the failure of the Germans to overwhelm the British defences by daylight bombing became apparent. Now that we can look back and see the events in better perspective it is becoming clear that the Battle of Britain ranks in importance with Trafalgar, Salamis, the defeat of the Spanish Armada and other battles of the past in which the invading forces of a seemingly invincible monarch or dictator have been beaten back and which have formed a turning point in history.
>
> *George Orwell, BBC Indian Service, 19 September 1942*

The Eton-educated Orwell, whose real name was Eric Blair, worked at the BBC in the Eastern Service, writing talks on the war to be broadcast to India. He left the Corporation in 1943 to become editor of *Tribune*; in the same year he famously said '"I heard it on the BBC" was almost like saying "I know it must be true".' In 1945 he published *Animal Farm* and four years after the end of the war *Nineteen Eighty-Four* came out. His nightmare vision of the future had some memorable phrases that have found their way into the language, and one at least has been applied to the BBC – 'newspeak'. He died in 1950, aged 47.

'THE FEW'

In all 2,353 British pilots and aircrew and 574 from overseas flew in the Battle of Britain. During the period of the battle 544, almost one in five, lost their lives. A further 791 were killed in action or died in the course of their duties before the war's end, making it close to 50 per cent who were killed during the Second World War. It was a remarkable achievement and an extraordinary display of courage and heroism on a scale the like of which we are never likely to see again.

Chapter 8

THE BLITZ

VIEWS OF THE BLITZ

Tonight, as on every other night, the rooftop watchers are peering out across the fantastic forest of London's chimney pots. The anti-aircraft gunners stand ready. I have been walking tonight – there is a full moon, and the dirty-gray buildings appear white. The stars, the empty windows, are hidden. It's a beautiful and lonesome city where men and women and children are trying to snatch a few hours sleep underground.

Ed Murrow, CBS News broadcast from BBC studios to the USA,
20 September 1940

In 2000 the veteran US broadcaster Robert Trout talked on America's National Public Radio about the importance of Ed Murrow's wartime broadcasts. 'America may still have been neutral, but CBS was not. There were many Anglophiles at 485 Madison Avenue, none more passionate than I, and I still have the isolationist hate mail to prove it. If we had failed to dramatise the Battle of France, we would not make the same mistake with the Battle of Britain.'

As the Battle of Britain reached its climax the RAF, if not winning outright, was establishing its supremacy. Success of another kind came when the BBC was finally accepted by public and press alike as the purveyor of the best quality news, far better than its German counterpart. Not, of course, that what the BBC broadcast was always correct, but much more often than not it wasn't the Corporation's fault. Postwar analysis of the number of aircraft lost in the Battle of Britain as reported on the radio has the BBC overstating the case by between 50 and 60 per cent, while German radio exaggerated by over 200 per cent.

As late summer turned to autumn and quickly to winter the German tactics continued to inflict casualties on the civilian population. At the same time Haw-Haw's broadcasts turned from something of a joke to something more sinister. German radio's boastful attitude, and clear exaggerations, caused more and more people to distrust what they said. The Germans' prediction of a number of imminent collapses – that of course never came about – were at the root of their problems. A fine example of the absurdity of Haw Haw, and a reflection upon the German view of the war, was this barmy rhetoric during a 'Germany Calling' broadcast:

> We have learned with horror and disgust that while London was suffering all the nightmares of aerial bombardment a few nights ago, there was a contrast between the situation of the rich and the poor which we hardly know how to describe. There were two Londons that night. Down by the docks and in the poor districts and the suburbs, people lay dead, or dying in agony from their wounds; but, while their counterparts were suffering only a little distance away, the plutocrats and the favoured lords of creation were making the raid an excuse for their drunken orgies and debaucheries in the saloons of Piccadilly and in the Café de Paris. Spending on champagne in one night what they would consider enough for a soldier's wife for a month these moneyed fools shouted and sang in the streets, crying, as the son of a profiteer baron put it, 'They won't bomb this part of the town! They want the docks! Fill up boys!'
>
> *Lord Haw-Haw, German radio, late August 1940*

As well as the bulletins that carried the news of the daily losses from German bombing in London and other cities there continued to be a steady flow of broadcast talks. These were, possibly, even more important than before in addressing listeners' issues and concerns. They struck a chord with the millions who heard them – bringing people together in a collective acknowledgement of their plight. Midway through September J.B. Priestley gave a talk on the 'Battle for London'. He began by musing on whether Hitler or Goering had ever read Charles Dickens's *Pickwick Papers* and whether or not they were acquainted with Sam Weller, who made his first appearance in the novel. Of course, if they had read Dickens, they may have understood better what made Londoners withstand the German bombing.

> . . . A lot of us, especially if we are from the north, and thought we knew everything, imagined that that old cockney spirit was dead and gone. We thought the Londoner of to-day, catching his tubes and electric trains, was a different kind of fellow altogether, with too many of his corners rubbed off, too gullible, easily pleased, too soft; and we were wrong. This last grim week has shown us how wrong we were. The Londoners, as the Americans say, can take it, and London itself – this grey sea of a city – can take it. The fact

that the savage, indiscriminate bombing of the city has seized the world's imagination is itself a tribute to the might and majesty of London. There was a time when, like many north-countrymen who came south, I thought I disliked London; it had vast colourless suburbs that seemed to us even drearier than the ones we had left behind. We hated the extremes of wealth and poverty that we found, cheek by jowl in the West End, where at night the great purring motor-cars filled with glittering women passed the shadowy rows of the homeless, the destitute, the down-and-out.

The life here in London seemed to us to have less colour, less gaiety than life in capitals abroad, and at the same time to have less character and flavour than the life we remembered in our provincial cities. And so on and so forth. But on these recent nights, when I have gone up to high roofs and have seen the fires like open wounds on the vast body of the city, I've realised, like many another settler here, how deeply I've come to love London, with its misty, twilit charm, its hidden cosiness and companionship, its smoky magic. The other night, when a few fires were burning so fiercely that half the sky was aglow, and the tall terraces around Portland Place were like pink palaces in the Arabian Nights, I saw the Dome and Cross of St Paul's, silhouetted in sharpest black against the red flames and orange fumes, and it looked like an enduring symbol of reason and Christian ethics seen against the crimson glare of unreason and savagery. 'Though giant rains put out the sun, here stand I for a sign.'

In a supreme battle for the world's freedom, and there can be no doubt that you and I are now in the midst of such a battle, there are only two capital cities in the world that are worthy of figuring in its portrait – one of them is Paris, city of quick barricades and revolutions, now temporarily out of the fight, not because its brave people lost heart but rather because they lost interest and so allowed banal men, intriguers greedy for wealth and power and all the enemies of a people on the march, to deceive and betray them . . .

. . . This, then, is a wonderful moment for us who are here in London, now in the roaring centre of the battlefield, the strangest army the world has ever seen, an army in drab civilian clothes, doing quite ordinary things, an army of all shapes and sizes and ages of folk, but nevertheless a real army, upon whose continuing high and defiant spirit the world's future depends.

We have not suddenly entered upon a new and quite lunatic way of living with the prospect of months and months and months of sirens and shelters and bombs before us, but we have been flung into a battle. As a kind of civilian life, this is hellish, but as battles go, it is not at all bad – with some shelter, meals arriving fairly regularly and a quick rescue of the wounded. But I am not giving advice to the cockneys. They can say to Herr Hitler and Marshal Goering what Sam Weller said: 'Sorry to keep you waiting, Sir, but I'll attend to you directly.'

J.B. Priestley, 'Sunday Postscript', BBC, 15 September 1940

On the same day as Priestley's 'Postscript', Robin Duff was on the Kent coast to record German long-range guns shelling a convoy from their French-based batteries; some of the shells actually managed to fall on Dover, and caused a number of casualties. This sporadic shelling was kept up until 1944 when the advancing Allies captured the guns. In all, well over 2,000 shells landed on Dover, and such was the intensity of attack on the Kent coast that it became known as 'Hellfire Corner'. This recording aired on 15 September 1940, but was probably recorded on 11 September, when Dover was shelled from about 3.45 p.m.

At the moment we can see two bright flashes, three flashes and three puffs of smoke, now a fourth and any moment now the shells will be arriving over this side. Four columns of smoke going up on the far side as the convoy goes past us here. And there's [bang] the first explosion, now the second just a very short way in front of us a tremendous column of water goes up. There's [bang] the third bomb, or rather shell, and one more to come and [bang] there it is. All of those four completely wide of the convoy as they've all been, so far, as the convoy steams slowly past us here. As you hear those explosions a great swirl of water goes up and clouds of smoke and spray in the air still. Extraordinary feeling as you see the flash right over on the far side of the coast and the little cloud of smoke goes up on it and you wait for the explosion on this side . . .

Robin Duff, BBC News, 9 p.m., 15 September 1940

BROADCASTING HOUSE ON THE FRONT LINE

The BBC found itself very much at war on 15 October when a 500lb delayed action bomb scored a direct hit on Broadcasting House. It was dropped by one of about 200 German aircraft involved in the raid on London. Ironically, Broadcasting House had just been given an exterior coat of camouflage paint. The bomb entered through a window of a room on the seventh floor that housed the switchboard at around 8.15 p.m., crashed through walls and floors and came to rest in the music library on the 5th floor, where it was found at around 8.30. Half an hour later someone tried moving the bomb, shortly after

Bruce Belfrage, who was down in the basement, began reading the nine o'clock news. He had got as far as saying, 'the postscript tonight . . .' when there was the smothered sound of an explosion and Belfrage paused. Lord Lloyd of Dolobran, who was in the studio to give the 'Postscript', is heard off-microphone saying somewhat urgently, 'It's all right'. Belfrage carried on with the news, as one newspaper later reported, 'quickly gathering confidence'.

Bruce Belfrage had been an actor and casting director with the BBC before he became a newsreader and before that had spent twelve years on the stage in Britain, the United States and Canada, so it may well have been this experience that helped him to remain so unflustered. The incident has passed into radio legend with all sorts of words being attributed to Belfrage as the bomb exploded. In his autobiography, written in 1951, he wrote about the remarks that had been attributed to him – they include 'God, what's that', 'Sod 'em', 'Christ', 'So what', and several more his publisher felt should be deleted to spare his readers' blushes. Seven BBC employees were killed in the explosion, including three women. The blast went down the lift shaft and through the ventilation system, covering everything with dust and dirt. The Senior Programme Assistant in charge of the BBC's output calmly spoke to the BBC studio in Bristol, telling them that they might have to take over at any moment, but in the end London kept broadcasting without a break, which in itself was remarkable.

On German radio the following night a pilot involved in the nightly attacks on London spoke briefly about the experiences faced by bomber crews. He also let the cat out of the bag as far as the military were concerned. German High Command had consistently denied that the RAF had any night fighter capabilities to oppose these raids. Clearly this pilot, and all those who risked their lives on a daily basis, knew differently:

During a night raid on London the anti-aircraft shell bursts. Nearer and nearer to our aircraft, until finally one of our engines was put out of action by a shell exploding close to the plane. We had to make for home and after some encounters with British fighters we made an emergency landing on the first patch of clear country we found on the French coast. Our crew had just time to get out of the plane without injury.

Luftwaffe pilot, German radio, 17 October 1940

On Sunday 8 December 1940 there was even greater damage inflicted upon Broadcasting House when a parachute mine came down in Portland Place, causing over fifty casualties but no fatalities among the three hundred or so Corporation staff who were on duty at the time. Fortunately, casualties were light because most people were either sleeping in the basement, a common practice throughout this period, or they were working in the adjoining offices. The same couldn't be said of the building; almost every single pane of glass was blown out of the windows of Broadcasting House. The mine had been spotted coming down by one of the roof spotters, who telephoned down to the control room saying, 'Look out, there's a big one coming.' Moments later it exploded. Soon there was water cascading down the main stairs of Broadcasting House, turning the lobby area into a pool. In one of the most remarkable broadcasts during this period of the war an unnamed BBC employee tells of his narrow escape and what it was like to be so close to an exploding bomb.

I left the BBC shortly after 10.45 and accompanied by a colleague, Mr Sibbick, went to the cycle-shed in Chapel Mews. The customary nightly air raid was in progress, and as we left the cycle shed we could hear the distant sound of aircraft and AA gun-fire. We were just entering Hallum Street from the mews when I heard the shrieking whistling noise like a large bomb falling. This noise continued for about three seconds, and then abruptly ceased as if in mid-air. There was no thud, explosion or vibration. I particularly remember this, as I'd heard this happen once before, and was curious as to what caused it and why it stopped. Then came the sound of something clattering down the roof of a building in the direction of Broadcasting House. I looked up thinking that it might be incendiaries, but this was not so. We slowly walked round to the entrance of Broadcasting House, and I estimate that we took about three and a half minutes in doing so. My colleague went inside, returned the cycle-shed keys, cycled off towards Oxford Circus. I remained outside the entrance, talking to two policemen, enquiring about possible diversions on my route home. Their names were Vaughan and Clarke. A saloon car was parked alongside the kerb some distance round from the entrance, and I could see to the left of the car the lamp-post in the middle of the road opposite the Langham Hotel. The policemen had their backs to this, so did not observe what followed. Whilst we were conversing I noticed a large, dark, shiny object approach the lamp-post and then recede. I concluded that it was a taxi parking. It made no noise. The night was clear, with a few small clouds. There was moonlight from a westerly direction, but Portland Place was mainly shadow. All three of us were wearing our steel helmets; my chinstrap was round the back of my head, as I had been advised to wear it so shortly after I was issued with the helmet.

A few seconds later I saw what seemed to be a very large tarpaulin of a drab or khaki colour fall on the same spot; the highest part of it was about ten or twelve feet above the road when I first saw it, and it seemed to he about twenty-five feet across. It fell at about the speed of a pocket-handkerchief when dropped, and made no noise. Repair work was being carried out on Broadcasting House and I, not unnaturally, concluded that it was a tarpaulin which had become detached and had fallen from the building into the roadway. There were no other warnings of the imminent danger. I drew the attention of the policemen to it. They turned round and could see nothing. It had collapsed, and from where we were it was partly screened by the car, and the roadway at that point was in shadow. They told me that they could not see anything. Then followed some banter, but I persisted in saying that I had seen something fall in the road. They then decided to go to investigate. A third policeman, Mortimer, had meanwhile approached us – he was about to conduct a lady across that part of the road. But after hearing that I'd seen something he told me that he was taking her inside the building while they found out what it was. Vaughan drew ahead of Clarke, who stopped at the kerb to ask me just exactly where it had dropped. I went over towards him; calling out that I would show him it. It was about a minute since I'd seen the dark object. I went towards the tarpaulin and had reached a spot to the left of Clarke about six feet from the kerb, and twenty-five to thirty feet from 'the thing', when Vaughan came running towards me at high speed. He shouted something, which I did not hear. At that moment there was a very loud swishing noise, as if a plane were diving with engine cut off – or like a gigantic fuse burning. It lasted about three or four seconds; it did not come from the lamp-post end of the thing, but it may have come from the other end.

Vaughan passed me on my left and Clarke, who apparently had understood the shout, also ran towards the building. Realising that I would have to turn right about before I could start running, I crouched down in what is known as prone-falling position number one. Even at that moment I did not imagine that there was any danger in the road, and thought that it was coming from above, up Portland Place. My head was up watching, and before I could reach position number two and lie down flat the thing in the road exploded. I had a momentary glimpse of a large ball of blinding, wild, white light and two concentric rings of colour, the inner one lavender and the outer one violet, as I ducked my head. The ball seemed to be ten to twenty feet high, and was near the lamp-post. Several things happened simultaneously. My head was jerked back due to a heavy blow on the dome and rim of the back of my steel helmet, but I do not remember this, for, as my head went back, I received a severe blow on my forehead and the bridge of my nose. The blast bent up the front rim of my helmet and knocked it off my head. The explosion made an indescribable noise – something like a colossal growl – and was accompanied by a veritable tornado of air blast. I felt an excruciating pain in my ears, and all sounds were replaced by a very loud singing noise, which I was told later was when I lost my bearing and had my eardrums perforated. I felt that consciousness was slipping from me, and that moment I heard a clear loud voice shouting: 'Don't let yourself go, face up to it – hold on'. It rallied me, and summoning all my will-power and energy I succeeded in forcing myself down into a crouching position with my knees on the ground and my feet against the kerb behind me and my hands covering my face. I remember having to move them over my ears because of the pain in them, doubtless due to the blast. This seemed to ease the pain. Then I received another hit on the forehead and felt weaker. The blast seemed to come in successive waves, accompanied by vibrations from the ground. I felt as if it were trying to spin me and clear me away from the kerb. Then I received a very heavy blow just in front of the right temple, which knocked me down flat on my side, in the gutter. Later, in our First Aid Post, they removed what they described as a piece of bomb from that wound. Whilst in the gutter I clung on to the kerb with both hands and with my feet against it. I was again hit in the right chest, and later found that my double-breasted overcoat, waistcoat, leather comb-case and papers had been cut through, and the watch in the top right-hand pocket of my waistcoat had the back dented in and its works broken.

Just as I felt that I could not hold out much longer, I realised that the blast pressure was decreasing and a shower of dust, dirt and rubble swept past me. Pieces penetrated my face, some skin was blown off, and something pierced my left thumbnail and my knuckles were cut, causing me involuntarily to let go my hold on the kerb. Instantly, although the blast was dying down, I felt myself being slowly blown across the pavement towards the wall of the building. I tried to hold on but there was nothing to hold on to. Twice I tried to rise but seemed held down. Eventually I staggered to my feet. I looked around and it seemed like a scene from Dante's *Inferno*. The front of the building was lit by a reddish yellow light; the saloon car was on fire to the left of me, and the flames from it were stretching out towards the building, and not upwards; pieces of brick, masonry and glass seemed to appear on the pavement, making, to me, no sound; a few dark huddled bodies were round about, and right in front of me were two soldiers; one, some feet from a breach in the wall of the building where a fire seemed to be raging, was propped up against the wall with his arms dangling by him, like a rag doll.

The other was nearer, about twelve feet from the burning car; he was sitting up with his knees drawn up and supporting himself by his arms – his trousers had been blown off him. I could see that his legs were bare and that he was wearing short grey underpants. He was alive and conscious.

I told him to hang on to an upright at the entrance and to shout like hell for assistance should he see or hear anyone approaching. I went back to look at the other soldier. He was still in the same posture and I fear that he was dead. I looked around. There was a long, dark body lying prone, face downwards close to the kerb in front of the building – it may have been Vaughan. There appeared to be one or two dark, huddled bodies by the wall of the building. I had not the strength to lift any of them. I wondered where the water was coming from which I felt dripping down my face, and soon discovered that it was blood from my head wounds. I could see no movement anywhere, and thought I would look round for my steel helmet and gas mask, which I had slung round me at the time of the explosion. I soon found the gas mask and picked up a steel helmet which was not my own.

I was then joined by my colleague who had returned, and went with him to the entrance where I shouted for assistance for those outside, and for someone to bring fire-fighting appliances to put out the car fire, as I was afraid the glare would bring down more bombs.

I walked down to our First Aid Post, where I was treated, and then to Listening Hall I where I rested until I was taken away by the stretcher party and sent to the Middlesex Hospital. Here I received every possible attention and kindness. Later on I was told that 'the thing' had been a landmine, and that its explosion or blast had lasted for nine seconds.

The effect of the blast on my clothes is possibly of interest. I was wearing bicycle clips round the bottoms of my trousers at the time; after the blast was over my double-breasted overcoat was slit up the back and torn in several places, but was being held together by the belt. My trousers and underpants were pitted with small cuts about an inch long, but presumably the bicycle clips had prevented the draught getting up my trousers and tearing them off. A woollen scarf, which was knotted round my neck, undoubtedly saved my neck and chest from small fragments such as were removed from my face, which was not covered.

Anonymous BBC employee, BBC, autumn 1940

The body lying face down in the kerb was PC John Vaughan, who had only become engaged two months earlier. Among the other employees who were hurt were the Controller of Programmes, and Sir Stephen Tallents, the Controller Overseas. A man who had gone to the door of Broadcasting House to 'see if it was quiet outside' had all his clothes blown off. The fires that broke out were brought under control by 4 a.m. and less than an hour after the explosion the BBC's European operation was broadcasting from an incomplete emergency studio at a disused ice-rink in Maida Vale, as well as using programmes broadcast from the BBC in Bristol. The only news bulletin that was missed was one in Norwegian. The BBC's ability to keep broadcasting throughout the Blitz was not a feat matched by German radio, which frequently went off the air during Allied bombing raids.

The bombing of Broadcasting House was not made public until almost two weeks later, when Harold Nicolson MP, Parliamentary Secretary to the Ministry of Information, paid tribute to the BBC staff. Another MP commenting on the work of the BBC showed how the tide had turned; people were now more ready to praise the Corporation than to condemn it. He spoke of the 'splendid reputation which the BBC had won throughout the world for its broadcasts'. His comments followed another bout of carping in *The Times* in which a retired brigadier-general wrote and complained of 'vulgar jeering and of sneering . . . in the worst possible taste'. His ire had been roused by a news bulletin in which the announcer had been perhaps a little too pleased to report a bombing raid on Berlin during the visit of Vyacheslav Molotov, Russian Foreign Commissar. The letter-writer said it was not just his opinion but also that of his 'domestics'. A week later another *Times* letter-writer spoke out for 'the other side'.

Letters of complaint to the Press frequently, if not generally, represent the views of a vocal minority. The contented majority has nothing to write about. I think that this is so in the case of your letters condemning the BBC News, and that it is time someone put in a word on the other side.

To me, and I believe to most people, the BBC announcers seem to be extremely efficient and admirably chosen for their work. Their voices are good, their knowledge of foreign languages exceptional, and their method of presentation free from any objection except of a carping kind. If they occasionally allow a human touch of exultation to colour good news, surely it helps to raise our spirits and should be encouraged. After all, what could be more jubilant in tone than their records of the exploits of our modest young airmen, yet nobody complains of them. To cavil at the way in which air raid casualties are announced is probably to put the blame on the wrong people.

H.C. Marillier, letter to The Times, *26 November 1940*

Interestingly a survey by Mass Observation during the late summer of 1940 showed that the newspapers were losing the battle with the BBC over the integrity of news provision. By a majority of three to one, people surveyed thought that the BBC's news bulletins were more reliable than the reports carried in the newspapers. Some of this was down to the speed at which things happened, which always gave the BBC the advantage – but there was also a political edge to the debate. Some newspapers supported certain political factions; most notably before Chamberlain's resignation there had been papers that sided with the Prime Minister. The *Daily Mirror* was one that went against Chamberlain and they had an upsurge in popularity – and sales – after his departure.

PROTECTION FROM THE STORM

While there were many people like those at the BBC who had to keep working through the Blitz the vast majority of Londoners took to the shelters during the nightly air raids. Some went to the large public shelters in the London Underground stations while others used Anderson shelters that they had erected for themselves in their own gardens.

It was a surface shelter that I went to and it's one of the most cheering sights I have seen since the raids started. I've been round the streets most nights on one job or another but I've never seen anything to equal this shelter for comfort and cheer. All the people come from a nearby block of flats, there's a family atmosphere and the place looks fine; there are flags on the wall and pictures of film stars and the children have hung paper streamers all around; along one side there are chairs and a few tables and when I went in all the women were knitting very busily. There was a babble of talk and most of the children were laughing and joking, and if there was a noise from outside they started laughing and singing. Their general motto seemed to be, 'take no notice'.

Robin Duff, BBC, 5 October 1940

During the bombing of London as many as 136,000 people slept each night in underground stations, although the number reduced from its peak in October 1940 to around 96,000 in January 1941. The Blitz lasted until May 1941 and about two million homes were destroyed in Britain, 1.2 million of which were in London. Almost 40,000 were killed and over 50,000 people were seriously injured. The majority of those who lost their lives were in London. The devastation to the City of London was terrible, with 30 per cent of this historic area totally destroyed. The numbers of people made homeless in the Blitz was enormous, and for some unfortunate people it happened more than once.

My mother and I were in the house alone when the bomb hit the house next door. We had to get out from beneath the wreckage as quickly as we could and went into a surface shelter where we stayed until the end of the raid. Then the next day we started out and we walked until we got to a place called Stoneleigh where they put us up for the night. Then two days later we got another house and I'm afraid that was bombed last night so now we're in the same situation . . .

Unidentified girl, BBC, autumn 1940

A few days before Christmas Robin Duff was again reporting on the bombing of London, broadcasting to a country that had largely not suffered like the capital.

St Paul's Cathedral was the pivot of the main fire. All around it flames were leaping up into the sky; there the cathedral stood, magnificently firm, untouched in the middle of all this destruction. As I walked along the streets it was almost impossible to believe all these fires could be subdued. I was walking between solid walls of fire. Roofs of shops and office buildings came down with a roaring crash. Panes of glass were cracking everywhere from the heat. Every street was criss-crossed with innumerable lengths of hose. Men were fighting the fires from the top of 100-foot ladders shot up from the street. Others were pushing their way into burning buildings taking their jet to the core of the fires . . .

 . . . I went to some of the public shelters, they were underground shelters mostly and the buildings on top of them were alight. The people had to be got away from them and quickly and then taken across to the underground station. Sparks were driving down the street like a heavy snowstorm. Obviously small children couldn't walk across to the station in this and so some of us went back and forward carrying them in our arms. I took off my macintosh covering them up completely in this. It must have been rather frightening to be carried across by someone they didn't know and not being able to see anything. But it was the only way to protect them from those sparks and by the time we got the last one across we would have had to do it anyway because the building above the station was on fire. Luckily the station escaped and they were all moved off in trains to get food and drink and some much needed sleep.

Robin Duff, BBC, 20 December 1940

Until the end of 1940, apart from London, it was just Coventry, Birmingham, Southampton, Bristol and Liverpool that suffered serious attacks. By the end of

May 1941 Cardiff, Clydeside, Merseyside, Plymouth, Portsmouth, Hull and Belfast all came in for some heavy bombing. The raid on Coventry on Thursday 14 November 1940 was the most significant outside the capital; 568 people were killed, and another 863 seriously injured, when over 400 bombers dropped 400 tons of bombs on the city centre and industrial areas. Thousands were made homeless and the city's famous cathedral, apart from its spire, was totally destroyed.

> That grand old parish church with its tower and spire soaring to the sky with its huge immense domestic building . . . Up on the top roof, the lower roof and on the ground floor we waited. Then bomb after bomb, incendiary bombs fell and we fought them with what we could, the equipment we had, it took a long time. Then a group of three fell on the roof and the fire blazed up and we had no more sand and no more water and no more strength to go on . . . By about 1.30 the whole thing was gutted. The nave of the cathedral was no more. All through that night the clock serenely struck the hours . . .
>
> *The Very Revd R.T. Howard, Provost of Coventry Cathedral,*
> *BBC, 15 November 1940*

In all Coventry suffered forty-one air raids and according to local records the alert sounded over 370 times; 1,236 people lost their lives in the city. Each British city that was attacked has a similar story to tell but none, other than London, as devastating as that one night when central Coventry was all but destroyed. 'It's almost like the day of judgement, as pictured in some of the old books', said an unnamed BBC correspondent who witnessed the air raid.

One night in early December Bristol was the target of a heavy German raid; it just happened to coincide with the 'Epilogue', which meant the regular studio could not be used and so the programme was switched to a tiny makeshift emergency room. The first casualties of the move were the musicians, who could not be fitted into the smaller studio. Undeterred, the announcer, Stuart Hibberd, introduced Dr Welch, the BBC's Director of Religious Broadcasting, to give the talk, accompanied by violinist Paul Beard, who played while crouching beneath the studio table. It demonstrates beautifully the wonder of radio. No one sees what's happening, and their imagination fortunately cannot always tell them exactly what it 'looks like' beyond the radio's speaker, and behind the microphone.

Of course it was not just Britain that was under attack. RAF bomber raids on Germany were taking place throughout most of the same period, and there was an element of tit-for-tat in what happened. On 8 November the RAF bombed Munich, and it was in revenge for this attack that the Germans launched Operation Moonlight Sonata – the attack on Coventry. The RAF raid on Munich involved fifty bombers, and the timing could not have been better, as Hitler was making a speech in the city on the anniversary of the failed assassination attempt at Bürgerbräukeller, a beer hall. The whole incident turned into something of a coup for the BBC as one of the pilots who took part in the raid, a New Zealander from Hawkes Bay, went into Broadcasting House and spoke of the experience just two nights later. He flew a Wellington bomber from 75 (New Zealand) Squadron – part of 3 Group, based at RAF Feltwell in Norfolk.

This was our first trip to Munich. Our target was the railway locomotive and marshalling yards, almost in the centre of the city and only a short distance away from the famous Brown House of the Nazi Party. Just before we took off the senior intelligence officer came rushing over and said he thought that we might be interested to know that Hitler and some of his gangsters were to be in Munich that night to celebrate the anniversary of the Beer Hall Putsch of 1923.

Everybody was flat out to get there. They had included in my bomb load one of the heaviest calibre bombs that we have so far carried. I talked things over with the observer and we decided before we left that as the station commander had been kind enough to entrust us with the delivery of this heavy calibre bomb we'd go in as low as possible to make sure of getting the target. It was a beautiful starlight night and there was almost a half moon. We were checking up our course by the stars as we went out. Round Munich itself there was not a cloud in the sky.

We passed an enemy aerodrome – all lit up for night flying – but on the way out we weren't wasting any bombs on that. We saw one of our fellows flying about five miles in front of us, getting a packet of stuff thrown up at him over Mannheim. He flew straight through it, but we turned away to the left and avoided the town. After Mannheim, Munich wasn't very far away and everybody was sitting up and taking notice. We were about twenty minutes' flying-time away when we first saw the flak and the searchlights coming up around the city. The navigator got a bit worried because we were ten minutes in front of our estimated time of arrival and he thought for a minute that we might have got off our course. Then we picked up a landmark – a goodish-sized lake to the south of Munich – and set course from there. Some of the other fellows had gone on ahead to light up the target and we could see their incendiaries bursting.

Flares were dropping all round as we went in. The guns on the ground were shooting quite well. I saw three flares shot down almost as soon as they had been dropped. We flew over to have a preliminary look at things and found we were about a mile south of the marshalling yards. We were low enough and it was so light that we could see houses and streets quite clearly. It was the bomb-aimer's dream of the perfect night. Altogether we stooged round for about twenty minutes, checking up on our target. We saw somebody else drop his stick of bombs slap on the target. The explosions lit up the locomotive sheds. We came down lower and they were shooting at us hard. In the light of one of our own flares I saw a stationary engine in the yard. I could make out the glow from its fires and I noticed, incidentally, that it had steam up. We had to turn round and come back over the yards, making our run from south-east to north-west. Then we went whistling down. Tracer seemed to be coming up right under the wings and the bomb-aimer said that he could see it coming up towards him as he lay in the nose of the aircraft looking down through his tunnel.

All the way down in the dive I could see these big black locomotive sheds in front of me. The front gunner was shooting out searchlights, which I thought was a pretty good effort, and the rear gunner was having a try at the same game, but it was more difficult for him. I'd told them that they could let loose with their guns and they didn't want telling twice. The bomb-aimer got the target right in his sight. He said: 'I can see it: I can see it absolutely perfectly.' Then he called out: 'Bombs gone. I've got it.' As a matter of fact I don't see how he could have missed at that height. Both he and the rear gunner saw the bombs burst. The rear gunner said that the heavy one made a dickens of an explosion. In the excitement I'd more or less forgotten that we had got this big bomb on board and the force of the explosion gave the aircraft a tremendous wallop. If we had come down any lower we should have been blown up. As it was we all thought we'd been hit. The effect was just as if a heavy shell had burst right under the rear turret. There was a stunned silence for a few seconds; then another babble of conversation when everybody decided that we were all right.

We were still low down. Searchlights kept popping up. The front gunner put out two and the rear gunner put out four. It was a remarkable sight to see the coloured tracer going down the beams of the light. After that, it was a race back because we'd been told that the weather would close down over our base and that after two o'clock we'd be very lucky if we got in there, so we beetled back pretty rapidly. Altogether it was a perfect trip.

RAF flight lieutenant, 'Air Log', BBC, 10 November 1940

The success of the raid on Munich, with Hitler in the city, was obliquely acknowledged by German radio at the end of the 7 p.m. bulletin:

The Führer to-day addressed old party members in the Löwenbräu cellar, in Munich. Owing to the early closing down of many German stations at 8.15 a record of the speech will be broadcast to-morrow after the 12.30 p.m. radio news bulletin.

German radio, 7 p.m., 8 November 1940

German radio frequently closed down because of air raids, and the RAF was definitely responsible for upsetting Hitler's plans.

This report of the raid on Munich was just one of a number of similar broadcasts by bomber crew during the second half of 1940. They included several talks on bombing Berlin, including one by a bomber squadron commander and another by a flying officer of a heavy bomber squadron; 'Bombing the Invasion Ports' by a pilot officer of a heavy bomber squadron, a tail gunner's story, 'Bombing Berlin' by a sergeant pilot, and '11½ Hours in a Dinghy after Bombing Berlin' by two pilot officers. Given the situation many at home were facing, these broadcasts greatly boosted morale by reinforcing the notion of the enemy getting a taste of what their air force was dishing out.

However, there was a sense of mounting frustration within both the Air Ministry and Bomber Command about the way in which the RAF's bombing campaign was being represented; they felt it lacked a coordinated approach. A meeting at the Air Ministry involving the BBC, the Foreign Office, the Ministry of Economic Warfare and Bomber Command was held in January 1941. What was clear to those attending from the BBC was that an element of inter-governmental wrangling was making it difficult for the Corporation to do their job. The Air Ministry wanted to put the bombing in a good light, something that the BBC had been helping them to achieve. However, the Foreign Office, in particular, wanted to be sure that things were not exaggerated, as it harmed the image of British propaganda to overstate the case. The Commander-in-Chief of Bomber Command, Sir Richard Peirse, was adamant that it was important to name targets so as to avoid listeners feeling that the bombing was indiscriminate or inaccurate. It was an issue that was to be even more hotly debated once Peirse's successor, Arthur Harris, embarked upon a bombing campaign far greater in scale than either the German Blitz or that which had been undertaken hitherto by the RAF.

In the year or so since the war had started the progress that the BBC had made in expanding its news service both at home and in broadcasting overseas was a remarkable achievement given wartime strictures. Even though broadcasting on the Home and Forces Programmes was not a 24-hour operation the BBC was on the air to somewhere in the world for every minute of every day during

1940; neither was the BBC 'off air' for one single minute because of enemy action. There were broadcasts in thirty-four languages, almost 70 per cent of which had been added since the outbreak of war. As a news service BBC radio had 'come of age', broadcasting close to eighty bulletins each day. The achievements of the Corporation are all the more laudable when you consider that when the war broke out 10 per cent of its staff had joined the forces. A further 200 of the Corporation's pre-war staff had joined up during 1940, although displaced foreign nationals working on overseas broadcasts replaced a good proportion of those that were lost.

Chapter 9

MANY QUESTIONS

With the start of a new year the BBC aired the first programme in a series that is still broadcast today, although it is not quite the same programme as was envisaged during wartime. 'Any Questions?' was launched on New Year's Day 1940 and on that opening programme not one of the panel was correctly able to name all Seven Wonders of the World – can you? The programme soon became known as 'The Brains Trust' and in that first year it received around 90,000 questions in the post and answered just 400; by the end of 1941 it was attracting between 8 and 10 million listeners. 'Any Questions?' was one more example, among many, of how the BBC's pattern of broadcasting on the Home Programme continued to evolve amid the constraints of wartime. Considerable changes had taken place during the course of 1940, with new programmes introduced to take account of the needs of the wartime audience.

The BBC had for the time a sophisticated audience research programme, which found out that there were some interesting listening patterns. In a typical week the BBC researchers found that nowhere in Britain were there people who listened to more than two bulletins each day. This is just one marked difference from today's listening patterns, and of course viewing habits, for news programmes. Contemporary research showed that people in the south were far more likely to listen to the news at 9 p.m. than at 6 p.m. – in the north it was the reverse. Overall, people living in Scotland listened to more news bulletins than those in any other part of Britain. The researchers also found that the appetite for news, not surprisingly, went up and down depending on what was happening on the various war fronts. In particular the period in mid-June between the evacuation of Dunkirk and the French capitulation was when most people listened to the lunchtime one o'clock news; on average 16.5 million adults listened each day. Even then the 9 p.m. news remained the most listened-to bulletin.

Variety shows of all types drew large audiences with almost 11 million people listening to 'Saturday Night Variety' each week. But alongside the public's appetite for fun was a seemingly insatiable appetite for talks and commentaries. 'War Commentary', on which 'Air Log' often featured regularly, drew audiences of over 7 million. 'American Commentary', with speakers such as Raymond Gram Swing, got close to 6 million listeners on Saturday nights after the 9 p.m. news, while 'In Your Garden' usually attracted around 3 million people most eager to learn how to be more productive in their back gardens or allotments.

ITMA

Ladies and gentleman, we don't care what he's been, we don't care what he's done, all we know is we're happy to welcome that man again . . .

[sung] It's that man again, it's that man again, Mr Tommy Handley is here.

His hundred and first appearance finds this sprightly centenarian as full as ever of beans, backchat and bonhomie . . .

[sung] Our pride and joy, Mrs Handley's boy.

'It's That Man Again', BBC, 7 October 1943

With catchphrases like 'Can I do yer now, sir?', 'I don't mind if I do', and 'Ta-ta for now' – which was shortened to TTFN and brought back into common usage by DJ Jimmy Young in the 1970s – ITMA became an essential part of the BBC's wartime output. Devised by Tommy Handley, a seasoned radio performer, and his scriptwriting partner Ted Kavanagh, ITMA ran for over 300 broadcasts – for millions of listeners it was the perfect antidote to the news.

ITMA did not begin during the war but merely carried on, and got better, having first been heard in July 1939. The show's title was lifted directly from a *Daily Express* headline of 2 May 1939 referring to Hitler's pre-war territorial scavenging. The second series began in September 1939, followed by a third in June 1941 – when it briefly became 'It's That Sand Again'. As well as catchphrases, the revolving cast of characters had some wonderfully inventive names; the best was arguably Hattie Jacques, who joined a later series as 'Sophie Tuckshop'. ITMA continued in the immediate postwar period and the final series began in September 1948, with the very last show on 6 January 1949 (310th edition). There was one more scheduled ITMA for the following week, but tragically Tommy Handley died on 9 January 1949, three days shy of his fifty-third birthday. The BBC decided the show should not continue – a wise decision, as Handley *was* ITMA.

The BBC was not only interested in entertaining on the Home Front. In May 1941 they introduced a new twist to try to win the hearts and minds of German airmen. According to the *Melody Maker*, a newspaper for musicians and fans of popular music, there was to be a 'Radio Dance Music Blitz' on Germany.

Every afternoon at 4 p.m., on 373 metres, a new form of Blitzkrieg descends on Germany. But it's not the RAF which delivers it this time, only the best dance orchestras in Britain, presented with the acme of showmanship.

Wednesdays are the high spot. For then the programme is specially presented for the entertainment of the German Luftwaffe and on several occasions bands composed of RAF players have actually broadcast to their German counterparts! A week ago an RAF band with some famous players included in the personnel aired on this programme, and the show they gave has already resulted in a surprisingly large number of letters from listeners, all over the world – and some of them from Germany.

For the daily airings Geraldo has become almost the house band, although Ambrose, Mantovani and Jack Payne have already broadcast in the series. On Wednesdays it is the BBC policy to include as many of the RAF combinations as possible.

The entertainment angle in these programmes is definitely swing, with only a small proportion of sweet tunes thrown in to make up the balance. The success of the Wednesday afternoons has caused the BBC seriously to consider two special Luftwaffe airings each week, and a neutral journalist who recently arrived in this country after touring Germany and Occupied France is said to have told the officials of the Corporation that he actually heard the programme being received in the officers' mess at a German aerodrome!

Too much credit has been given to Dr Joe Goebbels for his propaganda. We, for our part, tip our hats to the BBC for its realisation of the persuasive powers of really good dance music put over with imagination and skill for the cause of Britain.

Melody Maker, *31 May 1941*

The Italians attacked Greece in late October 1940 but Mussolini was very surprised that the Greeks, instead of capitulating immediately, resisted. In January 1941 the Italian Army was using Elbasan as a base for their operations.

This is the BBC Home Service, here is the news and this is Bruce Belfrage reading it. Elbasan, Italy's northern base in Albania, has had yet another

heavy raid by the RAF and there is news of the sinking of an Italian supply
ship in an earlier raid on Tripoli. Two German supply ships have been
bombed off Norway and aircraft of Coastal and Bomber Command have
carried out day and night attacks on the port of Brest . . .

                                    Bruce Belfrage, BBC News, 5 January 1941

The aircraft that attacked Elbasan were Bristol Blenheims of 211 Squadron,
which had been sent to assist and support the Greek Air Force. From their base
near Athens the Blenheims were in action almost every day, often flying in
atrocious winter weather. The day after the raid reported in the news one of
211 Squadron's Blenheims was shot down by an Italian Air Force Fiat CR-42
biplane; two more Blenheims crash-landed when returning to base owing to
damage inflicted by the Italians; and one of the RAF bombers was written off,
killing all three crew. The squadron stayed in Greece until April, when the
Germans' intervention in this particular theatre forced their withdrawal to
Egypt. They left in something of a hurry and to save the ground crew they
were squeezed into every, and any, available space on the aircraft – sometimes
two to a turret. But all this was not before the squadron lost six Blenheims, all
that had been sent on a raid; just one crew member survived from the six
aircraft, each with three crew members. During the short campaign in Greece
the two RAF Blenheim squadrons lost over ninety aircraft and 150 aircrew. It's
fascinating that behind one small snippet of wartime news there is a mass of
detail, and terrible losses to explain. It was also Blenheims of Coastal
Command that mounted the attack on the French port of Brest, mentioned on
the bulletin. They hit a German destroyer, and one of the Blenheims was lost
to enemy fighters. Blenheims were phased out in 1941 as they had proved to
be a less than adequate match for almost every type of Axis fighter.

Each and every news bulletin had fascinating detail behind what often seemed
like bland and sterile headlines and copy. The strictures of censorship meant
that greater detail was often impossible to give, which is what made the
commentary programmes so important in providing 'colour' to the news. The
talks, and commentaries, allowed listeners to get a little more understanding as
to the background to events and the realities, sometimes with a good dollop of
the 'gung-ho' spirit. It's another of those fascinating comparisons with the way
that news is served up in the twenty-first century. Of course what are set out
in the 5 January 1941 bulletin are the headlines, but there was nowhere near
the level of additional information that we are confronted with today. It's
arguable, though, that people may have been better informed during the
Second World War than we were during the last Iraq conflict. The sheer

volume of detail, expert comment, reports from all over the battle zone, GCHQ, London reporters, Washington reporters, defence analysts, former soldiers, Ministers, Opposition MPs *et al.* do not necessarily make for better news coverage. All too often, the news turns into a debate between experts. Where the BBC had it right in the period 1939–45 was very definitely to separate news from talks/commentary/expert analysis.

Away from the detail of specific wartime incidents there were the global political implications of President Roosevelt's re-election as US president. The ramifications for Britain, and the rest of the beleaguered European nations, were huge. Roosevelt's opponent for a historic third term was Republican Wendell Willkie, who charged his opponent with having made secret deals that would take America to war. Roosevelt's campaign countered with the slogan 'better a third-termer, than a third-rater'. Roosevelt famously said during the campaign, 'your boys are not going to be sent to foreign wars'. The President's inaugural address was relayed to London and broadcast on the BBC in the third week of January. At the close of his speech people in Britain and those who heard his speech on the BBC's Overseas Service would have had grounds for being somewhat heartened by its message.

The destiny of America was proclaimed in words of prophecy spoken by our first President in his first inaugural in 1789 – words almost directed, it would seem, to this year of 1941: 'The preservation of the sacred fire of liberty and the destiny of the republican model of government are justly considered . . . deeply . . . finally staked on the experiment entrusted to the hands of the American people.'

If we lose that sacred fire – if we let it be smothered with doubt and fear – then we shall reject the destiny, which Washington strove so valiantly and so triumphantly to establish. The preservation of the spirit and faith of the Nation does, and will, furnish the highest justification for every sacrifice that we may make in the cause of national defence.

In the face of great perils never before encountered, our strong purpose is to protect and to perpetuate the integrity of democracy. For this we muster the spirit of America, and the faith of America.

We do not retreat. We are not content to stand still. As Americans, we go forward, in the service of our country, by the will of God.

President Roosevelt, relayed from Washington on the BBC,
20 January 1941

Almost three weeks after the President's speech Churchill gave his first speech on the BBC in five months, his longest absence from the airwaves since the war had begun. He spoke of the progress of the war – the success of the Battle of Britain, the Blitz and how the country had won the respect of people in America. He gave a thorough review of the war in the desert, as well as in the other Mediterranean theatres, but much of his speech was directed at America. It was, in part, a response to the President's inaugural address, but Churchill also used the opportunity to make a very public plea:

> In war-time there is a lot to be said for the motto 'Deeds, not Words'. All the same, it is a good thing to look around from time to time and take stock. And certainly our affairs have prospered in several directions during these last four or five months far better than most of us would have ventured to hope. We stood our ground and faced the two dictators in the hour of what seemed their overwhelming triumph and we have shown ourselves capable, so far, of standing up against them alone . . .
>
> . . . Meanwhile, abroad in October a wonderful thing happened. One of the two dictators, the crafty, cold-blooded, black-hearted Italian who had thought to gain an empire on the cheap by stabbing fallen France in the back – he got into trouble. Without the slightest provocation, stirred on by lust of power and brutish greed, Mussolini attacked and invaded Greece only to be hurled back ignominiously by the heroic Greek Army, who I will say, with your assent, have revived before our eyes the glories which from the Classic Age gild their native land.
>
> While Signor Mussolini was writhing and smarting under the Greek lash in Albania, Generals Wavell and Wilson, who were charged with the defence of Egypt and of the Suez Canal in accordance with our treaty obligations, whose task seemed at one time so difficult, had received very powerful reinforcements, reinforcements of men, cannon, equipment and, above all, tanks, which we had sent from our island in spite of the invasion threat; and large numbers of troops from India, Australia and New Zealand had also reached them. Forthwith began that series of victories in Libya, which have broken irretrievably the Italian military power on the African Continent . . .
> Here, then, in Libya is the third considerable event upon which we may dwell with some satisfaction. It is just exactly two months ago to a day that I was waiting anxiously, but oh so eagerly, for the news of the great counter-stroke, which had been planned against the Italian invaders of Egypt. The secret had been well kept. The preparations had been well made, but to leap across those seventy miles of desert and attack an army of ten or eleven divisions, equipped with all the appliances of modern war, and who had been fortifying themselves for three months: that was a most hazardous adventure.

When the brilliant, decisive victory at Sidi Barrani, with its tens of thousands of prisoners, proved that we had quality, manoeuvring power and weapons superior to the enemy, who had boasted so much of his virility and his military virtue, it was evident that all the other Italian forces in Eastern Libya were in great danger. They could not easily beat a retreat along the coastal road without running the risk of being caught in the open by our armoured divisions and brigades ranging far out into the desert in tremendous swoops and scoops. They had to expose themselves to being attacked piecemeal.

General Wavell – nay, all our leaders and all their live, active, ardent men, British, Australian, Indian, in the Imperial Army – saw their opportunity. At that time I ventured to draw General Wavell's attention to the seventh chapter of the Gospel of St Matthew, at the seventh verse, where, as you all know or ought to know, it is written: 'Ask, and it shall be given; seek, and ye shall find; knock, and it shall be opened unto you.'

The Army of the Nile has asked, and it was given; they sought, and they have found; they knocked, and it has been opened unto them. In barely eight weeks, by a campaign which will long be studied as a model of the military art, an advance of over 400 miles has been made; the whole Italian Army in the east of Libya, which was reputed to exceed 150,000 men, has been captured or destroyed; the entire province of Cyrenaica, nearly as big as England and Wales, has been conquered; the unhappy Arab tribes who have for thirty years suffered from the cruelty of Italian rule, carried in some cases to the point of methodical extermination, these Bedouin survivors have at last seen their oppressors in disorderly flight or led off in endless droves as prisoners of war. Egypt and the Suez Canal are safe. And the port, the base and the airfields of Benghazi constitute a strategic point of high consequence to the whole of the war in the Eastern Mediterranean . . .

. . . Distinguished Americans have come over to see things here at the front and to find out how the United States can help us best and soonest. In Mr Hopkins, who has been my frequent companion during the last three weeks, we have the envoy of the President, who has been newly re-elected to his august office. In Mr Wendell Willkie we have welcomed the champion of the great Republican Party. We may be sure that they will both tell the truth about what they have seen over here, and more than that we do not ask. The rest we leave with good confidence to the judgement of the President, the Congress and the people of the United States.

I have been so very careful since I have been Prime Minister not to encourage false hopes or prophesy smooth and easy things, and yet the tale that I had to tell today is one which must justly and rightly give us cause for deep thankfulness and also, I think, for sound comfort and even rejoicing. But now I must dwell upon the more serious, darker and more dangerous aspects of the vast scene of the war. We must all of us have been asking ourselves what is that wicked man, whose crime-stained regime and system are at bay and in the toils, what has he been preparing during these winter months? What new deviltry is he planning? What new small country will he overrun or strike down? What fresh form of assault will he make upon our island homes and fortress? Which, let there be no mistake about it, is all that stands between him and the domination of the world.

We may be sure that the war is soon going to enter upon a phase of greater violence. Hitler's confederate, Mussolini, has reeled back in Albania. But the Nazis, having absorbed Hungary and driven Rumania into a frightful internal convulsion, are now already upon the Black Sea. A considerable German army and air force is being built up in Rumania and its forward tentacles have already penetrated Bulgaria with, we must suppose, the acquiescence of the Bulgarian Government. Airfields are being occupied by German ground personnel numbering thousands, so as to enable the German air force to come into action from Bulgaria. Many preparations have been made for the movement of German troops into or through Bulgaria. And perhaps this southward movement has already begun.

We saw what happened last May in the Low Countries – how they hoped for the best, how they clung to their neutrality, how awfully they were deceived, overwhelmed, plundered, enslaved and, since, starved. We know how we and the French suffered when at the last moment, at the urgent, belated appeal of the King of the Belgians, we went to his aid. Of course, if all the Balkan people stood together and acted together, aided by Britain and by Turkey, it would be many months before a German army and air force of sufficient strength to overcome them could be assembled in the south-east of Europe. And in those months much might happen.

Much will certainly happen as American aid becomes effective, as our air power grows, as we become a well-armed nation, and as our armies in the East increase in strength. But nothing is more certain than that, if the countries of south-eastern Europe allow themselves to be pulled to pieces one by one, they will share the fate of Denmark, Holland and Belgium, and none can tell how long it will be before the hour of their deliverance strikes.

One of our difficulties is to convince some of these neutral countries in Europe that we are going to win. We think it is astonishing that they should be so dense as not to see it as clearly as we do ourselves.

I remember in the last war, in July 1915, we began to think that Bulgaria was going wrong, so Mr Lloyd George, Mr Bonar Law, Sir F.E. Smith and I asked the Bulgarian Minister to dinner to explain to him what a fool King Ferdinand would make of himself if he were to go in on the losing side. It was no use. The poor man simply could not believe it, or couldn't make his government believe it. So Bulgaria, against the wishes of her peasant population, against all her interests, fell in at the Kaiser's tail and got sadly carved up and punished when the victory was won.

I trust that Bulgaria is not going to make the same mistake again. If they do the Bulgarian peasantry and people, for whom there has been much regard both in Great Britain and the United States, will for the third time in thirty years have been made to embark upon a needless and disastrous war.

In the Central Mediterranean, the Italian Quisling, who is called Mussolini, and the French Quisling, commonly called Laval, are both in their different ways trying to make their countries into doormats for Hitler and his new order, in the hope of being able to keep or get the Nazi Gestapo and Prussian bayonets to enforce their rule upon their fellow countrymen. I cannot tell how the matter will go, but at any rate we shall do our best to fight for the Central Mediterranean.

I dare say you will have noticed a very significant air action, which was fought over Malta a fortnight ago. The Germans sent an entire Geschwader of dive-bombers to Sicily. They seriously injured our new aircraft carrier *Illustrious*, and then, as this wounded ship was sheltered in Malta harbour, they concentrated upon her all their force so as to beat her to pieces.

But they were met by the batteries of Malta, which is one of the strongest defended fortresses in the world against air attack. They were met by the Fleet Air Arm and by the Royal Air Force and in two or three days they had lost, out of 150 dive-bombers, upward of ninety – fifty of which were destroyed in the air and forty on the ground. Although the *Illustrious* in her damaged condition was one of the great prizes of the air and naval war, the German Geschwader accepted the defeat. They would not come any more.

All the necessary repairs were made to the *Illustrious* in Malta harbour, and she steamed safely off to Alexandria under her own power at twenty-three knots. I dwell upon this incident not at all because I think it disposes of the danger in the Central Mediterranean but in order to show you that there, as elsewhere, we intend to give a good account of ourselves. But, after all, the fate of this war is going to be settled by what happens on the oceans, in the air and, above all, in this island.

It seems now to be certain that the government and people of the United States intend to supply us with all that is necessary for victory. In the last war the United States sent two million men across the Atlantic, but this is not a war of vast armies, hurling immense masses of shells at one another.

We do not need the gallant armies which are forming throughout the American Union. We do not need them this year, nor the next year, nor any year that I can foresee. But we do need most urgently an immense and continuous supply of war materials, and technical apparatus of all kinds. We need them here and we need to bring them here. We shall need a great mass of shipping in 1942, far more than we can build ourselves if we are to maintain and augment our war effort in the West and in the East.

These facts are, of course, all well known to the enemy, and we must therefore expect that Herr Hitler will do his utmost to prey upon our shipping and reduce the volume of American supplies entering these islands. Having conquered France and Norway, his clutching fingers reach out on both sides of us into the ocean. I have never underrated this danger and you know I have never concealed it from you. Therefore, I hope you will believe me when I say that I have complete confidence in the Royal Navy, aided by the air force of the Coastal Command, and that, in one way or another, I am sure they will be able to meet every changing phase of this truly mortal struggle, and that, sustained by the courage of our merchant seamen and of the dockers and workmen of all ports, we shall outwit, outmanoeuvre, outfight and out-last the worst that the enemy's malice and ingenuity can contrive.

I left the greatest issue to the end. You will have seen that Sir John Dill, our principal military adviser, the Chief of the Imperial General Staff, has warned us all yesterday that Hitler may be forced by the strategic economic and political stresses in Europe to try to invade these islands in the near future.

That is a warning which no one should disregard. Naturally, we are working night and day to have everything ready. Of course, we are far stronger than we ever were before – incomparably stronger than we were in July, August, and September. Our Navy is more powerful, our flotillas are more numerous. We are far stronger, actually and relatively, in the air above these islands than we were when our Fighter Command beat off and beat down the Nazi attack last autumn. Our Army is more numerous, more mobile and far better equipped and trained than in September, and still more than in July. And I have the greatest confidence in our Commander in Chief, General Brooke, and in the generals of proved ability who under him guard the different quarters of our land. But most of all I have put my faith in the simple, unaffected resolve to conquer or die which will animate and inspire nearly four million Britons with serviceable weapons in their hands.

It is not an easy military operation to invade an island like Great Britain without the command of the sea and without the command of the air, and then to face what will be waiting for the invader here.

But I must drop one word of caution, for next to cowardice and to treachery, overconfidence leading to neglect or slothfulness is the worst of martial crimes. Therefore, I drop one word of caution: A Nazi invasion of Great Britain last autumn would have been a more or less improvised affair. Hitler took it for granted that when France gave in we should give in. But we did not give in. And he had to think again. An invasion now will be supported by a much more carefully prepared tackle and equipment for landing craft and other apparatus, all of which will have been planned and manufactured during the winter months. We must all be prepared to meet gas attacks, parachute attacks and glider attacks, with constancy, forethought and practised skill.

I must again emphasise what General Dill has said and what I pointed out myself last year: In order to win the war, Hitler must destroy Great Britain. He may carry havoc into the Balkan States; he may tear great provinces out of Russia; he may march to the Caspian; he may march to the gates of India. All this will avail him nothing. He may spread his curse more widely throughout Europe and Asia, but it will not avert his doom.

With every month that passes the many proud and once happy countries he is now holding down by brute force and vile intrigue are learning to hate the Prussian yoke and the Nazi name, as nothing has ever been hated so fiercely and so widely among men before. And all the time, masters of the sea and air, the British Empire – nay, in a certain sense, the whole English-speaking world – will be on his track bearing with them the swords of Justice.

The other day President Roosevelt gave his opponent in the late Presidential election a letter of introduction to me, and in it he wrote out a verse in his own handwriting from Longfellow, which, he said, 'applies to you people as it does to us'. Here is the verse:

> . . . Sail on, O Ship of State!
> Sail on, O Union, strong and great!
> Humanity with all its fears
> With all the hopes of future years
> Is hanging breathless on thy fate!

What is the answer that I shall give in your name to this great man, the thrice-chosen head of a nation of 130,000,000? Here is the answer, which I will give to President Roosevelt.

Put your confidence in us. Give us your faith and your blessing, and under Providence all will be well. We shall not fail or falter; we shall not weaken or tire. Neither the sudden shock of battle nor the long-drawn trials of vigilance and exertion will wear us down. Give us the tools and we will finish the job.

Winston Churchill, BBC, 9 February 1941

Predictably German radio took a different tack from both Allied and neutral commentators on Churchill's speech.

This speech has done little to reassure the people of Britain. Past and present events showed no grounds for the optimism of Mr Churchill. General Wavell's successes, material as they may be, are not decisive. The situation will become critical as soon as the weather improves.

Bremen radio, 10 February 1941

The American press were unanimous in their support for Britain, and in the need for America to 'step up to the plate'.

One has only to set Churchill's speech beside the facts to compare it with the profound silence surrounding Mussolini, or the frenetic compound of rambling historical distortions and unsupported boasting which recently emanated from Berlin, to realise that in the slow, steady massing of the British sea, air, and land power there is tremendous force, which, if only it is provided with weapons, can strike with a crushing and decisive effect. One would not like to be an Italian Fascist or German Nazi listening to that broadcast.

New York Herald-Tribune

Churchill's voice, as it came over the radio, ran the gamut of every mood except despair, and those who listened on this side of the ocean to his ringing voice will take cheer and find renewed hope in the British will to victory.

Washington Post

Churchill gave a report which will live among the great orations of the twentieth century. Honest and frank as only a leader of a democratic people dare be, Churchill weighed the accomplishments and dangers confronting his people and the world.

Cleveland Plain-Dealer

Commenting on Churchill's plea to 'give us the tools and we will finish the job', the *New York Sun* said: 'A good many thousands of fires in a good many thousands of furnaces in a good many thousands of American factories are already kindled, so that with all due speed, those tools may be forthcoming.' These expressions of support for Britain were in Monday's newspapers – the day after Churchill's speech. The day before Churchill gave his speech Roosevelt's 'Lease and Lend' Bill to aid Britain and other countries fighting the Nazis had passed an important hurdle in the US House of Representatives. Despite a heated six-day debate, where the bill was delayed by an unusually large number of amendments, it was finally passed by 280 votes to 156. A leading Republican Representative said the Bill was 'the longest step America has yet taken towards direct involvement in wars abroad'. The House rejected Republican attempts to impose a $700,000,000 ceiling on the 'Aid Britain Program', to prohibit the sending of American troops outside the territorial waters of the Western hemisphere, and also defeated an amendment prohibiting the use of United States ports for repairing belligerent warships. The Lend-Lease Law was enacted a month later on 11 March; it would be of major importance to the prosecution of the war against Hitler. Argument has taken place ever since as to whether Britain would have been able to fight on without the act. Most now tend to agree that Britain would have kept on fighting, but Lend-Lease moved things along at a faster pace, which had benefits in all sorts of ways, not least in reducing the number of lives lost.

A week before the Lend-Lease Law was enacted British troops landed in Greece, but this news was not broadcast on the BBC until after German radio had told the world, including listeners to the English-language service of German radio. It was yet another example to stir up the critics of the BBC; at the same time it left the public somewhat baffled. The British landings had come the day after the Nazis began their Balkan campaign with attacks on Yugoslavia and Greece. This was in spite of the fact that Haw-Haw had broadcast a few weeks earlier, saying, 'Every German interest favours the maintenance of peace in the Balkans whereas England and France could only be interested in causing trouble in this region.' Two days before the German offensive had begun Lord Haw-Haw had revealed his identity as William Joyce, six weeks after he had become a German citizen.

In view of the fact that British land troops are pressing on from Greece towards the north, and of their union with Yugoslav forces, whose mobilisation has become known, units of the German Army have begun a counter-attack. The Greek and Serbian frontiers have been crossed at several points. Strong units of the German Air Force have attacked the fortress of Belgrade, and destroyed barracks as well as military objectives. At the same time, Italian bomber formations attacked important war objectives in

Southern Yugoslavia; with success . . . German troops have met stubborn resistance in the Struma Valley in Greece. There are favourable reports of the progress of the German attack.

German radio, 5 April 1941

After the entry of German troops into Bulgaria had brought to a head the long-threatened German invasion of the Balkans, His Majesty's Government in the United Kingdom, in full consultation with the Dominion Governments concerned, have sent an army to Greece, comprising troops from Great Britain, Australia, and New Zealand, to stand in line with the soldiers of our brave Ally, in defence of their native soil. The British Air Force, which has for some time been operating in Greece against the Italians, has been strongly reinforced.

BBC News, 6 April 1941

British newspapers were faced with the same dilemma in reporting the landing of the Allied troops in Greece. One paper reminded its readers that 'the German news is more propagandist than factual in its reporting'. Even with this proviso, there were those who argued that the BBC's reporting was tardy, albeit because of the policies and predilections of the Ministry of Information and other ministries. However, for most people listening to the radio it still gave the impression that the Germans were more on the ball. It was just the kind of thing that drove people to listen to Haw-Haw's ramblings. Given the pace of war, and the lines of communications, it was of course not possible for the newspapers to keep up with it all, or be first with anything. Back in October 1940 there had been discussion among BBC management that senior politicians and civil servants lacked confidence in the Corporation's news services. A.P. Ryan, the BBC's Home Policy Adviser, felt that instead of looking upon the Corporation as part of the problem, it should be looked upon as a definite part of the solution. He described an efficient news service as 'a fourth arm of this war'.

Not that the situation showed any rapid signs of improvement. A British Cabinet reshuffle in June was announced on German radio before the BBC was able to broadcast the news. The Corporation's management saw this as yet another sop to the newspaper barons who complained to anyone in government who would listen about the radio's ability consistently to 'get one up on them'. The newspapers had just not cottoned on to the new world order, and of course had no control over what foreign broadcasters had to say. According to Reith's diary, Churchill was among those with sympathy for the newspaper barons; he had been heard to give voice to the 'enemy within the gates' camp when talking of the BBC. But the power of radio was moving ever onwards and by the summer of 1941 the BBC was relaying every news bulletin, apart from the midnight news, on the Forces Programmes. It gave radio yet another advantage over the press in being, at least in Britain, first with the news. And just to be certain of their superiority the BBC gave regular news bulletins in both Welsh and Gaelic.

The continued expansion of the BBC's foreign and overseas services meant that space in Broadcasting House was at a premium, meaning that people had to work in the corridors, as well as in offices. This was despite the fact that around 60 per cent of the BBC's employees were based outside London; almost half of these were in Evesham, and a quarter in Bristol. During 1941 eight more foreign language broadcasts were added and many more hours of extra airtime were added to the majority of the existing language services. The result of all this expansion meant that the BBC during 1941 increased overseas output by close to 60 per cent. To ease the burden on space at Broadcasting House the studio at Maida Vale was being used for some of the foreign language broadcasts; in April a member of the German Service was killed when the North London studios took a direct hit. Another reduction in the pressures on space came in March when the majority of overseas services moved to Bush House in the Aldwych. Reception for listeners at home was also improved by the addition of a new wavelength – 203.5 metres. Wartime restrictions, and particularly those that meant German bombers could use the BBC's transmitters as direction finders, did not prevent the push for technical improvements. In early 1942 the BBC acknowledged that the war had helped them: 'In certain respects the war seems actually to have quickened the development of broadcasting in sound and to have enriched its content.'

One of the most interesting developments in 1941 on the BBC's European services was the 'V' campaign. In January 1941 Victor de Laveleye, a broadcaster with the BBC's Belgian language service, had a bright idea. 'I suggest that you should use the letter V as a rallying sign, because V stands for "victoire" in French and "Vryheid" in Flemish.' So began one of the most remembered ideas of the war – partly, of course, because Churchill was quick to adopt the idea and signal it with his fingers. Even before Churchill took up the idea of using the letter, Vs were appearing on walls and buildings in northern France as a sign of resistance – despite the best efforts of the police to remove them.

Soon after de Laveleye's broadcast someone noticed that the letter V in Morse code was represented by three dots and a dash – exactly the same rhythmic pattern as the opening bars of Beethoven's Fifth Symphony. It was taken up as an audio symbol of defiance, which apart from irritating the Germans also sounded great on the radio, car horns, blacksmiths beating an anvil, kids whistling, trains hooting and even audiences clapping.

> You wear no uniforms, and your weapons are different from ours, but they're not less deadly. The fact that you wear no uniforms is your strength. The Nazi official and the German soldier don't know you but they fear you. The night is your friend, the V is your sign . . . [opening bars of Beethoven's Fifth Symphony]
>
> *Colonel Britton, BBC, 27 June 1941*

'Colonel Britton's' broadcast took the campaign to a more prominent position with English-speaking listeners throughout Europe. As the campaign developed over the summer Churchill and other leaders from European countries spoke out in support of the idea. In one broadcast on 18 July 1941 Colonel Britton told listeners that in two days it was to be 'Europe's mobilisation against the Germans'.

This was too much for the German Propaganda Ministry and in retaliation they announced that in fact the V stood for 'Viktoria' in German – so there! It was about all they could do to counter the campaign, and in truth probably took some of the sting out of it. It wasn't something that could ultimately be delivered upon and so – apart from annoying the Germans – it could only really give people in Europe a feeling that there was some hope, although at this point the prospect of liberation was a fairly long way away. The 'Colonel' continued to broadcast until May 1942, when the Political Warfare Executive decided his activities ran counter to what they saw as their more sophisticated anti-Nazi activities – and they were right.

Douglas Ritchie, a 36-year-old BBC Assistant News Editor, was chosen to be the character of 'Colonel Britton'. During an ARP exercise in Edinburgh in September 1941 a piece of paper was found in the street and handed into the Regional Commissioner's office. Only one piece refers to the V campaign, but it's a brilliant example of humour in wartime. In fact, what was Spike Milligan doing in Edinburgh? He was supposed to be training in Kent.

ADVICE TO THE BRITISH PEOPLE

GERMANY'S EIGHT-POINT PROGRAMME

(1) In 1939 there were 8,000 British ships on the high seas. Since then, 22,000 British ships have been sunk by German troops and aircraft.

(2) We Germans know that the people of Britain are starving. You have no bread, no fats, no potatoes. As we sit each night before our nourishing meal of cornhusks and swill, we know that victory is near.

(3) The mighty German Army is fighting unceasingly an offensive war. Our soldiers are offensive. Our airmen are offensive. It is the duty of all who serve our beloved Führer to be offensive.

(4) All the World knows how the brutal British police have terrified the dejected dupes of Churchill. How different is the position of the Gestapo in the countries under the protection of Germany! In every part of Europe they tell us, 'We think your policemen are wonderful!'

(5) It is well known that Britain has no petrol left with which to run motorcars and buses. Instead, three Italian prisoners of war are yoked underneath every omnibus on the British highways. Thus these vehicles reverse readily. This will assuredly be avenged.

(6) Britain boasts that she always 'wins the last battle'. In this war there will be no last battle. In his divine wisdom our Führer will declare the war at an end when the second-last battle has been fought.

(7) Colonel Britton claims that the V for Victory campaign is his. He is wrong. Ve invented it, and ven the var is over ve will make you vash it off your valls.

(8) Our Führer's patience is exhausted. So are we. What is Britain's answer?

PEACE OFFERING?

One of the most unusual questions posed during 1941 was: just why did Rudolf Hess fly to Britain? He was a trusted friend of Hitler, which made it all the more incredible that he should take it upon himself to fly to Britain to negotiate a peace that no one in the German High Command wanted. He parachuted to the ground in South Lanarkshire, Scotland, on 10 May 1941 and within a couple of days the ploughman to whom Hess surrendered was on the BBC speaking about the incident.

I was preparing to go to bed shortly after eleven on Saturday night, when I heard the noise of a plane – the noise was loud – circling overhead. Putting out the lights I glanced out of the window and saw a parachute descending. Just then something crashed, and later I found out that the plane had struck the top of a hedge and bumped into a field, bursting into flames near the end of a field adjoining another farm . . .

. . . I went out to get a weapon and the first thing I picked up was a hayfork. The parachute had reached the ground about 50 yards from our back door, and the airman was on the ground. I went up to him cautiously, but he said that he had no weapon.

The airman had hurt his leg, and was trying to get out of his parachute harness. I helped him to the cottage, and my mother, who was standing at the door, helped him in. We put him in an armchair, and he kept on thanking us for our goodness. My mother made tea, but he declined it, saying that he did not drink tea so late at night, but would enjoy a glass of water . . .

. . . I told him I would have to get the police, and he agreed that would be best. Then he took out his pocket book and showed us a picture of a boy of about three or four. 'That is my son,' he said. 'I do not know when I will see him again.'

The officer gave his name as Albert Horn, and said he had taken a plane from Munich about four hours earlier. He was looking tired, and said his ankle pained him but otherwise was all right.

David McLean, BBC, 13 May 1941

For the government Hess's arrival raised the potential of a propaganda coup and the BBC's German Service, known as BBCD, was set to work almost immediately on maximising the opportunity. Up to ten times each day the BBCD carried reports detailing the arrival of Hess. As a BBC spokesman put it: '[we are] emphasising that he is talking freely and writing too – anything to make them nervous'. He added that 'Treat 'em rough' had become the BBC motto for 'Nazidom' – one of Churchill's favourite words to describe Hitler, his henchman and their philosophies.

Now that the first surprise of the arrival of Hess has worn off, it is possible soberly to consider the implications. Nothing precise will be known until Mr Churchill divulges as much as he thinks fit to divulge of what Rudolf Hess has been saying and writing in the military hospital where he now lies.

But, already, certain considerations should be borne in mind. First, consider the simple fact that the third man in the Nazi hierarchy leaves his Fatherland and goes, not to neutral Switzerland or Sweden, but to England. He does this, not on some whim but after careful consideration. The preparations for the flight from Augsburg to Scotland could not be made in a day or carried out by a single individual.

Secondly, Rudolf Hess was not a mere politician or administrator, but the most intimate friend of the Führer, who knows him in his every mood and has shared his most private thoughts from the first days of the NSDAP.

What can have made such a man desert that leader and betray the cause of National Socialism? What facts did he know which led him to break the friendship of a life-time and to endanger the structure of the Reich he had helped to build . . .

BBC German Service, 13 May 1941

Of course nothing came of either Hess's flight to Britain, or of the BBC's German Service's propaganda. Rudolf Hess was called insane by Hitler and the German propaganda machine, which did not prevent him from being tried for war crimes at Nuremberg. Hess was sentenced to life imprisonment, which literally meant what it said. Rudolf Hess committed suicide in Berlin's Spandau Jail aged ninety-two in 1987.

Not that his death put an end to the conspiracy theories as to why he was in Britain. Conspiracy theorists have said that he was here as the result of an MI5 invitation, although recent papers that have been released seem to put an end to that particular notion. However, others have tried to implicate the Duke of Kent, who died in a plane crash in Scotland during the war, as well as the King and Queen, in some kind of Machiavellian plot.

THE UNSINKABLE

Two weeks before the 'Hess Incident' Churchill, in a broadcast on the BBC, warned that the war was 'to become very fierce, varied and widespread'. He also counselled that it might spread 'eastwards to Turkey and Russia'. The Prime Minister finished his speech, heard by 77 per cent of the adult population of Britain, with some hard-hitting words, and one line, though not often quoted, that is pure Churchillian brilliance (underlined).

It is worthwhile therefore to take a look on both sides of the ocean at the forces which are facing each other in this awful struggle, from which there can be no drawing back. No prudent and far-seeing man can doubt that the eventual and total defeat of Hitler and Mussolini is certain, in view of the respective resolves of the British and American democracies. There are less than seventy million malignant Huns – some of them are curable and others killable – many of whom are already engaged in holding down Austrians,

Czechs, Poles, French, and the many other ancient races they now bully and pillage. The peoples of the British Empire and of the United States number nearly two hundred millions in their homelands and in the British Dominions alone.

They possess the unchallengeable command of the oceans, and will soon obtain decisive superiority in the air. They have more wealth, more technical resources, and they make more steel, than the whole of the rest of the world put together.

When we face with a steady eye the difficulties, which lie before us, we may derive new confidence from remembering those we have already overcome. Nothing that is happening now is comparable in gravity with the dangers through which we passed last year. Nothing that can happen in the East is comparable with what is happening in the West.

Last time I spoke to you I quoted the lines of Longfellow, which President Roosevelt had written out for me in his own hand. I have some other lines which are less well known but which seem apt and appropriate to our fortunes tonight, and I believe they will be so judged wherever the English language is spoken or the flag of freedom flies:

> For while the tired waves, vainly breaking,
> Seem here no painful inch to gain,
> Far back, through creeks and inlets making,
> Comes silent, flooding in, the main.
>
> And not by eastern windows only,
> When daylight comes, comes in the light;
> In front the sun climbs slow, how slowly,
> But westward look, the land is bright.

Winston Churchill, BBC, 27 April 1941

The words that Churchill used to finish his talk are from the English Victorian Arthur Hugh Clough's poem – 'Say not the struggle naught availeth'. Given the context of Churchill's speech it is interesting that Clough and his parents had moved to America when he was just three years old, although his parents brought him back to be educated at Rugby School when he was ten years old.

Clough stayed on in England before travelling to France in support of the revolution of 1848. Much of his later life was spent helping his wife's cousin, Florence Nightingale, in her efforts to reform hospitals and the nursing profession.

SUNK, THE *BISMARCK*

Fine words from Churchill on Britain's command of the high seas could not prevent HMS *Hood* from being sunk by the German battleship *Bismarck* less than a month later at what has become known as the Battle of Denmark Strait. The *Hood* opened fire on the *Bismarck* at 5.52 a.m. on 24 May; eight minutes later a gigantic explosion ripped the *Hood* in two and the British battlecruiser sank in less than two minutes. Only three men survived, while more than 1,400 died, including the former BBC correspondent Bernhard Stubbs, who had become a naval intelligence officer after leaving his job on radio. HMS *Prince of Wales* was also involved in the battle and was fortunate not to have met a similar fate to the *Hood*. However, the *Bismarck* was also damaged in the battle; she took a shell in a position that caused water to mix with the fuel, which impaired the battleship's performance.

In the evening after the sinking of the *Hood*, Swordfish torpedo bombers attacked the *Bismarck* but did little other than superficial damage. Having lost track of the German ship for some time she was eventually relocated, another Swordfish attack was mounted and one of their torpedoes damaged the rudder of the battleship, rendering her barely manoeuvrable. After the *Bismarck* was harried by British destroyers and torpedo attack, two Royal Navy battleships, HMS *Rodney* and HMS *King George V*, closed in on the German vessel. The two battleships, along with a number of destroyers, did tremendous damage to the *Bismarck*, rendering her little more than a floating wreck, unable to return fire or manoeuvre. With the Royal Navy ships running short of fuel they were ordered to return to their bases and the cruiser HMS *Dorsetshire* remained to try to sink the German raider. In the end rather than be sunk, or captured, the *Bismarck* was scuttled. Only 115 German sailors survived and over 2,200 were lost when the 'unsinkable' went down. More sailors may have been rescued had the *Dorsetshire* not been chased off by a German U-boat.

The First Lord of the Admiralty, Mr A.V. Alexander, addressed an ENSA luncheon in London.

I feel I am speaking on a rather important occasion. Members of the ENSA have entertained in the last few months officers and gallant men of the *Hood*. You will feel as I feel about their last great gallant sacrifice. But the British navy has in all its decades of history taken good care to avenge happenings of that kind, and that is why this morning at eleven o'clock the *Bismarck* was sunk. [Long and loud cheering] As Hitler has followed in the whole of his ill-gotten reign the precepts of Bismarck let us hope that destruction of the *Bismarck* – Germany's latest and greatest ship – marks the beginning of the end of his reign.

A.V. Alexander, BBC, 27 May 1941

Alexander was speaking of Otto von Bismarck, nicknamed the Iron Chancellor, who was the first to bring together a collection of loose states as a unified and powerful Germany.

SUITS YOU!

Within a couple of days of the news of the *Bismarck*'s sinking there was news on the Home Front that had a far greater, and more personal, effect on everyone in Britain; the bad news was spelt out by the President of the Board of Trade, Oliver Lyttelton.

> I want to talk to you this morning about clothes and boots and shoes. I have today made an order, which starts rationing these things, and you will see the details in the morning's newspapers. Coupons will now have to be given up when buying clothing in just the same way as when buying food. Everyone will have 66 clothing coupons to last them for twelve months. The first 26 coupons are in your present ration book. We all know that children grow out of their clothes, therefore they will be given more for their coupons than grown up people . . . I know everyone in these islands is prepared to undergo inconveniences and hardships if they are convinced of two things – that it is necessary and that it is fair. I want to assure you that the rationing of clothing is both.

Oliver Lyttelton, BBC, 1 June 1941

Lyttelton went on to explain what the allowance would buy, and the newspapers rapidly got to work telling both men and woman how their wardrobe could be enlarged in any one year. '26 COUPONS FOR MAN'S SUIT' announced one headline. In broad terms eleven coupons were required for a new woollen dress, while a pair of man's trousers or a shirt were eight, a pair of stockings two and socks three. All in all it meant that a woman could buy two dresses; one woollen and one silk for eighteen coupons, a skirt and a jumper for a further twelve coupons, a pair of pyjamas, and still have twenty-eight left for a year's supply of underclothes, stockings and shoes. As with any kind of system there were those that found ways around it. It was reported that in the first year of the scheme nearly 800,000 people claimed to have lost their ration books and were issued with new ones. It's even been claimed that some people adopted dual identities to get extra rations. I'm sure this was more prevalent among those who perhaps wanted extra to eat. I know in my own mother's house that she stopped taking sugar in her tea, and her mother stopped taking milk, in order that my grandfather could have what he thought were the prerequisite amounts of both. In any event black-marketeers found all sorts of ways to profit from rationing – and of course there was no shortage of customers. Such were the puzzles associated with rationing that there were many more broadcasts during 1941 in which Board of Trade officials attempted to explain the complexities.

EASTERN PROMISE

Three weeks later a major shift in the balance of the war took place, and it provided the BBC with a major coup. The newspapers had already gone to press on the morning of 22 June when monitors in London picked up a broadcast from Berlin by the Propaganda Minister, Dr Goebbels. He read a proclamation from Hitler to the German people in which were recited a number of complaints against Russia. Goebbels announced that Operation Barbarossa, an attack against Russia, was proceeding along a 1,700-mile front that stretched from Finland to the Baltic States and as far south as the southern Ukraine on the Black Sea. The BBC immediately ran with the details of Hitler's proclamation:

The greatest march the world has ever seen is taking place. German troops, together with Finnish divisions and the Conquerors of Norway, are marching together from East Prussia to the Carpathians. German and Rumanian forces extend from the Carpathians to the south. This front is not only a protection of single countries, but of Europe . . .

. . . For over 20 years – the Jewish Bolshevists wanted to set the whole of Europe on fire. It was not Germany who threatened Russia but the Jews, in their centre at Moscow, who wanted to spread their domination not merely in a spiritual but also in a military sense . . . Bolshevism is opposed to National Socialism in deadly enmity. Bolshevist Moscow desires to stab National Socialist Germany in the back while she is engaged in a struggle for her existence . . . In the coming struggle, the German people are fully aware that they are called upon not only to defend their native land, but to save the entire civilised world from the deadly dangers of Bolshevism, and to clear the way for social progress in Europe.

BBC News, 22 June 1941

By mid-morning in Moscow, shortly after Hitler's rhetoric had been aired, it was the turn of the Chancellor's former guest, the Soviet Vice-Premier and Foreign Commissar, Molotov, to have his say on Russian radio.

> This is not the first time that our country has had to deal with an arrogant invading foe. When Napoleon invaded Russia our country answered with the nationalist war, and Napoleon was beaten and met his doom. The same thing will happen to the arrogant Hitler, who has started a new attack on our country.
>
> M. Molotov, Moscow radio, 22 June 1941

At 9 p.m. that evening Churchill announced in his broadcast that 'England [sic] would make common cause with the Soviet Union'. Throughout the war on the Eastern Front the BBC continued to have a distinct advantage over the newspapers. TASS, the Soviet news agency, issued communiqués at 7 a.m. London time, which meant that the daily papers were always a day behind with the news, although the evening papers did help redress the balance. Russia seemed to provide an intense fascination for some people in Britain, and the BBC satisfied their hunger for more information with programmes such as 'I Worked in a Soviet Factory' by Eric Godfrey, while Sir John Russell, the Director of the Rothamsted Agricultural Experiment Station, spoke about Russian agriculture. While the BBC as a whole was happy to be beating the newspapers to the details of the war in Russia the newsreaders were not so happy. It's all very well reading complicated Russian names in print but many of them complained at having to say complex tongue-twisting names when communiqués were sometimes not received in the newsroom until the last minute.

SHUFFLE OFF TO NEWFOUNDLAND

The Cabinet reshuffle earlier in the summer that the BBC had failed to be the first to reveal included the appointment of Churchill's friend, Brendan Bracken, as Minister of Information. This appointment marked a positive shift in the BBC's position and a general improvement in their access to government at the highest level. The BBC found that the trust extended by the Cabinet improved, and in return there was a general upturn in the quality of the news reporting. A wind of change had begun blowing through Broadcasting House as early as 3 February, when Ivone Kirkpatrick was appointed Foreign Policy Adviser to the BBC. Kirkpatrick, a career diplomat, was both suave and at the same time a fighter, making him a tough man to do battle with. He mirrored the role of A.P. Ryan. Both men would be pivotal in the improvement of the Corporation;

simultaneously both men also worked for the Ministry of Information. As part of the Cabinet reshuffle Harold Nicolson lost his job at the Ministry of Information, which was also good news for the BBC. He was appointed to the BBC's Board of Governors in July and his relationship with Brendan Bracken, the new minister, and his contacts, helped improve the Corporation's standing. Nicolson joined other new appointees – Lady Violet Bonham Carter, Sir Ian Fraser MP, Dr J.J. Mallon and Mr Arthur Mann (a former editor of the *Yorkshire Post*) – all of whom had recently been added to the two-man board of C.H.G. Millis and Sir Alan Powell, the Chairman.

The 40-year-old Bracken, born in Kilmallock, Ireland, had helped Churchill in his attempt to return to Parliament in 1923 before he worked in publishing, becoming managing director of the *Economist*, among his other appointments. Bracken became an MP at 28 and Churchill's Parliamentary Private Secretary when war broke out. It would be unfair to single out patronage as the sole reason for his success; his achievements as Minister of Information owe something to his background as well as his innate talents. His understanding of both business and the media provided a more stable environment in which the BBC could function, both as an instrument of government and at the same time upholding the principles of its charter. His relationship with the governors, and especially Nicolson, played a key role in improving quality of output, as well as the quality and content of the input from the Ministry.

Besides reshuffles in the BBC hierarchy some of the evacuated departments, which had originally gone to Bristol, were moved to Bedford. Among them was the Religious Unit, which prompted an amusing headline in a Bristol newspaper – 'Religion leaving Bristol'.

During the course of the summer there was activity on all manner of fronts. On 13 July there were simultaneous broadcasts from London and Moscow announcing the signature of the Anglo-Russian agreement. The Prime Minister was also back on the radio talking about the need for even greater levels of wartime production; his speech was against a background of continuing heavy losses for the Merchant Navy on the transatlantic conveys. But as so often was the way in the war there was a lucky, or perhaps more aptly a timely, break, given the immense efforts of the code-breakers at Bletchley Park. They managed to crack the German encrypted messages sent to their U-boats on the Enigma machine; this allowed Allied convoys to be routed further away from the submarine menace and put on safer routes.

Four days after Churchill's broadcast a train left Marylebone station and went via Wendover, the station nearest to Chequers, where the Prime Minister got on board to join some of his most trusted advisers. Among the party of senior military and political aides on board was Major Ian Jacob, an Assistant Secretary to the War Cabinet; he would become Director General of the BBC from 1952 to 1959. Early the next morning the travellers arrived in Thurso in the north of Scotland; from here they transferred to Scapa Flow, where the party boarded HMS *Prince of Wales*, only recently repaired following its engagement with the *Bismarck*. It was the start of Churchill's journey to meet President Roosevelt. Besides the men, and all their luggage, there were forty-five brace of grouse, which Churchill was taking as a gift for the US President. Five days later after an uneventful transatlantic crossing, during which the party kept up with events listening to Bruce Belfrage and others reading the news on the BBC, Churchill met Roosevelt on board the USS *Augusta* in Little Placentia Bay, Newfoundland, on 9 August. Their talks continued on both ships, for several days, with the result of their meetings being announced on the BBC on 14 August by the Lord Privy Seal, Clement Attlee. He revealed to the world the terms of the historic Atlantic Charter:

I have come to tell you about an important meeting between the President of the United States and the Prime Minister which has taken place, and of a declaration of principles which has been agreed between them – Here is the statement which they have agreed to issue.

The President of the United States and the Prime Minister, Mr Churchill, representing His Majesty's Government in the United Kingdom, have met at sea. They have been accompanied by officials of their two Governments including high-ranking officers of their military, naval, and air services. The whole problem of supply of munitions of war, as provided by the 'Lease-and-Lend' Act, for the armed forces in the United States and for those countries actively engaged in resisting aggression has been further examined. Lord Beaverbrook, Minister of Supply of the British Government, joined in these conferences. He is going to Washington to discuss further details with appropriate officials of the United States Government. These conferences will also cover the supply problem of the Soviet Union.

The President and the Prime Minister had several conferences. They have considered the dangers to world civilisation arising from the policy of military domination by conquest upon which the Hitlerite Government of Germany and other Governments associated therewith have embarked, and have made clear the steps which their countries are respectively taking for their safety in facing these dangers. They have agreed:

The President of the United States and the Prime Minister, Mr Churchill, representing His Majesty's Government in the United Kingdom, being met

1. Broadcasting House became the BBC's headquarters on 15 May 1932. *(J.S. Havers)*

2. Former BBC Director General John Reith was appointed Minister of Information in 1940, much to his annoyance – he was hoping for greater things. *(Getty Images)*

3. Bush House. *(Author's Collection)*

4. With so many men being called up into the Armed Forces many more women were recruited by the BBC to do jobs that had often been seen as a male preserve. This young woman is working in the BBC's Engineering Division early in the war. *(BBC)*

5. Alvar Lidell came to epitomise the quintessential BBC 'voice'. He was a master of pronunciation; as one observer said, 'The Queen's English was never more safe than in the hands of, and at the microphone of, Alvar Lidell.' *(Getty Images)*

6. Edward Ward broadcasts an appeal for Aid for Finland on 31 March 1940 after his return to London. *(BBC)*

7. Although Wilfred Pickles, a 37-year-old Yorkshireman, was born in Halifax, in truth his 'news reading' accent was barely any different from the standard BBC English of his colleagues. *(Author's Collection)*

8. The Oxford-educated Freddie Grisewood, who had THE most impeccable BBC voice, went on to chair 'Any Questions?' from 1948. *(BBC)*

9. On 13 July 1940 Frank Phillips became the first reader to identify himself on air. *(BBC)*

10. Hard at it in the BBC newsroom. *(BBC)*

11. Tommy Handley. *(J.S. Havers)*

12. Sandy Macpherson at his organ. *(BBC)*

13. The BBC Handbook for 1940, published in early 1941. *(Author's Collection)*

14. *News Review*, which described itself as the first British news magazine. *(Author's Collection)*

15. J.B. Priestley, together with Leslie Howard, during his first broadcast on 'Britain Speaks', 17 July 1940. *(BBC)*

16. Charles Gardner commentates on the 'big fight' over the English Channel, 14 July 1940. *(BBC)*

17. Daily dogfights were a source of fascination for the British public. *(Imperial War Museum HU 810)*

18. St Paul's Cathedral in all its beauty, despite being surrounded by the destruction of the Blitz. *(Imperial War Museum HU 36220A)*

19. A staged photo opportunity to show the Home Guard in action against the Luftwaffe. *(Author's Collection)*

20. US broadcaster Ed Murrow. *(CORBIS)*

21. *Above:* On the right is S. Hillelson, Director of the BBC Near East Service; next to him is Mojtaba Minovi, who broadcast on the Iranian Service.

22. General Charles de Gaulle speaks to France on the BBC's European Service in a broadcast personally authorised by Churchill. *(BBC)*

23. Reg Pidsley (left) and Wynford Vaughan-Thomas just before take off in F-for-Freddie, 3 September 1943. (*Rob Clayton*)

24. A B-24 Liberator returning to its base in England after a raid. (*Getty Images*)

These three photographs were found in a camera of a wrecked B-26 Marauder near Great Dunmow in Essex.

25. Taken from the cockpit, this photograph shows two B-26s, one of which has just released its bombs. *(J.S. Havers)*

26. Nose and port engine of a B-26 named 'Weasel'. The nose-wheel has the legend 'The Lyon's Den'. The name of the pilot painted under the cockpit is D.W. Allen. *(J.S. Havers)*

27. Cockpit of a B-26 flying alongside another from 449 Bomb Squadron, named 'Truman Committee'. This aircraft was damaged beyond repair in an emergency landing on 27 May 1944 at Friston Airfield, Sussex, following battle damage over the target area of the Seine bridges. *(J.S. Havers)*

28. Wynford Vaughan-Thomas with his recording truck in Italy, January 1944. *(BBC)*

29. Field Marshal Montgomery is shown a midget recorder by Mr H. Bishop, the BBC's Controller of Engineering, at Broadcasting House shortly before D-Day. *(BBC)*

30. Frank Gillard using a midget recorder. *(BBC)*

31. Stanley Maxted and Guy Byam of the BBC, September 1944. *(BBC)*

32. Richard Dimbleby (right) broadcasting from a glider tug on 24 March 1945. *(BBC)*

33. Chester Wilmot (right) with engineer Harvey Sarney using a midget recorder on the banks of the River Elbe. *(BBC)*

together, deem it right to make known certain common principles in the national policies of their respective countries on which they base their hopes for a better future for the world.

First, their countries seek no aggrandisement, territorial or other.

Second, they desire to see no territorial changes that do not accord with the freely expressed wishes of the peoples concerned.

Third, they respect the right of all peoples to choose the form of Government under which they will live; and they wish to see sovereign rights and self-government restored to those who have been forcibly deprived of them.

Fourth, they will endeavour with due respect for their existing obligations, to further enjoyment by all States, great or small, victor or vanquished, or access, on equal terms, to the trade and to the raw materials of the world which are needed for their economic prosperity.

Fifth, they desire to bring about the fullest collaboration between all nations in the economic field, with the object of securing for all improved labour standards, economic advancement, and social security.

Sixth, after the final destruction of Nazi tyranny, they hope to see established a peace which will afford to all nations the means of dwelling in safety within their own boundaries, and which will afford assurance that all the men in all the lands may live out their lives in freedom from fear and want.

Seventh, such a peace should enable all men to traverse the high seas and oceans without hindrances.

Eighth, they believe all of the nations of the world, for realistic as well as spiritual reasons, must come to the abandonment of the use of force. Since no future peace can be maintained if land, sea, or air armaments continue to be employed by nations which threaten, or may threaten, aggression outside of their frontiers, they believe, pending the establishment of a wider and permanent system of general security, that the disarmament of such nations is essential. They will likewise aid and encourage all other practicable measures which will lighten for peace-loving peoples the crushing burden of armament.

Clement Attlee, Deputy Prime Minister, BBC, 3 p.m.,
14 August 1941

People's suspicions had been aroused when the heads of their respective governments had 'disappeared' from public view, despite President Roosevelt issuing some false statements about his fishing trip on his yacht *Potomac*. Just a couple of days into the transatlantic crossing Lisbon radio reported that a meeting was taking place, somewhere in the western hemisphere, between the two men. Among those back in Britain who knew exactly where Churchill was, was his wife, Clementine. In a letter to her husband written at Champneys, near Tring in Hertfordshire, she said, 'This morning my wireless told me that at 3 o'clock Mr Attlee would be making a statement on behalf of the Government and that simultaneously the same announcement would be given out from the White House in Washington – Great excitement and anticipation. It cannot be a declaration of war by America? Because the President cannot do that without Congress.' Clementine finished her letter at 3.20 p.m. after hearing the broadcast, saying simply: 'I have just heard your joint declaration. It is grand, God bless you.'

Millions of radio listeners in Britain, as well as on the European and Overseas Services of the BBC, shared Clementine's sentiments. Attlee's broadcast heralded what became known as 'a blueprint for a better world'. In respect of Britain's ability to fight more effectively against Hitler, and support the Russian war effort, it was a pivotal moment in the war. Ten days later, on his return to Britain, the Prime Minister spoke on the Home Programme about his journey to meet the President, and in more detail about what the North Atlantic charter meant to Britain, and the Allies. Churchill finished his speech by briefly talking of the journey home.

And when we were right out in mid-passage one afternoon a noble sight broke on the view. We overtook one of the convoys which carry the munitions and supplies of the New World to sustain the champions of freedom in the Old. The whole broad horizon seemed filled with ships; seventy or eighty ships of all kinds and sizes, arrayed in fourteen lines, each of which could have been drawn with a ruler, hardly a wisp of smoke, not a straggler, but all bristling with cannons and other precautions on which I will not dwell, and all surrounded by their British escorting vessels, while overhead the far-ranging Catalina air-boats soared – vigilant, protecting eagles in the sky. Then I felt that, hard and terrible and long drawn-out as this struggle may be, we shall not be denied the strength to do our duty to the end.

Winston Churchill, BBC, 24 August 1941

ATLANTIC BATTLES

The Battle of the Atlantic, involving the merchant ships, their escorts and the German U-boats, was the longest running engagement of the Second World War. In all 3,500 merchant ships were destroyed, along with over 170 warships; in excess of 30,000 Allied seamen were lost. The German losses were also very large: 700 U-boats were sunk, with over 7,500 of their crew killed. Two months after Churchill's broadcast on his return from meeting Roosevelt the first US Navy ship escorting a convoy, the destroyer USS *Reuben James*, was sunk by a U-boat; 100 US sailors died. It was the first loss for the US Navy in America's war with Germany; even before war was declared.

> We're now mixed up in, and I think I'm right in saying, the first attack on a convoy which has actually been recorded at sea. We've been attacked by bombers; there have been two runs over the convoy as yet. So all the ships have just been blazing off like mad. They've dropped a stick of bombs but no damage has been done. I have taken up a position by the gun in the stern, it's a twelve-pounder – and I'm right amidst the gun crew now, there are shells all around me too, and more are being handed up from the magazine below – I expect you can hear them. Wait a minute, here he comes, he's on our port quarter, not much more than 500 feet up, just about abreast of us now. There are tracer bullets bursting all around him, he's passing astern but you can still follow him through this light cloud, and there go his bombs. There's a stick of four of them hanging in the air a moment, they are dropping down over the convoy – wait a minute, he's missed. Columns of water spouting up but it looks as though we're all right, just a faint smell of gunpowder drifting across the water but we won't worry about that. He's missed and everything's OK.
>
> *Robert Dougall, BBC, 11 November 1941*

The Battle of the Atlantic has been characterised as U-boats attacking the convoys and it has often been forgotten that aircraft of both sides played an important part in its outcome. As early as August 1940 the four-engined, five-man Focke-Wulf 200C Kondor long-range bombers of the Luftwaffe began operating from France, and later from Norway as well, in support of the U-boats' attacks on the convoys. The Kondors would patrol off the coast of Ireland acting as spotter aircraft for the U-boats, as well as attacking convoys when the opportunity arose. They continued to be a threat until convoy escorts began carrying aircraft to act as a deterrent. The Kondors were essentially a modified pre-war airliner, having been the first plane to fly non-stop from Berlin to New York in the summer of 1938, and taking over a day to do so!

The decision to put Hurricanes, or 'Hurricats', as they became known, on board ships was taken in late 1940 and points up the extent to which the Kondors were more than just a nuisance. The plan was expedited by Winston Churchill, who, on 6 March 1941, issued a directive stating: 'Extreme priority will be given to fitting out ships to catapult, or otherwise launch, fighter aircraft against bombers attacking our shipping.' Launching the Hurricats from a merchant ship, or CAM (Catapult Aircraft Merchantman), with the aid of a rocket was both hazardous and expensive. Once launched there was nowhere for the aircraft to land and so the pilot either ditched his aircraft on the sea, or baled out; where he was usually picked up by an escort ship. The tactical trick was to wait until an approaching Kondor was sighted before launching the aircraft, a ploy that failed on the very first CAM ship, the SS *Michael E*; a U-boat sank it in May 1941 before the merchantman had time to launch its aircraft. Despite this setback, sixty pilots were trained and three months later a Hurricat from HMS *Mapplin* had its first 'kill' when a Kondor was shot down on 3 August 1941. The commander of the first squadron to shoot down an enemy aircraft with a Hurricat was Lieutenant-Commander P.H. Havers (no relation). He was killed in March 1943 when HMS *Dasher*, a converted American aircraft carrier, blew up in the Clyde Estuary and around 400 men were lost. Ironically aircraft carriers were usually a far better option for seaborne fighter operations.

GO EAST YOUNG MEN

The question of whether or not America would enter the war had largely been answered, and to some extent the time of its entry, given the physical support provided by the US Navy to the North Atlantic convoys. Bound up with the success of the North Atlantic convoy system was the war on the Eastern Front, a situation that was uppermost in many people's minds during the late summer, autumn and early winter of 1941. If Russia was overrun by Hitler's Blitzkrieg then the dangers facing Britain, and the rest of the world, from the Axis alliance between Germany, Italy, and Japan were very grave indeed.

Two broadcasts, not given in late 1941, but in 1943, illustrate the unusual nature of the fighting in Russia; they also provide two conflicting views of its likely outcome.

I had the luck to be in Russia as administrative officer – Wing Adjutant – with the chaps of the Fighter Wing of English Hurricanes that went out to Murmansk in the late summer of 1941. We were the first English contingent there in the first few weeks and months of Russia becoming our ally. We saw – in full measure – Russia at war. We lived and worked on an Arctic aerodrome with our Soviet opposite numbers – pilots, ground crews, senior officers, administrative personnel – each to each. We got to know them through and through, and believed in them, and trusted them, and liked them; and they got to know us, in those months, and they got to believe in us, and trust us – and I sincerely think, to like us, too.

I remember first the impression on landing, of welcome and co-operation. Curious memories mix together – the memory of one of our airmen having a tunic button sewn on by a Russian hospital nurse from a hospital train (with a couple of hundred Russians enthusiastically applauding). And the memory of the intensive and efficient arrangements made by high Soviet staff-officers to get us to our destination, from Archangel up to Murmansk, in destroyers, and cargo ships, and Russian trains. I remember a serious and solemn occasion at the end of our stay – when our pilots had shot down fifteen German aircraft for the loss of only one of our own, and had done forty escorts to Soviet bombers and we had never let them lose a single bomber. At the farewell luncheon-party, our own Wing-Commander got up and proposed and drank the health of Marshal Stalin – and the Russian General-of-Aviation who had commanded us all the time we were out there got up and proposed and drank the health of the King. I am not overstating this when I say that that was a serious and impressive moment. And I also remember the day when the same Russian General arrived for one of our operational conferences bringing with him a little baby reindeer, about two feet high, as a friendly and living testimonial of his regard for our Wing.

The Russians have a passionate enthusiasm for aviation. They would fly in any weather. And they worked up an extreme enthusiasm for the British game of darts once we had taught it them. They would throw the dart as though it were a harpoon, and the dartboard the body of a German.

I wish I could give you an idea of the tremendous sense of 'urgency' in wartime Russia. It impressed us, and shook us, and left something never to be forgotten in the memory. The Russian pilots gave our own pilots a series of parties, and nerve-shaking parties they were. Our own pilots gave the Russian pilots also some parties – and these were not bad parties either. And our senses of humour – British and Russian – turned out curiously the same. We had interpreters of course. But the pilots used to go and make diagrams in the snow. There were many lighter and off-the-record sides to the expedition. We'd laugh a lot but somehow we understood. But I still come back to that question of urgency. One day a little Soviet pilot – whom we knew well, and who had been to many of our parties – got into a fight with a couple of German machines. He shot down the first, and he rammed the second – and then, having baled out, he fought his two opponents on the ground; and killed them both – and then walked back, four days and four nights in the snow, with frost-bitten feet and his face slashed to pieces and then retired to hospital, where we went down to see him. This seemed to us not abnormal, but typical. It stood for so much that we had seen, with our own eyes, of the intensity with which Russia is taking the war. Kindness and courtesy to us as guests – certainly! Cordiality, and co-operation, and fun, and the endless excitement that aircrews always seem to find in one another's society. But, at the heart, steel – and black hatred of the Hun. They are in the war to the death – and it will be the death of their enemies. Our Wing is scattered now. Some of them are dead, for the RAF is always in continuous action. But the rest are left, believing a lot of good things about Russia, from our own personal knowledge and experience.

Flight Lieutenant Hubert Griffith, BBC, 7 November 1943

The Hurricanes were under the command of Wing Commander Ramsbottom-Isherwood, who reported to the local Russian commandant, Major-General Kuznetsov. The aircraft were based at Vaenga and ready for their first sortie on 11 September 1941. The idea was to train the Russians in preparation for an ongoing supply of Hurricanes for their air force; by war's end around 3,000 Hurricanes had been made available.

A month after the first action by the RAF Hurricanes in Murmansk there was a state of high excitement at the Propaganda Ministry in Berlin. Because the USA had still not officially entered the war Americans were still 'welcome' in the German capital, which is why Joseph Grigg, a United Press of America correspondent, was there. He, like everyone else who heard this information without the benefit of an opposing view, was concerned by what he heard.

On October 9th [1941], I was summoned by a phone call to a special press conference at the Propaganda Ministry in Berlin. The girl secretary in the Foreign Press Department said there was to be a statement by Dr Otto Dietrich, the Reich's Press Chief, better known to the foreign correspondents as 'Hitler's little Sir Echo'. She said Dietrich had just returned from Hitler's headquarters and that the conference would be historic. It was set for 12 noon, and I was warned not to be late.

At noon some 200 foreign correspondents were assembled in the great ornate Propaganda Ministry 'Theatre', crowded with expensive red plush chairs, and with an eight-feet-high map of Russia filling the stage. Behind the speaker's chair were grouped all Dr Dietrich's yes-men and stooges, resplendent in Nazi uniforms, pompous and self-important and smirking with anticipation at the news their boss was about to reveal to the world.

Just one half-hour late, Dr Dietrich bounced in, cocky and self-confident, flapping his right arm in an imitation of the salute Hitler uses at Nazi mass-meetings. The Nazi officials and Italians saluted and heiled. The rest of us just waited. Dr Dietrich is not the blonde Nordic giant type of Nazi. Actually, he is only a little man – about five foot three – with an ingratiating smile and cold, cynical eyes. Under Dr Goebbels his job is to run the whole tame Nazi press. He was wearing a grey uniform and high jackboots.

He opened with a long, tiresome tirade against the Allied leaders, whom he denounced as 'liars' and 'military illiterates'. The American and other neutral correspondents – Swedes and Swiss – began to wonder whether this wasn't going to be just another propaganda circus. I myself was beginning to think maybe I was wasting my time being there at all.

And then Dr Dietrich pulled out the rabbit he had been keeping in his hat to the very end. The great offensive, he announced, had resulted in the complete encirclement of Marshal Timoshenko's armies of some 60–70 divisions in two mighty rings before Moscow. I'll quote his exact words as I noted them down at the time:

'The entire Soviet front is smashed. With the destruction of Timoshenko's armies now proceeding, the last Soviet army group will be disposed of and wiped out. The campaign in the East', he shouted dramatically, 'is decided. Further developments will follow as we wish. With this last great blow we are dealing it, the Soviet Union is liquidated militarily. Gentlemen, I stake my professional reputation on this.'

The Nazi yes-men and the Italians leapt up, cheering and heiling, and scrambled to shake Dr Dietrich's hand. At the same time, the German radio began broadcasting with drums and trumpet fanfares a special communiqué telling the world the news Dr Dietrich had just told us. That afternoon and next morning the German papers came out with huge headlines splashed across their front pages proclaiming the military destruction of Russia.

Joseph Grigg, BBC, 9 October 1943

Following the news from the Eastern Front the BBC, like the newspapers, was quick to go on the counter-offensive, although it is clear from the tone of the news the following day that there is an element of hope in what is said, rather than a statement supported by irrefutable facts.

It has been authoritatively stated that the Germans are attacking towards Bzhev, north-west of Moscow, and are thereby extending the front along which the general offensive on Moscow is being massed to a total of 250 miles or more. German reports that 70 Russian divisions are encircled at Vyazma were described as preposterous. It was confirmed that the Germans have captured Melitopol, Berdyansk, and Mariupol on the southern front and it was added that possibly there is a considerable pocket of Russian troops encircled by the German advance from the north and along the Sea of Azov. North of Orel, the southern spearhead of the great pincer movement against Moscow has been held up. Above Vyazma, the northern claw of the German drive attempting to batter its way towards the railway town of Rhzev, about 130 miles west of Moscow, is suffering fearful losses. One sector alone cost the enemy 8,000 dead and 220 tanks in a five-day battle, while a German motorised unit routed in a counter-attack by General Lukin lost 4,000 men.

BBC News, 10 October 1941

TO HELMORE, AND BACK

Some of the very best talks during the first half of the war were given by a 47-year-old former First World War pilot on a series called 'Air Commentary'. The first of these was in early September 1941 and it, like most other talks, followed the 9 p.m. news. Group Captain William Helmore attracted large audiences with his easy and colourful style and in this first talk he looked at the situation in Russia, as well as telling the extraordinary story of a pilot's leg.

Nevertheless, at the beginning of this great third act the whole future of the war, whether by land, sea or air, is at this very moment balanced on a knife-edge of uncertainty, and on that knife-edge is poised the fate of our great ally, Russia. I cannot even start to comment on the air war without encountering the subject of Russia. It is in everybody's mind. Scarcely any two people meet at a street corner without mentioning it – wondering how we can aid Russia, and whether we are helping her enough and quickly enough.

From the start it was obvious that whatever we might want to do quickly – and for Heaven's sake and our own we wanted to do all we could – we were terribly impeded by geography. Land armies take time to move and assemble, whilst to move machinery and arms alone takes nearly as long. It was chiefly in the air that we could help most swiftly, and that is why for the past eleven weeks we have literally poured out our air forces on the job of harassing and distracting the enemy. Night after night, and day after day, in all weathers, our bomber sorties and fighter sweeps have been carried out against odds which have mounted with enemy resistance and with our increasing penetration into his territory.

Since 22 June, the day Hitler invaded Russia, eleven and a half weeks ago, we have more than doubled the weight of explosive dropped by our bombers on his territory as compared with the same period of eleven and a half weeks before that date. I give you these figures of the enormous spurt in our bombing effort in terms of weight because success in this grim commerce can obviously best be measured in terms of weight of goods delivered to the customer.

It must be remembered also in considering this swift doubling of our air attack that the hours of darkness during which our heaviest deliveries are made have been very short and to get these figures we have had to send out our roundsmen during most of the hours of daylight as well. It is the very daring of these daylight attacks which has sent a thrill through the hearts of Hitler's enslaved nations . . .

. . . On Sunday evening when I had begun to realise that in a few hours I must begin preparing for the ordeal of this commentary, I was standing in the garden of my house near London, watching our aircraft returning in the gathering dusk from their sweeps over occupied France. One or two squadrons had already passed overhead – they had re-formed after the unknowable experiences of their raid, and were flying wingtip to wingtip as if returning from a review. I had been wondering, in an analytical way, what were the prime essentials for success in this thing called air warfare.

Presently, a solitary machine, evidently detached from the main formation in some combat, came over almost at treetop level. A friend who was standing with me remarked: 'Look at that machine.' As I looked upwards, I suddenly realised what it was I was really looking at. It was not so much at a machine as at a young man in his early twenties surrounded with a certain amount of paraphernalia called an aeroplane, but the essential thing I was looking at was not that paraphernalia but at the man himself. With him the aeroplane was a thing alive with speed and destructive power, but without him, in a few seconds, it would have been a crumpled mass of burning wreckage. In that moment, I realised what is the first essential for success in air warfare. It is the flying man himself. The modern aeroplane is the product of a thousand pairs of hands, the fastidious skill of designers, the embodiment of materials collected from all over the globe, but in the end it is handed over to one man and his crew. The better it is – the more they can make of it.

And now that we are on the subject of our flying men, I want to tell you a story, which to my mind has something in it of the dash and romantic quality which has pushed down through history the tale of Nelson, his telescope and his blind eye. It is the story of what might some day be called 'The Battle of Bader's Leg'.

You have all heard of Bader, the legless fighter pilot who was shot down in France recently. I have before me the official report announcing this and it runs as follows: 'Wing Commander Bader is missing from patrol during the morning. Apparently he and Flight Lieutenant Casson dived down to attack twenty MEs below after ordering the rest of the Squadron to keep "top cover". Dogfights ensued; no more was seen of either of them. Combat took place between St Omer and Bethune.'

Before I come to the Battle of Bader's Leg, I must say something about Bader himself, and it is hard to do this without shocking oneself and everybody else by becoming emotional. Bader was, in fact, a human phenomenon, which can seldom have occurred in the world before. By all the ordinary laws of human conduct, when he lost both legs – one of them near the hip – in a flying accident, he should, had he obeyed those laws, have become virtually a bath-chair cripple, the object of pity and the subject even of self-pity. It is here that Bader achieved his first triumph – the triumph of character over disaster, for he found himself metal limbs and became almost an athlete once more. Then he achieved the physically and officially impossible feat of reinstating himself not only as a pilot, but as the pilot of fighting aircraft.

Everyone knows the standard of physical fitness and nervous stamina required to achieve even mediocrity as a fighter pilot. Bader outreached this seemingly impossible horizon and became an ace among aces. He became the leader of a fighter squadron – every member of which both worshipped and followed him unthinkingly. There was despair at a certain aerodrome on the South Coast when this terse official report I have just read you reached the Mess. Not one of that Squadron who, at Bader's own orders, had formed 'top cover' during that last attack on the enemy saw or knew his fate.

Some time later, according to the story which reached me, there filtered through from the other side a rumour that Bader was alive – that he had leapt from his Spitfire and had parachuted to earth in enemy territory – that in the process he had lost one of his metal legs. It had always been a joke of Bader's that with these legs he could get out through the safety hatch of his Spitfire quicker than anyone else could with normal legs. This time something must have gone wrong.

Just for a moment pause and imagine the reactions of the Huns who found Bader – a legless man with his left breast covered with decorations and a wrecked Spitfire on the ground near him. We shall not know until we see Bader's own combat report after the war whether or not there were some crashed MEs nearby as well. There were only two things the Huns could think when they found him. One was that we were so hard pressed for pilots that every man with arms was forced to take to the air. The other thing was that you may have to shoot off not only an Englishman's legs, but his arms as well before you have finished with him as a fighting pilot.

There was a popping of corks in that Mess on the South Coast when news of Bader's survival filtered through. There was a sense of frustration also at the hateful thought that Bader might have to spend the rest of the war short of one of his precious limbs. There was a conspiracy and much scratching of heads over the problem. In the end, a new leg was obtained, placed in a package, labelled and attached to a parachute. A few days later, a strange Air Argosy crossed the Channel flying at a height of 10,000 feet towards St Omer. It was one of our large-scale 'fighter-bomber' offensives in the course of its normal duties. They carried bombs and guns but they carried also that carefully labelled package whose safe delivery was ensured by a close escort of fighters from the very Wing which Bader had so often led in person across the Channel.

The bomber which dropped Bader's leg over St Omer spiralled down following the parachute in spite of heavy fire from the ground. This rite performed, the aggressive sweep went on, and not only was the parcel delivered on that journey but a number of MEs were sent down in flames after it.

Thus was Bader's leg delivered to their leader by his old Wing – together with a fiery reminder that their hands had not lost their cunning. There is one thing which every friend of Bader's and every admirer of Bader's – and that goes for the whole civilised world – will be glad to learn – Bader now has his leg . . .

Group Captain W. Helmore, BBC, 11 September 1941

Douglas Bader had lost both his legs in a flying accident in 1931 and the story of Bader's dogfight with the Me109s over France on 9 August 1941 has been made legend by the 1956 film *Reach for the Sky*, starring Kenneth More. Bader's aircraft was almost cut in half by one of the Me109s, and as he tried to bale out one leg became trapped; it was only when the artificial leg broke off that Bader managed to break free and parachute to earth, where the one-legged airman was captured by three German soldiers.

The man who 'dropped' Bader's leg from a Blenheim was a nineteen-year-old Canadian sergeant pilot named Jack Nickelson. He delivered the leg over an airstrip in France designated by the Germans, who had offered safe passage for the aircraft, on 19 August 1941. Nickelson was killed some months later, however, when he was on a low-level sortie against German shipping in the English Channel.

Within two days of having his second leg fitted Bader endeavoured to escape by knotting together a number of bed sheets and shinning down a wall. After two days on the run he was, not surprisingly, recaptured. After this he attempted several more escapes before he was finally sent to Colditz Castle, where he 'saw out' the war.

Group Captain Helmore had been heard on the BBC before the war when he commentated on the Schneider Trophy air races, as well as RAF displays. It meant that his broadcasts were not just well written, but also well delivered, from the experience he had gained. Following his first talk a W.E. Williams, writing in the *Listener*, commented: 'His version of "The Battle for Bader's Leg" . . . after this shemozzle is finished . . . will raise in us as compelling an emotion then as it did last week.' William Helmore became a Conservative MP for Watford in 1943, until he lost his seat in the 1945 election. In 1947 he chaired the Helmore Committee that looked into the airworthiness of British civil aircraft. He later became a director of Castrol, and worked for ICI and the Aluminium Association.

Chapter 10

LOOK EAST

On 10 November 1941, Lord Mayor's Day, the Prime Minister spoke at the Mansion House in London. The central theme of the speech was one of support for America in the event of any form of Japanese aggression – not that Hitler and the Nazis avoided coming under attack in the strongest possible terms from Churchill: 'Even the arch-criminal himself, the Nazi ogre Hitler, has been frightened by the volume and passion of world indignation which his spectacular atrocity has excited. It is he, and not the French people, who has been intimidated. He has not dared to go forward with his further programme of killing hostages.' Churchill then went on to explore the Japanese question:

I must admit that, having voted for the Japanese Alliance nearly 40 years ago – in 1902 – and having always done my very best to promote good relations with the island Empire of Japan, and always having been a sentimental well-wisher of Japan and an admirer of her many gifts and qualities, I would view with keen sorrow the opening of a conflict between Japan and the English-speaking world.

The United States' time-honoured interests in the Far East are well known. They are doing their utmost to find a way of preserving peace in the Pacific. We do not know whether their efforts will be successful, but if they fail, I take this occasion to say – and it is my duty to say – that should the United States become involved in war with Japan the British declaration will follow within the hour . . .

. . . Meanwhile, how can we watch without emotion the wonderful defence of their native soil, and of their freedom and independence, which has been maintained single-handed for five long years by the Chinese people under the leadership of that great Asiatic hero and commander, General Chiang Kai-shek. It would be a disaster of the first magnitude to world civilisation if the noble resistance to invasion and exploitation which has been made by the whole Chinese race were not to result in the liberation of their hearths and homes. That, I feel, is a sentiment which is deep in our hearts . . .

. . . We owe it to ourselves, we owe it to our Russian Allies and to the Government and people of the United States, to make it absolutely clear that whether we are supported or alone, however long and hard the toil may be, the British nation and his Majesty's Government at the head of that nation, in intimate concert with the Governments of the great Dominions, will never enter into any negotiations with Hitler or any party in Germany which represents the Nazi regime. In that resolve we are sure that the ancient City of London will be with us to the hilt and to the end.

Winston Churchill, BBC, 10 November 1941

While the Japanese press called Churchill's threats 'laughable' and labelled Britain and China 'the faithful dogs of the United States', just one month later Churchill's promise to side with America if Japan attacked – 'within the hour' – was put to the test.

A DAY OF INFAMY

It was a chilly 37 degrees in the twin cities of Minneapolis and St Paul in Minnesota, where the Columbia Broadcasting System (CBS) affiliate station WCCO was broadcasting a concert given by the New York Philharmonic of Shostakovich's Symphony No. 1, a work written in 1925 in Leningrad. The orchestra's conductor was the 49-year-old Croatian, Artur Rodzinski. Suddenly the music stopped in mid-bar and an urgent voice cut in . . .

Here is a flash just received in our news room, dateline Washington. A United States transport carrying lumber was torpedoed 1,300 miles west of San Francisco. Details of this news and other news that has been coming in on the Far East situation will be given to you at approximately 3.35 during the intermission of the New York Philharmonic concert. We return you now to the New York Philharmonic Orchestra.

[The music continues . . .] We interrupt this programme to bring you a special news bulletin. The Japanese have attacked Pearl Harbor Hawaii by air, President Roosevelt has just announced. The attack was also made on all naval and military activities on the principal island of Oahu.

[The music finishes . . .] Here is the Far East situation as reported to this moment. The Japanese have attacked Pearl Harbor Hawaii and our defence facilities in Manila, the capital of the Philippines . . . Columbia's correspondent in London, Bob Trott, heard the news for the first time from our report from New York. Up to that moment or very shortly before then the British capital had not been informed of the Japanese attack on the

Hawaiian Islands and Manila. In view of Prime Minister Churchill's recent pledge that a British declaration of war on Japan would follow almost immediately on the outbreak of war between Japan and the United States, a British announcement is expected soon.

John Daly, CBS News, 7 December 1941

There followed a series of conflicting messages which talked of fifty planes attacking Oahu; the planes were officially described as 'unidentified', although some other reports said 'at least two of the aircraft carried the emblem of the "Rising Sun"'. As we now know the attack on Pearl Harbor was a hammer blow for the US Navy and the United States in general. Meanwhile in London the first news of the attack was – some might say inevitably – read by Alvar Lidell.

Here is the news. Japan's long-threatened aggression in the Far East began tonight with air attacks on the United States naval bases in the Pacific. Fresh reports are coming in every minute; the latest facts of the situation are these. Messages from Tokyo say the Japanese have announced a formal declaration of war against the United States and Britain.

Alvar Lidell, BBC News, 9 p.m., 7 December 1941

The BBC's report went on to reiterate the confused scenario painted by American radio, specifically mentioning the lumber ship having been attacked. The BBC's bulletin finished with the news that both Houses of Parliament had been recalled for the following day. That next day, as Parliament was in session, President Roosevelt addressed Congress in Washington, delivering a speech that has passed into legend. On the afternoon of 8 December it was relayed live on the BBC.

Yesterday, December 7, 1941 – a date which will live in infamy – the United States of America was suddenly and deliberately attacked by naval and air forces of the Empire of Japan.

The United States was at peace with that nation, and, at the solicitation of Japan, was still in conversation with its government and its Emperor looking toward the maintenance of peace in the Pacific. Indeed, one hour after Japanese air squadrons had commenced bombing in the American island of Oahu, the Japanese Ambassador to the United States and his colleague delivered to our Secretary of State a formal reply to a recent American message. And, while this reply stated that it seemed useless to continue the existing diplomatic negotiations, it contained no threat or hint of war or of armed attack.

It will be recorded that the distance of Hawaii from Japan makes it obvious that the attack was deliberately planned many days or even weeks ago. During the intervening time the Japanese Government has deliberately sought to deceive the United States by false statements and expressions of hope for continued peace.

The attack yesterday on the Hawaiian Islands has caused severe damage to American naval and military forces. I regret to tell you that very many American lives have been lost. In addition, American ships have been reported torpedoed on the high seas between San Francisco and Honolulu.

Yesterday the Japanese Government also launched an attack against Malaya. Last night Japanese forces attacked Hong Kong. Last night Japanese forces attacked Guam. Last night Japanese forces attacked the Philippine Islands. Last night the Japanese attacked Wake Island. And this morning the Japanese attacked Midway Island.

Japan has therefore undertaken a surprise offensive extending throughout the Pacific area. The facts of yesterday and today speak for themselves. The people of the United States have already formed their opinions and well understand the implications to the very life and safety of our nation.

As Commander-in-Chief of the Army and Navy I have directed that all measures be taken for our defense, that always will our whole nation remember the character of the onslaught against us. No matter how long it may take us to overcome this premeditated invasion, the American people, in their righteous might, will win through to absolute victory.

I believe that I interpret the will of the Congress and of the people when I assert that we will not only defend ourselves to the uttermost but will make it very certain that this form of treachery shall never again endanger us. Hostilities exist. There is no blinking at the fact that our people, our territory and our interests are in grave danger. With confidence in our armed forces, with the unbounding determination of our people, we will gain the inevitable triumph, so help us God.

I ask that the Congress declare that since the unprovoked and dastardly attack by Japan on Sunday, December 7, 1941, a state of war has existed between the United States and the Japanese Empire.

President Roosevelt, BBC, 8 December 1941

That evening Churchill made a twenty-minute broadcast on the BBC's medium-wave transmitters, including the Forces Programme. He was also heard on six of the short-wave transmitters that reached almost every part of the British Empire, as well as the various overseas services of the BBC. It was virtually a repeat of the speech he had given to the House of Commons that afternoon:

As soon as I heard last night that Japan had attacked the United States, my first feeling was that Parliament should be immediately summoned. We are fighting for the maintenance of a parliamentary system, and it is indispensable to our system of Government that Parliament should play its full part in all the important acts of the state and on all the great occasions in the conduct of the war. The great number of members who attended in spite of the shortness of the notice shows the zeal and strictness with which the members of both Houses attend to their duties.

You will remember that a month ago, with the full approval of the nation and of the Empire, I pledged the word of Great Britain that should the United States become involved in a war with Japan, a British declaration would follow within the hour. I therefore spoke to President Roosevelt on the Atlantic telephone last night with a view to arranging the timing of our respective declarations. The President told me that he would this morning send a message to Congress, which of course as you all know is the instrument, the constitutional instrument, by which alone a United States declaration of war can be made.

And I assured him that we would follow immediately. However, it soon appeared that British territory in Malaya had also been the object of a Japanese attack, and later on it was announced from Tokyo that the Japanese High Command – not the Imperial Japanese Government – but the Japanese High Command had declared that a state of war existed with Great Britain and the United States.

There has been for a long time in Japan a number of military societies – secret societies – which have asserted their view of what the policy of Japan should be by murdering the Ministers whom they thought were not sufficiently 'jingo' for their tastes. And it is to these bodies that the most strange and violent action of Japan's, so fateful for her future, must be ascribed.

In view of the attack, and of this declaration, there was no need to wait for the declaration by Congress, and in any case there was the complication that American time is nearly six hours behind ours. The Cabinet, therefore, which met at half-past twelve today, have authorised an immediate declaration of war upon Japan. Instructions to this effect were sent to our Ambassador in Tokyo, and the Japanese chargé d'affaires in London and his staff have been given their passports.

Meanwhile, hostilities have already begun. The Japanese began a landing in British territory in Northern Malaya at about six o'clock – that's 1 a.m. local time yesterday – and they were immediately engaged by our troops who were there waiting for them.

The Home Office measures against Japanese nationals were set in motion a little after ten last night. You will see, therefore, that no time has been lost, and you will see also that we are actually ahead of our engagements . . .

. . . My friends, let me say this. It is of the highest importance that there should be no underrating of the gravity of the new dangers we have to meet, either here in this Island, or those dangers which the United States have to meet. The enemy has attacked with an audacity which may spring from recklessness, but which may also spring from a conviction of strength . . .

. . . The ordeal to which the English-speaking world and our heroic Russian allies are being exposed will certainly be hard, especially at the outset, and it will probably be long. But when we look around us, upon the sombre panorama of the world, we have no reason to doubt the justice of our cause, nor have we any reason to doubt that our strength and our will power will be sufficient to sustain it.

We have at least four-fifths of the population of the globe upon our side. We are responsible for their safety – we are responsible for their future. And as I told the House of Commons this afternoon, in the past we had a light which flickered, in the present we have a light which flames, and in the future there will be a light which will shine calm and resplendent over all the land and all the sea!

Winston Churchill, BBC, 8 December 1941

On the seven o'clock news, the day after Pearl Harbor was attacked, the newsreader had an accent that listeners to the BBC had been getting used to over the past couple of weeks – he came from 'up noorth'.

This is the BBC Home Service. Here is the news and this is Wilfred Pickles reading it. This morning's news of Japan's aggression is of successful counter-measures of invasion of Malaya. There have also been reports of enemy attacks on Thailand and Hong Kong. At Shanghai the Japanese have taken over the international waterfront and sunk the British gunboat *Petra* . . . The Japanese are reported to have lost an aircraft carrier and some of their bombers and submarines.

Wilfred Pickles, BBC News, 7 a.m., 8 December 1941

Today we take for granted that broadcasters with regional accents are heard on every radio and TV station in Britain, but until November 1941 the idea of such a voice reading the news had been an anathema to the powers that be at the BBC. Nowadays it would be inconceivable to listen to the radio and only hear what we have come to lampoon as a BBC accent. It was an amazing turnaround, given that the announcers had only just rid themselves of their dinner jackets – for the BBC, war was a huge catalyst for change. Pickles, a 37-year-old Yorkshireman, had been born in Halifax and in truth his 'news-reading' accent was barely any different from the standard BBC English of his colleagues. He seems to have softened his speech pattern slightly for news reading and to some extent his reputation as the 'first of the many' has been somewhat exaggerated. He did, though, become something of an overnight sensation by ending his broadcasts with a '. . . and to all in the north – Good-neet'. By the end of the war Pickles was a radio celebrity and his series, 'Have a Go', proved so popular that it ran for about twenty years and regularly attracted audiences of over 15 million.

The extent to which Roosevelt's speech has passed into legend was demonstrated over sixty years later when an article in the *Washington Post* in June 2004 suggested that the words 'so help me God' that the President used near the close of his speech had deliberately been left off the National World War Two Memorial that had been formally dedicated on 29 May 2004. The paper claimed that it was either motivated by political correctness or simply because 'We're not supposed to say things like that now'. In fact the words on the memorial are from a similar line of Roosevelt's speech that did not end with 'so help me God', making it a perfectly correct 'lift' from his speech.

HEARING IS BELIEVING

To further the BBC's avowed aim of keeping the public informed about its own activities a booklet was published at the end of 1941 to spread the gospel. Called *BBC at War*, it explained in some detail what the objectives of the BBC were and how it went about the important job of informing, not just the British public, but also its many listeners around the world. Read now, it shows how the BBC was still getting to grips with the task of war reporting, a task at which they would become even more adept over the next two years. However, the BBC's task was inevitably made more difficult by the expansion of the war into the Far East. In a slightly self-congratulatory, yet diffident, paragraph, the booklet ended:

> This is the story of the BBC at war. It is a human institution and therefore a fallible one. But the BBC now broadcasts about half a million words a day – as much as five full-length novels. It broadcasts them in forty languages and to nearly every nation in the world. These facts alone prove its efficiency and worth.

One example of how things were changing in the battle with German radio occurred when an advert appeared in a Portuguese newspaper in the latter part of 1941. Its proud boast was 'Germany speaks and the world hears her'. The BBC replied with an advert of its own – 'London speaks and the world believes her'.

At around the time the *BBC at War* booklet came out there were also some problems with the frequency on which the Home Programme could be heard in Britain. A wonderful BBC announcement, the very model of confusion, appeared in the newspapers.

The BBC announces that many listeners in various parts of the country are reporting that they can now get the Home Programme better on 203.5 metres than any other wavelength. When this is so, listeners are advised to make a practice of tuning to 203.5 metres. If, however, they do not get improved reception on this wavelength at present, they should remember to try it again later on.

Well that's all clear then . . .

HEARTFELT CHRISTMAS MESSAGES

On 11 December Italy and Germany, Japan's partners in the Axis Alliance, declared war on the United States; the US Congress immediately returned the favour. Two days later Churchill left Britain aboard the battleship HMS *Duke of York* and sailed to America for a meeting with Roosevelt and what became known as the Arcadia conference. The stormy and wild voyage lasted ten days and even before it was over Churchill was calling it 'the longest week I have lived since the war began'. Churchill spent most of each day in bed, not because he was seasick, but because there was little else to do but read and work. On 21 December as he was nearing America he began a letter to Clementine that he went on to finish on Christmas Eve at his room in the White House. 'I have not had a minute since I got here to tell you about it. All is very good indeed; and my plans are all going through. The Americans are magnificent in their breadth of view. Tender love to you and all – my thoughts will be with you this strange Christmas Eve.' A few hours earlier, at shortly after 5 p.m. Eastern Time, Churchill and Roosevelt, in front of 30,000 people, had performed the tradi-tional lighting of the White House Christmas tree by the south portico of the building. A relay of the event was carried to Britain and aired on the BBC. After Roosevelt had delivered greetings to the nation and the world, he invited Churchill to 'say a word to the people of America, old and young, tonight'.

Fellow workers in the cause of freedom. I have the honour to add a pendant to the necklace of that Christmas goodwill and kindliness with which my illustrious good friend – The President – has encircled the homes and families of the United States by his message of Christmas Eve, which he has just delivered.

I spend this anniversary and festival far from my country, far from my family; yet I cannot truthfully say that I feel far from home. Whether it be by the ties of blood on my mother's side, or the friendships I have developed here over many years of active life, or the commanding sentiment of comradeship in the common cause of great peoples who speak the same language, who kneel at the same altars and to a very large extent pursue the same ideals I cannot feel myself a stranger here in the centre and at the summit of the United States. [Applause]

I feel a sense of unity and fraternal association which, added to the kindliness of your welcome, convinces me that I have a right to sit at your fireside and share your Christmas joys.

This is a strange Christmas Eve. Almost the whole world is locked in deadly struggle, and, with the most terrible weapons which science can devise, the nations advance on each other. Ill would it be for us this Christmas if we were not sure that greed for the land or wealth of any other people, nor vulgar ambition, nor morbid lust for material gain at the expense of others had led us to the field.

Here, in the midst of war, raging and roaring over all the lands and seas, creeping nearer to our hearts and homes, here, amid all the tumult, we have, tonight, the peace of the spirit in each cottage home and in every generous heart. Therefore we may cast aside for this night at least the cares and dangers which beset us, and make for the children an evening of happiness in a world of storm. Here, then, for one night only, each home throughout the English-speaking world should be a brightly lighted island of happiness and peace.

Let the children have their night of fun and laughter. Let the gifts of Father Christmas delight their play. Let us grown-ups share to the full in their unstinted pleasures before we turn again to the stern task and formidable years that lie before us. Resolve that, by our sacrifice and daring, these same children shall not be robbed of their inheritance or denied their right to live in a free and decent world. [Applause]

And so, in God's mercy, a happy Christmas to you all.

Winston Churchill, relayed via the BBC, 24 December 1941

On Christmas day the King's message was likewise relayed around the world, and on the following day Churchill addressed Congress in Washington; it was another BBC relay back to Britain and was broadcast on all the Corporation's overseas networks. Speaking in broad terms about the relationship between Britain and America, as well as the particular problems confronting both countries, but particularly America in the Pacific, Churchill focused the middle part of his speech on the war in North Africa. It was a situation that Churchill thought would be the beginnings of something bigger to be played out across the whole of the Mediterranean region – and after that Europe itself.

. . . Not all the tidings will be evil. On the contrary, mighty strokes of war have already been dealt against the enemy – the glorious defence of their native soil by the Russian armies and people; wounds have been inflicted upon the Nazi tyranny and system which have bitten deep and will fester and inflame not only in the Nazi body but in the Nazi mind. The boastful Mussolini has crumpled already. He is now but a lackey and a serf, the merest utensil of his master's will. He has inflicted great suffering and wrong upon his own industrious people. He has been stripped of all his African empire. Abyssinia has been liberated. Our Armies of the East, which were so weak and ill-equipped at the moment of French desertion, now control all the regions from Teheran to Benghazi, and from Aleppo and Cyprus to the sources of the Nile.

For many months we devoted ourselves to preparing to take the offensive in Libya. The very considerable battle which has been proceeding there the last six weeks in the desert has been most fiercely fought on both sides. Owing to the difficulties of supply upon the desert flank, we were never able to bring numerically equal forces to bear upon the enemy. Therefore we had to rely upon superiority in the numbers and qualities of tanks and aircraft, British and American. For the first time, aided by these – for the first time we have fought the enemy with equal weapons. For the first time we have made the Hun feel the sharp edge of those tools with which he has enslaved Europe. The armed forces of the enemy in Cyrenaica amounted to about 150,000 men, of whom a third were Germans. General Auchinleck set out to destroy totally that armed force, and I have every reason to believe that his aim will be fully accomplished. I am so glad to be able to place before you, members of the Senate and of the House of Representatives, at this moment when you are entering the war, the proof that with proper weapons and proper organisation, we are able to beat the life out of the savage Nazi.

What Hitlerism is suffering in Libya is only a sample and a foretaste of what we have got to give him and his accomplices wherever this war should lead us in every quarter of the Globe.

Winston Churchill, BBC, 26 December 1941

Returning to the White House Churchill decided to open a window in his bedroom, but it proved to be a little stiff, and as he pushed it upwards he felt a pain move along his arm and he became short of breath. The following day Churchill's physician who accompanied him to America realised that the Prime Minister had suffered a mild heart attack, but didn't tell Churchill or anyone else. He simply told Winston to 'Ease up a bit on his work'. Naturally Churchill took his doctor's orders seriously, and so just four days later he was addressing the Canadian Parliament. In it he famously remarked:

When I warned them that Britain would fight on alone, whatever they did, their Generals told their Prime Minister and his divided cabinet that in three weeks, England would have her neck wrung like a chicken – Some chicken! Some neck!

IN WITH THE NEW

At the start of 1942 the BBC continued to strive to present a balanced mix of programmes that ensured that the audience in Britain would not become completely bogged down in thoughts of war. Simultaneously the BBC tried to make sure that there was no criticism of its ambition of providing the most effective news output. Just as 'Any Questions' was heard for the first time in January 1941, a year later another long-running BBC stalwart had its first broadcast. 'Desert Island Discs', according to all recognised sources, was first heard on Thursday 29 January 1942. The newspaper listings for that day do not carry news of the programme, but in the weeks that followed it was listed, airing sometime between 7.30 and 8 p.m. The newspaper listings for 29 January show the Forces Programmes as playing records at 8 p.m., sandwiched between 'Variety' and 'Join In and Sing'. The programme's first castaway was the 46-year-old, Austrian-born comedian Vic Oliver, which was an inspired choice. He was the son of Baron Victor von Samek, although Oliver had relinquished the title in 1922 and become an American citizen. Oliver married Sarah Churchill, the daughter of the Prime Minister, in 1936, although they would divorce in 1945.

Listeners to the Forces Programme that day would have heard a veritable potpourri of subjects and themes. Sandy Macpherson was still at the organ, the Central Band of the RAF played, there was an excerpt from *Cinderella*, a boxing commentary, Geraldo and his Orchestra, and a number of comedy shows – ample evidence to explain why a broadcaster on Germany's Australian and Far Eastern network said, 'London goes on with its radio programmes as if nothing has happened. People singing in the shelters, reports from cricket matches, nice and clever people make talks, there's more dance music than before. We must respect them for this.'

Apart from the developments in programming during January 1942 there was also a major change at the very top of the BBC. F.W. Ogilvie, who had been running the Corporation since 1938, resigned. Two men – Sir Cecil Graves, the former Deputy Director General, and R.W. Foot – replaced him; they were appointed Joint Directors General. Before joining the BBC the 53-year-old Foot had been head of the Gas Light and Coke Company; they had loaned him to the Corporation in October 1941 to help with wartime reorganisation. The decision to have two people running the BBC, like most such decisions to appoint joint chiefs, was not a recipe for success, nor for clarity of direction.

EDEN IN MOSCOW

Aside from the Prime Minister's visit to America, and the inevitable focus that it placed on the war in the Pacific, there was a lot of attention being paid to the war on the Eastern Front. By early December 1941 the German Army was just a few miles from Moscow, but the severity of the temperature, at minus 35 degrees Fahrenheit, forced Hitler to abandon the offensive thrust against the Russian capital. Within a matter of days, despite the weather, the Russian Army mounted a devastating counter-attack. As the Germans fell back against the Soviets' formidable onslaught, they abandoned frozen equipment that would not move, while many soldiers barely managed to save their own frostbitten selves. Hitler was disgusted with his generals and amid resignations in the field he assumed command of the army in Russia – not an awfully sensible option given Berlin's distance from the front line. The Führer's strategy was simple – there will be no withdrawal. The Russians continued to press and to probe making December 1941 a crucial month in this terrible war. It was the beginning of the end of Germany's designs on capturing Moscow – Russia was on the turn; it was a tidal flow that would ultimately carry them all the way to Berlin.

Against this background Anthony Eden, the Foreign Secretary, went to Moscow in mid-December for talks with Stalin and Molotov; discussions were made easier by the fact that Eden spoke Russian. His secret visit, which had only been decided upon on 4 December – the day before the Russian counter-attack – included a visit to see some of what the German Army had abandoned under the onslaught of General Georgy Zhukov's forces. Such was the extent of the German defeat, the worst they had suffered since the beginning of the war, that Eden took great heart from what he saw during his four days in Russia (16–20 December). Back home in London he broadcast on the BBC on 4 January about his meetings, and talked about some of what he had seen in Russia:

The spirit of these Russian troops is magnificent; their morale is higher than ever. They are striking at the retreating Germans without mercy and without respite. I saw a little of this myself. We drove along the Moscow–Leningrad road to Kiln and some miles beyond. There were plenty of signs of fighting by the roadside – shell-torn trees, derelict guns, and shattered homes. We saw something, too, of the scorched earth policy. Most of the houses in these parts are built of wood, the chimneys only being of brick, so that, when the houses have been burnt, gaunt brick fingers point solitary to the sky. 'Scorched earth' in a frozen land. The effect is even more awful than total destruction would be.

The German Army has been driven back fast and far. We reached Kiln at noon on a Friday. On the Monday fighting had still been going on in the town and, though we drove perhaps six or seven miles beyond it, I don't think that we were at any time within twenty miles of the nearest Germans.

Hitler has always liked a war of movement. He is getting it now. We saw what had evidently been the scene of pretty tough fighting some few miles north of Kiln. Russian and German tanks were knocked out by the roadside. In a ditch were frozen German corpses. On the way back we saw a small group of German prisoners, who had been captured the day before; I talked with some of them myself. They were young, not much more than boys, although three of them were NCOs, ill-clad and suffering bitterly from the cold. They were not a bit like the soldiers of a victorious army. They were just half a dozen more of Hitler's unhappy victims.

I had a look at their clothing, and they were quite ready to talk about it. Their overcoats were thinner and lighter than the service overcoat worn by British troops in this country. The tunics, too, were thin and of poor material. The boots were an imitation of the Russian top-boot, but not so stout or so warm. Even the tunic buttons were cheap and shoddy, and the whole turnout had an ersatz appearance. They had no gloves, and only thin cardigans, and they kept trying to pull the sleeves down over their frozen fingers.

But there is one exception I must make. Hitler's own personal SS troops are privileged, and have distinctly better equipment. Remember that the worst of the Russian winter has still to come. You will understand then that there is reason for this Russian confidence. Reason, indeed, for anxious, heavy hearts in Germany.

Anthony Eden, BBC, 4 January 1942

Eden clearly indulged in some jingoistic rhetoric, attempting to bolster the spirits of the listeners as to the 'waning power' of the enemy, but there was no doubting that the Russians had done an amazing job in countering the German advance.

Eden held a number of talks with Stalin; he was the first senior Western statesman to have face-to-face talks with the Soviet dictator. And while Eden happily spoke in his broadcast about the war on the Eastern Front, and did mention in broad terms his discussions with Stalin, he was less than candid about the precise nature of his meetings. At these meetings Stalin talked of how the British and the Russians would divide Europe in the postwar world; and all this with the Germans still less than fifty miles from Moscow.

The experience of my visit, the talks I had with M. Stalin and M. Molotov, have convinced me that closer political collaboration between us can and will be realised. We have to get rid of a legacy of suspicion on both sides. There is the contrast in forms of Government. But I will never accept that this need divide us. What matters in foreign affairs is not the form of internal government of any nation, but its international behaviour. The trouble with Hitler, for instance, was not that he was a Nazi at home. The trouble with him was that be would not stay at home. He was, and is, a ruthless aggressor, and an insatiable aggressor – with an insatiable appetite for world dominion . . .

Contrast this with Russia's attitude and our own. The Soviet Union is determined upon the utter defeat of Germany. So are we. The Soviet Union is determined to do all that is in its power to ensure that Germany cannot launch further war on the world. So are we. Out of the untold human suffering of the present war, the Soviet Union wishes to gain a lasting peace for all its people – so do we . . .

Anthony Eden, BBC, 4 January 1942

It is a fascinating insight into the pre-Cold War world, a world that Eden would become very familiar with when he became Prime Minister, ten years after the war ended. Eden had faced a very frosty Stalin during some of their

Moscow talks, and so he was not totally unprepared. 'I thought that the Atlantic Charter was directed against those people who were trying to establish world dominion. It now looks as if the Atlantic Charter was directed against the USSR,' said Stalin. Eden would not acquiesce to the Russian's request for all the Soviet borders to be as they were prior to the German attack and sent a telegram to Churchill in America, who was appalled at what he heard. 'Stalin's demands about Finland, Baltic States and Rumania are directly contrary to the 1st, 2nd, and 3rd Articles of the Atlantic Charter to which Stalin has subscribed. There can be no question whatever of our making such an agreement, secret, or public, direct or implied, without prior agreement with the United States . . . Foreign Secretary has acquitted himself admirably, and should not be downhearted if he has to leave Moscow without a flourish of trumpets.' In the pragmatic atmosphere of a war, which still had to be won, much of what Stalin wanted was a long way off for almost everyone, except possibly the Russians.

GRIM DEFEAT

Six weeks after Anthony Eden's broadcast, Winston Churchill gave one of only three broadcast speeches during 1942, in which he looked further east – specifically to Singapore, which had fallen to the Japanese.

Tonight I speak to you at home. I speak to you in Australia and New Zealand, for whose safety we will strain every nerve, to our loyal friends in India and Burma, to our gallant allies, the Dutch and Chinese, and to our kith and kin in the United States. I speak to you all under the shadow of a heavy and far-reaching military defeat.

It is a British and Imperial defeat. Singapore has fallen. All the Malay Peninsula has been overrun. Other dangers gather about us afar and none of the dangers which we have hitherto successfully withstood at home and in the East are in any way diminished.

This, therefore, is one of those moments when the British race and nation can show their quality and their genius. This is one of those moments when they can draw from the heart of misfortune the vital impulses of victory.

Here is the moment to display that calm and poise, combined with grim determination, which not so long ago brought us out of the very jaws of death. Here is another occasion to show, as so often in our long history, that we can meet reverses with dignity and with renewed accession of strength.

We must remember that we are no longer alone. We are in the midst of a great company. Three quarters of the human race are now moving with us.

The whole future of mankind may depend upon our actions and upon our conduct. So far we have not failed.

We shall not fail now. Let us move forward steadfastly together into the storm and through the storm.

Winston Churchill, BBC, 15 February 1942

This was far from one of Churchill's greatest speeches; it offered little that people could latch onto by way of turns of phrase. But it was one in which Churchill dug deep and embodied that spirit of self-belief and determination that was needed to keep people believing in ultimate victory – even in such a dark hour as this. Two weeks after the Prime Minister spoke, Group Captain Helmore was again on the radio giving one of his 'Air Commentaries'. He said, 'Priceless jewels of the East have rolled in the gutter', and spoke of the need to 'seize and nurture a mood of burning resentment'. Other talks by Ministers, politicians and regular BBC talk-givers all joined in this theme of pulling together in the 'utterly unshakeable belief in the greatness of our race'.

There are many historians who consider this to be the worst British defeat of the Second World War; others have gone as far as to say that it was the most awful defeat in the history of the British Army – it puts the rhetoric into perspective. The speed of the Japanese advance across the Malayan Peninsula, through incredibly hostile terrain, made Hitler's Blitzkrieg seem pedestrian. Such was the Japanese will to move with lightning speed that their troops were ordered to take no prisoners. British hopes that the jungle would prove impenetrable for the 70,000-strong Imperial Army proved groundless. The initial attack had begun on 9 December 1941, two days after Pearl Harbor, and its effects were relatively more devastating, as the RAF lost almost all its front-line fighters that day. Out of two squadrons of Blenheims all but one aircraft were destroyed on the ground at Alor Star. The Blenheim that survived the attack took off and raided a Japanese airfield. During the mission the pilot was badly wounded and when he returned to his base he died from his injuries; Flight Lieutenant Scarf was awarded the VC. The battleship *Prince of Wales* and the cruiser *Repulse* had put to sea the day before, but both were sunk on 10 December by Japanese torpedo bombers; over 800 officers and men were lost.

Fierce fighting took place on land, and the numerically superior British, Australian and Indian soldiers with hardly any battle experience were no match for the Japanese troops who had been honed from fighting with the Chinese. By 31 January the Allied soldiers had taken up their final position across the causeway that separated Singapore from Malaya. Churchill told his generals, 'There must be no thought of sparing the troops or population;

commanders and senior officers should die with their troops. The honour of the British Empire and the British Army is at stake.' With food stocks set to run out, and water being in even shorter supply Lieutenant-General Percival told his commanders 'we shall surrender'. At just after 5 p.m. Singapore time on 15 February Percival met with the Japanese commander, General Yamashita, and surrendered. Around 90,000 Allied troops were taken prisoner; many of these men would die in Japanese prisoner-of-war camps – including 10,000 during the building of the Burma railway.

There was a sort of joyous anarchical abandon about life in Singapore during those last days. For one thing possessions didn't count any more, money didn't matter either. The most you hoped for was to preserve your life, and possibly your freedom. And the old saying 'drink and be merry for tomorrow ye may die' was translated into a glorious irresponsible reality. I remember that after I'd seen my wife off to Java about a fortnight before the fall of Singapore I came away feeling naturally rather depressed to find my car had been requisitioned or stolen. So in desperation I asked a complete stranger for a lift, who was going the same way as I was. I told him what had happened and he said quite casually, 'Do you want this car, I've got two, so I don't really need it.' I thanked him very much and he gave me the keys and that was that. You see that was an illustration of the whole atmosphere of Singapore in those last days.

Giles Fairplay, BBC, 15 June 1942

Chapter 11

THE SCOURGE OF THE REICH

NO PARADE TO RAIN ON

Two days after Giles Fairplay's report on the last days of Singapore there was a broadcast by an RAF pilot who carried out one of the most bizarre missions of the war. He and his navigator dropped a French tricolour over the Arc de Triomphe in Paris in broad daylight. It was one of those wartime feats that used to be written about in comics like the *Victor, Hotspur* and *Boys' Own Paper.*

Paris looks exactly as I imagined it. Our visit only lasted five or six minutes, but I'd like to go again and see it on foot. The Eiffel Tower gave us a useful bearing when we were 40 miles away and over the Arc de Triomphe Sergeant Fern pushed the first furled flag down a flare shoot.

We'd experimented with the flags, and they were weighted and folded so that they would stream as soon as released. One of the things we wanted to look at particularly was the Ministry of Marine, because it was crammed with Hun and we had something for them. We came in as low as we dared, let fly with our four cannons at about 500 yards, and I saw sparks flying off the building. A great deal went through the windows. We sprayed the place from base to apex, cleared the roof by about five feet, and dropped our second flag.

We noticed one or two faces at the windows actually peering down at us and saw military cars stopped in the streets, with Huns standing by them, or dodging round trees in the avenue. We couldn't let fly at them, because there were too many civilians about – of whom most were waving to us. One very fat Hun shook his fist.

Flight Lieutenant Gatward, BBC, 17 June 1942

The solo raid on Paris was performed by a Beaufighter of 236 Squadron, Coastal Command, piloted by 27-year-old Flight Lieutenant Alfred Kitchener (Ken) Gatward and Sergeant F.F. Fern, at around midday on Friday 12 June. Their audacious raid, in which they targeted the former Ministry of Marine in

the Place de la Concorde, then being used by the Gestapo, was flown at
incredibly low level. They flew at the same height as the third-floor windows
on the Champs Elysées. The mission had been prompted after a secret agent
had reported a military procession used the Champs Elysées each day around
noon. Gatward volunteered for the mission, along with his observer. Fern was
a man with a dark secret, dark, that is, for an RAF flyer; he suffered from
airsickness and had to keep a bucket nearby for emergencies. The pair had
already tried the idea on a couple of earlier occasions, but cloud cover
prevented them from succeeding. The only things that actually went wrong on
the mission was the fact that there was no parade, and the starboard engine
ingested a crow and overheated – the price of low flying.

The Beaufighter was a derivative of the Blenheim with two distinct
advantages over its predecessor – speed and firepower. Gatward was awarded
the DSO and the DFC and Bar during the war and became a wing commander
in 1944, commanding a Royal Canadian Air Force squadron; he finished the
war as a group captain.

On 28 March the RAF bombed Lübeck; it was the start of what Air Marshal
Sir Arthur Harris, the Commander-in-Chief of Bomber Command, called 'the
scourge of the Reich from end to end'.

It is the first anniversary of the destruction of Coventry by Goering's
airmen, one of the most horrifying deeds with which Hitler's Germany
taught the world what total war means and how to conduct it.

It started in Spain, where the robots of death, that race with the blank,
inhuman faces, educated in National Socialism, prepared themselves for this
war. What sport was it thoughtlessly to dive-bomb and machine-gun the
fleeing masses of civilians who have no chance of defending themselves?
Neither will the massacres in Poland ever be forgotten; they can be called a
famous landmark in history, and so can Rotterdam, where 30,000 people
perished in 20 minutes, thanks to the bravado which is not easily distinguishable from moral insanity.

Did Germany believe she would never have to pay for the crimes which
her leap into barbarism allowed her to commit? She is paying already, both
over the Channel and in Russia. And what the Royal Air Force has
accomplished to date in Cologne, Düsseldorf, Essen, Hamburg and other
towns is only a beginning.

During the latest British raid over Hitler's Reich the old city of Lübeck had
to suffer. That concerns me, for it is my home town. The attacks were
directed against the harbour of Travemünde and the industrial plants there,

but fires were started in the town itself, and I would not like to think that the Marienkirche, the beautiful Renaissance town hall or the building of the Schiffer-Gesellschaft were damaged. But I think of Coventry and accept the principle of just retribution. There will be other natives of Lübeck, Hamburg, Cologne and Düsseldorf who likewise have no objection and who, on hearing the drone of the RAF planes over their heads, will wish them success.

It might even be that my sense of justice will be put to a special test by this bombing. Swedish newspapers report that my grandparents' house, the so-called 'Buddenbrook House,' in the Mengstrasse, has been destroyed during that raid. I do not know whether this information is correct. To many people outside Germany, the town of Lübeck is associated with this house since I wrote my book, *Buddenbrooks*, and they think of it when they hear that Lübeck has been bombed. Of course, in Lübeck itself it is no longer called the 'Buddenbrook House'. The Nazis, annoyed that visitors to the town were always asking about it, have renamed it 'Wullenweber House'. These illiterates do not even know that a house, which bears an inscription from the fifteenth century on its Rococo gable, cannot very well be associated with the bold burgomaster of the sixteenth century. Jürgen Wullenweber did much harm to his town by warring with Denmark. And the people of Lübeck did with him what the Germans might perhaps one day do with those who have led them into this war. They executed him. The occupants of the house which they called 'Wullenweber', to obliterate the name of Buddenbrook, have always, as I can testify, benefited the town. And I have in my own way followed their example. To follow an example in your own way is tradition. The old merchants' house, which is now said to lie in ruins, was to me the symbol of that tradition; but such ruins do not shock those who live for the future as well as for the past. The passing of an epoch need not destroy him who is rooted in it and who grew up in it, nor him who pictured it for you. Hitler's Germany has neither tradition nor future. It can only destroy.

May another Germany rise from its ruins, a Germany which can reflect and hope, which loves the past and the future of mankind. In this way it will win the regard of other nations instead of their bitter hatred.

Thomas Mann, BBC German Service, 11 April 1942

This remarkable talk was given on the BBC's German Service by an equally remarkable man. The Nobel Prize-winning author Thomas Mann was sixty-seven years old at the time of his passionate yet measured condemnation of the Nazi regime. He had exiled himself from Germany in 1933 because of his abhorrence of Hitler and the Nazis. He first went to Switzerland before moving to America, where he became a US citizen in 1944; later Mann moved back to Switzerland, where he died in 1955.

Air Marshal Sir Arthur Harris went on to earn the nickname 'Bomber' as a result of what he started with the raid on Lübeck. He had been promoted to the position at the start of 1942 and immediately set about reorganising the RAF's bombing strategy, which most considered to have been in disarray. Harris was a pilot in the First World War and it was from this experience that he developed a belief that bombing was vastly superior to the slaughter in the trenches. Two months after the Lübeck raid, on 30 May, there was the infamous Operation Millennium, the thousand-bomber raid on Cologne. The BBC news broadcast a recording of some of the bombers taking off; in the background a nightingale can be heard vainly trying to compete.

DEJA VU

The quality of broadcasting continued to improve – slowly, but not necessarily surely – in the sense that it was still a somewhat hit or miss affair; a fact of which the BBC was all too well aware. On 3 April 1942 A.P. Ryan wrote a gloomy private memorandum to Sir Cecil Graves and didn't mince his words: 'We have been criticised by the Board of Governors, by the Minister of Information, and by No. 10, for not having a high enough standard of news observing. We must, you will agree, admit that this criticism is justified . . .'. Ryan had switched from his job as the Home Adviser to become the Controller News Co-ordination Division and it was in this capacity that he wrote to the Director General. From this memorandum a revolution would be launched, one that would come to fruition in the early summer of 1944, when the War Reporting Unit went into operation – it was without doubt the jewel in the BBC's crown during the Second World War.

Despite the setbacks in the Far East there were some positive signs, as Churchill pointed out in March: 'It now seems very likely that we and our allies cannot lose this war, except through our own fault.' It pre-empted meetings in London between a high-level US delegation and their British opposite numbers on what was to be their future joint strategy. The Americans wanted to plan towards an Allied landing in the area of Antwerp in the summer of 1943, and there was talk of a smaller attack in 1942 to help relieve the pressure on the Eastern Front. There was one thing on which both sides readily agreed – the liberation of Europe was the Allies' key objective. As preparation for the invasion of Europe it was agreed that a raid on Dieppe in France made sense. It would enable everyone involved to test the logistics of such landings, albeit on a smaller scale. Under the command of Lieutenant-General Bernard Montgomery the planned attack was scheduled to go ahead in early July, but bad weather forced its cancellation, not once but twice. It was rescheduled for August but Montgomery was unhappy with such a proposal, and remained opposed to it going ahead because he thought too many people knew about the plan; as far as he was concerned just about every pub in the south of England knew what was happening and he wanted the whole affair cancelled. This was a view not shared by the Chief of Combined Operations, Lord Louis Mountbatten, and so it went ahead.

A raid was launched in the early hours of today in the Dieppe area of enemy-occupied France. The operation is still in progress. Meanwhile the French people are being advised by wireless broadcasts that this raid is not an invasion.

BBC News, 7 a.m., Wednesday 19 August 1942

On the one o'clock news there was a report of heavy fighting from an official communiqué and information on the raid on the right flank to destroy a six-gun battery.

As an English, or I should say as a Scottish war correspondent, I have trained with a Canadian for jobs like this and I had hoped I might go into battle with them but at the last minute I was transferred to a British Commando unit, a force of men from every regiment in these Islands. And now that I have landed in France and watched them fighting I wouldn't have missed it for a years pay. But for what these Commando boys did the whole Dieppe raid might have been a terrible failure. Don't misunderstand me, I have said this was an all-Canadian raid but there was a little job that had to be done before it could start. There was a German six-inch howitzer battery west of Dieppe that could have wrecked any force coming into Dieppe itself. Now, this battery lay beyond some high cliffs beyond the shore and there were nasty overhanging high cliffs, impossible to climb. There was only one thing you could do, go through them. And there were only two places to go through, two small gullies or cracks about 20 feet wide at the foot. I saw those cliffs and those cracks as I crouched with the Commando boys in one of their assault landing craft nosing inshore at the first light of day. I hated the sight of them, they made me feel more afraid than I had ever been in my life before, and I wasn't going to have to do any of the fighting.

But as we grounded on the shingle I heard a commando trooper whisper to his young mate, 'Don't forget these so and so's is twice as scared as you'.

Somehow that made me feel better, and it turned out to be true. So risky was the way we chose to attack the battery through those cliffs that the Germans just didn't believe we'd try it. And that was what the Commando leaders reckoned they'd believe. Half the Commando force was to go up one of these cracks, and the other half, under their young Scots colonel, was to land further down the coast and try to work their way round and take the battery in the rear. We soon found that one of the cracks was so stuffed full of barbed wire that we wouldn't have time to go through it so we blew up the two bands of wire in the other and went ahead. We fully expected to find a machine gun at the top of the crack – one platoon of men and one machine gun could have held it against us – but they weren't there. German snipers were there and they caused casualties, but snipers were not enough. The Commando boys broke through to the woods at the top and set up their mortars there. With mortar fire they blew up the howitzer battery's ammunition dump and it went up with such a bang that it made the worst of Hitler's bombs in the Blitz sound like a kettledrum.

Then the young colonel and his men working round with fixed bayonets charged across the open ground and across the badly fixed, careless barbed wire the Germans had laid and into the battery. They fought it out with the Germans hand to hand and the Germans fought gamely. Their battery commander died fighting in his office. I saw his typed orders for that day, and at that time his men should have been doing physical jerks. Instead they were all either dead or prisoners, and their great guns had been stuffed full of explosives and blown up. When we came back down the crack again and came on to the beach to find the boats the Commando boys had been fighting, climbing, or crawling for three hours; exactly the time they'd been given to do the job. Their young colonel sat down beside me on the rock and said, 'Well we've done it.' As they started out on their long journey back to Britain they knew they had made the Battle of Dieppe possible.

A.B. Austin, BBC, 24 August 1942

According to a communiqué released by Combined Operations Headquarters a short while ago reports received from the force commanders . . . show that as a combined operation the raid was a successful demonstration of coordination of all three services.

BBC News, midnight, 20 August 1942

Alexander Berry Austin worked for the *Daily Herald* and was one of twenty-two correspondents that went on the Dieppe raid, during which several of the reporters were wounded by shrapnel. The BBC's own man on the mission was

Frank Gillard, who actually stayed on one of the boats, and so it was Austin's report that would have added to the general feeling throughout Britain that the Dieppe raid had been something of a success; a similar story was reported by all the correspondents. Unfortunately it was in human terms a catastrophe. The force had been made up of around 5,000 Canadians and 1,000 British troops, and over 4,000 men were killed, captured or wounded. According to the *Official History of the Canadian Army in the Second World War*, 'the total of fatal casualties was 56 officers and 851 other ranks. Canadian casualties of all categories aggregated 3,369'. The Germans were reported to have lost around 600 men. There were a few American Rangers with the Commandos and among them was Lieutenant Edward Loustalot, who became the first American soldier to be killed in Europe during the Second World War.

Austin accompanied 4 Commando on the raid and theirs could be considered one of the few aspects of the operation that was successful, which is probably why it featured on the BBC. Austin referred to their 'young colonel': this was Shimi Fraser, his Christian name an Anglicisation of Shimidh, the Gaelic for Simon. Fraser was also the 17th Lord Lovat, Chief of the Clan Fraser, and a man from a proud tradition of Highland chiefs used to leading their men into battle. With Fraser were some of the American Rangers and one of them, Corporal Franklin 'Zip' Koons, from Iowa, was probably the first American soldier to kill a German in the Second World War. Following his return from Dieppe Lord Lovat made a speech in the House of Lords in which he attacked Lord Strabolgi, the Labour Party's Chief Whip in the Lords, who had written an article criticising the leadership of the British Army for an American magazine.

I had the honour to command representatives from 58 regiments of the British Army. They had no politics; theirs was the simple faith which made our forebears feared and respected on every foreign battlefield on which they fought. If any tub-thumping politicians came down to them and attacked their leader's policy, there would be only one answer – the nearest horse-trough.

Lord Lovat, House of Lords, 1 October 1942

It was also a disastrous day for the RAF; although not according to the BBC, whose broadcasts reported information from 'official sources'. One communiqué spoke of the results of 'the greatest air battle of the war', reporting that ninety-eight Allied aircraft were lost, and ninety-one Luftwaffe aircraft were shot down, along with 'probably twice that number destroyed'. Around seventy squadrons were involved, of which three-quarters were Spitfire units. In all the Allies lost 119 aircraft, the Luftwaffe 46; it all added up to the worst day for the RAF since the war had begun. In addition the Royal Navy lost a destroyer and over thirty landing craft, many of which carried tanks. It was a task at which they were singularly unsuccessful, and every tank that was landed on the beach was destroyed.

In part the reason for the failure of the raid was that the Germans knew it was coming, not because of spies in Britain, or careless talk, but from the accident of a German naval convoy running into the British force mid-Channel. At the time a brave public face was placed on the disaster and for a long while the truth was not out. Churchill was distraught; he had, after all, been living with the failure of Gallipoli for twenty-seven years. The best that could be said of the Dieppe raid was that an awfully expensive dose of experience was gained, which made the D-Day landings a less costly venture. According to Dwight D. Eisenhower, 'From it we learned a number of lessons that we later applied to our advantage, but the price paid by the Canadians still rankled,' while Mountbatten commented, 'For every soldier who died at Dieppe, ten were saved on D-Day'. British Intelligence was also satisfied that the Germans used up a lot of additional manpower on the Channel defences that could have been employed elsewhere, in the fear that there would be other attacks.

FUEL IS SOUGHT

The prosecution of the war, especially given the increasing size of the bomber raids on Germany, and undertakings like the Dieppe raid, used up huge amounts of fuel. It was rationed from the outbreak of war, but this was not such a hardship for the average British family. Car ownership was a fraction of what it is today and so the impact on daily life was much less than it would be now. There were about a million cars in Britain in 1930, which had doubled by the time war broke out; interestingly the number of cars roughly matched the number of telephones. But fuel didn't only mean that which was used by motor vehicles, and as the war went on consumption generally became an increasing issue. In the summer of 1942 the Minister of Fuel, Light and Power broadcast on the important need to save fuel in a 'Sunday Postscript'.

> The gap between coal production and consumption is just as serious as the gap made in our lines in Libya; it must be closed. This is the time of the year when we build up our stocks of fuel, and the more we can save the greater those stocks will be . . . The housekeeper is not by any means the largest consumer of fuel – generally speaking, she is an example to all of us in her

desire to help the country. The greatest consumers are our industries, and they must come in on this too. Indeed, it is because of the greatly increased consumption by essential industries that the domestic consumer is being asked to economise.

If the economies that can be made were made we should be able to ensure that every essential industry and every house got the necessary fuel next winter. If, however, my hopes are disappointed, then we shall have to have recourse to rationing. Obviously, no Government can take any chances in so vital a matter, and we are therefore proceeding with our plans for a rationing scheme, so that we shall be ready to put it into operation should the need arise.

Major Gwilym Lloyd George, Minister of Fuel, BBC, 28 June 1942

The Minister instituted a Defence Order that made the waste of fuel – either coal, gas, electricity or liquid fuel – an offence. The BBC got right behind the campaign, encouraged, of course, by the Ministry of Information, and initiated a series of talks and special features to encourage people to use less. As early as the following day tips and hints on savings were being offered on 'The Kitchen Front', as well as in between programmes, when the continuity announcers repeated items from the Minister's speech. After the 6 p.m. news 'Fuel Flashes' was introduced with the sole aim of encouraging people to use less. Announcer Freddie Grisewood called on people to send him ideas on how to conserve all types of fuel; he was inundated with all kinds of schemes, and was soon getting seventy-five letters a day from eager listeners keen to pass on their 'top tips'.

We've been getting a lot of letters from listeners who advise cooking with steamers and two-tiered saucepans if you have one. This is of course an excellent plan, and saves a lot of fuel. A listener from Belvedere, Kent, advises using an old saucepan lid, for they usually last longer than saucepans so you'll probably have one or two to spare. Turn it upside down and knock some holes in that from the inside. It balances marvellously on top of another saucepan and you can put in your vegetables and cover it with the lid belonging to the saucepan underneath.

Freddie Grisewood, 'Fuel Flashes', 17 August 1942

There were talks and discussions involving housewives from all over the country and these proved to be one of the most popular features concerning wartime strictures during 1942. Rationing of petrol for cars finally ended on 26 May 1950, to the jubilation of the owners of around 3.5 million motor cars. The Oxford-educated Grisewood, who had the most impeccable BBC voice, went on to chair 'Any Questions' from 1948. Like Alvar Lidell, Grisewood had trained as a singer before joining the BBC in 1929. He became synonymous with 'Any Questions', only stepping down in 1968 when heart trouble forced his retirement shortly before his 80th birthday. Although he was generally considered one of the safest pairs of hands there was one occasion when he was broadcasting and the script said 'His Holiness Pope Pius' – Grisewood could only manage 'His Holiness the Pipe'.

JUST DESERT

On 26 June Tobruk fell to Rommel's Afrika Korps and for a while things in the North African desert looked very bleak indeed. Not only was it a major strategic loss but the Axis powers captured over 30,000 Allied prisoners along with a massive amount of fuel, which was vital in fast-moving armoured warfare. The BBC's man in Egypt at this point was Richard Dimbleby, who had been sent to Cairo after his stint in France with the BEF, but for the most part he had not been the busiest of the BBC's overseas war correspondents. Some people went as far as criticising Dimbleby for his penchant for staying around the headquarters staff in Cairo, but in fairness a single reporter covering a war zone the size of the North African campaign was in a no-win situation. It was a similar to the situation in the war with Iraq in which correspondents were embedded with fighting units. They could only see the situation from the very narrow perspective of where they happened to be, while those reporting from GCHQ had the wider viewpoint. It is as much a comment on our need for news from the front line, a feeling of being an 'eyewitness to history', that correspondents are put with those doing the fighting. A man like William Howard Russell, War Correspondent for *The Times* and regarded by some as the greatest ever exponent of the art, has a lot to answer for. He reported on the war in the Crimea between 1854 and 1856, as well as the Zulu War in 1879, and did much to create this demand for reportage from 'our man at the front line'.

Another cast in the mould of William Russell was the BBC's correspondent Godfrey Talbot. He finally got his wish to be sent overseas at about the time of Tobruk's capture, having been released from the chores of reporting the war on the Home Front. Being told to get himself to Egypt to replace Richard Dimbleby was the easy part; actually getting there was another story altogether. He was first sent to Oban in Scotland to board a merchant ship before becoming part of a convoy bound for Lagos in Nigeria. Having hung around Lagos he eventually got a flight, via the Belgian Congo, and finally landed on the Nile in a flying boat; it had only taken six weeks. Talbot arrived shortly after Churchill visited the British troops at El Alamein and at just about the same time as Lieutenant-General Montgomery took over command of the Eighth Army. Montgomery, having objected to the planned Dieppe raid, had not been around to see the results of the Allied action. The 54-year-old Montgomery, whom the newspapers were fond of describing as 'the son of a Bishop, a teetotaller, non-smoking and a firm believer in spartan methods', arrived at the same time as Talbot; this turned out to be a good thing as the two men struck up a good working relationship.

Initially Talbot was told by others at the BBC's offices in Cairo not to bother rushing out into the desert as Hitler's 'Desert Fox', General Erwin Rommel, had been stopped at El Alamein. Much to his frustration as a professional reporter Talbot was encouraged to enjoy lunches at the Turf Club and sightseeing visits to look at the Sphinx. It all failed to meet with Talbot's view of what a war correspondent should be doing. He set about trying to organise some sorties to collect real 'war stories'. He attempted to accompany several naval missions and on one occasion was refused permission to go on a submarine mission, fortunately, as it turned out, because the sub disappeared with no survivors. To help broaden the coverage in North Africa the BBC sent another of their correspondents, Denis Johnston, to Egypt, but it will be Talbot's broadcasts that are forever remembered from this pivotal campaign.

Interestingly, Dublin-born Johnston was not really a 'professional broad-caster' but a playwright who helped establish the reputation of the Gate Theatre in his home city; his best-known work is *The Moon in the Yellow River*, written in 1931. He joined the BBC before the war and worked on its pioneering television broadcasts.

According to fellow correspondent Wynford Vaughan-Thomas Johnston was a far-from-typical reporter. After the North African campaign the two intrepid news hounds were stuck in the middle of a wintry Italian war. Vaughan-Thomas complained bitterly that there was no news and that he would have no choice but to inform London of the fact. Johnston was adamant that no desk-bound London editor would believe that in the middle of a war zone there could be nothing to report. For example, said Johnston, 'there's this report that a dog came over from the German positions north of Lanciano, and the Canadians have adopted it'. 'That's not news!' said Vaughan-Thomas. 'Wait and see,' said Johnston.

Reports from the Eighth Army front indicate that the Germans are now using trained dogs in an ingenious attempt to penetrate Canadian defences.

Frank Phillips, BBC News, January 1944

Despite the mood in the BBC's Cairo Office, where some people seemed to think the war would wait – either that or there was nothing much worth talking about anyway – Talbot finally got to the front line, but not before participating in one of the more surreal recordings of the whole war. He introduced a Services performance of Handel's 'Messiah' in the Anglican cathedral close to the River Nile. Although the sound quality was none too good it acted as a fanfare to what was to follow. At El Alamein there was stalemate so there were limited stories to report on, but this was just the lull before the inevitable storm. Montgomery and his senior commanders had been planning another assault against Rommel's men and it began at 9.40 p.m. on 23 October, with a thousand-gun bombardment of the positions held by the Afrika Korps and their Italian allies.

Here we will stand and fight. There will be no further withdrawal. I have ordered that all plans and instructions dealing with further withdrawal are to be burnt, and at once. We will stand and fight here. If we can't stay here alive, then let us stay here dead.

I want to impress on everyone that the bad times are over, they are finished. Our mandate from the Prime Minister is to destroy the Axis forces in North Africa – I have seen it. Written on half a sheet of notepaper. It can be done, and it will be done, beyond any possibility of doubt.

What I have done is to get over to you the atmosphere in which we will now work and fight. You must see to it that this new atmosphere permeates right down through the Eighth Army, right down to the most junior private soldier. The great point to remember is that we are going to finish with this chap Rommel once and for all.

Now, my forecast of this battle is that there will be three definite stages. First, the break-in to the enemy's positions. Then the dogfight, and then the breakout. We will do the break-in on the night of 23rd October. The dogfight battle will then begin and involve hard and continuous fighting. I believe the dogfight battle will be a hard killing match and will last for ten or twelve days. The enemy will crack. Then will come the breakout, and that will lead to the end of Rommel in North Africa. Make no mistake about it.

Lieutenant-General Bernard Montgomery,
BBC News, 24 October 1942

What Monty lacked in delivery skills – his speech impediment gave him a slight lisp and his voice was a staccato, flat monotone – was more than made up for by the absolute clarity of his instructions. The speech to the North African commanders was heard in Britain a few days later, during the news, having been recorded in the desert by Talbot and his engineer. There were many listening on the Home and Forces Programmes who must have been heartened, but at the same time those with loved ones, friends or family in the desert would have been filled with trepidation. The wife of a Royal Tank Regiment sergeant from Halifax in Yorkshire wrote to Talbot to explain how she felt. 'Your voice comes right into the room with us in the nine o'clock news and you tell us what our boys are doing, not that old flat communiqué stuff. I'm sweating out there with you, and it's a lovely link and comfort really, so God bless you and keep you safe.'

Monty's speech was one of Talbot's first significant broadcasts from the desert, but there would be many more. The recordings were made on heavy discs on to which four minutes of material could be 'cut' by 'Skipper' Arnell, the BBC engineer. The recording machinery was housed in a 30-cwt truck, nicknamed Belinda, that was driven by an army corporal. After a recording had been finished it was carried by motorbike to Cairo, from where it was radio-beamed back to London. The logistics of recording these discs were tested to the limit in the desert where the sand got into just about everything, although on the night of the thousand-gun bombardment there was another unexpected problem. Such was the ferocity of the firing, and the sheer explosive effect, that it ruined a number of precious discs before the engineer eventually managed to capture the sound. The problem was that the heavy pick-up arm just kept bouncing off the disc. Two nights after the battle began a report by Talbot in the morning news bulletin updated people with the state of play – all with that on-the-spot feel.

Dust storms are blowing over the face of the desert, and it's difficult to see far; but up above, very high in the blue sky, our aircraft are going over to gun and bomb the enemy – wave after wave filling the air with the steady, combined roar of the engines. It's almost a procession; sweep after sweep goes over, at frequent and regular intervals, like clockwork. No British land forces have ever had such a powerful air force with them as this.

Last night, when the campaign opened, was dramatic in the extreme. Up to the start, it was, to all appearances, just one of those normal, fairly quiet, desert nights, which we have known up here during the past weeks. The full moon shone down brightly; the scene was peaceful. Then, quite suddenly, with a crack and a roar, the barrage opened – our barrage – and in a minute or two, everything was let loose on the enemy. It went on, lifted, and went on again. It was terrific, flashing and roaring almost without pause, for hours. The desert has known nothing like it.

The guns were still going at dawn, and behind it our infantry had moved up, had cleared a gap for our armour to pass forward. So, very early in the morning, the tanks started to move. You couldn't see them – just clouds of dust on the stony plain, and a clattering rumble. Enemy guns didn't seem to be making a great reply to ours. Enemy aircraft were kept on the defensive.

The land forces engaged included, of course, a large number of British troops; all our very powerful armoured formations are British: then there is the 44th Division, with Home County units, the 50th Division, troops from the North of England, and also the 51st Highland Division. There are also the Australians, New Zealanders and South Africans, the 4th Indian Division, the Fighting French and the Greeks.

Godfrey Talbot, BBC News, 25 October 1942

Two days after Talbot's broadcast the 21st Panzer Division counter-attacked with the aim of pushing the Allied forces into the German minefields (around 4 million mines were laid in the area); it failed and they took a huge loss of panzer tanks. This left the Germans with a depleted armoured corps of close to eighty tanks, of which just over thirty were panzers. In the early hours of 2 November the Allies commenced Operation Supercharge – the final breakout at El Alamein.

This is Godfrey Talbot recorded in the desert. The sound you can hear now is the noise of British tanks moving into battle. It's the night of Sunday/ Monday November 1st/2nd in the early hours of the morning and I'm here on this desert; with the sand clouds whirling up behind them British tanks are moving into battle. Shells by the thousand are being pumped into the enemy and now here we are beside one of these desert tracks; here we are watching the armed might of the Eighth Army going forward to engage the enemy. The moon, just half a moon shining down here, a starry night, and overhead not only the moon but the flares that have been dropped which are shining down on the desert, which are illuminating this battleground. Tank after tank is going by just a few yards from the microphone as I speak now. One can't see very clearly, it's rather like being in a fog, it is indeed a fog, but it's a fog of sand. Because the sand is very soft here and each tank as it goes by churns up a great cloud.

Godfrey Talbot, BBC News, 2/3 November 1942

During the battle about half the remaining German tanks were destroyed and when Rommel signalled Berlin of his intent to withdraw Hitler ordered him to stand and fight.

This is the BBC Home and Forces Programme. This is Bruce Belfrage. Here's some excellent news, which has come during the past hour that has come in the form of a communiqué from GCHQ Cairo. It says. 'The Axis forces in the Western Desert after twelve days and nights of ceaseless attacks by our land and air forces are now in full retreat.' It's known that the enemy's losses in killed and wounded have been exceptionally high. Up to date we've destroyed more than 260 German and Italian tanks and captured or destroyed at least 270 guns. The full toll of the booty cannot be assessed at this stage of the operation.

Bruce Belfrage, BBC News, 4 November 1942

As well as reading the good news that had come in from North Africa Belfrage had other reasons to be happy. He had handed in his resignation letter just before reading the bulletin; he was off to join the Special Branch of the RNVR.

Over the next few days, with Rommel retreating as fast as he could, and down to just twelve tanks, the Allies took over 30,000 prisoners. The speed of the Allied advance, and their mounting success, caused even the normally unflappable Alvar Lidell to come over all excited: 'I'm going to read you the news – and there's some cracking good news coming.'

Such was the importance of this phase of the war that a lapse of the BBC's objectivity could be forgiven. By 14 November Tobruk had been retaken, an event that was marked in an unusual way. Denis Johnston and a BBC engineer had recorded the bells of the Anglican cathedral in Egypt as they were rung in celebration and they managed to get a recording back to London to be heard following the 9 a.m. news the next day, along with the bells of Coventry Cathedral. It marked the second anniversary of the destruction of Coventry. In fact, church bells all across Britain pealed in celebration of the victory. It was the first time that bells had been heard since 1940 when they had been stopped and people warned they would only be heard in the event of invasion. By the end of November the Allies retook large parts of Tunisia; the Axis powers in North Africa were finally on the wane. Four days before the fall of Tobruk Churchill spoke at the Lord Mayor's luncheon at the Mansion House – he could barely contain his feelings.

I notice, my Lord Mayor, by your speech you have reached the conclusion that news from the various fronts has been somewhat better lately. In our wars, episodes are largely adverse but the final result has hitherto been satisfactory. Eddies swirl around us, but the tide bears us forward on its broad, restless flood . . . We have not so far in this war taken as many German prisoners as they have taken British, but these German prisoners will, no doubt, come in droves at the end, just as they did last time. [Much laughter]

I have never promised anything but blood, tears, toil and sweat. Now, however, we have a new experience. We have victory – a remarkable and definite victory. The bright gleam has caught the helmets of our soldiers and warmed and cheered all our hearts . . . General Alexander, with his brilliant comrade and lieutenant, General Montgomery, has made a glorious and decisive victory in what I think should be called the Battle of Egypt. Rommel's army has been defeated. It has been routed. It has been very largely destroyed as a fighting force. This battle was not fought for the sake of gaining positions or so many square miles of desert territory. General Alexander and General Montgomery fought it with one single idea – to destroy the armed forces of the enemy and to destroy them at a place where the disaster would be most punishable and irrevocable . . .

. . . It was a deadly battle. The Germans have been outmatched and outfought with every kind of weapon with which they had beaten down so many small peoples and, also, larger, unprepared peoples. They have been beaten by many of the technical apparatus on which they counted to gain domination of the world. Especially is this true in the air, as of tanks and of artillery, which has come back into its own. The Germans have received that measure of fire and steel which they have so often meted out to others.

Now, this is not the end. It is not even the beginning to the end. But it is, perhaps, the end of the beginning . . .

. . . But this Battle of Egypt, in itself so important, was designed and timed as a prelude and a counterpart of the momentous enterprise under-taken by the United States at the western end of the Mediterranean, an enterprise under United States command and in which our army, air force and, above all, our navy are bearing an honourable and important share. A very full account has been published of all that has been happening in Morocco, Algeria and Tunisia.

. . . Let me, however, make this clear, in case there should be any mistake about it in any quarter: we mean to hold our own. I have not become the King's First Minister in order to preside over the liquidation of the British Empire. For that task, if ever it were prescribed, some one else would have to be found, and under a democracy I suppose the nation would have to be consulted. I am proud to be a member of that vast commonwealth and society of nations and communities gathered in and around the ancient British monarchy, without which the good cause might well have perished from the face of the earth. Here we are and here we stand, a veritable rock of salvation in this drifting world. There was a time not long ago when for a whole year we stood all alone. Those days, thank God, have gone . . .

. . . British and American forces continue to prosper in the Mediterranean. The whole event will be a new bond between the English-speaking people and a new hope for the whole world. I recall to you some lines of Byron which seem to me to fit event and theme:

> Millions of tongues record thee, and anew
> Their children's lips shall echo them and say,
> Here where sword the united nations drew
> Our countrymen were warring on that day.
> And this is much and all which will not pass away.
>
> *Winston Churchill, BBC, 10 November 1942*

The year 1942 was not a great year for Allied military operations and it's therefore unsurprising that the Prime Minister made as much as he did of the North African success. While the victory was not absolute, nor complete, it was enough of a success to crow about, particularly given the setbacks that had preceded it. As the fighting in Tunisia continued the battle-hardened Afrika Korps proved an extremely tough nut to crack. Given the importance of the fighting and the sheer scale of the theatre in which it was being played out the BBC had steadily added more correspondents, including Frank Gillard, Robert Dunnett and Howard Marshall. In early March Rommel was ordered to leave Africa, and never to return; his replacement could do nothing to stop the combined might of the British, Commonwealth, Free French and American armed forces. The Axis military losses in men alone during the first three months of 1943 were almost 70,000 killed, captured and wounded. On 9 May the unconditional surrender of all Axis troops took place in Tunisia. In all 250,000 prisoners were taken, of which 130,000 were German – the haul including twenty-six generals. It took three years, but finally the Afrika Korps was no more.

This is the Forces Programme. The War in North Africa is over – von Arnim has been captured. These were the brief but pregnant headlines of the News broadcast this morning. In celebration of this great victory, we are substituting for the miscellaneous orchestral programme advertised a tribute to our forces in Africa and those of our Allies. The concert is given by the BBC Symphony Orchestra, leader Paul Beard, conductor Sir Adrian Boult. It begins with the stirring march 'Stars and Stripes', by John Philip Sousa.

Stuart Hibberd, Forces Programme, BBC, 12 May 1943

The rest of the programme continued with Elgar's 'Enigma Variations' and concluded with Beethoven's Fifth Symphony.

THE RADIO DOCTOR

At the same time a new battle was just about to start on the Home Front. For all sorts of reasons, not the least of which was the poor quality of people's diet brought about by rationing, the Radio Doctor became an institution during wartime. He first broadcast in May 1942 and was never identified on air, but he was Charles Hill, from Luton in Bedfordshire, who worked for the British Medical Association.

'I cannot eat but little meat my stomach is no good.' No, no, it's not a confession. It's a poet's description of a pre-war Boxing Day, really pre-war for he wrote it 400 years ago. But how are you today? How's your tongue, is it smooth and red or knobbly and beige with an overcoat of a muddy hue? How's your stomach, is it firm and steady or somewhat warm or a little wobbly and a trifle windy? Or was your Christmas Day so spartan that today you're fighting fit with no twinge of remorse? Well, a word on digestion. It's the preparing of food for absorption into the body but nature has somehow arranged our digestions that we know not what they're doing.

Radio Doctor, BBC, 26 December 1942

Perhaps the Doctor's greatest claim to fame was being the first man to utter 'belly' on the BBC, and to survive! In 1943 he arranged to give a number of talks on the subject of venereal disease, although these were largely, one assumes, directed at the Forces, rather than at those on the Home Front. On one famous occasion, when talking of a man who had become gravely ill, he said, 'he took a turn for the nurse'.

Charles Hill later became a Conservative MP, going on to become Postmaster-General in 1955 and then Chairman of the Independent Television Authority. He was made Lord Hill of Luton in 1963, and from 1967 to 1972 he was Chairman of the BBC, having been appointed by Prime Minister Harold Wilson to 'sort out' the Corporation.

POLAND'S HORROR

At the end of May Poland's government in exile received news from the Polish Bundists (Jewish socialist movement) that the Germans had murdered 700,000 Polish Jews. On 2 June the BBC broadcast the same information, although they had stopped short of talking about the total elimination of the Jews in Europe by Hitler. There were a number of broadcasts on the BBC's European network in Polish and in Yiddish about the atrocities, but it was not something that featured much at all on the BBC. In recent years there has been some revisionism aimed at the BBC; it has accused them of duplicity, along with the Ministry of Information, about the whole question of the extermination of Jews in Poland. However, on 9 July Brendan Bracken, the Minister of Information, reiterated that 700,000 people had been murdered in Poland. He made it clear that once the war ended, the United Nations would ensure rapid and severe punishment of the persons responsible. 'They will be tried as murderers, which they are. These gangsters will be punished with the utmost rigidity of the law.' On 2 July there had been a BBC broadcast on the European Service by Szmul Zygielbojm, one of the Bundists' leading figures; he bluntly told of the Nazis' strategy in Poland, and the 'planned extermination of a whole nation by means of shot, shell, starvation, and poison gas'. When the full extent of the horror of what had happened in Poland became clear a year later Zygielbojm committed suicide.

In the midst of this delicate situation the BBC found itself in trouble for allowing a broadcast by Lord Wedgwood to America. The BBC admitted a 'serious error of judgement' in allowing the broadcast to go ahead, having not properly been through the process of censorship. The main thrust of his Lordship's speech was that America should take over the Palestine Mandate from Britain.

Ask no more from Britain . . . We want the Jews of Palestine armed, in the sure and certain conviction that, once armed, they will never surrender either to Hitler's Germans or to the British Administration in Palestine. The British Administration has been too strong for the British Parliament and conscience. The whole Administration, from the top to the Irish police who masquerade as British, are against the half-million Jews of Palestine. They will never let them have arms, nor land, nor free immigration, nor a refuge, nor a home. They don't like Jews and there are enough anti-Semites and crypto-Fascists still in Great Britain to back up the Hitler policy and spirit. Any change now must involve the whole Administration. They all have a vested interest in proving the Balfour Declaration unworkable – in proving themselves right.

Lord Wedgwood, BBC American Service, 26 May 1942

This highlights the difficulties that the BBC was facing, particularly when Lord Wedgwood went on the attack in the days after the broadcast, accusing the BBC of being made up of a Liberal group and a Tory group. He suggested the BBC wanted to 'get rid of one of their Liberal censors'.

On 27 September 1942 Thomas Mann gave a talk on the BBC's German Service in which he denounced the 'mass annihilation of European Jews with poison gas in territories occupied by Germany'. He went on to say that '16,000 French Jews had been gassed on a train after it had been hermetically sealed'. It largely fell on deaf ears. Three months later, on Christmas Eve, Marius Goring broadcast on the German Service of the BBC and repeated the information that Bracken had given to the Parliament. Goring read out the United Nations declaration condemning 'this bestial policy' and went on to tell listeners in Germany that the news of the extermination of the Jews in Warsaw could 'only serve to strengthen Allied determination to fight Nazism and punish all those responsible'.

A QUESTION OF BALANCE

The BBC was still receiving criticism in Parliament and in the press, but there were signs of it dwindling. The indications of a steady improvement in the quality of reporting the war, as well as a better standard of all-round output, were all there. In particular the BBC had gone from being little more than the relayer of communiqués to something closer to what we have come to expect from the news. As the historian G.M. Young said in 1943 of the BBC's news output, 'it had a standing without rival on the European Continent'.

Then just as it is now, it was impossible for the Corporation to provide a balanced pattern of broadcasting that hit all the right notes with every section of its audience. However, with sales of over three million each week for the *Radio Times*, which made it Britain's bestselling magazine, it was clear that many at least wanted to keep abreast of what was available. The BBC's own research indicated that people were enjoying a larger and larger proportion of the BBC's output. It was indeed fortunate because for many people the radio was almost their only source of entertainment. By 1943 German bombing raids were not the main issue, rather it was the logistics of keeping any semblance of normal life going. The strictures of rationing, the fact that many husbands and sweethearts were overseas, and a whole host of other priorities meant that it was very much a 'wireless world'. According to the BBC's own handbook, published in March 1943, the Corporation's most difficult task was in walking 'the tightrope of balanced controversy'. In wartime the imperative of doing everything possible to win did sometimes conflict with the mindset of many who worked for the BBC, some of whom felt it vital that all points of view be recognised – and broadcast. It was a sentiment clearly echoed by a proportion of its listeners too. It all boiled down to the old 'freedom of speech' argument. The former Parliamentary Secretary to the Ministry of Information, Harold Nicolson, in his dual role as an MP and a Governor of the BBC, gave a very well-balanced analysis during a discussion on the BBC in late 1942.

We are not a private concern in the sense that a newspaper is a private concern; we are a public concern; it is our duty not merely to inform and entertain our own public but to present a picture of British life and character which shall be coherent, balanced, representative, and true.

We must avoid, obviously, at any cost, taking political sides. I am always delighted when my friends of the Right tell me that the BBC is a seed-bed of Leftish opinions and when my friends of the Left deplore the fact that it should be a sanctuary of reaction. When I hear that, I feel satisfied that we are fulfilling our duty of being fair to all, of keeping the middle way . . .

. . . The wireless is a new and highly powerful invention. It is at the same time universal and intimate – by which I mean that whereas we are addressing some twenty million people we are also speaking to them in the intimacy of their homes. We are bound to respect such intimacy; we are bound constantly to reflect that we are not merely addressing a vast public audience but also being admitted into the privacy of countless families.

The BBC is not like a newspaper which can express its editorial opinion or repudiate responsibility for what it publishes; nor is it a Government Department like the Post Office, which is obliged to accept and carry any letter, however boring or silly that letter may be. The BBC is an organisation entrusted with the handling of the most potent instrument of publicity that has ever been devised. It must be inspired throughout by the utmost carefulness, which is something wholly different from timidity. And that carefulness must take constant account of the fact that when an idea or an opinion is broadcast it at once loses its true proportion and becomes magnified or amplified beyond life-size. In giving time on the air to some minority opinion (however sincere or useful that opinion may be; however ardently we may agree with it ourselves) it is our duty, as the BBC, to consider, not merely whether we are being fair to those who agree with this opinion, but whether we are also being fair to those to whom that opinion is a very abomination. It is for this reason that in controversial matters we generally try to adopt a round-table method. I do not call that cowardice; I do not call it a denial of free speech; I call it a careful and difficult maintenance of responsibility. We do make mistakes and sometimes we make blunders: but when you have to magnify opinion a thousand times beyond life-size it may happen that free speech does not turn out as fair speech; and our rule is, when in doubt, to prefer what is fair.

Harold Nicolson, BBC, October 1942

The governor's description of the dilemma facing the BBC and their way of handling it could not have been put more eloquently. Nicolson's argument resonates today when you consider the furore over the rights or wrongs of the BBC's activities. Nothing changes, whether it is controversy over the 'sexing up' of Iraq's weapons of mass destruction, or how much coverage, if any, certain minority groups should be given. The BBC would have been pleased with a letter-writer to Kent's *Tonbridge Free Press*, who in January 1943 stated, 'I never read the newspapers. I hear all the news I want over the wireless.' It was a view shared by H.G. Wells, who two months later told a conference that 'the day of the newspaper was done'.

As part of the Corporation's desire to improve its image it mounted the 'BBC At War' exhibition to tour the country, beginning in Scotland in late 1942 before moving on to visit the rest of Britain during 1943. Over 140,000 people visited the display in Glasgow, Edinburgh, Aberdeen and Dundee; it featured photographs and included concerts, talks and discussions. Naturally one of the concerns of people living north of the border was a possible bias towards the south, and especially the accents of the newsreaders. It's a debate that continues today, although it is more to do with the bias of the reporting than the accents of the announcers. Newsreader Frank Phillips was called upon to defend the accents of the newsreaders: 'I suppose we all talk Southern English.' He also added that because London was the capital it had not made 'Cockney speech the national tongue'. He went on to defend the BBC's view of how it used language: 'Pronunciation in any age is largely a matter of fashion, and it would probably be more true to say that the newsreaders of the BBC follow the general tendency rather than speak any particular regional brand of English. Mr Joseph MacLeod, for instance, who is of Skye descent and comes of a Gaelic-speaking family, is easily distinguishable from his colleagues by his pronunciation of the word "says" which he pronounces, with a careful regard for language which is perhaps a Scottish characteristic, as if it rhymed with "days" and not as most Englishmen do as "sez".' It is a subject that can still inflame passions, as a letter-writer to the *Liverpool Echo* in 2002 demonstrated.

> There is no place for regional accents on national radio. The newsreaders of the past, Stuart Hibberd, Godfrey Adams, Freddie Grisewood, John Snagge, Alwar Lidell [*sic*] and Frank Phillips were peerless. There are no equals today.

One matter they did not discuss in Edinburgh concerned the difficulties that were sometimes faced by the newsreaders in dealing with difficult foreign place-names, and the names of people – something that needed careful handling when it came to the names of Russian generals. There was an issue that was closer to home in its cause, and that was the wording of some of the official government communiqués. Bruce Belfrage was one day faced with saying 'The Italian battalions were scaling a precipitous escarpment'. He rang the offending Ministry and suggested to the officer who had apparently written the tongue-twister that he should perhaps think of how difficult it was to read these things on the news. 'Oh, you read these things, do you? We just stick them up on a green baize notice-board.'

During 1943 the BBC put great emphasis on increasing the quantity and quality of its broadcasts to Europe. During the year transmissions went up by around 40 per cent, with broadcasts in twenty-four languages, including for the first time regular programmes in Swedish, Spanish and Portuguese. But not all European programmes were produced by the BBC; some were supplied by the American Office of War Information, including 'America Calling Europe', which came direct from New York. The BBC paid particular attention to the listeners in France who wanted to hear an alternative vision of what was happening in the world to that supplied by the Vichy Government. In one of these broadcasts France was told of the atrocities against French Jews. All of these programmes to Europe were in one way or another underpinned by Allied propaganda. Sometimes they were explicit in their message, like the editor of the BBC's Italian broadcasts, who simply stated: 'We are addressing ourselves to all those Italians who are in any way fighting or working for the expulsion of the Germans and resurrection of a free and democratic Italy.'

BERLIN BOUND

On the night of 16 January 1943 the BBC's on-the-spot reporting entered a new phase when Richard Dimbleby flew with the RAF on a raid over Germany. He and six other men – correspondents from the Canadian press, the *New York Times*, Reuters, NBC, the *Daily Mail* and the *Sydney Daily Mirror* – flew in Lancaster bombers. Dimbleby got to fly with Guy Gibson, one of the most revered of wartime Lancaster pilots, on a mission to Berlin. Dimbleby was none too thrilled at the prospect of going on a bombing mission. Dimbleby's son Jonathan, writing about the incident in his biography of his father, said, 'He looked forward to the mission . . . with no excitement and considerable fear.'

. . . It was bursting away from us and much lower. I didn't see any long streams of it soaring into the air as the pictures suggest: it burst in little yellow winking flashes and you couldn't hear it above the roar of the engines. Sometimes it closes in on you, and the mid- or tail-gunner will call up calmly and report its position to the Captain so that he can dodge it . . .

. . . The flak was intense as we turned in for our first run across the city, it closed right round us. For a moment it seemed impossible that we could miss it, and one burst lifted us in the air as though a giant hand had pushed up the belly of the machine . . . white, and yellow and red incendiary bombs had hit the ground, all over the dark face of the German capital these great incandescent flowerbeds spread themselves.

'. . . Right – right – steady – left a little – left a little – steady – steady', and then, 'hold it – BOMB GONE.' The incendiaries turned to a dull, ugly red as the fires of bricks and mortar and wood spread from the chemical fires . . . This shimmering mass of flares and bombs and gun-flashes was their stronghold . . . I was filled with a great exultation.

Richard Dimbleby, BBC, 18 January 1943

After the bombs dropped and Gibson turned the Lancaster for home such was Dimbleby's mixture of fear and relief that he was sick, narrowly missing the bomb-aimer. Given that this was his 'first mission' it is totally explicable; but in fact what would prevent any one of us from feeling that way on every mission? It was perhaps a pity that his trip to Berlin was not recorded, but then again was it something that the people listening back home needed to know? The 'tally-ho' mentality of the Battle of Britain pilots had been replaced by the dour determination of the bomber crews – a stoic attitude that focused on getting the job done. In fact Dimbleby showed amazing courage and went on to fly twenty missions with the RAF; given the attrition statistics for bomber crews in the Second World War he certainly chanced his luck. After the Berlin raid Dimbleby had to take a train back to London from the RAF base from which he had flown. He was apparently slumped in his seat, looking very much the worse for wear, and feeling completely exhausted, only to be told by a woman passenger: 'I should have thought that a lucky young man like you would have the good manners to give up his seat to one of our fighting men.'

The 'Dimbleby raid' on the night of 16/17 January involved over two hundred aircraft, almost all Lancasters, but there were about a dozen Halifaxes as well. It was the RAF's first attack on Berlin in over a year, and was also the first time that all the aircraft involved in the raid were four-engined bombers capable of packing an extra punch. In military terms the raid was far from successful. There was thick cloud over the German capital and the bombs were scattered far and wide. On the positive side the German air-raid precaution system failed and the aircraft arrived over Berlin practically unopposed. Bizarrely, almost half of the anti-aircraft gun personnel were away on a course, which contributed to the fairly light flak. Those gun crews still at their posts may have been surprised at the height at which the bombers were operating. In any event it all added up to fairly light casualties, with just 200 people killed in Berlin, although about a quarter of them were British prisoners of war.

Two months after Dimbleby flew with Guy Gibson the wing commander was ordered to form 617 Squadron, the famous Dam Busters. In May 1943 their specially modified Lancasters attacked the Möhne, Eder and Sorpe dams, and following the raid Gibson was awarded the Victoria Cross; he was also told to stand down from operational flying. His enforced 'rest period' was not total and he managed to fly occasional missions over the coming year until he was officially authorised to undertake one more sortie. On 19 September 1944 Gibson flew a Mosquito, with Squadron Leader Jimmy Warwick DFC acting as his navigator, as the master bomber (the aircraft that identified and marked the target), but on their return they were spotted over Holland with failing engines. The aircraft crashed in flames and both men were killed.

THE WORLD'S BIGGEST-EVER BATTLE

On the Russian front the German Army stared catastrophe in the face. The Russian defenders of Stalingrad achieved the unthinkable and had defeated overwhelming German odds.

The triumphant conclusion to the Battle of Stalingrad with the capture of eight more German Generals, and 45,000 other prisoners, in the past two days has overshadowed the rest of the news from Russia. Our Allies have kept up their great advance on the Donetz front. The programmes of the German radio were interrupted this afternoon to broadcast a special communiqué. It was followed by sustained funeral drum rolls and slow music, then by the national anthem and a three-minute silence. A little later it was announced that Goebbels had ordered all places of entertainment to be closed for three days. When this announcement was broadcast it was followed by more slow music. It has also been announced that the whole public life of Germany was being given over to mourning.

Robert Robinson, BBC News, 9 p.m., 3 February 1943

The streets of Stalingrad if you can give the name to open spaces between ruins still bear all the marks of battle. There's the usual litter of helmets and weapons, stacks of ammunition, papers fluttering in the snow, pocket books from dead Germans, and any number of smashed corpses lying where they fell or stacked up in great frozen heaps for later burial. Stalingrad can never be repaired, it will have to be rebuilt from the beginning. But even though all its buildings are wrecked there's life in it still. Along the narrow strip of cement-coloured cliff by the river, which the Russians held through the long months of assault, there's a city of dugouts. Dugouts occupied by the soldiers who have not yet left and by a few women who stayed behind to launder and cook for the men. There's a real holiday atmosphere among these people today. They're the proudest men and women I have ever seen. They know they've done a terrific job, and have done it well. Their city's been destroyed but they smashed the invader by sheer stubbornness and unconquerable courage. These men and women fought for months with their backs to the river that they'd sworn never to cross. Facing an enemy who occupied the only dominating height in Stalingrad and could pound them with shells and mortars unceasingly by day and night.

Paul Winterton, BBC, 9 February 1943

In his definitive book on the battle, *Stalingrad*, Antony Beevor calls this the 'most catastrophic defeat hitherto experienced in German history'. When Robert Robinson, one of the wartime intake of newsreaders who had been invalided out of the army after Dunkirk, read the news he, like most people listening, could probably not fully comprehend the enormity of the Soviet victory. It certainly made a mockery of William Joyce's boast just a few weeks earlier:

The extent of the enemy's sacrifices has been colossal and cannot be maintained. In the Stalingrad Sector, above all, the Soviets have been employing heavy forces and their losses have been proportionately high. Day after day, more Soviet tank losses have been reported and at the same time, the ratio between the German and Soviet air losses is incomparably in favour of the Luftwaffe. For example, it was reported yesterday that sixty-seven Soviet aircraft had been shot down as against four German losses; on Tuesday, the ratio was fifty-two to one in our favour. As might be expected, the Luftwaffe's superiority has dealt a hard blow at the enemy and it is now reported that the Soviets are being compelled to use untrained personnel in their larger bombers.

William Joyce, German radio, 16 January 1943

Haw-Haw was not wrong; the Russians' losses were enormous, but they had more manpower and Stalin rightly assumed that sheer force of numbers would eventually win out. The actual German losses in the battle have been debated ever since the 200-day battle ended, but a figure of 500,000 seems about right – the Russians lost half as many again. On top of that there were civilian casualties of anything between 1.5 and 2 million. Included in the German losses are 45,000 prisoners who died when the Russians force-marched them to Siberia, about half of the number that started out; by the end of the war 38,000 more of them had died, leaving just 7,000 survivors.

> To Field Marshal of Artillery Voronov and Colonel-General Rokossovsky, commanding the forces of the Don Front: I congratulate you and the forces of the Don Front on the completion of the liquidation of the enemy troops surrounded at Stalingrad. I am grateful to the troops, commanders and political workers of the Don Front for the excellence of their military achievements. Signed Stalin, Supreme Commander in Chief.
>
> *Moscow Radio, 2 February 1943*

As a footnote to the Germans' sense of dejection over their defeat it is interesting to note the music that they played on their radio network. First up came 'Ich hatt' einen Kameraden' (I had a comrade), a march that was usually played at military funerals; it was repeated three times. Inevitably there was 'Deutschland über Alles' and the Nazi hymn 'Horst Wessel', played in slow time. After a three-minute silence came Wagner's beautiful 'Siegfried Idyll'. After also playing the Rumanian and Croatian national anthems there was, somewhat ironically, Beethoven's Fifth Symphony – with its 'V' campaign opening.

JUST LIKE REAL WAR

Three weeks after the German Army's devastating defeat at Stalingrad there was an exercise in southern England. Codenamed Spartan, it was designed to replicate an Allied army assault on a bridgehead 'somewhere in central Europe'. It began on 1 March, lasted for twelve days and involved ten British and Canadian divisions; four of the divisions were armoured.

This was not only an exercise for the military in anticipation of the opening of the 'Second Front', but also one for the BBC. They got permission to have two reporting teams cover Spartan and decided to treat it just like a 'real war'. The flow of information was sent back from the 'front' to Broadcasting House, where two special teams had been set up to process the stories and the recordings into news bulletins. Spartan was of critical importance to the military in their planning for D-Day, and it proved to be no different for the BBC. They had to be able to prove that they could do the job with total professionalism if reporters were to accompany troops in the front line when the European invasion was launched.

The BBC put Seymour de Lotbinière, their long-time Director of Outside Broadcasts, in charge of the exercise. They did this because while the information collected and processed was news, it was to all intents and purposes an outside broadcast. Richard Dimbleby, fresh from his success over Berlin, was one of the reporters to capture the stories as the exercise went about its business. The teams used Austin saloon cars to hurtle about the south of England, but as a vehicle for war it proved to be totally inadequate. The Austins were overloaded with equipment and were insufficiently rugged, or speedy, to operate on a real front line. That aside, the reporters and their back-up teams managed to collect an impressive amount of information that they rapidly sent to back to Broadcasting House where it was sifted into news items, as well as material to be saved for a documentary-style hour-long programme called 'War Report'. It all worked brilliantly and all that was left to be done, to avoid any doubt as to the success of the trial, was to play their material through loudspeakers, to replicate a broadcast, for the Secretary of State for War and the C-in-C Home Forces; they too agreed that it was a huge success. The BBC had proved itself ready for combat.

About the only thing that failed to come up to the Corporation's exacting standards, standards exemplified by Dimbleby, was the fact that many of those who filled the positions of engineers or features men seemed totally unable to wear a uniform. '[They] would never have passed the eliminating tests of officer cadetship,' wrote Dimbleby in his report on the exercise. Dimbleby went on to chastise his compatriots for their slovenly language: 'He addressed private soldiers, military policemen and sentries as "old boy". He addressed an elderly War Office general by calling at him "I say", with a cigarette dangling . . . when he finished he gave a friendly wave and turned away.'

Aside from these slight lapses in discipline the BBC decided to begin the task of assembling teams to be attached to the various units of the Allied forces as soon as the invasion of Europe began. All was proceeding well with the planning until November 1943, when General Eisenhower was appointed Supreme Commander of SHAEF (Supreme Headquarters Allied Expeditionary Force). It meant that the BBC effectively had to 'renegotiate their contract', as the Americans had a very different perception of broadcasters. In the US there were a number of different networks, all competing for news, which meant to the American top brass that the BBC was just another news gatherer. Naturally the Corporation's senior management found this a bit mystifying – after all, the BBC was 'purveyor of news to the world'! And so simultaneously the Corporation set about training key personnel to accompany an invading army, as well as justifying its special status to SHAEF. A.P. Ryan's vision had begun to come to fruition and would be carefully nurtured over the coming fourteen months before spectacularly bearing fruit.

TOTALITARIAN INSTRUMENT

On 8 April 1943, three weeks after Spartan was over, there was a debate in Parliament in which the BBC came in for yet more criticism. This was not the normal kind of condemnation of the broadcaster's output, however. It was from some Independent Labour Party (ILP) members who seemed to be motivated along doctrinaire lines. However, with the BBC seeming to have turned the corner, a public rebuke was the sort of thing that could stir the pot in some other quarters.

John McGovern had been a member of the Anti-Parliamentary Communist Federation before becoming the Independent Labour Party MP for Glasgow Shettleston; he had been expelled from the Labour Party proper. Like his colleagues in the ILP, he consistently opposed the war, refusing to recognise the coalition of all parties that were fighting the Axis powers and generally making a nuisance of himself. McGovern put forward the motion 'That this House is gravely concerned at the partiality of the propaganda and choice of propagandists by the BBC, and the way in which it is being directed on totalitarian lines; and is of the opinion that the Government should take the necessary steps to secure that more opportunity should be given for the propagation of the different shades of opinion on political, social, religious and medical questions, so that the Corporation should be used as an instrument of democracy, instead of one for the creation of an authoritarian regime in this country.' War clearly was not going to get in the way of this man's fight for justice in broadcasting. When the debate opened McGovern accused Churchill of 'dictatorship' and 'complete authority over the BBC and the Press'.

John McGovern went on to say, 'We get a one-sided hash all the time. It shows a complete lack of faith in democratic institutions.' He pleaded that the BBC should provide expression for even extreme points of view. He had no objection to a Fascist speaking over the radio, if he was answered by a representative speaker in reply. 'I do claim that this is a totalitarian instrument wielded for the benefit of the Government and particularly at the dictation of the Prime Minister. Everybody seems to be afraid to face up to this individual and he appoints in every phase of public life those who can be depended on to carry out his own wishes.' One of McGovern's colleagues in the ILP, Campbell Stephen, MP for Camlachie, who seconded the motion, spoke about an outrage against the Glasgow Orpheus Choir. According to him his fellow Scots were still suffering a certain amount of victimisation because of the anti-war views of its conductor, the Revd Dr MacLeod of Glasgow. 'A man of great influence in the Church of Scotland, [who] was very often at the microphone, but evidently the BBC decided that he was unsafe when he became a disciple of Dick

Sheppard, who took an anti-war point of view.' It meant that Dr MacLeod was 'no longer a welcome visitor to the microphone'. In finishing his speech he accused the BBC of using propaganda to 'create a nation of robots, instead of a nation of thinking people'.

A Liberal member, Professor Gruffydd, making his maiden speech in the House said, 'The BBC was becoming the great cock-shy or Ye Old Aunt Sally . . . it gives the nation a service such as no other broadcasting corporation gives in the world.' Lord Hinchinbrooke for the Conservatives suggested 'that proceedings in the House should be broadcast. After the war the BBC should be further divorced from Government control and associated more intimately with the people, or an alternative network should be set up.'

In both these comments there is perhaps the first mention of some tried and trusted chestnuts. Was this the first time the BBC had been called 'Auntie'? The idea of broadcasting parliament would be hotly debated for the next thirty or so years. It was not until 1975 that Parliament was first broadcast live. The first commercial radio stations in the UK, and the first legal alternative to the BBC, beat the broadcasting of Parliament by just two years.

Following a lively debate Brendan Bracken, who some felt fitted McGovern's barb of being a Prime Ministerial patsy, set out his vision of the BBC's conduct during the war. He began by suggesting that some people who hated the BBC treated it as a hair shirt and felt that they must listen in to exacerbate their own feelings. When he got down to the serious business of defending the Corporation he did so powerfully and gave as good an insight into the role of the BBC in wartime as has been given.

Broadcasting is a more complicated business than newspapers, but you will never be wanting a supply of persons unhampered by any technical knowledge who are quite certain that they could run the BBC better than the men and women who have given a fair portion of their lives to broadcasting and are responsible for it now.

The charter of the BBC is not affected by the Emergency Powers Act except in this limited sense that in common with all other people it is forbidden to publish information that might be of value to the enemy. The existing arrangement depended upon the goodwill and good sense of the Ministry of Information and the BBC. It afforded infinite opportunity for friction, but in the time that I have been Minister of Information the only difference I have ever had with the Governors of the BBC was about finance . . .

. . . As for the Ministry taking over all the services of the BBC, I am absolutely opposed to that. The British public does not want Government-edited news, whether in the Press or in the BBC news bulletins. If the news bulletins of the BBC were suspected of being given a Government slant, they would lose all character and be discounted in the ears of millions of listeners.

Bracken also went on to say that he knew that discussion and entertainment programmes would be ruined if they were taken over by the Ministry of Information. The Minister then talked about the power of the BBC's European services.

It was estimated that 20 to 35 million people in Europe defied the Nazis to listen in to the BBC at least once a day. I think that is an over-statement, but nevertheless it has a very considerable audience in Europe, and any big news story put out by the BBC is known to most people in western Europe, excluding Germany, within three hours of the time at which it is put out. It is also true to say that in Germany itself, where the BBC have well over one and a half million listeners, no news story put out by the BBC and suppressed by Dr Goebbels fails to have currency in the length and breadth of Germany within one week. In Italy our audiences are greater, and in recent times I have had most remarkable evidence of the effect of BBC broadcasts to Italy.

As to the provision the BBC made for clandestine newspapers in Europe, there were at least five hundred of these newspapers being mainly dependent upon the BBC for their text and guidance. Germans tried desperately to smother this voice of Free Europe, but the BBC have shown great wisdom and foresight in this matter, and the power of their transmission has been altered to overcome this, and, with the co-operation of listeners in many parts of Europe, many devices have been introduced for combating jamming.

The BBC's European news service was one of the best and liveliest news organisations in the world, Bracken said, and he wished he could find words to praise the intelligence, energy, and resourcefulness of its staff. After complaining about Mr McGovern's 'vile slanders' against the BBC bias Bracken finished by saying:

So long as I am Minister of Information, I am resolutely determined that no outside influence shall deflect the editors of the BBC news bulletin from editing the news according to their own judgement. Some of the things the Governors had done deserved criticism, and some things they had left undone exposed them to blame. But in all their doings they strove to be fair to all sections of the community. They had no political partisanship and no religious bias.

If devotion to duty and willingness to work long hours in uncomfortable conditions, and intelligence and ingenuity are qualities which appeal to the House, every fair-minded member must acclaim the work of the staff of the BBC. Let us recognise the BBC as one of our greatest war assets.

While not everything the Minister said about controlling the BBC was absolutely true within the limitations of trying to have a free press in a wartime scenario, the achievements of his Ministry and of the BBC were considerable. The motion was defeated 134 votes to three, those against being McGovern and his two colleagues in the ILP.

THE FLIGHT OF THE IBIS

With the war in North Africa over, an incident took place off the coast of Spain that has attracted the attention of conspiracy theorists ever since.

The British Overseas Airways Corporation regrets to announce that a civil aircraft on passage between Lisbon and the United Kingdom is overdue and must be presumed lost. The last message received from the aircraft stated that it was being attacked by an enemy aircraft. The aircraft carried thirteen passengers and a crew of four; the next of kin have been informed. Later it was announced that among the passengers was Leslie Howard . . . and now a personal tribute by J.B. Priestley.

'I was his colleague very often in overseas broadcasts; in fact the first one he ever did was with me nearly three years ago. I know well how he succeeded in conveying to distant audiences the same easy charm and quiet sincerity that marked his performances on stage and screen.'

BBC News, 3 June 1943

The fifty-year-old English actor Leslie Howard, one of the stars of *Gone with the Wind*, became the first film star to lose his life during the Second World War. Howard, as well as giving talks on the BBC, had also been a member of the 'Brains Trust' since October. The BOAC DC-3 had been owned by KLM, the Dutch airline, and the aircraft with its all-Dutch crew of four had left Lisbon at 9.40 a.m. on a regular flight to Bristol. Named the *Ibis*, the DC-3 had been airborne for a little over three hours and was flying low over the Bay of Biscay. The aircraft normally kept radio silence on these flights but at 12.54 p.m.

Cornelis van Brugge, Flight 777's radio operator, sent a Morse code message: 'I am followed by unidentified aircraft . . . I am attacked by enemy aircraft . . .' It was the last message from the *Ibis*. Flight 777 had been attacked by eight Junkers Ju88s, which had no difficulty shooting down the unarmed airliner. This flight was far from unique, as airliners had been flying from Lisbon to the UK since 1941. On one occasion when Godfrey Talbot travelled between London and North Africa he took this route. Staying overnight in Lisbon he had dinner in his hotel, but had to share a table with a Luftwaffe officer.

On 4 June the *New York Times* ran a story stating, 'It was believed in London that the Nazi raider had attacked on the outside chance that Prime Minister Winston Churchill might be among the passengers'. This is not such a wild theory. One of the passengers was called Alfred Chenhalls, whose name may have been mistaken for Churchill by German spies, who were known to scrutinise aircraft manifests regularly. Chenhalls, who bore a passing resemblance to the Prime Minister, was actually an accountant who looked after Howard's business affairs. The potential for Winston Churchill to be in this area – or even on this aircraft – existed, because he was in North Africa in late May. The Germans may have put two and two together, although quite why they imagined the Prime Minister would travel under his own name and in broad daylight on a scheduled flight with no fighter escort is anyone's guess.

Lisbon during the war was a hotbed of spies, informants and double agents and subsequent research has revealed that just about everyone on board the aircraft probably had connections of one sort or another with one or another of the Allied secret service agencies. It's hypothesised that even Howard had some associations himself, and certainly Chenhalls seems to be linked to those involved in espionage through his association with Anthony Eden. It was Eden who had encouraged Howard to make a month-long tour of Spain and Portugal to give lectures on film-making for the British Council. It is highly likely that the Germans knew Howard was on board and that may have been incentive enough to shoot down the aircraft, given his position as a leading light in the British cinema with a penchant for roles that were 'anti-Nazi'.

A fact probably unknown to the Germans was that the English film legend was born Leslie Howard Steiner in London on 3 April 1893 to a young Jewish couple; Howard's father was of Hungarian descent. Howard throughout his life maintained his parents' name was Stainer, perhaps to avoid any possibility of anti-Semitism. Howard had been a second lieutenant in the cavalry on the Western Front in the First World War but had returned to England with a severe case of shell shock. It was at the end of the war that he made his stage debut as an actor, before graduating to films. One of his best-known wartime movies was *The First of the Few* about R.J. Mitchell, the designer of the Spitfire.

The day after the DC-3 had been shot down an RAF Sunderland of Coastal Command was attacked in almost the same position. The Sunderland was searching for survivors of the previous day's crash and one of its crew was killed before the aircraft returned to its base. This suggests that either the Germans had information that Churchill was going to be on a particular plane or that the Luftwaffe was shooting at anything that moved, or flew, across the Bay of Biscay. In recent years there has been increasing evidence suggesting that the aircraft on which Howard was travelling was sacrificed to save ULTRA, the codename given to the secrets that the British gleaned from deciphering German messages.

Perhaps most interesting of all to conspiracy theorists is the fact that the papers associated with Leslie Howard's estate, due to be released in 1980, have been reclassified until 2056. Was Howard sacrificed to protect Churchill, or was it just an aberration of war and an accident, as the Germans claimed? The smart money is on a link with ULTRA, and yet much more sensitive information has been declassified. So why keep something secret for 113 years?

As with most things during the war that had a whiff of controversy, speculation in the media over Howard's death soon abated. There was always something new coming along to take its place in the news spotlight.

THE ITALIAN JOB

Ten days after the DC-3 was shot down the Allies invaded Pantelleria, a small volcanic island in the Straits of Sicily. It marked the start of the campaign to conquer Europe on the Western Front, albeit initially from the south. On 9 July under cover of darkness Allied troops landed on Sicily by parachute and glider. The following day Operation Husky began, involving 160,000 men of the British Eighth Army under General Montgomery, along with the US Seventh Army commanded by Lieutenant-General George Patton; 2,700 landing craft began disgorging their men and machinery on the Italian island.

> Darkness fell. The destroyers of Group V quartered the sea like grey ghosts guarding a ghost fleet. And from every port in Tunisia there would be other ghost fleets dashing through the darkness in this gigantic jigsaw puzzle to slip into their respective places at zero hour, 2.45 a.m.
>
> There was a steady droning sound in the air, and we knew that our airborne troops were passing over in droves, high up in the starlit sky. Our ship, the destroyer *Blencathra* would have the post of honour by leading the landing craft in to a small bay between Cape Passero and Pozallo, and knock

out of action a powerful battery overlooking the bay. We were expecting casualties, of course, and preparing for it in the way usually done in small ships. Our dining table was turned into an operating table, with a big, powerful electric light suspended over it, and stacks of instruments were made ready in glittering metal trays.

We had finished by about 11.00, and then had a little singsong, as I had brought my guitar with me. At twelve I thought I had better take a nap, for when operations started I would probably have a couple of days and nights on deck and on the bridge without sleep or rest. So I lay down on the settee for forty winks. I was suddenly roused by the 'Doc' shaking me: 'Ras, wake up and see what the wind blew in. Our first patients.' I sat up and blinked at eight wet, naked men, with blankets over their shoulders, who were drinking tea and chatting.

They were a fine crowd of men, without a trace of weakness or fear after their terrible ordeal. They had been dropped short from a glider and fell into the sea three miles from shore. After tearing their way through the fabric of the submerged glider, they drifted about for over three hours before we found them. They had then given up hope, as the glider was sinking under them. Four of them were strong swimmers who could have made shore, but they would not leave the others who could not swim. One man had been lost in the crash.

It was getting on towards zero hour, and I had to go up on the bridge. The steward came in and asked: 'About your cocoa, Sir. Would you like it before or after action?' It was said so naturally and in such a matter-of-fact way as if knocking out shore batteries was an everyday occurrence in the *Blencathra*. I replied: 'Thank you, Steward. I will have it after action. I think it will taste better then.' He said: 'Very good, Sir,' with a puzzled look on his face. To him the cocoa was purely a routine matter and, as such, more important than the action.

As I left the wardroom, Action Stations was sounded. It was a beautiful starlit night with a waning moon. The *Blencathra* was ripping through the water ahead of the convoy and closing the shore rapidly. Suddenly from the lighthouse at Cape Passero, the long luminous finger of a searchlight started to probe the darkness. It moved slowly towards us and stopped just short of our position, a long lane of blinding, glaring light, surrounded by pitch-blackness. Another move forward of that beam would floodlight the whole invasion fleet a quarter of an hour too early. I held my breath and watched. Then as suddenly as it had been turned on it was switched off and left us half blinded in the pitch dark. It had been a narrow squeak, for the island fortress Coranti was within rifle shot.

On the bridge, every eye was now turned towards shore, where the massive outline of the fortifications could be picked out against the skyline. We were inside a bay, and it was getting on to zero hour. The gunners were ready to open fire, and the range was being called out in rapidly shortening distances. The moon had by now gone down.

The blackness and silence ashore was suddenly broken by a burst of machine-gun fire and long arcs of white and red tracers. Here and there Verey lights, white and green, cut through the darkness, followed by the sharp rattle of firing. To the eastward, but far away, great fireworks lit up the sea and sky and were followed by the full rumble of heavy gunfire. In the twinkling of an eye the scene had changed from utter silence to a growing pandemonium of sound. One moment the *Blencathra* was alone in the bay. The next, dark shadows were racing for the beaches and the waters were alive with craft and roaring with engines. It was zero hour, and our gunners were on the point of opening fire when the radio crackled and the army ashore reported: 'Situation well in hand. Batteries captured – bombardment unnecessary.' The airborne troops had done their job well, and apparently the landing had come as a complete surprise.

We turned to meet the troopers, due to anchor at 3.00, and at 3.00 to the tick I heard the rattle of many anchor chains. Then across the bay towards Pozallo, where a great fleet of supply ships were due at 3.15, and at 3.15 I could see the bow of the first ship coming out of the darkness. The firing to eastward had increased, and the sky was filled with long arcs of red tracers crossed by sprays of white tracers from the shore. Far out to sea the air trembled with the thunder of heavy guns, and the flickering flames of gun flashes made the stars pale.

An arc of flaming guns almost a hundred miles long marked the steel ring of the Royal Navy and the American Navy. A ring of battleships, monitors, cruisers and fleet destroyers were guarding the landing fleet from any naval interference, and pouring a deadly fire into the strongpoints inland to secure the beachheads. The low, rolling hills shook under the impact of this avalanche of shells and glittered with their explosions.

As dawn broke, the black waters gave up their secrets, and the fleets of shadow ships took shape. Far out, the towering bulk of big fighting ships, and within their protecting ring the sea was black with ships as if all the shipping of London, Southampton and Liverpool had suddenly been assembled off the Sicilian beaches by a magician. There were famous liners and unknown tramps. There were ships from every known shipping company of every Allied nation. Destroyers were dashing about here, there and everywhere looking for trouble, like terriers with their hackles up. Close inshore they were shooting up strongpoints and pill-boxes, putting up barrages for advancing troops or blinding enemy gun positions with smoke shells. That was over towards Pozallo where the situation was still a bit sticky. There, some of the destroyers of our Group acted as mobile field artillery in close support of the troops, and did a magnificent job. The *Blencathra* was doing an anti-submarine sweep round the invasion fleet with the rest of Group V.

The sun rose like a big red-hot ember, and across its face moved a stately procession of cruisers, like jet-black etchings. The whole bay glowed with the first sunrays and the fleet lay in a rosy haze. The air vibrated with sound. Aircraft swarmed overhead, guns rolled like thunder in the distance and banged off broadsides near the beaches, and in between, hundreds of winches clacked and grated, davit falls crackled as small landing craft were lowered from the troopers and joined the stream towards the beaches. From the army ashore came this signal: 'All operations proceeding as planned. Forts and airfields captured.'

And now it was also possible to see how the land lay. To eastward the long low tongue of Cape Passero reached out into the sea with wide stretches of golden beaches. To the north a wide half-moon bay backed by low grey foothills, stippled with dull, dusty green of olive groves and orchards. Small villages of cream-coloured houses nestled in the dips and down by the beaches. Dominating this were the squat, massive fortifications and barracks on the rising ground above the bay. At the western end of the bay I could see Pozallo town and fortifications where a battle was in full swing. Further inland and beyond the nearest ridges nothing could be seen except clouds of yellow dust from the heavy shells of the big ships.

The bay itself was alive with craft, coming and going, and the beach itself was already a vast storehouse of supplies, crawling with men, tanks, trucks and Bren carriers in orderly converging streams. The beach roads were packed with convoys racing towards the front line just beyond the first ridge of hills where our field artillery and tanks were already in action.

Out to seaward were new fleets coming in, the vanguard of the ferry service between North Africa and Sicily. More landing craft, more supply ships, more special equipment, each wave carrying special gear, supplies and men required for the successive stages of the operations. There seemed to be a bridge of ships between the landing beaches and North Africa.

It was while we were pumping shells into Pozallo that the first air attack on the invasion fleet came. But that fleet could take care of itself. A solid sheet of flame shot skyward, like a volcano in eruption, as every ship went into action. No aircraft could face that barrage, and the attack soon fizzled

220 HERE IS THE NEWS

out after two planes had come hurtling down in flames. All the bombs fell wide. We kept on bombarding at regular intervals all through the night. It was essential to knock out opposition there, because Pozallo was the junction between the Canadians and the Highland Division.

All Sunday morning, the 11th, the bombardment continued, when suddenly at 13.18, HMS *Brissenden* signalled: 'The town of Pozallo wishes to surrender.' The Senior Officer signalled back: 'Proceed in and accept surrender.' Later on the Senior Officer signalled to the *Brissenden*: 'Hand over Pozallo to army now approaching.' Pozallo was ours; the rest was now plain sailing, and the *Blencathra* returned to her 'ack-ack' duties with the invasion fleet.

Lieutenant A.H. Rasmussen, BBC, late July 1943

The Allied raid on Hitler's Fortress Europe, as it was dubbed at the time, did not get off to an auspicious start. The men that appeared naked on board the *Blencathra* were some of the lucky ones. Due to some atrocious weather, only twelve out of almost 150 gliders carrying the British troops managed to land on target. Sixty-nine crashed into the sea and the other gliders were dispersed far and wide. The American paratroops, who were on their first jump in anger, were equally scattered; their colonel landed twenty-five miles away from his intended drop zone. It was a testament to the resilience of all the airborne troops that they managed to create such havoc among the garrison troops on Sicily.

The landings took place in very windy conditions but went very well; the Italian defenders lived up to their reputation and put up little in the way of resistance. On a second wave of parachute drops by the Americans thirty-seven aircraft were shot down by 'friendly fire', around a quarter of the total number of planes. The drop had followed an Axis air attack and the Allied gunners had not all been informed of the planned descent. Operation Husky was a success in the end as Sicily was taken with far greater numbers of German and Italian casualties and captured than Allied troop losses. Probably the most important lessons learned regarded airborne invasion techniques, by both parachute and glider. These resulted in changed training and communications programmes, which would prove vital if operations on D-Day and beyond were to succeed.

At the end of June Churchill gave a speech when he was awarded the freedom of the City of London.

Three years ago all over the world, friend and foe alike – everyone who had not the eye of faith might well have deemed our speedy ruin was at hand.

Against the triumphant might of Hitler with the greedy Italian at his tail . . .
more than 40,000 of our people were killed and more than 20,000
wounded. But now those that sowed the wind are reaping the whirlwind. In
the first half of this year which ends today the Royal Air Force alone has
cast upon Germany alone thirty-five times the tonnage of bombs which in
that same six months of this year has been discharged upon this islands.

Winston Churchill, BBC, 30 June 1943

In mid-July with the attack on Sicily in full swing Churchill and Roosevelt sent
a joint radio communiqué to the Italian people. In the names of Prime Minister
Churchill and President Roosevelt they were told that the sole hope for their
survival was in

honourable capitulation to the overwhelming power of the military forces of
the United Nations. The time has come for you to decide whether Italians
shall die for Mussolini and Hitler – or live for Italy and civilisation.

BBC Italian Service, 16 July 1943

This was not the first time the Italians had received such a message. The
first approach by Churchill had been made during a broadcast in December
1940, when he read to the Italians a message of goodwill and appealed to
them 'to stop a river of blood from flowing between the British and Italian
people'. In another broadcast in November 1942, the Prime Minister warned
the Italians that when Tunisia was captured, North Africa would be the
springboard from which to get to closer grips with the enemy: 'It is for the
Italian people, all 40 million of them, to say whether they want this terrible
thing to happen to them or not.'

When the island of Pantellaria, close to Sicily, surrendered, President
Roosevelt made a strong appeal to the Italian people to rid themselves of their
Fascist Government and make peace; this was followed up by numerous leaflet
drops urging an Italian surrender. After the 16 July broadcast there was
something of a radio silence, which was out of character for Italian radio.
There was not the immediate rebuttal, the usual bluster or tough-talk and
threats.

Nine days later news came through of a partial harvest; the 'greedy Italian'
had got his just deserts.

Here's an important piece of news that has just come in. Rome Radio has
announced that the King of Italy has accepted the resignation of Mussolini.

Maurice Shillington, BBC News Flash, 11.15 p.m., 25 July 1943

When the Allies seized Palermo on 24 July Mussolini's fate was sealed. After Italy failed to accept the Allies' call to surrender a massive air raid involving 500 bombers was launched against Rome's factories, industrial and military facilities. Benito Mussolini missed it as he was away in Verona having a meeting with Hitler. Upon Il Duce's return to Rome on 25 July he was met by the King Victor Emmanuel, and an armed escort, who promptly took the sixty-year-old dictator into custody. While it proved not to be the end of his 'reign' it was the end of his power. He was rescued by the Germans after Italy announced their surrender and briefly took 'control' of northern Italy as the Nazis' puppet. A new Italian government led by Marshal Pietro Badoglio was sworn in and within two days the new Premier announced that Italy was no longer a fascist state; secret negotiations for an armistice commenced almost immediately.

Two minutes ago the ceasefire was ordered and here is General Patton the Commander-in-Chief of the US Seventh Army speaking to you from the hill-top overlooking Messina.

'General Truscott I appreciate very much your asking me to accompany you on entering the city that you have so gallantly captured. I cannot find words with which to express my admiration of your drive and enthusiasm, nor to express my appreciation of the magnificent fighting qualities and super-human endurance of the soldiers of the 3rd Division. I certainly thank you.'

Gerry Marsh interviewing Lieutenant-General Patton,
BBC, 17 August 1943

Lieutenant-General Patton had been having a war of his own during the invasion of Sicily. He clashed with both Alexander and Montgomery over almost everything. It even came down to a lot of silly posturing, with Patton going to absurd lengths to prove that as a general he knew how to behave more correctly. He had a US Army band play when Montgomery came to meet him at his HQ – all because Monty didn't give him lunch or seemingly show him enough respect on Patton's earlier visit to the British General's HQ. The 'contest' between the two men extended to who was going to capture Messina. Patton simply issued orders that his army were going to do it and wrote in his diary on 1 August: 'It is a miracle that our men can get through them [the mountains] but we must keep up our steady pressure. The enemy simply can't stand it, besides we must beat the Eighth Army to Messina.'

It was during the race to Messina that Patton made a huge error of judgement when visiting a field hospital. He slapped a soldier with his glove and accused the man of cowardice. A week later there was a more serious incident when Patton pulled a gun on an enlisted man at another hospital. Having taunted him he hit him in the head, a scene witnessed by several newsmen. General Eisenhower managed to keep the thing under wraps and personally intervened with both the newsmen and Patton. It remained a well-known secret until November, when the incident was reported on an American radio show. Patton kept his job, and did not even face disciplinary charges, despite the fact that hitting an enlisted man was a court-martial offence. In January Patton was removed from Italy and sent to England to work on the planning for D-Day. It would come back to haunt the 58-year-old general and his career would be dogged ever after.

Whatever Patton's personal foibles the fact that Messina was taken and Sicily finally captured opened the door for the Allies to plan and execute an attack on the Italian mainland. It was executed in double-quick time.

Today the 3rd September we enter the fifth year of the war. And today the Eighth Army having fought its way from Egypt to Tunisia then crossed the seas to Sicily have landed on the mainland of the Continent of Europe. We have a good plan and air support on a greater scale than we've ever had before. There can only be one end to this next battle, and that is another success. Forward to victory, let us knock Italy out of the war.

General Bernard Montgomery, BBC, 3 September 1943

As for knocking Italy out of the war, it was totally unnecessary, as Marshal Badoglio's secret negotiations had come to an end and an armistice was agreed on the very day that the invasion began. It was, however, kept secret until the Allies' invasion was in full swing. With Montgomery's Eighth Army gaining a foothold in the toe of Italy the main invasion force followed on 9 September; it was the day after the Italian surrender was announced. Given that the Germans expected this to happen their plans were well advanced and their troops took over the main defensive positions, previously occupied by Italians, and disarmed their former ally at the same time.

This is the Home and Forces Programme. Here is the news and this is Frederick Grisewood reading it. Two hours ago Italy declared war on Germany. A proclamation by Marshal Badoglio brands the Germans for savagery against the civilian population and says there can be no peace while a single German remains on Italian soil. Italy's new step has been acknowledged in London, Washington and Moscow. Her status will be that of a cobelligerent, not an ally.

Freddie Grisewood, BBC News, 13 October 1943

The announcement of Italy's change of side came at a time when Allied forces were in the midst of an offensive push to cross the River Volturno in southern Italy, After the Allied landings Naples had fallen on 1 October and the German Tenth Army fell back to their defensive positions at the river. After some hard fighting the Germans eventually withdrew across the Volturno but it was to be the start of some desperate fighting in which every ridge, every valley and every river crossing on the road to Rome was bitterly contested.

For the remainder of 1943 the war in Italy ebbed and flowed, with the Germans winning some victories over the Allies in the worsening weather conditions. Not everyone was happy about the way in which the BBC covered the Italian campaign. In late September the historian G.M. Young, who had helped Winston Churchill with his book *The English-Speaking Peoples*, wrote to A.P. Ryan complaining about the broadcasts. It was not the first time that Young had complained and in he did so partly in his capacity as a 'language scrutineer'. The BBC in 1941 decided to pay Young £200 a year to 'watch the English of our news bulletins'. For Young this was *carte blanche* to comment on just about anything. It wasn't just in private letters and memos to BBC managers and governors that he let his feelings be known. In June 1943 Young wrote an article for the *Sunday Times* in which he asked what people in 2043 would think of the BBC's coverage of the war, and its output in general: 'would the picture be fair and representative?' Given that he was writing in the *Sunday Times*, and that he was a historian, Young's predilection was towards the historical veracity of the Corporation's output. In fact by this time the quality of the BBC's newsgathering machine had improved immeasurably from the rather amateurish early attempts at reporting the very narrow field of conflict that was France. With the war now really a 'world war' the BBC was doing a remarkable job in what may have been less trying physical circumstances than the post-Blitz scenario; even so, they did not have the technology to sift and sort, and cut and paste, that we now have. Every news bulletin, every programme, every talk, every minute of every day was a triumph of ingenuity and personal dedication over considerable odds.

At the time of Young's *Sunday Times* article there was a change of management at the top of the BBC. On 24 June 1943 Sir Cecil Graves, the Joint Director General, resigned because of ill health. Robert Foot became sole Director General, with William Haley appointed to the new post of Editor-in-Chief. Haley had been the editor of the *Manchester Evening News* before becoming a director of the *Manchester Guardian* and later Reuters. Two weeks before Young's critique of the Italian coverage Ryan had written to the professor and said: 'When we think we have been reasonably colloquial, people say we are vulgar. When we feel we have been dignified they tell us we are pompous.' It neatly sums up the BBC's wartime dilemma. They were doomed whatever stance they took. Such was the importance of news – and such was the BBC's importance as a provider of news – that they were constantly in the bright, white glare that is the spotlight of public opinion.

THE AMERICAN FORCES NETWORK

With so many American military personnel in Europe a radio station dedicated to their needs was a must. The American Forces Radio Service began broadcasting in 1942 but a move to Europe did not take place until the following year. At 5.45 p.m. on 4 July 1943 Corporal Syl Binkin became the first man to be heard on the newly renamed American Forces Network. The new service used studio facilities and technical support from the BBC, with initially around five hours of programming every day, along with news bulletins provided by the BBC. AFN could be heard across the whole of the UK, much to the delight of American service personnel – who were probably bemused by the humour of the BBC's Forces Programme, and confused by some of the sports commentaries, such as the Army versus Navy cricket match!

There were some tensions between the BBC and the AFN, with the Corporation feeling – perhaps strangely – under threat as the national broadcaster. Given that the broadcasts went out on the medium wave there was nothing stopping anyone in Britain listening to the AFN shows, whether they were a soldier or a civilian. Because of the popularity of the American big bands and their singers, like Frank Sinatra and Ray Eberly, it was none too surprising that British people tuned in. With the large numbers of black GIs stationed in the UK some of their favourite artists were introduced to British audiences. Nat King Cole, and from 1944 onwards the great Louis Jordan, were just two who found an audience in Britain, in part because of the AFN.

The BBC did in fact make a rod, or perhaps a baton, for its own back in that the Corporation was not keen to broadcast American big bands – in particular, the most famous and perhaps the best of them all, Major Glenn Miller and the American Band of the American Expeditionary Force. In October 1944 the BBC decided that Miller's music was 'unsuitable for the British public'. It sparked a furious row with many of the biggest stars in British music, including the band leaders Harry Roy, Geraldo, Victor Sylvester and Jack Hylton, who all demanded that the BBC should feature Miller's band.

BOMBS AWAY

Shortly before the capitulation of Italy one of the most remarkable broadcasts of the war took place, a live recording of a bombing raid on Berlin. Richard Dimbleby's report of his flight with Guy Gibson earlier in the year, and other subsequent reports, were recorded after he got back to Britain. This time an engineer and a correspondent flew together on a mission and captured something of what it was really like to be on board an RAF bomber. According to Wynford Vaughan-Thomas's memoirs, the engineer had even volunteered – he wanted to give 'my two youngsters something to talk about'. Thirty-five-year-old Vaughan-Thomas, on the other hand, had been 'hand-picked' by his superiors.

Last night on the fourth anniversary of Great Britain's entry into the war a strong force of Royal Air Force Lancasters made a concentrated attack on Berlin. Among that force was a bomber that carried in addition to its bomb load and its crew of seven, two BBC men and recording gear. The Recording Engineer was Reginald Pidsley and the Observer Wynford Vaughan-Thomas.

WVT:	And here we go to drop our bombs on Berlin.
Navigator:	Hello Skipper.
Pilot:	Hello Navigator.
Navigator:	Half a minute to go.
Pilot:	OK, thanks very much.
Bomb-aimer:	OK, keep weaving Ken.
Unknown:	There's quite a lot of light stuff coming up as well, falling off a bit low.
Pilot:	Ah . . . hello engineer, Skipper here.
Engineer:	Yeah.
Pilot:	Will you put the revs up please?
Engineer:	Yeah.
Bomb-aimer:	OK, keep weaving.
Unknown:	There's a lot of searchlights and fighter planes, Skipper, over there.
Bomb-aimer:	Yeah, keep on.
Pilot:	OK, boys, OK.
Bomb-aimer:	Left, left . . . Bomb doors open.
Pilot:	Hello Bombardier. OK when you are.
Bomb-aimer:	Bomber doors open.
Pilot:	Bomb doors open, Bombardier.
Bomb-aimer:	Right . . . Steady . . . steady.
Navigator:	It's a long time yet, a little bit longer yet.

Unknown:	Lob one down in the centre.
Bomb-aimer:	OK, steady . . . steady . . . Right a little bit . . . right . . . steady . . . Bombs going in a minute . . . One, two, three . . . bombs still going.
Rear Gunner:	Hey, Jerry tracer behind us boys.
Bomb-aimer:	Bombs jettisoned. [GUNFIRE]
Pilot:	Where is he . . . ah . . . rear gunner, can you see him? [GUNFIRE]
Rear Gunner:	Down! Down!
Mid-upper Gunner:	Down!
Rear Gunner:	He's gone down! He's gone down.
Mid-upper Gunner:	Yes, he's going down.
Pilot:	Did you shoot him down?
Rear Gunner:	Yeah.
Mid-upper Gunner:	Yes, he's got him, boy, right in the middle. Bloody good show.
Crew:	[Cheers and shouts]
Bomb-aimer:	Photograph.
Crew:	[Cheering]
Bomb-aimer:	Photograph taken. Keep weaving, there's some flak coming up with . . .
Pilot:	OK. Don't shout all at once!
Unknown:	All right.
Bomb-aimer:	Photograph taken.
Pilot:	OK, photograph taken.
Navigator:	Hello, Skipper. Will you turn on to 081?
Pilot:	All right. 081, navigator. Don't all speak at once now, keep quiet, it's OK.
Unknown:	OK Ken.
Pilot:	Ahh . . . hello, mid-gunner, did you recognise that fighter you shot up?
Mid-upper Gunner:	I . . . no, I didn't recognise it but it's definitely going down now.
Pilot:	Good, Jimmy, I can see him boys, good show! I can see him now.
Rear Gunner:	Look at him burning: doesn't he look lovely?
Pilot:	Good show lads now keep your . . .
Pilot and bomb-aimer:	. . . eyes open.
Unknown:	OK Ken.

Now we can see him too, he's going down all right, he's burning a huge flare, and the searchlights get on to him, there's a cone getting on to him, we can see him falling right into that central glow. As he does the whole searchlight cone is swinging back, it is swinging on to us, probing all the time. The whole searchlight cone is swinging back, our pilot's weaving. Getting out of it. Down goes the nose of the Lancaster, we feel like we're being flung around. That main beam is getting further and further away – we're out of it and once we were through that searchlight I got a glimpse of that furious glowing carpet of light, it's all we can now see of Berlin.

Wynford Vaughan-Thomas, 5 September 1943

The raid took place on the night of 3/4 September with the BBC men flying on board a 207 Squadron Lancaster, EM-F for Freddie, from RAF Langer, nine miles south-east of Nottingham. There were 316 Lancasters and four Mosquitoes on the raid; the Mosquitoes were there to act as decoys by dropping flares far away from the main bombing force in order to attract the night fighters. The pilot of the Lancaster was Flight Lieutenant Ken Letford, a 25-year-old who had flown over fifty missions. The remaining crew members were Charlie Stewart, engineer; Bill Bray, the bomb-aimer; James Fieldhouse, mid-upper gunner; Con Connelly, navigator; Bill Sparkes, wireless operator; and Henry (Harry) Devenish, rear gunner, who shot down the Messerschmitt Me110.

This raid was the last in a two-week phase of attacks that formed the opening moves in Bomber Command's 'Battle of Berlin'. On this raid twenty-two Lancasters were lost, around 7 per cent of the total, and it was not terribly successful. Most of the bombs fell in Charlottenburg and Moabit, which were predominantly residential areas. Several factories in the Siemensstadt area were damaged, but perhaps most damaging was of all was the fact that one of Berlin's largest breweries was put out of commission.

Two months after F for Freddie's famous raid Ken Letford was awarded the DSO, to which a Bar was added in 1945. These were added to the DFC the flight lieutenant was given a week after the raid. In 1949 he was uniquely awarded a Bar to his DFC when he flew a Sunderland to take supplies to HMS *Amethyst*, which had been damaged by Chinese Communist artillery fire on the River Yangtze. Letford was a good airman, but what is impossible to convey in just the transcript is the maturity and sense of dependability that comes over in the recording made by Reg Pidsley – but it's there, believe me. Ken Letford finally made it to squadron leader, but not until after the Yangtze incident. He later retired from the RAF and went to live in Canada.

One unexpected bonus of the raid was the fact that all five of the German domestic stations went off the air before midnight, which was 'almost a record', as Reuters reported. There was an additional benefit from the recording on board F for Freddie, although this was much closer to home. The BBC's own research discovered that the audience for this one-off documentary was exceptionally large, only bettered by their programme about the Battle of Britain several years earlier. Nor did people worry about the quality of the recording; they were more than happy with it, given that they got to hear real war. Those people questioned for the research were very impressed with the calm way in which the crew went about their business; a feeling extended to Vaughan-Thomas and Pidsley.

All in all this was a historic recording; for the first time ever the British public heard the reality of war captured through the heroism of those actually fighting in it – not a recording after the event, where the inevitable 20/20 vision of hindsight masks and in some cases sanitises what's heard. For many people this was the finest piece of radio that the BBC had managed since the war began; this was real radio!

Wynford Vaughan-Thomas wrote about the recording in his autobiography, including a lovely closing touch that was not, as you will see, included in the final broadcast for obvious reasons. As the aircraft was approaching its base in Nottinghamshire the mid-gunner started to sing 'Bless 'em All' – with different lyrics.

> There's many a Lancaster back from Berlin
> Bound for old Blighty's shore
> Carrying its cargo of terrified men
> Shit-scared and prone on the floor.

Blighty was popular in the First World War to signify Britain, among men serving overseas. It's an Urdu word, bilāyati – meaning 'foreign' – that had been brought home by British troops serving in the Indian subcontinent.

The campaign to bomb Germany into submission – or at least to try to make more and more people want a change from the Nazi regime – had many critics. It was also an extremely delicate issue for the BBC to handle. In October there were some complaints against the reporting of a raid on Leipzig. The news bulletin had apparently sought to justify the fact that not just military targets but also civilian targets were bombed. Marshal of the RAF Sir Charles Portal, Chief of the Air Staff, was anxious to make it clear that it was policy from the highest level that saw German industrial cities as a military objective. This was an incredibly sensitive subject that touched the consciences of everyone at the highest level in both the government and the military. The BBC found itself caught between policy, propaganda and the truth, and they found it extremely uncomfortable.

Two days after F for Freddie's Berlin raid a Swedish reporter talked to a Berlin resident who spoke 'of sullen despair' in Germany. Over 1.5 million people would leave the city each night to spend the time in the suburbs. The desperate Berliner said, 'For almost a week following a raid I could not eat or sleep properly and trembled all the time'.

Among the other correspondents who flew on Lancasters was CBS's reporter Ed Murrow. Other reporters flew with USAAF Flying Fortresses in daylight bombing raids over the Reich. Murrow's report, like Vaughan-Thomas and Pidsley's broadcast, is among the most famous pieces of radio from the Second World War. The full-length broadcast, which has become known by the name 'Orchestrated Hell', runs for almost twenty minutes; here are two short extracts.

The captains of aircraft walked out. I noticed that the big Canadian with the slow, easy grin had printed 'Berlin' at the top of his pad and then embellished it with a scroll. The redheaded English boy with the two-weeks'-old mustache was the last to leave the room.

Late in the afternoon we went to the locker room to draw parachutes, Mae Wests and all the rest. As we dressed, a couple of Australians were whistling. Walking out to the bus that was to take us to the aircraft, I heard the station loudspeakers announcing that that evening all personnel would be able to see a film: *Star-Spangled Rhythm*. Free.

We went out and stood around the big, black four-motored Lancaster, 'D for Dog'. A small station wagon delivered a thermos bottle of coffee, chewing gum, an orange, and a bit of chocolate for each man. Up in that part of England the air hums and throbs with the sound of aircraft motors all day, but for half an hour before takeoff the skies are dead, silent and expectant. A lone hawk hovered over the airfield, absolutely still as he faced into the wind. Jack, the tail gunner, said, 'It'd be nice to fly like that.' D-Dog eased around the perimeter track to the end of the runway. We sat there for a moment. The green light flashed and we were rolling – ten seconds ahead of schedule . . .

. . . There were four reporters on this operation. Two of them didn't come back. Two friends of mine, Norman Stockton of Australian Associated Newspapers, and Lowell Bennett, an American representing International News Service. There is something of a tradition amongst reporters, that those who are prevented by circumstances from filing their stories will be covered by their colleagues. This has been my effort to do so. In the aircraft in which I flew, the men who flew and fought poured into my ears their comments on fighters, flak, and flares in the same tone that they would have used in reporting a host of daffodils. I have no doubt that Bennett and Stockton would have given you a better report of last night's activity.

Berlin was a thing of orchestrated Hell; a terrible symphony of light and flames. It isn't a pleasant kind of warfare – the men doing it speak of it as a job. Yesterday afternoon, when the tapes were stretched out on the big map all the way to Berlin and back again, a young pilot with old eyes said to me, 'I see we're working again tonight.' That's the frame of mind in which the job is being done. The job isn't pleasant; it's terribly tiring. Men die in the sky while others are roasted alive in their cellars. Berlin last night wasn't a pretty sight. In about thirty-five minutes it was hit with about three times the amount of stuff that ever came down on London in a nightlong Blitz. This is a calculated, remorseless campaign of destruction. Right now the mechanics are probably working on D-Dog, getting him ready to fly again.

Ed Murrow, CBS, 3 December 1943

This raid by a force of 458 aircraft, mostly Lancasters but including eighteen Mosquitoes and fifteen Halifaxes, was the continuance of the Battle of Berlin. A total of forty bombers were shot down, partly because the Germans had accurately forecast the target as Berlin and had fighters in position. The winds too played a part and a number of aircraft were blown off course resulting in their bomb loads being scattered far and wide across the south of Berlin. The two reporters who were killed were with 460 (RAAF) Squadron who lost five of the twenty-five Lancasters that took part in this raid. Somewhere around 55,000 men from RAF Bomber Command lost their lives in the Second World War; although not all were during raids on Germany, that aspect of their operations certainly counted for the majority. There were 7,377 Avro Lancasters built and almost 3,500 were lost in action – it is thought that only thirty-five aircraft completed more than 100 missions. By comparison 6,176 Handley Page Halifaxes were constructed during the war and close to 1,900 were lost; only four Halifaxes made it to one hundred or more missions.

ONE HALIFAX, FOUR MISSIONS

My uncle was a flight engineer, a sergeant, with 466 Squadron, a Royal Australian Air Force unit that flew Halifaxes; this despite the fact that he had been born in South London and was English through and through. Between 15 February and 18 March 1944 he and his fellow crew-members, who were all Australian, flew four missions against targets in France and Germany. The other six members of the crew were flight sergeants with the exception of the wireless operator/gunner who was a warrant officer. On their first mission they bombed Augsburg in Germany; they took off at 2103 and landed again at 0514 hours, meaning that they were airborne for over eight hours.

Their fourth mission, on the night of 18/19 March, was as part of a raid against Frankfurt. Twelve Halifaxes from 466 Squadron got airborne that night, although two returned early owing to hydraulic trouble. Seven of the remaining ten aircraft bombed the primary target and returned safely; three failed to return, including my uncle's aircraft. A German fighter attacked HX231, killing the mid-upper gunner, Noel Lees, and probably the other gunners, Jack Dansie and George De Fraine. With the fuselage a mass of flames the Captain, Johnny Richards, told the crew to bale out, which Bill Bray, Ken Wilson and Doug Wooldridge all did. Richards pushed Wooldridge out of the aircraft, causing him to strike the tail, which knocked him out and broke his teeth. He came to in a snowdrift covered by his parachute, which in view of the very cold conditions undoubtedly saved his life. He was eventually discovered by German troops and admitted to a hospital run by Sisters of Mercy. Richards went down with the aircraft. Ironically the news bulletins the following day said that the bombers 'met fewer fighters than usual'. All three men who baled out became POWs and separately passed through the Luftwaffe interrogation centre at Oberursel, near Frankfurt-on-Main, before moving on to Stalag Luft 3 at Sagan in south-east Germany, where they were reunited. They were later moved to Stalag Luft 6 at Heydekrug, East Prussia, before being marched back west in the wake of the advancing Red Army; they were found by Allied troops. The four men that died, including the pilot, were all twenty-one years old with the exception of Jack Dansie who was just twenty; they are buried at Rheinberg War Cemetery in the Ruhr. My uncle, Doug Wooldridge, was a month shy of his twenty-third birthday – today, at eighty-five, he still enjoys playing golf and travels the world. He is just one example that illustrates the random nature of survival in Bomber Command; the same can be said of every aspect of war.

PACIFIC HELL

Following the catastrophe at Singapore, and what seemed like a never-ending stream of setbacks in the Far East, the Allies steadily began to turn things round. The war in the Pacific seemed to many in Britain a long, long way away, which of course it was. It was also because the war in the Far East involved fewer British forces that coverage was not as fulsome. When you add to this the logistics of getting material back to London it is obvious that the 'on-the-spot' style of reportage was less suited to the war in the East:

General MacArthur's campaign in the last islands of the Solomons group and in New Guinea is moving along very nicely to its ultimate objective, the expulsion of the Japanese from all of these islands between the Australian mainland and Truk – where the Jap navy is skulking. Here you are looking at a combined operation where sea, land and air forces are blended and where good staff work, marvellous timing and gallantry of all involved enable an amphibious operation to succeed.

Now the pattern for these operations, the really classic instance where they have brought great victory, was laid down at the Huon Gulf on the north-east of New Guinea. I was there, as a matter of fact. I had marched with the Australians through the rain, forests, and over the razorbacks of the Owen Stanley Mountains from the pretty little township of Wan, set amid the hills in the heart of the New Guinea goldfields, to Salamaua at the coast. So I am going to start the story for you in the third week of August last.

We had arrived just two or three miles from Salamaua. The Japs occupied the last high features; they are well defended with pillboxes and many machine-guns, and they had their backs to the sea. It would have been easy, of course, for General MacArthur and General Sir Thomas Blarney, the Australian Commander, to bound forward and seize Salamaua, but they were after bigger fish. To have gone straight for Salamaua, you see, would simply have alarmed the Jap High Command, who would have taken extra precautions to save Lae, which lies just north of Salamaua in the bend of the Huon Gulf, under the mouth of the mighty Markham River. General MacArthur was really anxious to seize Lae and Salamaua, and to the north-east, Finchhafen, and the whole of that Huon Gulf peninsula. He desired actually at one stroke to cut the remnants of the Jap force, which had been operating there all year against us. Let me tell you how I watched him set about it.

First of all, through the latter half of August, he mustered all his air power to smash the Jap air bases. They had a number of airfields along that north New Guinea coast. They have still got four at Rabaul on the northerly tip of New Britain, and several on the south coast of that island just across the straits which separate New Guinea from New Britain. From all these, Jap airplanes could converge to attack our troops or upset the amphibious plan. So MacArthur set upon them with all his resources. On one day alone in August I remember he caught nearly 300 aircraft on the ground, at the airfields at Wewack, destroyed them all in a midnight to dawn attack of great intensity and slew some skilled personnel who were all lined up waiting to take off.

These attacks reached their highest intensity on the night of September 3rd, the anniversary of the war's outbreak. On that night, all of these airfields were attacked at once to deprive the Jap of his eyes, when the grand manoeuvre for encircling the whole Jap force was to commence. At 6.30 a.m. on that Saturday, September 4th, while General Sir Thomas Blarney was describing to some of us in the jungles of New Guinea details of the plan, it had already started. Australians of the famous 9th Division had moved along the north New Guinea coast in barges, protected by air cover and by the United States Navy. Their task was to land at two beaches above Lae. One part of this force marched along the coast and cut the Jap supply line. The other part turned in the opposite direction along the beaches towards Lae. These landings were protected by a smoke screen, laid by the American warships in the Huon Gulf. The Japs didn't have wind of the plot for half an hour, which is a very long time in amphibious operations.

Now MacArthur hoped that when he halted his troops in front of Salamaua, the Japs would be tempted to believe they still had a sporting prospect of holding it, and that they would bring the defences of Lae to send men to Salamaua to reinforce it, and this was precisely what happened, just what the doctor had ordered! It made Lae an easier target, and of course once Lae fell, you'll see that Salamaua must automatically go, because its sole supply line came through Lae.

But the attack on Lae still gave the Japs one avenue of escape. That was to move inland from the coast. Now this was just what MacArthur and Blarney desired to avoid, for if the Japs escaped into the interior of New Guinea, we should have to face more of these heartbreak marches next year. So the plan for the encirclement included a daring parachute exercise; American paratroops were to descend behind the enemy's lines, just a few miles inland from Lae, along the Markham River to seal the back door to Lae, and prevent an escape along the river. This paratroop exercise was designed to take place on Sunday morning, September 5th, just 24 hours or so after the Australians had successfully landed on the beaches above Lae.

But there was also a third exercise. Another Australian force had been secretly landed at an advanced airfield in the mountains. They had 800 New Guinea boys with them carrying pontoon bridge equipment. This force commenced marching actually on September 1st, marching northwards along the course of the snake-like Wampit River, towards the lower bank of the Markham River, which they were due to reach by dawn on September 5th. This was the most gruelling of all the razorback marches of this war, because the forest-clothed mountains reared their ridges in solid ranks, the gradients were almost one in two. In fact the trail along the creek bed dare not be followed because of the risks of detection from the air. The Australians were without a supply line or any staging camps, crawling with heavy packs on their hands and knees over these mountains in the green ghost-like tunnels, which they carved as they marched. Each man had got to carry his five days' rations. Each one, in fact, was told there would be no turning back, even the wounded had to march onward until the Markham was reached. And at the Markham River they were to hide in the jungle awaiting their cue to cross.

That cue was to be the spectacle of the American paratroops descending. I spent Saturday, September 4th, among the American paratroops in New Guinea, attended their final briefing. I met and talked with General MacArthur, and that night under flitting storm lanterns amid the ghost gums and eucalyptus, I saw the officers being given their final instructions. We all turned in by ten, you see it takes several hours to move a parachute unit; so by 2.30 next morning the stillness of the jungle was rent with the sound of bugles calling us from our blanket-rolls. The birds of paradise uttered shrill protest at this indecent disturbance of their rest. Hot breakfast was served to us at 3.15, and by the play of torchlights, looking very much like fireflies in the trees. I remember, the Captains assembled their men in the ghostly jungle, called the rolls and marched them to their waiting lorries.

I should explain that each of the Douglas planes holds 21 men, so each lorry held the same number. Each lorry and each aircraft were given identical numbers. We were all seated in these vehicles by 4.30, and by 4.35 in the morning, before dawn, a long procession of lorries moved out of its jungle hide to the main road. I was to fly in the last of the troop carriers, so was given a seat in the last lorry. We commenced to move by ten past five. By six we were due at the airstrip, just as dawn was breaking in the Owen Stanley Mountains – Zero hour was to be at any time over seven, but now we had to wait upon weather reports. Our route was to take us for 300 miles above the wild headhunters' lands, and to 10,000 feet over the Bismarck ranges, and it was essential to have good weather. Not until 8.30 was the signal given to start. So for an hour and a half the paratroops had to face the ordeal of self-discipline sitting in those transport planes all waiting to go, keyed up after eighteen months' training.

Well, the transport lined up in a long line on the taxiway. Just like taxicabs at a railway station, and when the signal to start comes at last, all the propellers start whirring together. The long line, nose to tail, moves forward, turns into the runway at the end of the taxiway and the aircraft take off at thirty-second intervals, close together. Within a few minutes a

vast armada of troop-carrying aircraft are in the sky. At the end of the
taxiway at the end of the jungle I saw a lone figure. It was General
MacArthur; he, too, had risen at 2.30 that morning to salute his men as
they started. Then I saw him jump into a Fortress bomber, which led the
host into battle. He was first over the battle line, last to leave and he spent
seven hours in the air that morning. The great adventure had begun. We
were now joined by bombers, which were to hammer the Lae defences up to
sixty seconds prior to the drop; by Bostons which were to drop a smokescreen sixty seconds before this event, and by a cloud of fighters stepped up
to thirty thousand feet. The whole armada met above a razorback to
rendezvous and then we all turned on course. Then we commenced the
300-mile flight high over the mountains, maintaining radio silence, every
man tense. All were wondering if we would see any Jap Zeros, and how far
secrecy and supplies were with us. Soon after ten we crossed the mighty
Bismarcks, and then commenced the great wheeling movement over the
beautiful Markham Valley within full view of the foe at Lae, which we could
see so clearly only a few miles away at the coast. We had to descend to
within a few hundred feet of the dropping area. The glorious valley looked
very green and English this warm Sunday morning; the folds of the hills,
gentle and velvety, reminded me of Sussex Downs. But this, of course, was
the dangerous period and not an enemy aircraft was in sight. At ten-past-
ten, a green light appeared over the doorway of my Douglas plane. The 21
paratroops silently rise, blacken their faces, adjust their 'chutes, and form up
in line, just as if they are in an omnibus which has reached its terminus. I
shook hands with the Lieutenant in command; the officers, of course,
always jump first. At ten-twenty the green light changes to red. Without
looking over his shoulder, the Lieutenant calls out, 'Follow me, men', and
hurls himself through the open doorway. One by one the twenty men follow
as the jumpmaster calls out the signal – Go-Go-Go – to each of them in
turn. Within two minutes all of the hundreds of paratroops had left their
aircraft. I could see the great mass of men floating down to earth. A
smokescreen between us and the enemy was laid to time as six Bostons
lashed past underneath me, and everybody dropped and disappeared into
twelve-foot high jungle grass, which, of course, hid each man from his
neighbour – secrecy and supplies had been maintained to the end. The Japs
were trapped and encircled. The Australians waiting at the lower bank of
the river bridged the 800 yards-wide Markham and rushed across. The two
armies met and embraced upon the airfield.

Next day seventy air transports flying more Australians landed at an
airstrip which the Aussies, who had marched so far, had cleared of its jungle

grasses. Within 24 hours it had become one of the busiest airports in the world, after it had lain hidden for eighteen months in silence beneath its tall jungle coverage. So falls Salamaua, Lae, Finchhafen, and the whole Huon peninsula.

William Courtenay, BBC, 25 November 1943

By the middle of September the Japanese retreated through the mountains but such was the difficulty of the terrain that they lost 40 per cent of their men to exhaustion, disease and hunger. The BBC's man in New Guinea worked for the *Daily Sketch* and his reports were shared among all the British media. There's no evidence to suggest a relationship with his more famous namesake, Sir William Courtenay, the man who led a workers' rebellion in 1838. That affair climaxed with the last battle to be fought on English soil, at Bosenden Wood, in Kent.

While the grinding slog of taking island after island in the Pacific continued one of the most significant meetings of the Second World War took place: Churchill, Stalin and Roosevelt met in Teheran to discuss the final push against Nazi Germany. The American President left the USA in mid-November and travelled on board the USS *Iowa* to Cairo, where he met Churchill and General Chiang Kai-shek from 23 to 26 November. The British and American leaders then flew to Teheran, where talks began on 28 November. Negotiations were difficult and there were some very prickly moments, including one night at dinner when Stalin said that it might be necessary to execute 50,000 German officers after the war was won. It was said in the context of the Russian leader thinking that the Prime Minister was not hard enough on the Germans. Churchill said it would be a 'barbarous act' and something he could never ever agree to; Roosevelt apparently laughed and said, 'Perhaps 49,000 would be enough.'

The declaration by President Roosevelt, Mr Churchill and Premier Stalin after last week's Teheran conferences is published this evening. Military and Diplomatic staffs were there and common policy for war and peace was shaped and confirmed. Complete agreement was reached on the scope and timing of operations to be undertaken from the east, west and south – with common understanding as a guarantee of victory. The declaration also invites all nations dedicated to the elimination of tyranny and slavery into a world family of democratic nations . . . Their joint communiqué closed with these words. 'We came here with hope and determination. We leave here friends in fact, in spirit, and in purpose.'

Freddie Grisewood, BBC News, 6 December 1943

Chapter 12

THE BIG PUSH

In January 1944 the BBC expressed, in a few well-chosen words, what the year was likely to mean, not just for the Corporation, but also everyone in Britain: 'The prevailing emotion of 1944 is best described by the words "forward looking".' There was a growing feeling of wanting it all to be over; although Churchill had warned everyone that the war was likely to be long, the strain of living under such circumstances increased from year to year. For Churchill himself the strain of it all had brought about a bad cold, which developed into pneumonia shortly before Christmas. When the newsreader announced the fact on the one o'clock news on 16 December the Director General immediately sent a message to the newsroom: 'Don't be too solemn about the PM.'

It was not a case of new year, new idea, as things had been building towards the final push and everyone – whether in the military, or working in a factory, or simply keeping families together on the real Home Front – was being encouraged to get involved. New schemes tried to focus people's efforts towards the 'guarantee of victory'. In October 1943 the Saturday edition of 'The Kitchen Front' on the Home Programme had a name change, and a change of emphasis. It became 'Make Do and Mend' and the radio campaign was supported by a Board of Trade exhibition that travelled around the country encouraging everyone to take part. Sir William Darling, the Lord Provost of Edinburgh, said, 'We have reached the stage of the war when we must find the last reserves on the domestic front' when he opened the 'Make Do and Mend' exhibition in the city's Martin Hall in November. A by-product of the campaign was a Mend for Victory Committee, which frankly didn't have the same cachet as 'Dig for Victory'. 'Make Do and Mend' was not only aimed at women: 'Men would be interested and they would have to resort to the needle for their own comfort. Nothing should be allowed to lie idle in this time of need!' stated the Lord Provost. Mrs Anne Lee-Mitchell, a Somerset housewife, noted in her diary: 'The Board of Trade issues a moral little booklet *Make and Mend* exhorting us to cut the feet from old stockings, pick up the stitches and knit new feet, with creased turn-downs to hide the joins. Am doing this, but for other tips such as

"Reinforce all elbows, knees and pockets on new clothes before putting them on", I've little use and less time.'

ROMAN HOLIDAY

The slow progress of the Allied soldiers in battling their way northwards towards Rome during the winter of 1943/4 was great news for the Germans. Every week gained by impeding the Allies meant a week more to construct better defensive positions on the approaches to Rome. The Gustav Line, as these defences were known, stretched across Italy from Ortona to Minturno and consisted of man-made bunkers and pillboxes that complemented the natural terrain, as well as extensive minefields. Hitler gave Field Marshal Albert Kesselring command of the German army in Italy; his task was easier to say than to do – keep the Allied armies south of Rome. Kesselring's opponent was General Sir Harold Alexander, who commanded an army group made up of the British Eighth Army and the US Fifth Army.

On the morning of 22 January 1944 American and British troops landed on the beaches to the south of Rome around the small port of Anzio. They established a beachhead to the north of the German lines; this area would become one of the bloodiest battlefields of the Italian campaign. The Germans knew that they needed to push the Allied troops back into the sea in order to be able to concentrate on the main attack from the south. The forces at the beachhead knew they had to hold on in order to give the main Allied army a better chance of success.

Churchill, who was the main advocate for the Anzio landings, carried Roosevelt along with him, but he failed to impress the commander in the field, US Major-General John Lucas. He called Churchill an 'amateur' in his diary, adding, 'Unless we can get what we want, the operation becomes such a desperate undertaking that it should not, in my opinion, be attempted.' The landings involved around 40,000 men supported by tanks and other armoured vehicles. By midnight on the first day most of the troops and their support equipment had landed, the port had been captured and there were surprisingly few casualties. Military historians remain sharply divided about what happened next, or rather what didn't. Having gained the advantage Lucas failed to push on and halted his troops in order to establish defensive positions around Anzio; it became an impregnable beachhead cordon. Perhaps Lucas's view of the plan affected his thinking. Whatever was the case it became a long-drawn-out affair.

The BBC's man sent with the troops on the Anzio landings was Wynford Vaughan-Thomas, fresh from his triumph over Berlin. He had been dispatched to Italy where Denis Johnston was his mentor, although perhaps not the best of teachers. Having left Naples with the invasion armada the BBC's man, like everyone else, had only one thought on his mind when he landed shortly after dawn on 22 January – 'Rome in ten days'. In one of his earliest reports from the beachhead Vaughan-Thomas makes an accurate prediction of what the Battle of Anzio would be all about – digging in. Anzio became the Second World War's answer to the trench warfare in the First World War.

The position here is that we are extending the bridgehead to gain elbow room, and the Germans are trying to contain us. The Appian Way is under our shell-fire but no troops are yet across. The Germans hold Litloria, possibly with elements of the Hermann Goering Division. Their rush arrival is proved by supply parachute dropping. There are also signs of digging in the central sector.

Wynford Vaughan-Thomas, BBC, 24 January 1944

Hello BBC. Wynford Vaughan-Thomas speaking with Herbert Waldon recording. That's the sound, first sounds of our ack-ack and it's a sign of the usual night raid on our positions here coming in. Right above us the sky has suddenly become as bright as day, the German flares burning, hanging on motionless overhead in the night sky, with a shower of glittering silver lights coming down from them. Here on the ground we feel as if we're standing under the flares on a fairground. Every tree, every house is lit up. Our own flak is getting furious and fierce . . . First bombs going down, it's away to the left of us. But even back here the ground is shaking furiously and Waldon's recording truck is now rocking on its springs. [Sounds of aircraft low overhead]

Wynford Vaughan-Thomas, BBC, 26 January 1944

We regrouped today after Friday's heavy enemy counter-attack. We now know the enemy took advantage of the cloudy weather and the curtailment of our air cover to move troops for the attack against the British advanced units in the salient north of Carrocetto (Aprilia).

Tanks, possibly Tigers, got across the road, and our forward troops were cut off and caught in the enemy fire. In the withdrawal they badly mauled the enemy, and took many prisoners. Anti-tank gunners caught enemy tanks as they made off in the light of dawn. They presented a perfect target and smashed at least five. The whole plain was filled with the reeking oily smoke of burning tanks.

In the darkness one group of enemy guards with prisoners mistook the way, and guided them back into our lines. The guards and prisoners then changed places.

Our troops are firmly in their new positions. With a clear sky there is a renewal of air activity on both sides. Enemy fighter bombers nipped in for a morning raid, and to see our fighters pouncing on them was a heartening sight again to our men on the ground.

There have been heavy artillery duels all day. On the Pontine flank the Germans attempted to seize a half bridge and blow it up. A counter-attack drove them off and cut off a force of the enemy. These were either killed or captured.

Wynford Vaughan-Thomas, BBC, 5 February 1944

The German attack goes on, and the thunder of guns still echoes over the beachhead. I have been up watching the battle. From the edge of a patch of heath I could see the whole area where the Germans are seeking a vital decision. It surprising how small it is – plough land on either side of a straight road is the cockpit of the struggle. There is hardly a yard of this cockpit without its shell-burst, with thick columns of white smoke where the German shells are falling on our forward positions.

Down the coverless road, German tanks start to crawl into the battle storm. Our guns plaster them, and the road becomes a line of leaping earth fountains. Black specks – men jump out and into the elusive shelter of a ditch as the leading tanks flare, with oily smoke pouring out.

Wynford Vaughan-Thomas, BBC, a.m., 18 February 1944

The enemy is accepting heavy losses in an effort to continue his attack, and is supporting it with heavy artillery concentrations and tanks. On Thursday our Air Forces intervened in the battle with the heaviest close support we have yet seen here.

Today is cloudy, and heavy rain fell in the night. Some units have been engaged in continuous fighting since the German attack was renewed. There is no doubt that this is a real all-out attack, but our men are resisting bitterly. A square mile of battle-torn plough land was a blazing hell of shellfire this morning and our tanks and the German infantry fought a furious battle. Kesselring's main tank forces are probably not yet committed, but a big armoured clash cannot now be far away.

The enemy is keeping up the intensity of his air attacks, with all-night raids on the port of Anzio and the heaviest long-range shelling.

Prisoners keep arriving at an assembly point behind our lines. An American soldier from New York, who had fought in Sicily and Tunisia, told me 'Aprilia was the hardest fighting I have ever been in.'

Wynford Vaughan-Thomas, BBC, p.m., 18 February 1944

Fighting in the gullies around the Molleta River (on the northern part of the bridgehead front) continued on Tuesday. British troops are now firmly established on ground won on Saturday night. There has been no spectacular forward move. The advance can be measured in yards, but in this difficult 'wadi country' yards can be important, and even a minor ridge a few feet higher than the surrounding country can give observation into the tangled undergrowth in the gullies below.

Much of this fighting has been hand-to-hand, especially when one of our units met a German unit counter-attacking at the same time. Both sides suffered casualties.

But we are now in the ascendant in an area where the enemy had been continually aggressive since his last big push against the bridgehead fizzled out over a fortnight ago.

Wynford Vaughan-Thomas, BBC, 20 February 1944

This short sequence of reports by Vaughan-Thomas from the Anzio beachhead had been selected from dozens of similar broadcasts covering months of fighting; it was that repetitive. One historian has called it 'a symbol of heroic tenacity', and there's no doubt this was far from the Allies' finest hour on the battlefield, yet it can be argued that the job done by the troops at the Anzio beachhead took many Germans away from defending against the main Allied thrust. Did it save lives? Five thousand men from the Allied armies and navies lost their lives, another 18,000 were wounded and over 6,000 were taken prisoner or went missing – and it is impossible to say whether it would have been more if the attacks had not gone ahead. After the war Wynford Vaughan-Thomas wrote his own book, called simply *Anzio*; in it he argued the case strongly that if there had been a speedier push inland to the north of the landing area then things would have gone very differently, as the area was lightly defended. Again, who knows, although according to Kesselring's own book, the area was well protected. No doubt on-line war gamers and armchair strategists could tell us the answer, but then again it would change from war game to war game.

Two days after the last of the broadcasts reported above, on the insistence of General Alexander, Lucas was replaced by Brigadier General Lucian Truscott. There was an almost immediate change in the mood of the troops, stemming from Truscott's more visible style of commanding his men. The stalemate, however, continued until early May, when the major part of the Allied army began its push from the south. The march for Rome was finally in full swing, even if it was closer to 140 days, rather than the ten days that had been predicted. Whatever the realities on the battlefield there was no doubt that

Vaughan-Thomas's coverage of the fighting was closer to what A.P. Ryan had called for when demanding a far higher standard of news observing.

CHANGED DAYS

All this was good news for the BBC, whose staff numbers in March 1944 hit a wartime peak of 11,663 – well over double what they were at the start of the war. There were also changes at the very top of the Corporation; William Haley, formerly the BBC's Editor in Chief, was appointed Director General, succeeding Robert Foot, who became Chairman of the Mining Association of Great Britain. A month later Clement Attlee announced to Parliament that Sir Allan Powell was to be reappointed as a Governor and Chairman of the BBC. On the six o'clock news the following day, 26 April, it was announced that the American Broadcasting Station in Europe (ABSIE) would broadcast for the first time four days later. ABSIE was under the control of the US Office of War Information and the programmes were of American origin beamed to Europe from Britain. Within a month the Supreme Allied Command gave what was the first of a series of talks for European listeners on both ABSIE and the BBC's frequencies.

Prior to these changes in both broadcasting and the management of the BBC there had been one of the most significant changes to the Corporation's wartime output.

One of the important respects in which this war differs from all others is that broadcasting enables the fighting man to have a daily link with home. For British soldiers, sailors, and airmen, wherever they may be, that link is provided by the BBC. As the war progresses, the need will not only be extended but deepened. From more than one quarter there has come confirmation of the bet that the men and women serving overseas wish to share with their families at home the same programmes, thus securing a community of spirit between them and their homes.

The BBC has decided that starting on 27 February, the General Overseas Service, organised and designed for the British men and women serving abroad, shall be broadcast as the second programme throughout the United Kingdom. It will be called 'The General Forces Programme'. The present Forces Programme will be dropped, but listeners will find that the new service contains its most popular features.

As a result of this change, home listeners will have the Home or General Forces Programme to choose from. They will be able to hear what the BBC is broadcasting to their kin abroad. The British fighting services will know that their daily listening is the same as that of their families, and their families will know it too. The new arrangement will also have the benefit of providing listeners within the United Kingdom, throughout all normal hours of broadcasting, with two self-contained and contrasting services.

BBC, 20 January 1944

It meant that from February, and for the first time in four and a half years, the people in Britain and the armed forces would hear the same programmes, wherever they were serving in the world. Stuart Hibberd had closed down the Forces Programme the night before with the words, 'It's eleven o'clock, and so we have come to the end of the Forces Programme.'

This was the first day's schedule for the General Forces Programme that was broadcast on Sunday 27 February:

6.30 – Solo and Orchestra. 7 – News. 7.15 – Boston Promenade Orchestra. 8 – News. 8.15 – Cairo Calling. 8.45 – Orchestral Music (Records). 9.10 – Greetings from South Africa. 9.30 – Scottish Variety Orchestra. 10.15 – Service. 10.30 – Calling all Canadians. 11 – Announcements and News. 11.2 – Weekly Newsletter. 11.12 – London Calling. 11.15 – Records. 11.30 – Service. 12 – News. 12.15 – Kay on the Keys. 12.20 – ITMA.

1 – News. 1.1 – BBC Orchestra. 1.30 – Brains Trust. 2 – News. 2.10 – Forces' Favourites. 2.30 – Radio Newsreel. 2.45 – Football Results and News. 3 – Primo Scala and Accordion Band. 3.30 – Palestine Half-Hour. 3.55 – Records. 4 – News. 4.15 – Books, Plays, and Films; A Talk. 4.30 – Harry Fryer and Band. 4.55 – London Calling. 5 – Calling Malta. 5.30 – Variety Band-Box. 6.15 – BBC Scottish Orchestra.

7 – News. 7.15 – Forces' Favourites. 7.45 – All Together Now. 8.15 – Happidrome. 9 – News. 9.1 – Sunday Half-Hour. 9.20 – Parliamentary Summary. 9.40 – Records. 9.45 – World News and News from Home. 9.55 – News from Canada. 10 – Conductors at Their Best (Records). 10.25 – Epilogue. 10.30 – Phil Green and Band. 10.59 – News.

On the same day on the Home Programme at half past midday, and therefore head to head with 'ITMA', was a thirty-minute recital by the Scottish violinist David McCallum. His ten-year-old son David may have been listening; he would later become an actor and star as Illya Kuryakin in the sixties TV series *The Man From U.N.C.L.E.*

CALLING ON EUROPE

A broadcast by a spokesman for Supreme Allied Command, on both the ABSIE and the BBC networks, was more than just an indication of the way things were heading – these were referred to as 'First Invasion Orders'. It was also more than just propaganda, it was an appeal to those in the 'underground army' on the Continent to take direct action – albeit subtler than perhaps many would have liked. Speaking on behalf of General Eisenhower, the spokesman said:

> When the Allies come to liberate you they will rely on your help in many ways. In a no more valuable way can this be given than by information about the enemy. Take minute and detailed note of every single move of the enemy, his men, tanks, and guns, their markings and strength. Let nothing escape you; pool your knowledge. Take the utmost care to give information to none but known patriots. Be patient above all and hide your actions until the word is given.
>
> *Philip Cohen, ABSIE and BBC, 20 May 1944*

The message from the Supreme Allied Command finished with the warning that the enemy would try to discover their intentions and destroy their organisations before they could co-operate with the Allied forces. For those who were listening it engendered mixed emotions. On the one hand news that an invasion was coming was wonderful, but at the same time, given what had happened during the preceding years to those who had either sided with the Allies or were thought to have done, some must have been fearful too.

While this very public pronouncement was a confirmation of things to come no one had been under any illusion as to what it was that was coming. Two months earlier Churchill, in his first BBC Sunday evening talk for a year, almost to the day, had spoken about what was looming. 'The hour of our greatest effort and action is approaching. It will require from our own people here, from parliament, from the press, from all classes, the same cool, strong nerves, the same toughness of fibre, which stood us in good stead in those days when we were all alone under the Blitz.' It was not a speech that went down well, in part because Churchill was by this point very tired – at sixty-nine years old the strain was intense. According to the MP and BBC Governor Harold Nicolson he sounded like 'a worn and petulant old man'. The first part of his speech dealt with a review of the current situation, much as if 'a Mosquito aircraft on reconnoitring duty' was taking listeners across the many theatres of war. But a significant part of his speech dealt with what would happen after the war was over, a matter that was of great importance, but for many listeners not necessarily top of their agenda. In America the press seemed generally pleased with what Churchill had to say, and in particular his support for the Allied efforts against the Japanese. Churchill's praise for the toil of the Russian armed forces was not a view shared in Germany, as shown by this 27 March broadcast on German radio: 'The allegedly dangerous situation in the East front to which the British Premier referred will be mastered, and the foundation laid for one of the greatest victories in the world's history.' Perhaps the most interesting view expressed from around Europe was that of a Swedish commentator in the *Allehanda* newspaper: 'It had been hoped that Mr Churchill would copy Hitler's dramatic methods, and announce, "As I am speaking, Allied troops are streaming ashore in France".'

BY DAY AND BY NIGHT

The Lancasters and Halifaxes of RAF Bomber Command, and the B-17 Flying Fortresses and B-24 Liberators of the US Eighth Air Force continued to take it in turns to bomb Germany by both night and day. Regular reports by the BBC correspondents, and those of US reporters, spoke of the heroism of these crews. In May there was an unusual talk on the BBC that looked at the job being done by the bomber crews from a different perspective from most of the coverage.

If you live in Sussex or Kent nowadays (or I suppose in a good many other counties besides), you know before getting out of bed and pulling aside the black-out if it's a nice day. A clear dawn has a new clarion – the deep and throbbing roar of hundreds of planes, outward bound. They may be sailing high towards the coast, flashing or shining in the light of the sun that's not yet up over the horizon. Sometimes they look white and as graceful as gulls against the blue; at others they look black and sinister as they come and go between the clouds. But the impressive thing – the thing that makes land-girls pause in their stringing of the hop fields and makes conductors of country buses lean out and look up from their platforms – the impressive thing is the numbers. Never in the Battle of Britain, in the days when the Luftwaffe was beaten over these fields and woods, did the Germans send over such vast fleets. Never were their bombers four-engine monsters, such as these of the Americans, which go out in their scores and hundreds. Sometimes you will see one big formation coming, say from the north, others from the north-east, others from the west, all heading for a common rendezvous. Their courses often converge, and a stranger to the scene might hold his breath seeing the approach of disaster as the formations close in. At the moment when it looks as if they must collide, he sees with relief, that they're at different heights; and they make a brief, fascinating cross-over pattern and sail on as easily as an express train flies over complicated points. As their roar fades with them, another rises until things on the kitchen mantelshelf tinkle and rattle as they catch the vibration. Up over the beech woods on the hill, the leading formation of a second wave of heavies appears, followed by others and still others. Some days it will go on like this pretty well all day – not all heavies, of course, but twin-engined bombers of various kinds, fighter-bombers and fighters. There are always lots of Marauders, packed together, flying very fast – reminding one of those sudden clouds of migrating birds which appear from nowhere and as quickly vanish. They have an appointment abroad, and they're keeping it.

Quite often I have noticed that some time after the heavies have gone out, fighters will follow them, flashing across the sky, seeming to leave their noise behind them. I always imagine that they're the escort; whose pilots might still have been having breakfast long after the heavies took off, knowing that with their much greater speed, they'd be there at the rendezvous in plenty of time.

On some of the really big days, you'll see the first of the raiders coming home, still in formation, as others are going out, and it will be more or less like that till well after sundown.

I remember how thrilled people were, and how they even stood in the streets and fields and cheered, as German planes were shot out of the sky over this part of England in the Battle of Britain. Now, all this time later, you find people looking up and counting the homecoming Allied bombers. I went into our little village shop the other morning just as one big formation was coming back. The old lady behind the counter said, 'I wonder if they're all there?' and made her way out of the shop to shade her eyes, look up and count. 'Twelve there,' she said, 'twelve there, twelve there, and twelve there. Oh dear, only eleven here. Another twelve, another twelve. That's one missing. I do hope he's all right.' We went hack into the shop and chatted for a few minutes about what it must be like on the other side. The roar of the heavies had died away. But there was one single plane some-where around. We strolled across to the door again and looked up. 'Oh good,' said the old lady, 'it's the missing one.' She was probably right, too. It was a Fortress with a hole in its tail and one engine stopped, flying much lower than usual, but getting home just the same.

Pat Smithers, BBC, 5 May 1944

No matter that Pat Smithers's talk was a romantic, 'fluffy' view of war, one in which everyone got back home; it showed that the recording by Charles Gardner, for which he received a lot of criticism, still resonated four years later.

Today it seems that the media covers every tit bit of information, every event no matter how trivial, and most certainly every death. In the Second World War there was so much happening and comparatively so little coverage that much of what took place went unreported. One incident on 21 January 1944 graphically illustrates the changing times. USAAF B-26 Marauders of 322 Bomber Group were night-flying when one of them crashed following a touch-and-go at Andrews Field in Essex. It came down near Great Dunmow in Essex and exploded. The aircraft, named 'Radie Baby', belonged to 451 Bomber Squadron; the crew of four – Lieutenant Gene Jones, Lieutenant Raymond Spencer, Lieutenant Ralph Eltzroth and Sergeant Paul Rotes – were all killed. A camera was found in the wreckage and it was given to my grandfather, Inspector Charles Havers, who developed the film in an effort to identify the camera's owner. My grandfather had been an amateur photographer since 1922 and processed the film in his usual darkroom, the bathroom at the Police Station! It only contained three exposures, which failed to provide any clues to the ownership; these are reproduced in the plate section.

The US Eighth Air Force was a formidable and powerful weapon, arguably the most feared fighting machine that the world had seen. By 1944 there were over 200,000 people serving with the 'Mighty Eighth', capable of putting 2,000 four-engine bombers and 1,000 fighters in the air for a single mission. During the war the Eighth Air Force suffered almost 48,000 casualties, of which 26,000 were fatalities, and they lost over 5,000 aircraft – but at the same time they dropped close to three-quarters of a million tonnes of bombs on enemy, mainly German, targets.

Chapter 13

HITLER'S EUROPEAN FORTRESS

T he build-up to D-Day for the BBC's War Reporting Unit (WRU) had been taking place simultaneously to that of the Allied Armed Forces, and while not quite as complex a scenario as that faced by the military it was, by the standards of broadcasting, a massive undertaking. At one end of the equipment spectrum was building and kitting out the trucks on which the larger recording and transmitting units would be carried, down to the pencils and paper that were the tools of a radio reporter's trade, just as much as a microphone and a midget recorder.

The midget recorder was to prove one of the success stories of the BBC's coverage of D-Day and beyond. It had been developed by the MSS Company (Marguerite Sound Studios) in conjunction with BBC engineering personnel and had first been used at Anzio – it was a major hit. Weighing in at 40lb it had twelve double-sided discs that were stored in its lid, which allowed a correspondent to record up to an hour's worth of material on location. It was so simple to use that there was no need for an engineer to be available. Many of the remarkable recordings that were heard in 'War Report' would have been impossible without the midget recorder.

Recording material was one thing; transmitting it back to the UK from the field was quite another. The BBC engineers designed a 250-watt transmitter that could be fitted on to a Bedford truck. This proved unacceptable as its clearance was too low and so it was remounted on a three-ton truck with better clearance. Just a week after D-Day the first transmitter, call sign MCO (Mike Charlie Oscar), was operating from France, having been landed at the Mulberry harbour at Arromanches.

With events moving very quickly the engineers struggled to get larger transmitters operational and in the period after Operation Market Garden two more trucks were delivered to the Continent, with the call signs MCN and MCP. These three transmitters carried thousands of transmissions back to London during the course of 1944–5 and were a pivotal part of the BBC's broadcasting campaign. They were truly a triumph of ingenuity and their consistency of performance was testament to the engineers who designed them and those who kept them operational on the battlefield. The very last transmission from Germany was made by MCN. It was news of Heinrich Himmler's suicide and was yet another world exclusive for the BBC during a wartime of scoops.

Besides training the members of the WRU in map reading, physical training and using the new machinery developed for the task, there was a great deal of time devoted to giving the correspondents the correct guidelines about what to report, and how to report it. The old adage that reporters are born not made may be true, in part, but trying to develop a sense of style and cohesion was of the utmost importance. It was particularly important to train corres-pondents to produce reports that would pass the censors and much time, and effort, was spent in getting this aspect just right. The situation that existed in the early days of the war, when nearly every report was written down and then cleared by the censor before being recorded, was a luxury that was unavailable in the fast-moving warfare that was expected after D-Day.

The simple fact was that the BBC lacked enough experienced reporters to cover the war on the 'Second Front', as the D-Day landings were inexplicably called – the Allies were already fighting on a second front in Europe, moving steadily north through Italy. It was not just the correspondents that had to be trained, but also engineers and other personnel who made up the teams that worked together to support 'the voice'. Careful plans were in place to secure the mission and those that were detailed to cover the D-Day land-ings had a bag packed and kept at Broadcasting House. According to John Snagge one was labelled 'Florence Nightingale – Crimea' to put people off the scent!

While much of the training concerned what would happen after the landings, when the hoped-for advance was in full swing, there were particular issues surrounding the build-up to D-Day and the landings themselves. There was undoubtedly going to be a huge demand for news from around the world and a need to provide something akin to coherent coverage was a mission more complex than any undertaken by the BBC in its existence to date. At least one historian has made the point that the BBC's push to report D-Day and its aftermath was motivated by the fear that if reporting was left to the American radio networks then Britain's role would have been downgraded. There may be a grain of truth in this, but it seems much more likely that no one but the BBC had the wherewithal, the experience, or the ability to pull the task together. The American networks were competing companies, and by definition found working together difficult; this isn't to say they did not co-operate, but it was usually on the basis of 'needs must'.

In the middle of May the BBC broadcast an appeal of an unusual kind:

The Admiralty now want photographs of every inch of coastline, and more than that, every road, every railway bridge and every factory in the world. Look out all your snapshots and postcards from abroad. All three services use our files, and you who are listening to me now may have one photograph which will provide a vital missing part of the whole picture. Please send them to the following address – Photographs – Admiralty – London.

Stuart Hibberd, BBC, 15 May 1944

The photographs that were sent in proved incredibly useful on D-Day. Two weeks later the BBC was warned of the impending invasion, with John Snagge telling newsreaders to start sleeping at Broadcasting House. In the build-up to the landings they were kept busy reporting good news from the war in Italy.

The first 'War Report' was heard at 9.15 p.m. on D-Day, immediately following the news. As many as seventeen to twenty million people tuned in that night and throughout the eleven months that the programme was on the air it regularly had ten to fifteen million attentive listeners in Britain. In addition, men serving around the world, wherever they could hear the BBC's General Forces Programme, heard the same broadcast. Belgians, French and Dutch, many of whom illicitly tuned their radios to the BBC against the direct orders of the German armies of occupation, also listened to 'War Report'. On D-Day over seven hundred American radio stations carried 'War Report' and much of the BBC's coverage of the day's events.

The BBC's mission was to provide the 'latest and fullest picture of the war' directly to the homes of the men fighting on the front line. 'War Report' was deliberately made in a more relaxed presentational style than the authoritarian voice of the BBC news bulletins. By mixing the sound of battle with the reporter's own voice it provided a powerful soundtrack, like that pioneered by Charles Gardner's 'Battle of Britain' commentary or Wynford Vaughan-Thomas's 'Raid on Berlin'. Listeners literally heard history happen; they eavesdropped on ordinary fighting men speaking about their own experiences and personal stories, often recorded at the point of battle. Hardly anything like this had ever been heard before, and after 'War Report' the media's coverage of conflicts would never be the same again.

The best way to get a flavour of what the D-Day reporting was like is to read what was said. These reports were not necessarily heard in this order, which particularly applies to those that describe events before the invasion, but they carry the story of one of the most ambitious, daring and extraordinary events of the Second World War – a statement that applies in equal measure to the military forces and the BBC.

All contact with the shore has ended, no one may come aboard, no one may go ashore. In Navy jargon the ship and all of us aboard here are sealed. We're sealed because we've been told the answers, the answers to the questions the whole world's been asking for two years and more; where, and how, and when. Troops swarmed up the rope ladders last night, strong, healthy, formidable men, many of them going into battle for the first time.

Robin Duff, recorded 3 June 1944, BBC, broadcast after D-Day

Somewhere in Britain on the eve of Invasion. This is from one of the many airfields from which the first wave of invasion is being launched tonight. Within a very short time the airborne forces – the spearhead of the Allied assault – will be heading for France. They'll land by parachute and glider behind the German coastal defences and they'll carry the battle well into enemy territory before the seaborne attack comes in. If all goes well, the airborne forces will make considerably easier the task of those who'll attack from the sea some hours after we land.

More than a week ago the airborne troops were moved from training camps to marshalling areas near the 'dromes from which they'll fly. When they left camp they were nominally on an exercise, but when they reached here they knew it was the real thing. They were issued with live ammunition, boxes of concentrated battle rations, paint for camouflage webbing and equipment; they got field dressings and phials of morphia, and then – to leave no doubt – they drew French money and a booklet about France, which began with these words: 'A new BEF, which includes you, is going to France. You are to assist personally in pushing the Germans out of France and back where they belong.'

This was the occasion that these troops have been training and planning for ever since Dunkirk – just four years ago last week. Now – fit, eager, determined, there'd be no holding them. This was quite evident when their general spoke to his men in this camp last week. He gave them the broad outline of his plan and their task, told them how much depended on their success. He didn't belittle their task – in fact he ended by saying this: 'I don't think the Hun'll expect us to land where we're going to land. He's obstructed the whole area so thoroughly that no doubt he thinks no one but a bloody fool would try to go there; but I'm going.' The general stepped down from his rostrum; a thousand soldiers rose as a man, whipped off their red berets and cheered . . .

I saw the same eagerness when the troops were fitting their parachutes and making up their battle kitbags yesterday. They had crammed so much ammunition into their pouches and pockets, so many weapons into their webbing that they could barely struggle into their parachute harnesses. But they'll be ready to go into action the moment they hit the ground. Grenades were festooned around them, hanging from any spare inch of webbing. No man was carrying less than 80lb – some had more than a hundred. And yet they had trained themselves to move and fight with loads like these. I talked to one section of men that had marched in training – ten miles in two and a half hours – fully laden. With endurance like that, these walking human arsenals will lead the attack tonight. But they won't have to rely wholly on the arms and ammunition they bring down. Heavier arms, medical supplies, explosives for making demolitions and other stores will come down in containers on parachutes or else in gliders. I've watched them packing the gliders these last few days. They're crammed to capacity and they carry an amazing tonnage. Jeeps and guns specially designed to fit in gliders will be towed out in the same way.

The troops haven't had many spare moments since they came to the marshalling areas. Four or five hours a day they have been poring over maps, aerial photographs, models of the ground on which they'll land. They've been most fully briefed in the whole operation until they know the exact plan for the force and their part in it.

The last few days of waiting have been long-drawn-out. As the sky clouded over and a gusty wind whipped across the airfield during the weekend, the troops' faces lengthened. The day they thought was the day came and went, and this morning dawned blustery as before. But about noon the word came through, and long faces broke into broad smiles.

Now the troops, aircrews, glider pilots have had their final briefing. After these many months of training it's difficult for them to believe that this at last is the day. This morning I heard one paratroop say to another: 'Think of it – to-night we'll really be in France – fighting.'

Chester Wilmot, recorded 5 June 1944, 'War Report',
BBC, broadcast 6 June 1944

This is London calling in the European news service of the British Broadcasting Corporation. Here is the news. But first here are some messages for our friends in occupied countries. The Trojan War will not be held. John is growing a very long beard this week. The long sobs of the violins of autumn wound my heart with a monotonous languor . . .

BBC European News, 5 June 1944

The messages broadcast to Allied agents and resistance groups in Europe may well have given them advance news of the proposed invasion, or then again they may have been very specific in what they were asking the Special Operations Executive's agents to perform. For real news of the actual invasion it was ironic, and far from unusual, that the first news of the D-Day landings was broadcast on German radio:

Here is a special bulletin. Early this morning the long awaited British and American invasion began when paratroops landed in the area of the Seine Estuary. The harbour of Le Havre is being fiercely bombarded. Naval forces of the German Navy are off the coast fighting with enemy naval vessels. We just brought you a Special Bulletin.

Berlin radio, 6.37 a.m., 6 June 1944

Later in the day American radio listeners were reminded that, despite the fact that the Germans' radio had been first with the news of the invasion, listeners should not believe that their broadcasts were more accurate. 'Joseph Goebbels is in business for his health, and not ours.' When the Allies' announcement finally came it was hardly news, just an official confirmation of what many people had heard during the evening and night of 5/6 June, when thousands of sorties were flown by the RAF and the USAAF. As well as hearing the roar of the bombers overhead, those in the south of England witnessed the constant flow of traffic heading towards the coast to act as the second and subsequent waves of troops set out to cross the Channel and support the invasion. Of course it wasn't 'news' to those on duty at the BBC. During the late evening on 5 June they had been alerted to the fact that the landings were going to happen next day; John Snagge and Stuart Hibberd had worked on various aspects of the next day's scripts into the early hours. Freddy Allen read the 8 a.m. news in which there was no direct mention of the landings having taken place, but there was a warning to the people living on the western seaboard of France that 'a new phase of activity was about to begin'. Allen had also reported that German radio had announced that troops had landed in France. But it was eighty-something minutes before Britain would hear the official word, and when it came it was almost anti-climactic.

This is London, London calling in the Home Overseas and European Services and through United Nations Radio Mediterranean, and this is John Snagge speaking. Supreme Headquarters Allied Expeditionary Force have just issued Communiqué No. 1. Under the command of General Eisenhower, Allied naval forces, supported by strong air forces, began landing Allied armies this morning on the northern coast of France. I'll repeat that communiqué . . .

John Snagge, BBC Home Service, 9.32 a.m., 6 June 1944

Following this bulletin Joseph MacLeod announced that 'Music While You Work' would not be heard that day – so bang went the production levels in the factories.

People of western Europe: A landing was made this morning on the coast of France by troops of the Allied Expeditionary Force. This landing is part of the concerted United Nations plan for the liberation of Europe, made in conjunction with our great Russian Allies.

I have this message for all of you: Although the initial assault may not have been made in your own country, the hour of your liberation is approaching. All patriots – men and women, young and old – have a part to play in the achievement of final victory.

To members of resistance movements, whether led by nationals or by outside leaders, I say: Follow the instructions you have received. To patriots who are not members of organised resistance groups I say: Continue your passive resistance. Do not needlessly endanger your lives. Wait until I give you the signal to rise and strike the enemy. The day will come when I shall need your united strength. Until that day I call on you for the hard task of discipline and restraint . . .

General Eisenhower, broadcast to Europe, BBC, 10.30 a.m., 6 June 1944

Eisenhower went on to give a special message to the French in whose country the landings were taking place. He again urged people not to act foolishly, but he also added a warning: 'Those who have made common cause with the enemy and so betrayed their country will be removed.'

We have a great and a righteous cause. Let us pray that the Lord, mighty in battle, will go forth with our armies and that His special providence will aid us in the struggle. I want every soldier to know that I have complete confidence in the successful outcome of the operations that we are now about to begin. With stout hearts and with enthusiasm for the contest, let us go forward to victory; and, as we enter the battle, let us recall the words of a famous soldier spoken many years ago. These are the words he said: 'He either fears his fate too much, or his deserts are small, who dare not put it to the touch, to win, or lose it all.' Good luck to each one of you – and good hunting on the mainland of Europe.

General Bernard Montgomery, BBC, 6 June 1944

This is the BBC Home Service and here is a special bulletin read by John Snagge. D-Day has come; early this morning the Allies began the assault on the north-western face of Hitler's European Fortress. The first official news came just after half past nine when Supreme Headquarters of the Allied Expeditionary Force, usually called SHAEF by its initials, issued the following communiqué . . . it was announced soon after the Allied Communiqué that General Montgomery was in charge of the army group carrying out the assault. This army group includes British, Canadian and United States forces. Correspondents at Supreme Headquarters said the landings were in Normandy and they took place between six o'clock and a quarter past eight . . .

John Snagge, BBC Home Service, midday, 6 June 1944

Air Commodore Helmore gave the first eyewitness report of the landings, flying in an RAF Mitchell bomber over the beaches. He had arrived back at 'War Report's production office, housed in what had been the pre-war artists' Green Room, shortly before lunch with a batch of discs he had recorded on a midget recorder.

We're going across to bomb a target which is a railway bridge, which may help those good fellows down below in those boats. I know that it's what they do today that matters, but every little bit that the RAF can do to help is going to mean something.

We're coming down right low to attack our target; it's a pretty job, we're looking out for the markers now. I don't think I can talk to you while we're doing this job; I'm not a blinking hero. I don't think it's much good trying to do these flash running commentaries when you're doing a dive-bombing attack. I can see flashes where the Bomber Command stuff is falling down: a lot of Bomber Command are pounding this invasion spot like hell, doing their best to tear it to pieces.

I've just heard the navigator say 'OK. On it.' Now we're getting our nose down, and we've got to go down and give this bridge the works. We're in a colossal static storm at the moment, which is rattling in my ears like mad – what with the engine noise I can't hear myself speak at all. We're losing height rapidly – we're just going in. There's something ahead of us there – do you see – do you see that light? Oh, I thought I was talking to the pilot, I recorded that. There's a funny light, I thought it was the markers going down – instead of talking into the intercom. I talked into the record. I just heard the navigator say, over the intercom, 'We're over there', and I also heard the bomb-aimer say 'Shall I give it a cosh the moment I see it?' And the pilot said, 'Yes'.

We're just going in to drop our bombs; it's a very tense moment – just the dawn of the moment when our troops are going in on the French beaches; I've seen them with my own eyes, practically in the act of touching down on the beaches. I feel it a great privilege to be here. I'll be glad to get home all the same. Never mind, we're just getting ready to go in and bomb, and I'd better shut up. Hold it! My God, there's some bloody nasty flak round this place – very nasty flak, blast it!

Never mind, I heard the bomb-aimer say just now, 'Go in and do your stuff. Right o.' Ah, he hasn't let them off, I hear him telling the pilot to go 'Straight and steady, straight and steady'. Oh, there they go – my God, what a good lift, what a good lift up into the air! We feel much lighter now. The best thing is to get out of here. We're pointed the right way round now anyway. Hello, the rear-gunner's reported – or the bloke at the back rather – has reported a night fighter after us. I hope we make this cloud ahead of us. I don't feel very belligerent. We're heading for the coast now. There's been a constant traffic of aircraft coming to and fro. Bomber Command's been out, we've passed a lot of them. There's great open patches in the cloud through which one can get a pretty good view. Now I can see the invasion craft out on the sea, like a great armada attacking France. This is history; it's a thing I can't be eloquent about in an aeroplane, because I've got engine-noises in my ears. But this really is a great moment for us, and to feel that I sit here with this weird means of telling you about what I'm seeing gives me a feeling of witnessing a strange pageant – something unreal. I feel detached, and that awful feeling that the great history of the world is unfolding before us at this very moment.

Air Commodore Helmore, BBC News, 1 p.m., 6 June 1944

From now on it will be of even greater importance than heretofore to hinder and impede the enemy by all subtle and covert means that do not expose yourselves or others! . . . This order does not apply to organised resistance groups who are in touch with the Allied military authorities; they have been given their orders, and they will receive further orders.

King Haakon of Norway, BBC European Service, 6 June 1944

Wherever invisible and unrecognisable passive resistance is possible, it must be inexorably forthcoming. As soon as more forceful action is required of you, this will be made clear from here in unmistakable fashion.

Professor J. Gerbrandy, Prime Minister of the Netherlands,
BBC European Service, 6 June 1944

The watchwords we send you are courage, discipline, unity, and confidence.

M. Hubart Pierlot, Prime Minister of Belgium,
BBC European Service, 6 June 1944

Frenchmen – American and Anglo-Saxon forces have landed on your soil. France has thus become a battlefield. Civil servants, officials, railwaymen, workers, remain at your posts to maintain the functioning of services in order to fulfil your duties. Frenchmen, do not aggravate our misfortunes by acts which must lead to tragic reprisals. It will be an innocent French population which will have to suffer the consequences. Do not listen to those who, after having abandoned their country to her defeat, are trying to lead her into disaster.

France can only be saved by observation of the most rigorous discipline. Obey the order of the Government. Everybody's to stay at his post. Circumstances of the battle may result in the German High Command taking special decisions in the battle zone. Accept these as necessities. I am impressing upon you these recommendations in the interests of your safety. I implore you, Frenchmen, to think beforehand of the mortal danger France will be incurring if this solemn warning of mine is not heeded.

Marshal Pétain, German-controlled Paris radio, 6 June 1944

In between the regular announcements there were constant news updates and reports from correspondents accompanying the invasion troops. Some of the reports were not by WRU correspondents, but by newspaper reporters. This one from Ward Smith is movingly straightforward in the way it describes what were incredibly tense moments for the American paratroops, as well as for Smith himself, on an aircraft that could have come under attack at any time from anti-aircraft fire or German fighters.

Paratroops, steel-helmeted, black-faced, festooned from head to feet, covered the long line of bucket seats on either side of the fuselage. As I climbed aboard the co-pilot Major Cannon was reading a farewell message from General Eisenhower. It spoke of 'the great crusade' and ended 'let us all beseech the blessing of Almighty God'. As the door clanged to on us, sitting there in the dusk we realised suddenly that we'd passed from one world to another. Perhaps that was partly the effect of the all-red lights in the plane. We had a sinking feeling in the pit of the stomach but that didn't last long. Somehow that seemed to be left behind on the ground . . .

We exchanged cigarettes and we talked on, but somehow never about things that mattered – we just thought about them. Suddenly the red lights went out and I wasn't consciously thinking about anything but I found the phrase 'thy rod and thy staff' moving through my mind over and over again – just that.

. . . Corporal Jack Harrison of Phoenix Arizona who was opposite me stepped over and thrust a packet of cigarettes in my hand. 'You might need them on the way back,' he said. Then he lined up with the others. Well just in case Corporal Harrison happens to hear this I'd like him to know that I'm keeping those cigarettes for him, he might like a smoke on the way home. But if he can spare them I'd like to keep them always.

Ward Smith, BBC, 7.15 p.m., 6 June 1944

Smith worked for the *News of the World* and after flying with the American airborne troops early in the morning he returned to London to make his broadcast. He later escaped the Arnhem pocket and stood as a Liberal candidate for Bexley in Kent during the 1945 elections.

The US Air Force have concluded in postwar studies that only about 10 per cent of the troops of the 82nd and 101st Airborne Divisions actually hit their drop zones; over half of the paratroops landed up to several miles away. It all contributed to a confused state of affairs with individuals and small groups trying to link up in order to find their units. Problems like these all contributed to the total of around 9,000 casualties on D-Day – although experts have argued long and hard about exactly what the number should be; about a third of the 9,000 were fatal.

Four year ago our nation and Empire stood alone against an overwhelming enemy, with our backs to the wall. Tested as never before in our history, in God's Providence we survived that test. The spirit of the people, resolute, dedicated, burned like a bright flame lit surely, from those unseen fires which nothing can quench.

Once more a supreme test has to be faced. This time the challenge is not to fight to survive, but to fight to win the final victory for the good causes. Once again what is demanded from us all is something more than courage – more than endurance. We need a revival of spirit, a new unconquerable resolve. After nearly five years of toil and suffering, we must renew that crusading impulse on which we entered the war and met its darkest hour.

King George VI, BBC News, 9 p.m., 6 June 1944

Following the King's speech the National Anthem was played and this was followed by the tune 'Lilibulero', which introduced the first of the 235 editions of 'War Report' that were heard on the BBC, although there had actually been a kind of trial edition following the 1 p.m. news earlier in the day; that is when Helmore's report had first been heard.

War Report – Night by night at this time, this programme will bring you news from correspondents and fighting men. It will contain live broadcasts and recordings made in the field, special broadcasts from forward areas and dispatches and expert comment to give you the latest and fullest picture of the war on all fronts . . .

Joseph McLeod, BBC News, 9.15 p.m., 6 June 1944

There were further elements of Helmore's report repeated in that first edition, as well as the first coverage of the forces on the ground in France; this last element had been brought back by Howard Marshall, the BBC's Chief War Correspondent, who faced some daunting difficulties before completing his mission. He had capsized twice, and his notes had become so waterlogged that they were illegible. As well as being heard on 'War Report' Marshall's eyewitness account was relayed on the 725 US radio stations that took the BBC's D-Day broadcasts.

I'm sitting in my soaked-through clothes with no notes at all; all my notes are sodden, they're at the bottom of the sea, so as it's only a matter of minutes since I stepped off a craft, I'm just going to try to tell you very briefly the story of what our boys had to do on the beaches today as I saw it myself. I won't go into the build-up, which was taking place as you know for a very long time, but I'll start with first light of this morning. The landing craft were lowered and, as the light broke and we really could see around us, we began to become aware of the formidable character of this invasion fleet of which we were a part. I was in a barge, which was due to pick up the brigadier of an assault group, and we were going in with the first assault wave. So we circled round with the various types of vessels opening fire on the beach, which we could see quite plainly in the dim morning light, opening fire on the beach in their own manner and at the appointed time.

First of all the cruisers started with rather a loud bang. And soon the air grew heavy with the smell of cordite and loud with the sound of explosions, and looking along the beach we could see the explosions of our artillery creating a great cloud and fog of smoke.

Well, we in my particular craft picked up our brigadier not easily because the sea was very rough and we headed straight for our appointed portion of the beach. We could see as we went in that that particular portion of the beach wasn't altogether healthy, but we drove towards it with our planes overhead giving us the sort of cover we'd been hoping for, and which we'd been expecting.

As we drove in we could see shell bursts in the water along the beach, and just behind the beach, and we could see craft in a certain amount of difficulty because the wind was driving the sea in with long rollers and the enemy had prepared anti-invasion, anti-barge obstacles sticking out from the water – formidable prongs, many of them tipped with mines, so that as your landing barge swung and swayed in the rollers, and they're not particularly manageable craft, it would come in contact with one of these mines and be sunk. That was the prospect which faced us on this very difficult morning as we drove into the beach. And suddenly, as we tried to get between two of these tripart defence systems of the Germans, our craft swung, we touched a mine, there was a very loud explosion, a thundering shudder of the whole craft, and water began pouring in.

Well, we were some way out from the beach at that point. The ramp was lowered at once, and out of the barge drove the Bren gun carrier into about five feet of water, with the barge settling heavily in the meanwhile. Well, the Bren gun carrier somehow managed to get through it, and we followed wading ashore. That was one quite typical instance of how people got ashore, and when they got ashore seemed to be in perfectly good order, because the troops out of that barge immediately assembled and went to their appointed places, and there was no semblance of any kind of confusion. But the scene on the beach until one had sorted it out was at first rather depressing because we did see a great many barges in difficulties with these anti-tank screens, and we noticed that a number of them had struck mines, as ours had struck mines. But then we began to see that in fact the proportion that had got through was very much greater, and that troops were moving all along the roads, and that tanks were out already and going up the hills, that in fact we dominated the situation; and that our main enemy was the weather and that we were beating the weather; that we had our troops and our tanks ashore, and that the Germans weren't really putting up a great deal of resistance.

Howard Marshall, 'War Report', BBC, 6 June 1944

This first edition of 'War Report' was not the smooth, well-oiled programme of reportage that it would become. There was so much going on, so many reports and recordings coming in during the day that the staff at Broadcasting House did well to get anything on air at all. There were over fifty reports to sift through and edit into something that resembled a seamless programme. From a technical standpoint it was a miracle that the machinery stood up to the job – and some of the staff manning the machines, with barely time for a break, were brought close to breaking point. At least one of the female secretarial staff needed a stiff whisky to pull her through. However, the next morning the news from France appeared to be positive – although hard facts and detail were in short supply.

> . . . At points our troops have advanced several miles inland, and tanks have been reported as moving on the town of Caen 10 miles from the coast where fighting was reported earlier. When BBC reporter Frank Gillard came through from General Montgomery's headquarters there was no report of the violent reaction when Field Marshal von Rundstedt concentrates his forces against our operational area. It's early yet to get any firm assessment of the general situation over on the French coast but our reporter says there was an atmosphere of confidence at General Montgomery's headquarters fully justified by the news flashed back from our troops so far. One of the things everyone wants to know about is how our airborne troops are faring. There's no hard news yet about their part but at least it's known that the operation of landing them, the biggest airborne operation in history, was most successful . . .
>
> *Alvar Lidell, BBC News, 8 a.m., 7 June 1944*

> The die is cast. We do not know yet what portion of his forces the enemy has already thrown into battle – a question of great moment to the defender, particularly at the beginning of a large-scale offensive. Certainly the battle in the Seine Bay constitutes only the first act of the invasion. This will not be an affair of 'Here today and gone tomorrow'. The troops which we have to face now are fighting with the traditional Anglo-Saxon bulldoggedness. Let us never forget that there are other theatres of war which demand our full attention. The grim battle in Italy is continuing with undiminished fury. Our eyes have constantly to be strained towards the east and south-east of the Continent, it is only a matter of time when Stalin will switch the lever, and unleash his armies on a grand-scale offensive. Sooner or later the Balkan coasts may become the target of yet another diversionary invasion. We have no illusions about the difficulties in store. The stakes are high.
>
> *Lieutenant-General Dietmar, High Command spokesman,*
> *German radio, 7 June 1944*

Over the next few days the WRU teams were hard at it with the air forces, the navy and before long on the ground with the troops in the front line of battle. 'War Report' soon started using the voices of the fighting men themselves to add that crucial ring of authenticity demanded by the audience at home and overseas, all hungry to hear 'real stories' – and, most of all, success in battle. Interestingly the reports did not always sound as though the Allies were winning.

I was crouched in the barge and the sergeant shouted 'OK this is it'. So I jumped up and grabbed my gear and jumped into the water. It was a long way from the shore, further than I thought, about 200 yards – it was deeper than I thought and so I started to swim. I eventually made the sea wall and just as I got alongside our tank a Jerry 88-millimetre gun hit our tank.

British tank crewman, 'War Report', BBC, 8 June 1944

We're over the coast now and the run-in has started – one minute – 30 seconds. Red light – green and out – get on out – out – out fast into the cool night air out over France – and we know that the dropping zone is obstructed. We're jumping into fields covered with poles. And I hit my parachute and lower my harness. And then the ground comes up to hit me. And I find myself in the middle of a cornfield. I look around and even with my compass I can't be sure where I am – and overhead hundreds of parachutes and containers are coming down. The whole sky is a fantastic chimera of lights and flak and one plane gets hit and disintegrates wholesale in the sky, sprinkling a myriad of burning pieces all over the sky.

The job of the unit with which I jumped was to occupy the area and prepare the way for gliders – we were to rendezvous near a copse, but I could not find it. It's a tricky business this moving about the countryside at night. But we are well in hand and at the most I shall only meet my own patrols. I find the unit after having been sniped at once and challenged a number of times. They are assembling under a hedge. And things are happening all around and it's difficult to guess what exactly is happening. The sky is crossed and recrossed by tracer, and the distinctive splutter of a light machine-gun is quite near us.

Like a tentacle into the air was the radio set aerial, and the major was signalling, and the radio messages cross the fields – Allied soldiers talking to each other through the night.

Things are going well for our troops; at this early hour they have deployed and infested the whole area around the dropping zone. A tremendous bombardment has started now on the coast defences from the sky, and hundreds of Lancasters are raining their blockbusters down on the coast. It's an awe-inspiring sight, for in another few hours or so the navy will bring the men to the beaches.

Meanwhile on the dropping zone, shock paratroop engineers are finishing blowing the poles that obstruct the dropping zone, and soon the gliders come in scores, coming out of the sky like a sign.

Guy Byam, 'War Report', BBC, 8 June 1944

Byam's report may well have described a drop on the night of D-Day itself and his discs had only managed to make it back to London in time for the Thursday night edition of 'War Report'. Chester Wilmot was in a glider just behind Byam, although it's unclear whether they landed in the same area.

This is Chester Wilmot broadcasting from a glider bound for France – and invasion. We've just passed over the coast of France and all around us along the coast ack-ack fire is going up – away to the right and away off to the left but in front of us there's nothing coming up at all. I can see away off to the right the river that is our main guide for coming into the landing zone. And there now I can see the light that is to guide us in . . .

. . . With grinding brakes and creaking timbers we jolted, lurched, and crashed our way to a landing in northern France early this morning. The glider in which I travelled came off better than most. The bottom of the nose was battered in . . . the wings and tail assembly were slashed here and there, but she came to rest on her three wheels, even though she had mown down five stout posts that came in her path, and virtually crash-landed in a ploughed field. No one was even scratched.

We shouted with joy . . . and relief . . . and bundled out into the field. All around us we could see silhouettes of other gliders, twisted and wrecked – making grotesque patterns against the sky. Some had buried their noses in the soil; others had lost a wheel or a wing; one had crashed into a house, two had crashed into each other. And yet as we marched off past these twisted wrecks – thanking heaven for our good fortune – troops were clambering out almost as casually as they might leave a bus. Some had to slash away the wooden fuselage before they could get out their jeeps and trailers; but almost without exception they soon had them on the road.

But as we moved off the landing zone we were promptly reminded that we were still in the middle of enemy territory. We could hear Germans shouting excitedly at a church nearby, starting a car and driving furiously off. A quarter of a mile away a German battery was firing out to sea . . . from positions all around us German ack-ack batteries sent up streams of tracer. The airborne forces had gained their first foothold in France by a daring night landing . . . but all of us knew that it'd be harder to hold the ground than to take it.

Chester Wilmot, 'War Report', BBC, 8 June 1944

Among the many reports that aired on D-Day, and for the weeks that followed, were those by Richard Dimbleby. Picking just two at random shows the power of his mind, and the way he seemed to manage to make each broadcast sound like a description of a coronation or some other state occasion. Dimbleby had the ability to imbue momentous events with a simple grandeur and it comes as no surprise that he made many of the Corporation's broadcasts that needed that 'sense of occasion' – both during the war and until his untimely death in 1965, aged just fifty-two.

I saw the shining blue sea. Not an empty sea, but a sea crowded, infested with craft of every kind; little ships, fast and impatient, scurrying like water-beetles to and fro, and leaving a glistening wake behind them; bigger ships, in stately, slow procession with the sweepers in front and the escort vessels on the flank – it was a brave, oh, an inspiring sight. We are supplying the beaches all right – no doubt of that. We flew on south-west, and I could see France and Britain, and I realised how very near to you all at home in England is this great battle in Normandy. It's a stone's throw across the gleaming water.

I saw it all as a mighty panorama, clear and etched in its detail. There were the supply ships, the destroyers, the torpedo boats, the assault craft, leaving England. Halfway over was another flotilla, and near it a huge, rounded, ugly, capital ship, broadside on to France. There in the distance was the Cherbourg peninsula, Cherbourg itself revealed in the sun. And there, right ahead now, as we reset course, were the beaches. Dozens, scores, hundreds of craft lying close inshore, pontoons and jetties being lined up to make a new harbour where, six days ago, there was an empty stretch of shore.

Richard Dimbleby, 'War Report', BBC, 11 June 1944

This is Richard Dimbleby calling you from over the English Channel flying between England and France. We're on our way out south from the coast crossing over towards Normandy with a wing of Spitfires on its way to take over the patrol and the protection of the Allied armies on the beaches and inland. A very lovely sight the Spitfires on our port side, ranged in their ranks of three, and now we're going in over the cliffs and the green fields of France and over there to starboard the big warships firing inshore towards the Cherbourg Peninsula where the Americans are – A flash of their guns just gone now – another flash from a ship further down the line. And now we're winging in behind the Spitfires, they're spreading out now, right and left, searching for German aircraft as we follow them inland.

Right ahead of us are great fires burning on the ground, and clouds of white smoke coming up from the battlefront. There's a great pattern of France, cratered and recratered where our bombs have fallen in the past. Here is the new landing strip lying out, looking for all the world like an old-established and magnificently prepared aerodrome.

We're diving down and coming in over it right now – flying straight over the top. And there, in the distance, and all around us in a great semi-circle is the battlefront. I can see the whole of it from east to west. Fires are burning in every direction. There's smoke going up in clouds. We've seen the guns firing and the ships firing inshore. And we're flying so low now that I can see individual people on the ground, there are anti-aircraft guns, there are some cows sitting in a field. More guns and at that road junction just below us a Military Policeman waving 'em on. You know I can even see his red cap from here, because he's wearing that and not his tin hat . . .

Richard Dimbleby, 'War Report', BBC, 12 June 1944

These two broadcasts, a day apart, offer a unique insight into Dimbleby's supreme skills as a broadcaster. The first was written on his return and delivered in the studio, while the second was recorded live, on board what was probably a Mosquito, using a midget recorder. For a man who had a fear of flying he was superb.

MEANWHILE OVER TO ROME

The amazing news of D-Day had all but swept news of Rome's liberation from the radio, as well as the newspapers. Godfrey Talbot had only gone to Italy because, having been assigned to Burma, a virus kept him in London and another correspondent was sent to the Far East. It fell to Talbot to give listeners back home a flavour of what it was like to be in a city freed from the clutches of an enemy – even if Germany had been an ally a few months before. Such was the delight of many Romans that Talbot reported that he was 'kissed and hugged to suffocation point, my battledress is torn with the violence of this welcome'.

This is Godfrey Talbot speaking from Rome. I am standing in the middle of the Palazzo Venezia on this day of our occupation. And at this moment the windows of the balcony of the Palazzo Venezia from which Mussolini used to make his speeches, the windows have been opened and there's come out on to the balcony – not Mussolini, who incidentally has never made any appearance on that balcony since July of last year, not Mussolini, but three

Allied soldiers with their steel helmets on and their rifles in their hands. Beside them, two Romans, two people who have gone up from this square, two of the Italian people and those four are standing there and they are waving the Italian and the Allied flags, a vastly different scene from the one that that balcony has staged in the past.

Godfrey Talbot, BBC News, 8 a.m., 6 June 1944

Apart from the problem of Talbot's mathematics – there were five people on the balcony according to his build-up – the fact was that Rome's liberation was only of passing interest. It was not so true of some of his earlier reports in the post-Anzio breakout period. The siege of the monastery at Monte Cassino had aroused great interest around the world – partly because the Allies were shelling a holy site.

Now as for today's taking of the great Abbey at Monte Cassino on Monastery Hill, this was an enormously hard-won triumph for Polish troops against an enemy from whom they had suffered much. In the mountain heights through which the Poles broke to get round the back of the ruined Monastery fortress fighting had been severe in the extreme. Men fought till they dropped, dropped exhausted or dropped killed or wounded. They had to get through appalling mountain tracks with the Germans commanding them and pouring streams of fire on them at every move. The Poles were counter-attacked time after time when they gained the height and there was all the time no way up to the hill positions except by mule and finally on foot. Always the supply, ammunition and water parties had to go up through heavy German fire. In many positions you could by day remain alive only in a hole in the ground. To show yourself and move in daylight in these forward positions was death.

I was at a Polish headquarters on the morning of the capture when the news came through. 'We're in the Abbey, Monastery Hill is occupied.' It was an historic moment and the drama was heightened when an officer put the good news right in front of my eyes. He handed me a small piece of paper. 'It's come from the monastery by one of our carrier pigeons,' he said. And I looked at the crumpled scrap of paper. All that was on it was a 'V' for victory and it was signed by a Lieutenant of Signals who had reached the abbey.

Godfrey Talbot, BBC News, 18 May 1944

In other parts of this broadcast Talbot spoke movingly of the desecration of the abbey and the sight of so many bodies that lay everywhere after the struggle for Monte Cassino came to an end; although it was actually four separate battles and lasted for five months. The abbey occupied a strategic position in the German defensive line about 80 miles to the south of Rome. It was pulverised from the air and during the first three phases of the battle, between January and March 1944, 54,000 Americans, British, New Zealanders, Indians, Canadians, French, South Africans and Australians were killed. When the Poles and the Indians finally captured Monte Cassino it allowed the final advance on Rome to begin and brought about the effective displacement of the Germans from Italy. In all there were around a quarter of a million casualties at Monte Cassino, including 30,000 Germans killed.

Florence was captured in August 1944 after bitter fighting. The men of the British Eighth Army were issued with an eight-page booklet and a map of the city. Inside it says, 'Respect FLORENCE for what it is, a city famous in history and possessing some of the finest artistic and cultural achievements of man. Take inspiration also from the thought that this Eighth Army with every fresh success is hastening the day when the arts can flourish again in all its beauty and magnificence.'

HITLER'S SECRET WEAPON

Perhaps the most interesting part of a Churchill speech on the BBC in late March 1944 was a small reference to what might happen in the near future. 'There will be many false alarms, many feints, many dress rehearsals. We may also ourselves be the objects of new forms of attack from the enemy. Britain can take it.' It was a prediction that sadly was to become all too true.

A week after the D-Day landings men on duty at a Royal Observer Corps station in Kent's Romney Marshes saw a strange glowing black object in the sky heading towards them – they were baffled as they had never seen anything like it. It was a sight that was to become all too familiar. It was the first V1 flying bomb, one of ten pilotless 'aircraft' fired from launch sites in France. On this first occasion only four made it across the Channel, and only one managed to reach London, where it crash-landed in Grove Road in Hackney, killing six people. It was the start of the shorter, but no less frightening, Blitz. The first confirmation for most of Britain of this new aerial threat was on the 1 p.m. news on Friday 16 June, and even then it was not the first item on the bulletin. Given the potential threat that this could have posed, and against a background of the Normandy landings, the need to maintain domestic morale was an overriding consideration for the government. It was one of those situations where the news needed to be managed, and the extent of the threat examined, before saying too much, too soon. Initially some sections of the press called them 'robot machines', which somehow made them sound even more sinister. Later in the day, on 16 June, Herbert Morrison, the Home Secretary, made a more measured statement and this was read on the evening news bulletins.

> The enemy has begun to use his secret weapon – the pilotless aircraft. The damage it has caused has been relatively small, and the new weapon will not interfere with our war effort and our sure and steady march to victory. The enemy's aim is clearly, in view of the difficulty of his military situation, to try to upset our morale and interfere with our work, It is essential that there should be the least possible interruption in all work vital to the country's needs at this time, and the Government's counsel is that everyone should get on with his or her job in the ordinary way and only take cover when danger is imminent.
>
> *BBC News, 16 June 1944*

Four days later they had been christened 'doodlebugs', which made them seem less threatening than the earlier 'robot machines', although it did nothing to reduce their effectiveness. By the end of June around eighty V1s were hitting the London area every day, over 120 reaching their target on some days; one hit the Air Ministry in the Aldwych and killed close to fifty people. At the forefront of Britain's defence was once again the RAF; it became almost a mini-Battle of Britain, or the 'doodlebug summer' as some have named it. Given the need to support the land forces in France, as well as in many other theatres of war, it was a major task to combat the doodlebugs, but a vital one given the threat to the civilian population, and particularly those living in the south-east. Such was the threat to morale that Churchill personally ordered that the RAF's Tempest pilots would fly in any and all weathers in order to reinforce the will of the people on the ground. He deduced that it was important for people on the ground to hear the sound of the RAF defending them.

> We patrol at between 5 and 6,000 feet, that's about 3,000 feet higher than the path of the average flying bomb. The first thing we usually see is a small light rather hard to distinguish from a star coming in from the sea, then the searchlights light up and point out the direction from which the bomb is coming. The guns go into action and we wait for the bombs that get through the gun belt, as soon as we spot a bomb that's run the gauntlet successfully we make a diving turn and go down after it, finishing our dive just behind the bomb and opening fire at a range of about 250 yards.

The Doodle Bug doesn't go down easily. It will take a lot of punishment, and you have to aim at the propulsion unit – that's the long stovepipe, as we call it, on the tail. If your range and aim are dead on, you can see pieces flying off the stovepipe. The big white flame at the end goes out, and down goes the bomb. Sometimes it dives straight to earth, but at other times it goes crazy and gives a wizard display of acrobatics before finally crashing.

Sometimes the bomb explodes in mid-air, and the flash is so blinding that you cannot see a thing for about ten seconds. You hope to be the right way up when you are able to see again, because the explosion often throws the fighter about and sometimes turns it upside down.

Squadron Leader Joe Berry DFC, BBC, 8 September 1944

Joe Berry, aged twenty-four, was credited with sixty doodlebug kills flying a Hawker Tempest for 501 Squadron, which he also commanded. As the threat of V1s subsided Berry and his squadron were reassigned to ground attack duties on the Continent, which is where he was shot down by small-arms fire from the ground – bullets ruptured his glycol tank. His aircraft crashed in flames and he was pulled, dead, from the blazing wreckage by two German civilians.

The Typhoon was the only fighter capable of getting anywhere near close enough in low-level flight to the flying bombs, and they often had to operate at night. Initially there were very few of these high-performance fighters available, but by the end of the year one hundred or so were in service. Other aircraft were also modified to allow them to get within range of the doodlebugs, but it was the Tempest that had the greatest success, shooting down close to 700 of them. The RAF's first jet fighter, the Meteor, was rushed into service to counter the menace, but only accounted for around a dozen kills; its speed wasn't the issue, just its guns that jammed all too regularly. The anti-aircraft batteries also played a valuable part in countering the V1 menace.

This report from Ed Murrow of CBS at the height of the doodlebug summer captured the mood perfectly. He always managed to paint a bigger picture while never losing sight of the stories of individuals – the mark of a great broadcaster.

This is London. These doodlebugs come over, sounding like a couple of dissatisfied washing machines hurtling through the air. They come at every hour of the day or night. Living here is like being under unobserved artillery fire.

The other night one of them hit a hospital. Hit it smack on the roof. Most of the nurses were sleeping downstairs, but one of the maids, a 30-year-old, sallow, squint-eyed individual was sleeping on the top floor. These doodles explode on impact and have very little penetrating power. This one went off when it hit the roof. A few minutes later, before the dust had settled, a doctor friend of mine was making a round of the wards. There he found the maid, pretty well bespattered with glass. She was the only casualty. She had never been considered very bright and she said to the doctor, 'I'm so ashamed. I should have been sleeping downstairs, but I wasn't, and now I am the only one to be hurt. And what will the hospital think of me, being such a nuisance and all.'

Early the next morning, workmen were replacing the windows and patching the walls. And the men doing the job came from Scotland. No one had ordered them to come down here. They had volunteered, just because there was a job of work to be done. My doctor friend told me they were using some kind of American, plastic glass. And they gave him some of it to repair the windows of his home. He hadn't thought to tell me that his house had been blasted.

Ed Murrow, CBS, August 1944

In all over 9,000 doodlebugs were fired against Britain but less than 40 per cent managed to reach their target; even so, over 6,000 people were killed in the capital, and a further 18,000 were injured – and it was not only London that was hit. In the autumn the Luftwaffe found a new way of delivering V1s by launching them on specially converted Heinkel He111 bombers. On 24 December 1944 forty-five doodlebugs were launched from over the North Sea; their target was Manchester, where over thirty landed in the area – of which half landed on Manchester itself.

To add to the threat the Germans pressed the more deadly V2 rockets into service in early September. Weighing almost 13,000kg they came down from the stratosphere at 3,000 miles per hour – with no warning. These were psychologically more potent than the V1s, but less effective against the civilian population, but only owing to the fact that many fewer were fired against London. In all around 2,700 people were killed and 6,000 injured by the 520 V2s that hit London. Such was the government's level of concern about the V2 rockets that a plan for the evacuation of London was even considered. Thankfully the advancing Allied armies in Europe nullified the threat of both the doodlebug and the V2 when they captured the majority of the launch sites.

In the midst of the V1 and V2 attacks there was one welcome piece of information broadcast on the morning of 7 September:

From September 17, when British Double Summer Time ends, window black-out will be replaced by 'hall-lighting' over the whole country except in a few special coastal areas. Under the new requirement, windows other than skylights will only need to be curtained sufficiently to prevent objects inside the building from being distinguishable from the outside. This will enable ordinary peacetime curtains or blinds to be used, except the flimsiest kind, and from the streets a diffused light will be seen. On an air-raid warning, complete obscuration will be required, either by drawing black-out curtains or extinguishing the lights.

BBC News, 8 a.m., 7 September 1944

It was also announced that from 12 September daylight Fire Guard duties would end everywhere, while in most of Britain night duties would also be suspended; in addition there were big cuts in Civil Defence duties.

FREEDOM

While the war had very definitely returned to the Home Front the work of the WRU was busier than ever across the battlefronts of Europe. Frank Gillard and Chester Wilmot had been kept hard at it reporting from the very front of the front line in France during June and July. Even when the advance had moved through an area there were still stories to report, like the one filed by Robin Duff in early July on the work of the French Resistance.

Yesterday they were at work routing out the Germans themselves. They were searching a deserted farmhouse, when one of them saw a boot sticking out of a corner of an attic. They fired through the floor and nineteen German soldiers, fully armed, surrendered to four soldiers of the Resistance.

As you stand in their headquarters and talk to them, to men who have just come back from the Maquis, to boys who are so young that they have only just been allowed to join the movement, you begin to realise something of what this movement really means. You understand why they all ask the same question: 'When are we going to be called up for the regular army?' They all say the same thing. They want everyone to know of their gratitude to the armies that have liberated them, but they want still more to show that Frenchmen are ready and able to take their full part in the fight. Their chief summed it up: 'Il y a encore des bons Français en France.' – 'There are still good Frenchmen in France.'

While he was in the courtyard of this headquarters a report came in that a German parachutist had been seen nearby. These parachutists are dropped to carry out sabotage and spying. As soon as the report came in, the chief ordered out three men. They were very young Frenchmen and they wore much-patched suits. On their arms was their uniform – a red, white, and blue band with the Cross of Lorraine. Armed with rifles, they started out and two of us went with them. With three combatants and two correspondents, it looked like being the most heavily reported engagement in history.

As we went along, searching as best we might, three small children joined us. There was a boy of fifteen and his two little sisters. They asked us whether they could help us to look for les Boches. Armed with some chewing gum, some toffee, and a cigarette, they tagged along. And suddenly, we wanted to laugh.

It was a serious job, and the three young Frenchmen were going about it in a business-like way. They were thankful to be able to lend a hand to stalk with rifles the men who'd bullied them until a few days before.

But the picture of this incongruous little band, the little girl stumping seriously along chewing her toffee, was just a bit too much. We left without having captured the German parachutist and without having disgraced ourselves by laughing in the presence of these three enthusiastic, determined young men who might have misunderstood that laughter. Because it would have been laughter that hid a very real admiration and respect.

Robin Duff, 'War Report', BBC, 11 July 1944

As Robin Duff was reporting on a sideshow of the campaign, Chester Wilmot and Frank Gillard were with the British troops who captured Caen. Wilmot had been recording the sound of what soldiers called 'the Sobbing Sisters' – the German missile-launchers. Unfortunately he was so close to the impact of the missiles that it caused the sapphire-tipped cutting head to jump so violently that it stopped the midget recorder from recording.

A month later, with the Allies approaching Paris, Godfrey Talbot was busy reporting on the attack on the Mediterranean coastline of France. He watched gliders land in the area between Nice and Marseilles; it was an attack that took the Germans by surprise and almost at once they began retreating. A few days later on 23 August and the news of the liberation of Paris was broadcast on the 12.30 p.m. news bulletin of the BBC's French Service; when the BBC's Home Service relayed the news they did so to the accompaniment of the bells of St Paul's. Anxious to be there to share the moment, General de Gaulle had flown to France and was at the head of the column of troops that drove into the city. A couple of days later, on Saturday, 40,000 people were amassed around Notre Dame Cathedral; many were there to cheer the General, who had established the rule of the Free French Forces in France. A BBC reporter was able to provide radio with another first – an assassination attempt live on air.

> . . . The general's now turned to face the square, and this huge crowd of Parisians [machine-gun fire]. He's being presented to people [machine-gun fire]. He's being [shots] received even while the general is marching [sustained firing] – even while the general is marching into the cathedral . . . [a gap in the recording]
>
> Well, that was one of the most dramatic scenes I've ever seen. Just as General de Gaulle was about to enter the cathedral of Notre Dame, firing started all over the place. I'm afraid we couldn't get you the noise of that firing because I was overwhelmed by a rush of people who were trying to seek shelter, and my cable parted from my microphone. But I fell just near General de Gaulle and I managed to pick myself up. General de Gaulle was trying to control the crowds rushing into the cathedral. He walked straight ahead in what appeared to me to be a hail of fire from somewhere inside the cathedral, somewhere from the galleries up near the vaulted roof. But he went straight ahead without hesitation, his shoulders flung back, and walked right down the central aisle, even while the bullets were pouring around him . . .
>
> Robert Reid, 'War Report', BBC, 27 August 1944

Some newspaper reports that followed played down the attempt on 54-year-old de Gaulle's life. The *Daily Telegraph* even spoke of a 'few stray bullets' and implied that it was not that serious. All over the weekend in the streets of Paris there were sporadic gun battles between small bands of concealed snipers and the Resistance. Even though the Germans had surrendered to General Leclerc there were still isolated groups of fanatical Nazis or the Darlan Militia that carried on the fight. When the shooting occurred at Notre Dame the Maquis turned all their available firepower on where the shots had come from, which included the gallery of the cathedral. As calm was restored, four men, who Reid described later in his report as 'very obvious Germans', were marched out from inside Notre Dame with their hands above their heads. The shooting at the cathedral appeared to have been a signal for similar activities in other areas of Paris. The *Daily Telegraph*'s reporter said: 'As we drove back to the Ritz Hotel, shots rang out in several streets. Despite these alarms, all Paris was in a holiday mood. The streets were filled with crowds of people all wearing their best, thousands of cycles were weaving in and out among the French and American army vehicles.'

Chapter 14

CALLING ON GERMANY

Less than a month after the relief of Paris another crucial phase of the Allied advance on Germany took place. Stout German resistance in Belgium had allowed the Nazi forces to organise for a new defensive line to be taken up in Holland. Problems with the supply lines to the advancing Allies also played a part in slowing the advance. The plan hatched by Montgomery, and rather surprisingly favoured by the US President, was called Operation Market Garden. It was audacious and risky in that most of First Allied Airborne Army was to be parachuted or carried by glider behind enemy lines. Their mission was to capture key bridges in Holland across the Rhine. In all it involved 30,000 men and was to be the biggest airborne operation ever staged.

Besides the ambitious nature of the plan, which was effected in far too short a space of time, luck also went against the Allies, and particularly the British 1st Airborne Division. The spot chosen by the Germans for II Panzer Corps to regroup and refit was Arnhem – exactly where the British were to be dropped.

About two hours ago Supreme Headquarters gave the news of our airborne landing in Holland in this brief announcement. Strong forces of the First Allied Airborne Army were landed in Holland this afternoon . . .

John Snagge, BBC News, 6 p.m., 17 September 1944

I want to-day – the 17th September – to speak to all soldiers in the group of Armies under my command. What a change has came over the scene since I last spoke to you on the 21st August. Then we were moving up towards the Seine, having inflicted a decisive defeat on the German armies in Normandy. Today, the Seine is far behind us, the Allies have removed the enemy from practically the whole of France and Belgium, except in a few places, and we stand at the door of Germany.

And, by the terrific energy of your advance northward from the Seine, you brought quick relief to our families and loved ones in England, by occupying the launching sites of the flying bombs. We have advanced a great way in a short time – and we have accomplished much. The total of prisoners captured is now nearly 400,000, and there are many more to be collected from those ports in Brittany and in the Pas de Calais that are still holding out. The enemy has suffered immense losses in men and material. It is becoming problematical how much longer he can continue the struggle.

A more historic march of events can seldom have taken place in history in such a short space of time. You have every reason to be proud of what you have done. Let us say to each other, 'This was the Lord's doing, and it is marvellous in our eyes.'

And now the Allies are closing in on Nazi Germany, from the east, from the south, and from the west. Her satellite Powers have thrown the towel into the ring; they have had enough of the Nazis, and they now fight on our side.

Our American Allies are fighting on German soil, in many places. Very soon we shall all be there. The Nazi leaders have ordered the German people to defend their country to the last, and to dispute every inch of ground. This is a very natural order, and we would do the same ourselves in a similar situation, but the mere issuing of orders is quite useless. You require good men and true to carry them out. The great mass of the German people know that their situation is already hopeless and they will think more clearly on this subject as we advance deeper into their country. They have little wish to continue the struggle.

Whatever orders are issued in Germany, and whatever action is taken on them, no human endeavours can now prevent the complete and utter defeat of the armed forces of Germany. Their fate is certain, and their defeat will be absolute. The triumphant cry now is 'Forward into Germany'. Good luck to you all and good hunting in Germany.

Field Marshal Bernard Montgomery, BBC, 9.15 p.m.,
17 September 1944

Montgomery's biblical quote came from Psalm 118 and we can presume some of his confidence stemmed from the fact that Market Garden was his idea. However, while what he said was to come true the forecast of a German collapse was undoubtedly premature. Over the next week he probably rued his words.

By now we were getting towards the dropping area and I sat looking down the length of the fuselage. The crew chief is on his knees back in the very rear talking into his intercom, talking with the pilots. The rest of the men have folded up their yellow Mae Wests, as there is certainly no possibility of our ditching in the water on this trip. They're looking out of the window rather tirelessly, almost as though they were passengers on a peacetime airliner. You occasionally see a man rub the palm of his hand against his trouser leg. There seems to be just that – oh – sort of a film over some of their faces, as though they were just on the verge of perspiring but they aren't. Every man the whole length of the ship is now looking down at this Dutch countryside. We see a few stacks down there that seem to be wheat. There's a small factory off to the right, about half of it demolished. The country is perfectly flat of course; a little while ago we saw some of those big thirty-passenger British Horsa gliders being towed in, and it looks much better glider country than it did in Normandy.

. . . There go the parapacks from the formation ahead of us – yellow, brown, red, drifting down gently, dropping their containers. I can't see, we're a little too far away – I can't see the bodies of the men – yes, I can, just like little brown dolls hanging under a green lamp-shade they look.

Just before our men dropped we saw the first flak. I think it's coming from that little village just beside the canal. More tracer coming up now, just cutting across in front of our nose. They're just queued up on the door now, waiting to jump. Walking out of this aircraft with no flak suits, no armour plating on the ship, we're down just about to the drop altitude now – there are more tracers coming up – nine ships ahead of us have just dropped – you can see the men swinging down – in just about thirty seconds now our ship will drop and those fighting men will walk out on to Dutch soil – you can probably hear the snap as they check the lashing on the static line – there goes, d'you hear them shout '3–4–5–6–7–8–9–10–11–12–13–14–15–16–17–18' – there they go – every man out – I can see their 'chutes going down now – every man clear – they're dropping just beside a little windmill near a church – hanging there very gracefully – they're all going down so slowly it seems as though they should get to the ground much faster – we're now swinging about making a right-hand turn.

As we came out there was the blue-grey haze of battle smoke. The parachutes dappled the green fields. And more planes and more gliders were going in. Only a few minutes after the drop we looked down and saw parachutists moving along the road towards a village. They had formed up, were properly spaced, and were moving on their first objective.

Ed Murrow, 'War Report', CBS and BBC, 17 September 1944

The confident tone of Murrow's broadcast in 'War Report' on the evening of the first day of the Allied attack must have given everyone listening the feeling that this was indeed the final push into Germany – it was just like the D-Day landings. Over the next few days the fierce fighting at the bridges targeted by

Allied forces saw heavy casualties. What was not made clear at this point was the fact that the British troops had been dropped too far from their targeted bridges, which hindered their mission. The US airborne forces were far more successful. The British troops did manage to get to the north side of the bridge at Arnhem but it was the only one.

> The position of the hard-pressed airborne troops at Arnhem is still not clear. Correspondents with the forces at Arnhem report that they are fighting on magnificently, although they are short of ammunition and water – some have had no food for several days. War correspondent Alan Wood writes: 'If in the years to come any man says to you "I fought at Arnhem", take off your hat to him.'
>
> *Robert Robinson, BBC News, midnight, 23 September 1944*

Alan Wood of the *Daily Express* was one of six correspondents who dropped with the Allied paratroopers at Arnhem; included in the six were Stanley Maxted and Guy Byam of the BBC. In the ensuing withdrawal from Arnhem the Reuters correspondent was captured and Byam only escaped by swimming across the Rhine, avoiding the machine-gun fire targeted against the bridge. Tragically a little over four months later Byam went missing while he was on a US Eighth Air Force daylight raid on Berlin. The aircraft in which he was flying crashed on its return flight, probably over the North Sea. Maxted, who gave some wonderful broadcasts in which he covered the attempts to drop supplies to the beleaguered British paratroops, was out of action for a while, having been stunned by a mortar blast. Another correspondent with the American forces at Nijmegen was Walter Cronkite, who after the war became one of the most famous newsmen on American television.

Despite heroic attempts to get through to the troops pinned down at Arnhem the Allied effort proved futile. On 25 September Montgomery admitted that there was no point in continuing to try, and the withdrawal of the British airborne troops began. Only around a quarter of the 10,000 that had landed escaped; over 1,000 were killed and over 6,000 captured. The US airborne forces captured the bridge at Nijmegen, which helped in allowing the British troops to escape from the Arnhem pocket. When Maxted and Byam got back to London and the safety of Broadcasting House Maxted gave a wonderful broadcast about escaping from Arnhem. This and a number of other BBC reports from Arnhem told of the heroic efforts of the soldiers who had been pinned down. Three decades later the film industry took several hours to do the same thing in *A Bridge Too Far*.

About five kilometres to the west of Arnhem, in a space 1,500 yards by 900 on that last day, I saw the dead and the living – those who fought a good fight and kept the faith with you at home, and those who still fought magnificently on. They were the last of the few. I last saw them yesterday morning as they dribbled into Nijmegen. They had staggered and walked and waded all night from Arnhem about ten miles north, and we were busy asking each other if this or that one had been seen. Everyone wondered what the final check-up would amount to. I walked up to one young lieutenant to ask him about his sergeant – a stout lad if ever there was one – and he started to explain what had happened and then turned away. Remember all of these men had been practically ten days and ten nights under the most murderous concentrated fire I have seen in two wars. Then he turned again and said: 'It's hell to be pulled out when you haven't finished your job, isn't it?' That's the way they all felt. It didn't occur to them that if they hadn't held that horde of enemy force at Arnhem, that force would have been down at Nijmegen upsetting the whole applecart.

That was yesterday morning. Late on the afternoon before we were told that the remnants of the 1st Airborne Division were going to pull out that night. The enemy was making it impossible for the elements of the Second Army to relieve us. We were told to destroy all our equipment with the exception of what would go into a haversack, to muffle our boots with bits of blanket, and be ready to move off at a certain time. When the various officers were told to transmit this news to that thin straggle of hard-pressed men around the pitifully small perimeter, a great silence seemed to come upon them even in the middle of the shelling – day or night the shelling and mortaring never stopped. The ones I saw just drew a deep breath and said: 'Very good, sir.' Then those staring eyes in the middle of black muddy masks saluted as they always would, and faded away to crawl out on their stomachs and tell their men.

Perhaps I should remind you here that these were men of no ordinary calibre. They had been nine days in that little space I mentioned being mortared and shelled, machine-gunned and sniped from all around. When a tank or a self-propelled 88 gun broke through, two or three of them had detached themselves and somehow or another had put it out of business. For the last three days they had had no water, very little but small arms ammunition, and rations cut to one-sixth. Luckily or unluckily, it rained and they caught the water in their capes and drank that. These last items were never mentioned – they were airborne, weren't they? They were tough and knew it. All right, water and rations didn't matter. Give them some Germans to kill and even one chance in ten and they'd get along somehow.

At two minutes past ten we clambered out of our slit trenches in an absolute din of bombardment – a great deal of it our own – and formed up in a single line. Our boots were wrapped in blanket so that no noise would be made. We held the tail of the coat of the man in front. We set off like a file of nebulous ghosts from our pockmarked and tree-strewn piece of ground. Obviously, since the enemy was all round us, we had to go through him to get to the River Rhine. After about two hundred yards of silent trekking we knew we were among the enemy. It was difficult not to throw yourself flat when machine-gun tracers skimmed your head or the scream of a shell or mortar-bomb sounded very close – but the orders were to 'keep going'. Anybody hit was to be picked up by the man behind him. A major had reconnoitred the route earlier on with a headquarters officer and had it memorised.

The back of my neck was prickling for that whole interminable march. I couldn't see the man ahead of me – all I knew was that I had hold of a coat-tail and for the first time in my life was grateful for the downpour of rain that made a patter on the leaves and covered up any little noises we were making. At every turn of the way there was posted a sergeant glider pilot who stepped out like a shadow and then stepped back into a deeper shadow again. Several times we halted – which meant you bumped into the man ahead of you – then, when the head of our party was satisfied the turning was clear, we went on again. Once we halted because of a boy sitting on the ground with a bullet through his leg. We wanted to pick him up but he whispered: 'Nark it; gimme another field-dressing and I'll be all right, I can walk.'

As we came out of the trees – we had been following carefully – throughout footpaths so far – I felt as naked as if I were in Piccadilly Circus in my pyjamas, because of the glow from fires across the river. The machine-gun and general bombardment had never let up. We lay down flat in the mud and rain and stayed that way for two hours till the sentry beyond the hedge on the bank of the river told us to move up over the dyke and be taken across. Mortaring started now and I was fearful for those who were already on the bank. I guessed it was pretty bad for them. After what seemed a nightmare of an age we got our turn and slithered up and over on to some mud flats. There was the shadow of a little assault-craft with an outboard motor on it. Several of these had been rushed up by a field company of engineers. One or two of them were out of action already. I waded out into the Rhine up to my hips – it didn't matter, I was soaked through long ago – had been for days. A voice that was sheer music spoke from the stem of the boat saying: 'Ye'll have to step lively boys, it ain't healthy here.' It was a Canadian voice, and the engineers were Canadian engineers. We helped push the boat off into the swift Rhine current and with our heads down between our knees waited for the bump on the far side – or for what might come before. It didn't come. We clambered out and followed what had been a white tape up over a dyke. We slid down the other side on our backsides; we sloshed through mud for four miles and a half – me thinking, 'Gosh! I'm alive, how did it happen?'

In a barn there was a blessed hot mug of tea with hot rum in it and a blanket over our shoulders. Then we walked again – at night. After daylight we got to a dressing station near Nijmegen. Then we were put in trucks and that's how we reached Nijmegen. That's how the last of the few got out to go and fight in some future battle. No matter what battle that is, I know they won't let you down.

Stanley Maxted, 'War Report', BBC, 27 September 1944

SUPPLY CHAIN

The problem of supplies for the 1st Airborne Division fighting at Arnhem was a microcosm of far larger logistical nightmare – that of delivering materials, food and every other piece of equipment for the Allied armies on the Continent. The Mulberry harbours, the vast artificial ports that began to be put in place just twenty-four hours after D-Day, were the solution to the challenge. Two Mulberries were constructed off the coast of France, one near Arromanches-les-Bains, the site of Gold Beach, and the other off Omaha Beach. Close to a hundred severely damaged merchant ships were sunk to form a breakwater, before the huge concrete blocks that had been towed across the Channel, having been built off the coast of Sussex, were put into position. The harbour was then connected to the shore by a series of pontoons. Within ten days of the Mulberries being in place the one off Omaha Beach was all but destroyed in a severe gale, but the other remained intact and did sterling work in becoming the gateway to France for over two million Allied soldiers and four million tonnes of equipment.

It was no longer a confused assortment of bits and pieces. The jigsaw had come together, and now it was a harbour in operation. The outer breakwater was almost complete. Nearly a mile out to sea coasters were tied up alongside landing stages now fixed firmly in position – landing stages that could be lifted and lowered with the tide. Within the sheltered water ducks were plying to and from the Liberty ships. Harbour craft were busy everywhere. There were all the masts, the funnels, the cranes, the derricks, the smoke, the din, the traffic, and the shouts of the Merseyside, of Glasgow, of Southampton – where a month before there had been nothing but a deserted expanse of sea. And for three-quarters of a mile across that sea connecting the landing stages with the new inland roadways, two floating bridge roads ran right into the shore, clanking and undulating a little under a two-way stream of heavy trucks. An all-weather harbour was in being and supplies to the fighting armies were assured. Britain's most momentous secret weapon was in use.

Michael Standing, 'War Report', BBC, 16 October 1944

The delay in broadcasting Standing's report was because the whole Mulberry project had to be kept as secret as possible. The Allied strategy called for the capture of the ports in northern France and Belgium, Antwerp in particular. The Germans grimly held on to these ports to allow them time to re-group and to slow the Allied advance as best they could. Simultaneously the Allied bombing campaign against Germany's heavy industry in the Ruhr brought horrendous civilian casualties in late October and early November. It was a strategy that culminated in the huge bombing raid of Dresden in February 1945 in which somewhere close to 30,000 people lost their lives. It is difficult to see precisely what the purpose of this attack was, and with hindsight it seems indefensible. In recent years others have argued that it was genocide; a few people in Germany have used it as a political symbol to raise passions and emotions in some kind of ultra-right-wing revivalist movement. The bombing, like many other actions throughout the war, just goes to underline the horror that is war, and the evil that evil, or sometimes misguided, men can do.

The autumn bombing campaign was linked to the onset of bad weather, an attempt to get things moving before the anticipated severe winter weather actually started. By mid-November the armies on the ground set about trying to breach the German defences in the area around Metz. The defences in the German Siegfried Line were formidable, with an interlocking network of pillboxes, all protected by large minefields; progress was slow along the 400-mile front. By early December the advance had just about halted, every yard was bitterly contested and both the Allied and German armies took heavy losses.

Against the background of a war that was almost on hold, if ground gained is the yardstick, Hitler had a new plan. Although it wasn't so much a plan, more a redeployment, in that he put Field Marshal von Rundstedt in charge of the Western Front. With twenty divisions at his disposal, almost every tank on the Western Front and a large part of what was left of the Luftwaffe the

Germans planned to smash through the American lines. The Battle of the Bulge in the Ardennes Forest was about to take place.

During the night the town had been bombed a little, strafed a little, and a siren had wakened us to give warning of paratroop activities. In the morning there was a rumour that German tanks were just over the hill. Armed patrols went out on to the roads, trees were felled as roadblocks, and Thunderbolts and Lightnings came low over the town and began wheeling and searching in the woods just east of us. Then the order that everyone hoped would never come, came. We had to move out quickly. Somehow the news spread around the little border town and the people came out to see the leave-taking. Some of the troops had been there for three months, many had made friends. There was handshaking and many questions. How near were the Germans? Did we think that they'd come to their town – again? Was it true that the German tanks were just over the hill? There were awkward silences, GIs couldn't answer those questions.

Robert Barr, 'War Report', BBC, 18 December 1944

The German attack began at dawn on 16 December, and Barr's report was recorded on the following day. The fighting over the next few days was desperate and reports by Barr and other correspondents in the front line spoke of the immense struggle to stop the German breakthrough. The German advance was helped by atrocious weather and bad visibility, which hampered the Allied planes from disrupting the Axis supply lines. Two days before Christmas the weather changed and from that moment the battle began to turn the Allies' way.

Yesterday the greatest force of heavy bombers ever flown on a single mission by any air force – more than 2000 Flying Fortresses and Liberators of the US Eighth Air Force – attacked communication and supply centres just opposite the bulge driven into the US lines by the Germans, a number of Luftwaffe aerodromes in the Frankfurt area, and other military installations in western Germany.

More than 900 Mustangs and Thunderbolts of the Eighth Air Force escorted the bombers, bringing the total number of planes engaged in the operation to approximately 3,000. The bombers dropped approximately 10,500,000 pounds of bombs on road and rail supply lines from Euskirchen south to Trier and on 11 Luftwaffe aerodromes in the Frankfurt area. Incomplete reports from returning fighter pilots revealed that at least 70 enemy aircraft were destroyed in aerial combat.

In the afternoon strong forces of Halifaxes and Lancasters of RAF Bomber Command, escorted by Spitfires and Mustangs of RAF Fighter Command, made concentrated attacks, in clear weather, on two airfields in the Ruhr. Spitfires of RAF Fighter Command attacked V2 storage, erection, and launching sites in enemy-occupied Holland yesterday.

BBC News, 25 December 1944

The improvements in the weather no one could have predicted, but one prophecy that Hitler had made – that General Eisenhower would fail to recognise the strength of the German advance – proved hopelessly wrong. The Commander-in-Chief poured in men and supporting armour to shore up the Allied defences and as can be gathered from the BBC Christmas Day bulletin, nothing was spared in the air either. A German counter-offensive on New Year's Day led by the Luftwaffe proved to be a temporary blip for the Allies, but a more permanent one for the Germans. Nevertheless the BBC carried a report that was less than optimistic: 'I think it would be wise to abstain from predicting . . . that this year will see the end of the fighting either in Europe or Asia.'

During the offensive the Germans lost close to 300 aircraft and it effectively marked the end of the Luftwaffe as an effective fighting force. The Ardennes offensive finally finished on 7 January when Hitler agreed that von Rundstedt should pull back. On the same day Field Marshal Montgomery, wearing a Parachute Regiment red beret, gave an interesting press conference at his headquarters. At this point he was unaware of the order to withdraw; he just felt von Rundstedt was beaten.

As soon as I saw what was happening I took certain steps myself to ensure that if the Germans got to the Meuse they would certainly not get over the river. I carried out certain movements so as to provide balanced dispositions to meet the threatened danger . . .

Then the situation began to deteriorate. But the whole Allied team rallied to meet the danger; national considerations were thrown overboard. General Eisenhower placed me in command of the whole northern front. I employed the whole available power of the British group of armies. This power was brought into play very gradually and in such a way that it would not interfere with the American lines of communication. Finally it was put into battle with a bang, and to-day British divisions are fighting hard on the right flank of the US First Army . . .

. . . The first thing to be done was to 'head off' the enemy from the tender spots and vital places. Having done that successfully, the next thing was to 'see him off' – that is, to rope him in and make quite certain that he could not get to places he wanted, and also that he was slowly but surely removed away from those places. He was therefore 'headed off' and then 'seen off'. He is now being 'written off' and heavy toll is being taken of his divisions by ground and air action.

You must not imagine that the battle is over yet. It is by no means over, and a great deal still remains to be done . . . No one can tell for certain. The only guide we have is the message he issued to his soldiers before the battle began. He told them it was the last great effort to try to win the war – that everything depended on it, that they must go all out.

On the map you see his gains – that will not win the war. He is likely slowly but surely to lose them all. He must have scraped together every reserve he could lay his hands on for this job, and he has not achieved a great deal. One must admit that he has dealt us a sharp blow, and he sent us reeling back. But we recovered. He has been unable to gain any great advantage from his initial success.

He has therefore failed in his strategic purpose unless the prize was smaller than his men were told. He has now turned to the defensive on the ground, and he is faced by forces properly balanced to utilise the initiative, which he has lost.

. . . I shall always feel that Rundstedt was really beaten by the good fighting qualities of the American soldier and by the teamwork of the Allies . . . And now I come to my last point. It is teamwork that pulls you through dangerous times, it is teamwork that wins battles, it is victories in battle that win wars.

Nothing must be done by anyone that tends to break down the team spirit of our Allied team – if you try to 'get at' the captain of the team you are liable to induce a loss of confidence and this may spread and have disastrous results. I would say that anyone who tries to break up the team spirit of the Allies is definitely helping the enemy.

The captain of our team is General Eisenhower. I am absolutely devoted to 'Ike'. We are the greatest of friends. It grieves me when I see un-complimentary articles about him in the British Press. He bears a great burden. He needs our fullest support, he has a right to expect it, and it is up to all of us to see that he gets it.

Field Marshal Bernard Montgomery, BBC, 8 January 1945

The reports of Montgomery's press conference gave no inkling of the issues that were present between the British field marshal and the senior American generals in the field. Some of what Monty said at his press conference grated with the American generals, Bradley and Patton. Both generals threatened to resign if Montgomery wasn't held in check by the Supreme Commander – it was possibly something that Montgomery was well aware of, and hence his somewhat sycophantic comments at the close of his speech. The longer-term effect of all this was a whispering campaign by some on the American generals' staff, designed to undermine Montgomery.

During the Battle of the Bulge the Americans and the Germans took casualties in the order of 90,000 each, but all it achieved for the Germans in military terms was a delay. Soon the Allied armies were on the move again; crossing the Rhine was the next objective.

ONE BIG RIVER

During the first few days of March various units of the US Army reached the Rhine and on 7 March the US First Army made a speedy advance and captured a bridge over the Rhine at Remagen. It was not the ideal spot to cross the river, but the point was that the Americans were across; psychologically it was a hammer blow for the Nazis.

> The Allies are across the Rhine. Troops under General Hodges established a bridgehead on the east bank, south of Bonn, yesterday afternoon. A Reuters report from the First American Army says that the crossing was made at Remagen about twenty-five miles south of Cologne between Bonn and Koblenz.
>
> *Freddie Grisewood, BBC News, 8 March 1944*

Hitler was incandescent and ordered the court-martial of those in charge. Five officers were sentenced to death and four were executed. The Allied armies were firmly in control along the western bank of the Rhine and three days later there was news of just how much in control they were.

> This is Chester Wilmot speaking from Field Marshal Montgomery's headquarters. The German bridgehead west of the Rhine opposite Wesel has been wiped out. Yesterday afternoon three columns of Canadian, British, and American troops broke through the last German defences 5 miles south-west of Wesel and reached the west end of the two bridges which the Germans had blown yesterday morning. The end was sudden and swift.
>
> On Friday evening the Germans were still resisting strongly, holding a line across the neck of the bend on which Wesel stands. But during the night they evidently withdrew the bulk of their forces, and when Montgomery's

troops attacked yesterday morning they found little more than rearguard parties covering roadblocks. During the day the Germans were driven back more than 5 miles, and in the evening British infantry of the First Canadian Army linked up with Ninth Army troops opposite Wesel.

This means that the Allied armies now control the west bank of the Rhine from Arnhem to Endernacht, 4 miles north of Koblenz. Though there may still be a few German stragglers at odd points along the west bank, and one pocket in an old fort upstream from Wesel had not been fully cleaned up last night. The 21st Army Group began its drive to the Rhine 33 days ago. In that time it captured more than 50,000 prisoners – of these 29,000 have been taken by the Ninth Army and 21,000 by the British and Canadian.

Chester Wilmot, BBC, 11 May 1945

Thirteen days after the news from Montgomery's headquarters the operation to cross the Rhine at Wesel began. Codenamed Varsity, it would eclipse the airborne landings of Market Garden both in scale and, more importantly, in their success. The plan was to advance towards the Baltic coast some 350 miles away once the bridgehead on the eastern bank of the Rhine had been secured. Six parachute battalions of the 6th Airborne Division, supported by troops in gliders, were dropped on 24 March 1945; in addition, men of the US Army's 17th Airborne Division took part. In all it involved over 500 C-47 Dakotas and C-46 Commandos, as well as over 1,300 gliders.

The Rhine lies left and right across our path below us, shining in the sunlight, wide and with sweeping curves; and the whole of this mighty airborne army is now crossing and filling the whole sky. Down there is the smoke of battle. There is the smokescreen laid by the army lying right across the far bank of the river; dense clouds of brown and grey smoke coming up. And now our skipper's talking to the glider pilot and warning him that we're nearly there, preparing to cast him off.

Ahead of us, another pillar of black smoke marks the spot where an aircraft has gone down, and – and yet another one; it's a Stirling, a British Stirling; it's going down with flames coming out from under its belly – and more parachutes are coming out – one, two, three, four – four parachutes have come out of the Stirling; it goes on its way to the ground. But we haven't got time to watch it further because we're coming up now to the exact chosen landing ground where our airborne forces have to be put down; and no matter what the opposition may be, we have got to keep straight on, dead on to the exact position. Our glider has gone: we've let her go . . .

Richard Dimbleby, 'War Report', BBC, 24 March 1945

Our period of waiting is over, this is the time.

In the Buffalo, that's a strange all-purpose vehicle that's taking us over the Rhine, I'm crouching with the commanding officer of the Assault Battalion in his Bren Gun carrier fills the Buffalo, on the Bren Gun Carrier piles his men, tin-hatted, and we're watching gazing to that far bank of the Rhine. It's a fantastic sight, we've broken out, first through the bund, the wall that retains the floodwaters of the Rhine, and we're out in the open spaces. Overhead goes an absolute criss-cross pattern of our tracers firing in as fast as they can into the German bank. The thunder of our guns echoing and crashing in our ears. As we waited we were deafened by the noise and blinded by their flashes, but now we seem alone out here on the water's edge waiting for the final signal. The Buffalo – the driver in charge – a man of the Royal Tank Regiment is receiving the signal – the captain's waving to him, and this is where we move.

The Buffalo driver gives an extra rev as he feels for the edge of the water – we're guided up right to the very edge by a long little line of small green lights that have been laid to take us to the jumping-off ground. A last look back at the shore we're leaving. The searchlights are playing, the moonlight's filling the sky, but here ahead of us there's no effect of moonlight at all, we've reached the water's edge and we see the Rhine – not running, as we thought it would, bright under the moon, but running red; because right on the opposite side of the village every single house and haystack you can see is burning, beaten down by the fury of our barrage.

Slowly, carefully, we come down to the water's edge. We're in – the Buffalo tips its nose down the bank and now it's opening up full power. Three minutes to go and we're racing across, and side by side with us go racing the other Buffaloes: racing for that hell on the other side. The searchlights cast a white beam, they go right across the river on one side of us, but ahead of us is only red water. The current's carrying us down and we're putting up our nose against it, going clean across it all the time, and the tracer is making a path on either side of us, beating down the opposition. Now we're utterly alone it seems – right out in the midst of this swirling stream. You get a complete feeling of detachment, waiting all the time for the enemy to open up: waiting all the time for them to spot us as we lie helpless, as it seems, out here in this wide stream. The Buffalo springs and points its nose upstream now – we're drifting – fighting the current to get over . . .

Wynford Vaughan-Thomas, BBC, 24 March 1945

Vaughan-Thomas wrote about the crossing in his autobiography and revealed that his brother, who was a brigadier in the Army, was in the Buffalo alongside him on his trip over the Rhine. The only thing that marred the crossing was that when they landed on the east bank of the river the pipe major found that a bullet had gone clean through his bagpipes and rendered them useless. It was the first time in 150 years that the Royal Scots Fusiliers had gone into battle without the skirl of the pipes.

The following day one of the war's stranger incidents took place; it involved Winston Churchill. Dressed in the uniform of a colonel in the Royal Sussex Regiment he had gone to visit Montgomery at his headquarters and from there he took a trip to the Rhine, crossed over to the east bank and even took a short cruise on the river. It's an incident that is either ignored or barely mentioned in passing by many of Churchill's biographers and yet the area was still very much a war zone. Can you imagine one of our leaders going so close to the front today? Health and Safety would be apoplectic!

In warm, brilliant sunshine this afternoon the Prime Minister, Mr Churchill, basked on his balcony overlooking the Rhine and discussed casually with General Eisenhower and Field Marshal Montgomery just how the Ninth Army bridgehead had been established. Downstream he could see the town of Wesel, which the British Commandos had just completely cleared. Through his binoculars the Prime Minister was inspecting the bridgehead just across the slow-flowing Rhine, when quite suddenly he decided to cross. Our planes were still pounding the German positions across the river when Mr Churchill walked down to the river's edge and got into a landing craft. With him went Sir Alan Brooke, Chief of the Imperial General Staff, Field Marshal Montgomery, General Omar Bradley, and General Simpson, Commander of the Ninth Army, which had forced the river at this point. We cruised across the Rhine in the tracks of the infantry, and the Prime Minister scrambled up the gravel bank on the other side along the same narrow wired path that the infantry had used, and scaled a high earth dike to get a good view. He studied the bridgehead and discussed the morning's battle with the American generals and then he decided to have a short cruise on the Rhine. It was his first cruise on the Rhine since he sailed it in a motor torpedo boat at the end of the last war. After the short cruise, the landing craft turned back to shore. The Prime Minister went to Wesel along the river road. At the approach to the great steel and concrete Wesel bridge (the one the Germans destroyed when they retreated across the river) the cavalcade of staff cars halted and the Prime Minister got out. Leaving the party, he found a path through the debris, and climbed up on to the first span of the wrecked bridge. The ruins of Wesel were just across the water,

and the sound of machine-gun and rifle fire was still coming up spas-
modically from the town. Through binoculars the Prime Minister watched
the crouching infantry moving through the streets, while Field Marshal
Montgomery explained how the British assault had been made.

Robert Barr, 'War Report', BBC, 25 March 1944

Churchill had told the men of Montgomery's 21st Army Group that 'once
the river line is pierced and the crust of German resistance is broken decisive
victory in Europe will be near'. It was a significant moment in his life and one
that should be more often spoken about. Perhaps the fact that the Prime
Minister decided to 'take a leak' in the Rhine may have discouraged some from
mentioning the affair.

There is a picture of Churchill and the commanders walking about on the
east bank of the Rhine featuring a young woman who is simply identified as a
'female war correspondent'. It seems likely to have been Marguerite Higgins, a
24-year-old American who had been born in Hong Kong and was working for
the *New York Tribune*. She had only managed to inveigle her way into the job in
late 1944 and had only been transferred to the front a matter of days before.
Higgins went on to cover the Korean War, and the war in Vietnam, winning a
Pulitzer Prize for her book about the Korean War. Shortly after crossing the
Rhine with Churchill she witnessed the liberation of the concentration camp at
Dachau and was decorated by the US Army for her help during the surrender
of the SS guards. She died in 1966 at the prematurely young age of forty-five
after catching a tropical disease.

From a military standpoint the most important task was to get bridges
across the Rhine to carry men and machinery forward as quickly as possible.
The race to Berlin, as it was dubbed, was very much on and while it seemed
inevitable that the Russians would win the competition from the east, the
contest to be quickest in the west was more than just a sideshow. Before March
was out eight bridges had been established across the Rhine; all carried vast
amounts of traffic under the direction of the Military Police, in what was one
of the largest movements of vehicles ever. Besides trucks, guns, armoured
vehicles, bulldozers and ambulances, there were huge quantities of
ammunition, food, and every other conceivable consumable that an army
needs when it's stationary, let alone advancing at the speed of the Allies, and
in some areas fighting against bitter, last-ditch opposition.

One has only to spend a few minutes among our advancing troops on the
far side of the Rhine to feel the almost frenzied spirit of offence that is
running through every single formation. This morning I went across one of

the Rhine bridges and all along the route I was staggered by the hustle and dash of every single formation, right down from the Military Police to squadron commanders who were racing tanks across the river and far beyond on the other side. Up to the time of the Rhine push it had always been a good idea to slow down when approaching a bridge for that was the direction that was glaring at you in bold red letters of a snow-white signboard, but no more – things have changed. I had hardly put the nose of the car down towards the start of the bridge when an English policeman shouted 'Come on mate, flat out across that bridge'. Halfway across the river another Red Cap had shouted even louder, 'Come on mate, you're holding traffic up, show a pace, show a pace . . .'

Stewart McPherson, BBC, 28 March 1945

SPECIAL RELATIONSHIP

At the start of April 1945 the Russians were twenty to thirty miles from Berlin, and the Allies were 200 miles away in the west and so, despite the Russians facing stiffer opposition than the American and British forces, it was really no contest. Despite much urging from Churchill to Eisenhower to set Montgomery free to make the final dash to Berlin the Supreme Commander ordered the 21st Army Group to halt at the River Elbe – they were some 60 or so miles from Berlin, and the Russians still hadn't made it. Churchill had cabled Roosevelt arguing that it was important that the British and Americans got there first, but on 11 April Roosevelt disagreed in a reply to Churchill, just as he had done over the zoning of Germany at the Yalta conference two months earlier.

This is Dora Bateman speaking to you from a BBC studio in London. I really don't know how to express the horrible shock I had on listening to the seven o'clock news this morning to hear the death of Mr Roosevelt. It seems like a personal loss and I'm sure we English feel it almost as much as if it had been our leader . . . To have worked so hard and long for victory and to be taken when it is within sight is tragic. I think everyone in England liked and respected Mr Roosevelt and personally I have never heard a soul speak an unkind word about him.

Dora Bateman, BBC North American Service, 13 April 1945

The news of President Roosevelt's death was keenly felt by many in Britain, where he was recognised as being a true friend at a time when the country was desperately in need of one. His death had nothing to do with the order to halt at the Elbe issued by Eisenhower, who was still being urged by Patton to let the 21st Army Group go all the way to Berlin. While some have seen this decision to call a halt as a mistake Eisenhower always insisted that it was to save lives. The Russians took large numbers of casualties – in excess of 300,000 during that last push to Berlin; the Supreme Commander's view was simple and pragmatic. Why risk the lives of soldiers to capture Berlin when it was going to be in the Soviet zone once the fighting had finished, this having been agreed at Yalta? At the same time Eisenhower was under orders from Washington not to take the city and risk the wrath of Russia being brought to bear on America. It's another of those 'what ifs' of history.

After talking about President Roosevelt Mrs Bateman, a regular giver of such talks on the North American Service, spoke of the good news that was gladdening the hearts of British and American mothers; prisoner-of-war camps were being overrun and their captives released. One POW who had a release – not by the British or Americans, but by the Russians – was Edward Ward, the BBC correspondent who had been captured in North Africa two years earlier:

The moment of relief was without any doubt the greatest in my life and in the lives of my fellow prisoners of war of Oflag XIIB. We'd been moved from the camp for eighteen weary months and had gone through a somewhat anxious period expected a further move from day to day . . .

. . . To us of Oflag XIIB, the senior British officers' camp in Germany, which included eleven Brigadiers, it meant the end of a long weary term of imprisonment dating back to Dunkirk days for some. To the French, Belgian, Dutch, Russians, Poles and others it meant emancipation from slavery. Rumours had been flying around for days about where the American troops were. German trucks returning from the front were continually claiming to have missed capture by minutes. But early on Wednesday afternoon it became plain that the Americans were very close. Our temporary camp was a group of huts out in an open field, with a slagheap and an arms factory which had long since ceased active production behind us. About three o'clock in the afternoon things began to warm up; shells began to fall ahead of us in the field, and machine-gun fire began to get more and more intense. Soon we could see figures appearing on the horizon. It was decided to evacuate the camp to the German air-raid shelters, which were dug deep under the slagheap. Our German guards no sooner entered the shelters than they unbuckled their arms and threw them in heaps in corners of the shelter. They'd been a little bit embarrassed about their arms for some time; they thought they wouldn't get a very good reception from the Americans if they were armed. I dumped my belongings in the shelter and went outside. The noise of the battle increased; and then suddenly out of a wood came the American tanks and tracked troop-carriers. Everyone became delirious with excitement.

'Come on and see the American tanks,' I shouted to some Russian girls who'd been working in the station restaurant. 'American tanks? Nievos mosno!' they cried. 'Pas possible,' cried the French – but it was possible, it was true. One of the troop carriers stopped, two men jumped out and came down to the far bank of the Lahn River, which separated us from them. I ran down the steep bank on my side. By the greatest piece of luck there was an old barge tied up there. 'How's things over there with you?' the Americans asked. 'Fine,' I said, 'do you want to come across?' 'Yeah, can you get that boat over?' 'You bet your life I can.' And with three others, including the only American POW in the camp, I poled the rickety old craft across. 'How are your guards?' the Americans asked when we were about in midstream. 'Like lambs,' I said, 'you needn't worry about them.' 'Oh, we're not worrying,' said one of the Americans, fingering his gun. We nearly upset the boat on the return trip, but we got our deliverers safely and dryly across. They forced their way through a cheering crowd of POWs and foreign workers. Relief lit up the faces of even the Germans. No more bombs – no more alarms for them. The worst of the war was finished as far as they were concerned.

Edward Ward, BBC, 31 March 1945

Oflag XIIB, which is an abbreviation of Offizier Lager, was at Hadamar, north-east of Limburg on the Lahn; Oflags were normally for officers only. In addition to the eleven brigadiers there were 261 other officers and 324 other ranks. There were also two other correspondents besides Ward; Patrick Crosse of Reuters had been captured in January 1942 and Godfrey Anderson of the Associated Press had been held captive since November 1941. Having had such a promising start to his wartime broadcasting career Ward, like everyone else held captive, was frustrated by his incarceration. Other broadcasts he made after his release told of how even the German guards listened to the BBC for scraps of news, despite it being prohibited. This they traded with the POWs for bits of soap or a cigarette. Ward told of one guard he would talk to as the Americans were nearing their camp who had lost relatives in the Cologne bombing, had a 17-year-old son missing in U-boat service and who was profoundly angry with the Nazi Party: 'They are not men, they are beasts.' On his return to London Ward was soon back on the radio; he gave a talk at lunchtime on 9 April about foreign workers in Germany.

Captain Adam Farquhar of the Royal Army Medical Corps was at Oflag XIIB with Ward; he told the *Scotsman* about life in the camp and in particular their diet.

Breakfast was at 8.30 a.m. and consisted of mint tea. Lunch, two potatoes and about 2 or 3 spoonfuls of dried turnips. Supper at 7 p.m. was a larger ration of potatoes and some mixed dried vegetables. In addition to this, there was a daily ration of 5½oz of black bread and a little ersatz margarine. The guards had the same diet, except for an additional ration of bread. On occasions the prisoners had Red Cross food parcels. After August 1944, however, no parcels arrived until the middle of February, owing to our bombing having hindered communications.

In many ways Ward was one of the lucky ones, in that the Commandant of Oflag XIIB kept them in their camp until the last few weeks, when he transferred his prisoners to a nearby camp for 'foreign workers'. Other prisoners were marched for days on end to avoid the advancing Russians. In a broadcast on 10 April a South African sergeant talked of being marched by his guards for forty-three days, averaging twelve miles a day, from Breslau to evade the Russians. Nothing, however, compared with the horror that was to face some reporters who visited the Nazi concentration camps.

Here over an acre of ground lay dead and dying people You could not see which was which except by perhaps a convulsive movement, or the last quiver of a sigh from a living skeleton too weak to move. The living lay with their heads against the corpses and around them moved the awful ghostly procession of emaciated aimless people with nothing to do and no hope of life – unable to move out of your way, unable to look at the terrible sights around them. There was no privacy, nor did men or women ask it any longer. Women stood and squatted stark naked in the dusk, trying to wash themselves, and to catch the lice on their bodies. Babies had been born here, tiny wizened things that could not live. A woman driven mad screamed at a British sentry to give her milk for her child and thrust the tiny mite into his arms and ran off crying terribly. He opened the bundle and found the baby had been dead for days. This day at Belsen was the most horrible of my life . . .

Richard Dimbleby, BBC, 19 April 1945

When Dimbleby sent his report back to London it had not been played immediately, as was normal procedure. There was consternation in the BBC as to how to deal with it. Subsequently there have been some who have argued that the BBC played down the Holocaust, but there are others who argued that the editorial staff were shocked into incredulity and even questioned whether it was true. Dimbleby himself was traumatised. Vaughan-Thomas, whom he met as he left the camp, says, 'He was a changed man.' Dimbleby even had trouble beginning his report and broke down before his engineer, Harvey Sarney, whom he had worked with back in the days of the BEF in France in 1939, could get anything on to a disc. When London did not transmit his report Dimbleby is reported to have called Broadcasting House and said he would never make another recording in his life if it did not air. When it did it was edited, but it still resonated with everyone who heard it. What is clear from reading the newspaper reports in the days following Belsen's liberation is that no one could grasp the enormity of the crime. The *Daily Telegraph* simply called it, 'a spectacle of absolute evil'.

Belsen was in north-western Germany near Hanover, and for many years had somewhat better conditions than some of the other concentration camps. It had been set up as a holding point for Jews that could be exchanged for German citizens who were being held by the Allies. It was only as the war was coming to an end that the horror of Belsen descended to the level that Dimbleby witnessed. Prisoners from other camps had hugely inflated the camp's numbers, many moving ahead of the Russian advance, and this exaggerated the awful human catastrophe at Belsen. Designed for 10,000, the camp held six times that number when the Allies reached it and already disease was rampant; it was typhus that claimed Anne Frank's life at Belsen in March 1945. As this was the first camp liberated by British troops – the Americans had so far liberated none – it received major publicity, which is what helped in making it so difficult for so many to comprehend.

Ed Murrow gave as moving a report as Richard Dimbleby had done of the Buchenwald camp:

There surged around me an evil-smelling stink, men and boys reached out to touch me. They were in rags and the remnants of uniforms. Death already had marked many of them, but they were smiling with their eyes. I looked out over the mass of men to the green fields beyond, where well-fed Germans were ploughing . . .

I asked to see one of the barracks. It happened to be occupied by Czechoslovaks. When I entered, men crowded around, tried to lift me to their shoulders. They were too weak. Many of them could not get out of bed. I was told that this building had once stabled 80 horses. There were 1,200 men in it, five to a bunk. The stink was beyond all description. They called the doctor. We inspected his records. There were only names in the little black book – nothing more – nothing about who had been where, what he had done or hoped. Behind the names of those who had died, there was a cross. I counted them. They totaled 242 – 242 out of 1,200, in one month.

As we walked out into the courtyard, a man fell dead. Two others, they must have been over 60, were crawling toward the latrine. I saw it, but will not describe it. In another part of the camp they showed me the children, hundreds of them. Some were only 6 years old. One rolled up his sleeves, showed me his number. It was tattooed on his arm. B-6030, it was. The others showed me their numbers. They will carry them till they die. An elderly man standing beside me said: 'The children – enemies of the state!' I could see their ribs through their thin shirts . . .

We went to the hospital. It was full. The doctor told me that 200 had died the day before. I asked the cause of death. He shrugged and said: 'tuberculosis, starvation, fatigue and there are many who have no desire to live. It is very difficult.' He pulled back the blanket from a man's feet to show me how swollen they were. The man was dead. Most of the patients could not move. I asked to see the kitchen. It was clean. The German in charge . . . showed me the daily ration. One piece of brown bread about as thick as your thumb, on top of it a piece of margarine as big as three sticks of chewing gum. That, and a little stew, was what they received every 24 hours. He had a chart on the wall. Very complicated it was. There were little red tabs scattered through it. He said that was to indicate each 10 men who died. He had to account for the rations and he added: 'We're very efficient here.'

We proceeded to the small courtyard. The wall adjoined what had been a stable or garage. We entered. It was floored with concrete. There were two rows of bodies stacked up like cordwood. They were thin and very white. Some of the bodies were terribly bruised; though there seemed to be little flesh to bruise. Some had been shot through the head, but they bled but little. I arrived at the conclusion that all that was mortal of more than 500 men and boys lay there in two neat piles. There was a German trailer, which must have contained another 50, but it wasn't possible to count them. The clothing was piled in a heap against the wall. It appeared that most of the men and boys had died of starvation; they had not been executed.

But the manner of death seemed unimportant. Murder had been done at Buchenwald. God alone knows how many men and boys have died there during the last 12 years. Thursday, I was told that there were more than 20,000 in the camp. There had been as many as 60,000. Where are they now?

I pray you to believe what I have said about Buchenwald. I reported what I saw and heard, but only part of it. For most of it, I have no words. If I have offended you by this rather mild account of Buchenwald, I'm not in the least sorry . . .

Ed Murrow, BBC, 16 April 1945

Postwar estimates put the number of people who died in the camp at somewhere around 65,000. That's the same number of people who live in Wrexham today, and slightly more than the population of either Maidenhead, or Folkestone, or Bognor Regis. On 5 May 1945 the BBC's 'Radio Newsreel' carried a half-hour documentary programme presented by Patrick Gordon Walker, who recorded much of the programme at Belsen, where he interviewed soldiers and inmates just a few days after the camp had been liberated. It is a testament to the job that the soldiers had to do, and most of all the terrible suffering of those who were in the camp. The first soldier he interviewed was Jewish and he spoke movingly of what he had to face.

BERLIN TRILOGY

On St George's Day, 23 April, a report was received at Broadcasting House that the Russians had finally broken through the bitter resistance of the Germans on the eastern outskirts of Berlin. Two days later Russian and British troops finally met up – but not in Berlin.

This is the BBC Home Service. Here is the news, read by Frederick Grisewood. We begin by taking listeners over direct to one of our trans-mitters in Germany where Frank Gillard is waiting to speak.

[Frank Gillard] East and west have met, at twenty minutes to five on Wednesday afternoon April 25th 1945 American troops of General Bradley's 12th Army Group made contact with Soviet elements of Marshal Konev's 1st Ukrainian Army Group near the German town of Torgau on the Elbe. This is the news for which the whole Allied world has been waiting. Nazi Germany tottering to her final collapse has been split clean in half . . .

BBC News, 25 April 1945

Hello BBC, Hello BBC, this is Edward Ward speaking from Corps Headquarters of the Russian Army on the east bank of the Elbe. You can hear this music, it's the Red Orchestra playing; we've got some dancing here, the Russian dancers dancing around. We've just had a very, very big lunch – with the Red Army – As I said we've just had a very great lunch from the

Red Army, we've joined up with them today, General Hodges and the Russian General have given some big speeches – and we're all here – and everything is beautiful.

Edward Ward, BBC, 25 April 1945

Ward's report was perhaps the only time in the war where there was a noticeable lack of self-control during a broadcast. It wasn't of course fear, rather euphoria that seems to have got the better of the man who had by this time become Viscount Bangor. Quite understandably – after a 'very, very big lunch' with the Russians that probably included enormous amounts of vodka, and so soon after his release from the POW camp – he sounds ever so slightly merry.

Torgau, where the armies met, is about one hundred miles south-west of Berlin, where bitter fighting continued. Goebbels had declared Berlin the front line and those soldiers that remained in the city were fighting for their lives. On 28 April, with the Red Army at the gates of his Chancellery, Hitler married his lover Eva Braun and named Admiral Dönitz as his successor. Two days later Hitler shot himself and his wife poisoned herself – as did Goebbels and his wife, who were with Hitler in his bunker, but not before poisoning their six children.

We are interrupting our programmes to bring you a news flash. [Sound of pealing bells] This is London calling. Here is a news flash. The German radio has just announced that Hitler is dead. I'll repeat that the German radio has just announced that Hitler is dead.

Stuart Hibberd, BBC, 1 May 1945

The announcement on the BBC followed hard on the heels of a broadcast made on German radio at 9.40 that evening. It said, somewhat euphemistically, 'Adolf Hitler has fallen this afternoon at his Command Post in the Reich Chancellery fighting to his last breath against Bolshevism, and for Germany.' Immediately preceding the announcement on Hamburg Radio they played Wagner's 'Götterdämmerung' ('The Twilight of the Gods'). Admiral Dönitz broadcast immediately following the news of Hitler's death and finished his speech by saying: 'German soldiers do your duty. The very life of our people is at stake.'

The following day Broadcasting House was its usual busy self, with the news staff coming and going for their appointed shifts. Stuart Hibberd was instructed to be there by 5 p.m. by John Snagge, who had gone to see film of some of the atrocities committed in the concentration camps, and so Hibberd was the senior announcer on duty. Shortly after he had arrived in the news room R.T. Clark, the Home News Editor, told him to arrange with the engineers to allow them to break into a programme because reports of the German Army's unconditional surrender in Italy had just come through. Freddy Allen did the honours, making the announcement at 7 p.m. Just over three hours later, at 10.15, the news everyone had been expecting was telephoned through to Broadcasting House. Stuart Hibberd went on the air himself to make the announcement.

> We are breaking into our programmes for a second time to-night, this time with some splendid news from Moscow: Berlin has fallen. Marshal Stalin has just announced the capture of the capital of Germany, the centre of German imperialism, and the cradle of German aggression. The Berlin garrison laid down their arms this afternoon. More than 70,000 prisoners have been rounded up so far to-day.
>
> *Stuart Hibberd, BBC, 2 May 1945*

Somewhat peculiarly, given all the news of Germany's defeat, and more so given the horrors that had been exposed in the concentration camps, the BBC was once more under attack. Lord Ailwyn, who according to newspaper reports described himself as a 'plain Englishman with a profound distrust of Germany and the Germans', complained at the large numbers of Germans employed by the BBC. He went on to say that their 'infiltration is most sinister. One sees it in almost every sphere of our national life, in Government Departments, the BBC, the Press, the universities, and factories. More and more they appear to be penetrating into positions where they are able to exert a pernicious influence.' The Marquess of Reading said it was a 'deplorable and ungenerous attack. Many of the refugees were in British uniforms and had won campaign medals for their gallantry. About 90 per cent of the 40,000 he had mentioned were Jews, who if they had not been in Britain would have been in Dachau, Belsen, or Buchenwald.'

In the real world, two days after the news of the fall of Berlin, Stuart Hibberd read the 6 p.m. news – a bulletin of quite significant proportions. It was the last news of the war in which the newsreader gave his name. By the time of the 9 p.m. news, read by John Snagge, the BBC was back to its pre-war method of simply saying 'Here is the news'. With no threat of invasion, there was no need to ensure that listeners knew the news was genuine; it was all perfectly understandable – at least according to the BBC's management.

Following the news with an anonymous John Snagge was 'War Report', the last one in the series that had been on the air every night since D-Day, barring a short break from 4 February until the Rhine crossing on 23 March.

Hello BBC, this is Chester Wilmot speaking from Field Marshal Montgomery's tactical headquarters on a high windswept hill on the wild Luneburg Heath near the River Elbe. It's ten minutes past six on Friday May the 4th. The Commanders of the German forces opposing Field Marshal Montgomery's 21st Army Group have come to this headquarters today . . .

Chester Wilmot, 'War Report', BBC, 4 May 1945

At this point Broadcasting House lost the transmission from Germany and 'War Report' ended somewhat abruptly. Communications were regained at 10.25 when a recording of the Field Marshal was heard in its entirety.

The German Command agrees to the surrender of all German armed forces in Holland, in north-west Germany including the Frisian Islands, and Heligoland and all other islands, in Schleswig-Holstein and in Denmark to the Commander-in-Chief 21st Army Group. This includes all naval ships in these areas. These forces to lay down their arms and to surrender un-conditionally. All hostilities on land, on sea or in the air by German forces in the above areas to cease at 0800 hours British Double Summer Time on Saturday 5th May 1945 . . .

Field Marshal Bernard Montgomery, 'War Report', BBC, 4 May 1945

Over the weekend news bulletins continued to be packed with information from everywhere covering Germany's final collapse. They were also filled with news of the war in the Far East where Japan was still putting up stiff, if declining, resistance. In Okinawa the American advance continued and the Japanese lost 3,000 men killed during their counter-offensive, which brought the total Japanese dead to 33,462 for the 35-day campaign on the island. While this news had a place on the radio it was almost totally eclipsed by the plans for VE-Day.

At about 4.30 p.m. on Monday 7 May news came in from General Eisenhower's headquarters about the signing of the surrender terms. Because of some confusion among the Allies the details of the German surrender were not broadcast until the 9 p.m. news, but what nearly everyone in Britain cared about was VE-Day. Finally at 7.45 p.m. the Ministry of Information gave permission for the following statement to be broadcast.

This is the BBC Home Service. We are interrupting programmes to make the following announcement. It is understood that in accordance with arrangements between the three great powers an official announcement will be broadcast by the Prime Minister at three o'clock tomorrow, Tuesday afternoon the 8th of May. In view of this fact tomorrow, Tuesday, will be treated as Victory in Europe day and will be regarded as a holiday. The day following, Wednesday the 9th of May, will also be a holiday. His Majesty the King will broadcast to the people of the British Empire and Commonwealth tomorrow, Tuesday, at 9 p.m. British Double Summer Time.

John Snagge, BBC, 7.45 p.m., 7 May 1945

Three months later, following the tumultuous celebrations in Britain, ten days of triumphant BBC broadcasts, and a gradual wearing down of the Japanese forces in the Far East, the Second World War came to an end.

British and American scientists have made the Atomic Bomb at last. The first one was dropped on a Japanese city this morning . . .

Frank Phillips, BBC News, 6 August 1945

EPILOGUE

ollowing the week-long 'broadcasting party' to celebrate the victory in Europe the radio got back to its day job. A relatively normal service of presenting the news and a balanced variety of programming was resumed, albeit against the background of the war in the Far East, which still involved British forces, not forgetting the large numbers of British prisoners-of-war in Japanese camps.

Two months after VE-Day there were elections in Britain in which the radio played an important part. It was not the first time that the wireless had been used by the political parties and there was an agreed formula for how much time should be allotted to each party. For four weeks both the Home and Forces Programmes carried twenty- to thirty-minute speeches by the party leaders. Whereas in the past the BBC had seen its role as purely a purveyor of electoral news it now entered a new phase by offering comment on the political process. Things would never be the same again.

Following the Labour Party's landslide victory the new Prime Minister, Clement Attlee, was the one to give the news of the surrender of the Japanese. This was done in far less dramatic terms than Germany's surrender, mostly because it was at midnight in Britain, although the news was carried simultaneously on all the BBC's transmitters at more listenable times around the world.

Before the year was out the most important change, in broadcasting terms, came with the announcement in October that the Hankey Report had been adopted and that the government had made a decision on the future of television. Back in September 1943 a committee under Lord Hankey had been set up to review how television should develop in the postwar era. In early 1945 work commenced on the refurbishment of Alexandra Palace, ready for the service to be reinstated in 1946. Initially the television could reach a radius of about forty miles from the transmitter atop the Victorian People's Palace in North London.

The BBC's *Yearbook* for 1946 spoke confidently of the future of television. Maurice Gorham, who had been appointed to take charge of BBC television, proudly announced that while radio can be listened to in the background the television 'demands your attention', and because of this there is a limit to the amount of time that 'an ordinary viewer can give to his viewing'. On that basis the BBC naturally decided that there was no need to broadcast beyond limited periods in the afternoons and evenings. Mr Gorham and the BBC were also very clear about what type of programmes they would be supplying the viewers with:

> As for programmes, there is no limit to what viewers can hope to see. Judging from previous experience, the most popular items will probably be television 'outside broadcasts' of sporting events – Cup Finals, the Derby, big boxing, tennis, cricket, seen whilst they are actually taking place – and from theatres, with of course big public events such as the opening of Parliament and the Lord Mayor's Show. These outside shows will always appeal, particularly to the new viewer. The old hand may in time come to earmark his evenings primarily for full-length television plays, which were the other great attraction in pre-war days. And then of course there will be variety, cabaret, ballet, fashion shows, demonstrations of everything from cooking to carpentry, talks, discussions, and quiz programmes, art shows, personality interviews, visits to the zoo, street interviews with ordinary Londoners, jazz sessions, recitals, and films.

No mention of the news – I think they may well have had a point!

Bibliography

Beevor, Anthony, *Stalingrad*, London, Viking, 1998

Belfrage, Bruce, *One Man in his Time*, London, Hodder & Stoughton, 1951

Briggs, Asa, *The War of Words 1939–1945*, The History of Broadcasting in the United Kingdom, Vol. 3, London, Oxford University Press, 1970

British Broadcasting Corporation, *BBC Year Book 1940*, London, 1941

——, *BBC Year Book 1941* , London, 1942

——, *BBC Year Book 1942*, London, 1943

——, *BBC Year Book 1943*, London, 1944

——, *BBC Year Book 1944*, London, 1945

——, *BBC Year Book 1945*, London, 1946

——, *BBC Year Book 1946*, London, 1947

Brown, Richard, *Mr Brown's War: A Diary of the Second World War*, ed. Helen Millgate, Stroud, Sutton Publishing, 1999

Gardiner, Juliet, *Wartime Britain 1939–1945*, London, Headline, 2004

Garfield, Simon, *We Are at War: The Remarkable Diaries of Five Ordinary People*, London, Ebury Press, 2005

Gilbert, Martin, *Finest Hour*, London, Heinemann, 1983

Harrisson, Tom, *Living through the Blitz*, Harmondsworth, Penguin, 1990

Hibberd, Stuart, *This is London*, London, Macdonald & Evans, 1950

Hylton, Stuart, *Their Darkest Hour: The Hidden History of the Home Front*, Stroud, Sutton Publishing, 2001

Jacob, Sir Ian, *From Churchill's Secret Circle to the BBC*, ed. C. Richardson, London, Brassey's, 1991

Jenkins, Roy, *Churchill: A Biography*, London, Macmillan, 2001

Kenny, Mary, *Germany Calling: A Personal Biography of William Joyce*, London, New Island Books, 2003

Krabbe, Henning, *Voices from Britain*, London, George Allen & Unwin, 1947

Lean, Tangye, *Voices in the Darkness*, London, Secker & Warburg, 1942

Mitchison, Naomi, *Among You Taking Notes*, London, Oxford University Press, 1986

Moynihan, Michael (ed.), *People at War*, Newton Abbot, David & Charles, 1988

Musto, Walter, *The War and Uncle Walter*, London, Bantam, 2004

Price, Alfred, *The Hardest Day: Battle of Britain, 18 August 1940*, London, BCA, 1979

Sinclair, W.A., *The Voice of the Nazi*, London, White Circle Newsbook, 1940

Speaking for Themselves: The Personal Letters of Winston and Clementine Churchill, ed. Mary Soames, London, Doubleday, 1998

Talbot, Godfrey, *Permission to Speak*, London, Hutchinson, 1976

Various, *War Report: A Record of Dispatches Broadcast by the BBC's War Correspondents with the Allied Expeditionary Force 6 June 1944–5 May 1945*, Oxford, Oxford University Press, 1946

Vaughan-Thomas, Wynford, *Trust to Talk*, London, Hutchinson, 1980

Ziegler, Philip, *London at War*, London, Sinclair Stevenson, 1995

INDEX